THE GOSPEL ACCORDING TO JOHN

The Gospel According to John

VOLUME II
(Chapters 8-14)

by

Oliver B. Greene

The Gospel Hour, Inc., Oliver B. Greene, Director
Box 2024, Greenville, South Carolina 29602

First printing, November 1966 — 10,000 copies
Second printing, October 1968 — 15,000 copies

$6.00

FOREWORD

This is the second of three volumes comprising a verse-by-verse commentary on The Gospel of John, the "Salvation Book." It is, however, also an independent study covering chapters eight through fourteen of John's Gospel.

The chapters dealt with in this volume follow a central theme pointing to the unity of the Godhead—Father, Son, and Holy Spirit—and of the union of the believer with Christ. Throughout these passages Jesus the Son stresses His complete and perfect union with the Father, and passes on to His disciples the truth that though He did nothing independently of the Father, He nevertheless had life in Himself, as the Father had life.

In the last chapters included in this volume, as our Lord neared the end of His earthly ministry, His teaching reached a plane of high and holy intimacy with His disciples as He gradually withdrew from the public eye and concentrated His teaching upon the little band of men who were soon to represent Him on earth. Tender and gentle are His teachings in those passages, revealing not only the "express image" of Almighty God, but the compassionate Son of man and His understanding of human frailty.

This volume is sent forth with the prayer that Christians may be strengthened and encouraged, and the lost may be brought to Jesus through these pages.

The Author

CONTENTS

THE GOSPEL ACCORDING TO JOHN

CHAPTER VIII

1. Jesus went unto the mount of Olives.

2. And early in the morning he came again into the temple, and all the people came unto him; and he sat down, and taught them.

3. And the scribes and Pharisees brought unto him a woman taken in adultery; and when they had set her in the midst,

4. They say unto him, Master, this woman was taken in adultery, in the very act.

5. Now Moses in the law commanded us, that such should be stoned: but what sayest thou?

6. This they said, tempting him, that they might have to accuse him. But Jesus stooped down, and with his finger wrote on the ground, as though he heard them not.

7. So when they continued asking him, he lifted up himself, and said unto them, He that is without sin among you, let him first cast a stone at her.

8. And again he stooped down, and wrote on the ground.

9. And they which heard it, being convicted by their own conscience, went out one by one, beginning at the eldest, even unto the last: and Jesus was left alone, and the woman standing in the midst.

10. When Jesus had lifted up himself, and saw none but the woman, he said unto her, Woman, where are those thine accusers? hath no man condemned thee?

11. She said, No man, Lord. And Jesus said unto her, Neither do I condemn thee: go, and sin no more.

12. Then spake Jesus again unto them, saying, I am the light of the world: he that followeth me shall not walk in darkness, but shall have the light of life.

13. The Pharisees therefore said unto him, Thou bearest record of thyself; thy record is not true.

14. Jesus answered and said unto them, Though I bear record of myself, yet my record is true: for I know whence I came, and whither I go; but ye cannot tell whence I come, and whither I go.

15. Ye judge after the flesh; I judge no man.

16. And yet if I judge, my judgment is true: for I am not alone, but I and the Father that sent me.

17. It is also written in your law, that the testimony of two men

is true.

18. I am one that bear witness of myself, and the Father that sent me beareth witness of me.

19. Then said they unto him, Where is thy Father? Jesus answered, Ye neither know me, nor my Father: if ye had known me, ye should have known my Father also.

20. These words spake Jesus in the treasury, as he taught in the temple: and no man laid hands on him; for his hour was not yet come.

21. Then said Jesus again unto them, I go my way, and ye shall seek me, and shall die in your sins: whither I go, ye cannot come.

22. Then said the Jews, Will he kill himself? because he saith, Whither I go, ye cannot come.

23. And he said unto them, Ye are from beneath; I am from above: ye are of this world; I am not of this world.

24. I said therefore unto you, that ye shall die in your sins: for if ye believe not that I am he, ye shall die in your sins.

25. Then said they unto him, Who art thou? And Jesus saith unto them, Even the same that I said unto you from the beginning.

26. I have many things to say and to judge of you: but he that sent me is true; and I speak to the world those things which I have heard of him.

27. They understood not that he spake to them of the Father.

28. Then said Jesus unto them, When ye have lifted up the Son of man, then shall ye know that I am he, and that I do nothing of myself; but as my Father hath taught me, I speak these things.

29. And he that sent me is with me: the Father hath not left me alone; for I do always those things that please him.

30. As he spake these words, many believed on him.

31. Then said Jesus to those Jews which believed on him, If ye continue in my word, then are ye my disciples indeed;

32. And ye shall know the truth, and the truth shall make you free.

33. They answered him, We be Abraham's seed, and were never in bondage to any man: how sayest thou, Ye shall be made free?

34. Jesus answered them, Verily, verily, I say unto you, Whosoever committeth sin is the servant of sin.

35. And the servant abideth not in the house for ever: but the Son abideth ever.

36. If the Son therefore shall make you free, ye shall be free indeed.

37. I know that ye are Abraham's seed; but ye seek to kill me, because my word hath no place in you.

38. I speak that which I have seen with my Father: and ye do that which ye have seen with your father.

39. They answered and said unto him, Abraham is our father. Jesus

saith unto them, If ye were Abraham's children, ye would do the works of Abraham.

40. But now ye seek to kill me, a man that hath told you the truth, which I have heard of God: this did not Abraham.

41. Ye do the deeds of your father. Then said they to him, We be not born of fornication; we have one Father, even God.

42. Jesus said unto them, If God were your Father, ye would love me: for I proceeded forth and came from God; neither came I of myself, but he sent me.

43. Why do ye not understand my speech? even because ye cannot hear my word.

44. Ye are of your father the devil, and the lusts of your father ye will do. He was a murderer from the beginning, and abode not in the truth, because there is no truth in him. When he speaketh a lie, he speaketh of his own: for he is a liar, and the father of it.

45. And because I tell you the truth, ye believe me not.

46. Which of you convinceth me of sin? And if I say the truth, why do ye not believe me?

47. He that is of God heareth God's words: ye therefore hear them not, because ye are not of God.

48. Then answered the Jews, and said unto him, Say we not well that thou art a Samaritan, and hast a devil?

49. Jesus answered, I have not a devil; but I honour my Father, and ye do dishonour me.

50. And I seek not mine own glory: there is one that seeketh and judgeth.

51. Verily, verily, I say unto you, If a man keep my saying, he shall never see death.

52. Then said the Jews unto him, Now we know that thou hast a devil. Abraham is dead, and the prophets; and thou sayest, If a man keep my saying, he shall never taste of death.

53. Art thou greater than our father Abraham, which is dead? and the prophets are dead: whom makest thou thyself?

54. Jesus answered, If I honour myself, my honour is nothing: it is my Father that honoureth me; of whom ye say, that he is your God:

55. Yet ye have not known him; but I know him: and if I should say, I know him not, I shall be a liar like unto you: but I know him, and keep his saying.

56. Your father Abraham rejoiced to see my day: and he saw it, and was glad.

57. Then said the Jews unto him, Thou art not yet fifty years old, and hast thou seen Abraham?

58. Jesus said unto them, Verily, verily, I say unto you, Before Abraham was, I am.

59. Then took they up stones to cast at him: but Jesus hid himself, and went out of the temple, going through the midst of them, and so passed by.

The scribes and Pharisees had just failed in their attempt to have Jesus arrested—and so bitter was their anger against Him, I do not doubt that they spent *hours* thinking and planning, finally deciding on the scheme set forth in the first part of this chapter, in further effort to do away with Him and silence Him completely. They hoped by their newly devised plan to cause Him to bring condemnation upon *Himself,* thereby causing the public to turn against Him and continue their loyalty to the Law of Moses. If they could entangle Jesus as they hoped to do, they would have at least a pretense for bringing Him to trial before the Sanhedrin. But their plan was doomed to total failure, and was destined to bring embarrassment and humiliation upon themselves rather than upon this One who knew their hearts, every *secret* of their wicked hearts.

The Woman Taken in Adultery

Verses 1 and 2: *"Jesus went unto the mount of Olives. And early in the morning He came again into the temple, and all the people came unto Him; and He sat down, and taught them."*

The last verse of the preceding chapter told us that "every man went unto his own house," but evidently not one person invited Jesus to spend the night in a home, for in this first verse we are told that He *"went unto the Mount of Olives."* Very possibly He spent the night there, since it would not have been uncomfortable at that time of year to spend the night in the open air. In fact, according to Luke 21:37, Jesus spent a good many nights in the Mount of Olives: "In the day time He was teaching in the temple; and at night He went out, and abode in the mount that is called the Mount of Olives."

"Early in the morning He came again into the temple."

The record does not tell us at what *hour* Jesus came to the temple, but I personally believe it was at daybreak. Since He came *"again"* to the temple it would not be unreasonable to conclude that it was His custom to come there in early morning. This is borne out by the fact that members of the Sanhedrin knew He would be there at that time; otherwise they could not have laid such detailed plans to trap Him.

"All the people came unto Him." Jesus had been teaching at the feast of tabernacles for the past few days and His fame as a teacher had spread through the great crowds that thronged Jerusalem at that time. Thus a multitude of people came to hear Him in the temple.

"He sat down and taught them." Apparently it was customary in that day for a teacher to sit while teaching, for in Matthew 26:55 Jesus said, "I *sat daily with you teaching in the temple."* In Luke 5:3 we read, *"He sat down, and taught the people out of the ship."* In Acts 16:13, when Paul and Silas were at Philippi, we read, "On the Sabbath we went out of the city by a river side, where prayer was wont to be made; and *we sat down, and spake unto the women which resorted thither."* The teacher sat down, and the people gathered around him to hear his teaching. Since the people in that day did not have books and an abundance of printing as we do today, almost all information was gained by listening to public speakers.

Verses 3 and 4: *"And the scribes and Pharisees brought unto Him a woman taken in adultery; and when they had set her in the midst, they say unto Him, Master, this woman was taken in adultery, in the very act."*

It is interesting to note that this is the only place in the Gospel of John where the *scribes* are mentioned. The Pharisees are named twenty times, four of those times they are mentioned in connection with the chief priests; but scribes are not named except in verse 3 of this chapter.

The scribes and Pharisees *"brought unto Him a woman*

taken in adultery." Notice that this woman did not come willingly. She was *"brought"*—which means that she was carried or dragged—before the crowd of people who had gathered to hear Jesus teach. They *"set her in the midst"*—more than likely they flung her down in front of Jesus. Most assuredly she was put where she could be seen by all.

The scribes and Pharisees did not address Jesus as "Lord." They said to Him, *"Master* (teacher), *this woman was taken in adultery, in the very act."*

Verse 5:   *"Now Moses in the law commanded us, that such should be stoned: but what sayest thou?"*

The apparent zeal of these men to administer the Law of Moses could not fool the Lord, for He (the Word in flesh) "is a discerner of the thoughts and intents of the heart" (Heb. 4:12). He knew of their plan to trap Him, but He also knew that they were quoting only *part* of the law—the part that suited them and their purpose. What *did* Moses say in the law concerning a woman taken in adultery? Suppose we look at that part of the commandments and *read* what he said:

In Leviticus 20:10 we read, "The man that committeth adultery with another man's wife, even he that committeth adultery with his neighbour's wife, the *adulterer AND the adulteress shall surely be put to death."*

In Deuteronomy 22:22—24 we read, "If a man be found lying with a woman married to an husband, then they shall *both of them* die, both the man that lay with the woman, and the woman: so shalt thou put away evil from Israel. If a damsel that is a virgin be betrothed unto an husband, and a man find her in the city, and lie with her; then ye shall bring them *both* out unto the gate of that city, and ye shall stone them with stones that they die; the damsel, because she cried not, being in the city; and the man because he hath humbled his neighbour's wife: so thou shalt put away evil from among you."

Moses clearly said that both the man AND the woman

should be put to death if they were found guilty of the act of adultery. Why did not these scribes and Pharisees bring the *man* along with the woman? Jesus did not *ask*, "Where is the man?" because He already *knew* why they had not brought the second party involved in this incident. Could it have been that they did not accuse this woman's partner in the act because he was *one of their own group?* It is not difficult for me to believe that those who would go to such lengths to ensnare the Son of God would not hesitate to dupe a poor sinful woman into helping them in their scheme to find cause to have Him brought before the authorities.

Verse 6: *"This they said, tempting Him, that they might have to accuse Him. But Jesus stooped down, and with His finger wrote on the ground, as though He heard them not."*

The Holy Spirit makes it clear that these men were not interested in cleaning up the community, nor in stamping out immorality. They were tempting Jesus, trying to find something with which to accuse Him. What was the temptation here? How did these members of the Sanhedrin hope to find legal grounds for arresting Jesus and bringing Him before the authorities? They thought they had Him *trapped,* because if He said, *"Take the woman out and stone her"* He would openly deny what He preached. In Luke 19:10 He had announced, "The Son of man is come to seek and to save that which was lost." In Luke 9:56 He said, "The Son of man is not come to destroy men's lives, but to save them." He had also declared that publicans and harlots would enter the kingdom of God before the Pharisees (Matt. 21:31). He had proclaimed Himself as the Son of God, speaking the *words* of God. Therefore, if He invoked the Law of Moses against the woman and had her stoned, He would prove Himself an impostor and a false prophet.

On the other hand, if He said, "She shall NOT be stoned," He would be pouring contempt on the law! If He

told them to let her go free He would be condoning sin
and they could proclaim Him an enemy to righteousness.
Their plan was carefully laid; they thought they had Jesus
in a trap from which He could not escape—but He knew
their scheme, even before they devised it, and He did not
answer them audibly. Instead, He *"stooped down, and with
His finger wrote on the ground, as though He heard them
not."*

We are not told what Jesus wrote on the ground. Perhaps He wrote what Moses actually *did* say in the law concerning people guilty of adultery. Or perhaps He wrote
something from the Old Testament prophets, such as Isaiah
1:18: *"Come now, and let us reason together, saith the
Lord: Though your sins be as scarlet* (even the scarlet sin
of adultery), *they shall be as white as snow; though they
be red like crimson, they shall be as wool."* He might
have written something from His own sermons, something
they had heard Him proclaim with compassion and love
toward sinners. But *whatever* He wrote, His writing was
the Word of God.

Verses 7 and 8: *"So when they continued asking Him,
He lifted up Himself, and said unto them, He that is without sin among you, let him first cast a stone at her. And
again He stooped down, and wrote on the ground."*

The scribes and Pharisees were being energized by the
devil, and they were determined to get an audible answer
from Jesus—an answer they could use against Him to get
Him out of their way; but the malicious motive behind their
questions was not hidden from Jesus, and when He finally
answered them His words shocked them: *"He that is without sin among you, let him first cast a stone at her."* This
caused the finger of their conscience to point to themselves,
and it also assured them that Jesus had perfect understanding of the law. He was pointing them to the Old Testament Scriptures: "The hands of the witnesses shall be first
upon him to put him to death, and afterward the hands of

all the people. So thou shalt put the evil away from among you" (Deut. 17:7).

Jesus did not condemn the adulteress, neither did He justify her sin. At the same time, He gave honor and reverence to the Law of Moses. He said to these men, "I am not here to sentence this woman. I came *to seek and to save* sinners. YOU know the law, therefore you know that you have no right to judge and condemn her because you yourselves are not without sin. You profess to honor Moses and the Law of Moses, therefore I point you to what that law requires concerning an adulteress AND an adulterer."

The fact that He stooped and again began to write on the ground signified that insofar as He was concerned, the case was closed. He had neatly and wisely avoided their trap and was now waiting for the man without sin to cast the first stone at the woman they had brought before Him! Again, the Holy Spirit did not see fit to tell us what Jesus wrote on the ground the second time, but whatever it was, it convicted the enemies of the woman and *convinced her* that she was in the presence of the Lord, as she confessed a bit later.

Verse 9: *"And they which heard it, being convicted by their own conscience, went out one by one, beginning at the eldest, even unto the last: and Jesus was left alone, and the woman standing in the midst."*

When Jesus stooped the second time to write on the ground, the woman's accusers slipped out, silently, one by one, *"beginning at the eldest, even unto the last."* Why? The Word answers, *"being convicted by their own conscience!"* Every man has a God-given conscience. Paul speaks of those "having their conscience seared with a hot iron" (I Tim. 4:2), but the conscience is *there* — and the words of Jesus struck these men so forcibly, stirred the conscience to such conviction, that they slipped out as quietly as possible. When He said, "He that is without sin among you, let him first cast a stone at her," I believe He referred

to the sin of which the *woman* was accused, the sin of
adultery; and some of these men, if not *all* of them, were
guilty of that sin. No wonder they left the temple without
saying anything or attracting further attention to themselves! *"And Jesus was left alone, and the woman standing in the midst."*

Verses 10 and 11: *"When Jesus had lifted up Himself,
and saw none but the woman, He said unto her, Woman,
where are those thine accusers? Hath no man condemned
thee? She said, No man, Lord. And Jesus said unto her,
Neither do I condemn thee: go, and sin no more."*

When Jesus saw that the woman's accusers were gone,
He turned to her with a question—but you will notice that
He did not ask her, "Are you guilty as charged?" No, He
displayed mercy, compassion, and wisdom in what He asked:
*"Woman, where are those thine accusers? Hath no man
condemned thee?"*

Her reply is interesting: *"No man, LORD."* How did
this woman know that Jesus was the Lord? She was *evidently* a woman of the streets, a fallen woman, and it is
very unlikely that she had ever attended one of the meet-
ings Jesus conducted—either on the street or in the temple.
She may have *heard* about Him, but it is very doubtful that
she had ever heard Him preach. So how could she have
known that He was the Lord? There is but one answer:
"Faith cometh by *hearing,* and hearing by *the Word of
God"* (Rom. 10:17). Jesus had twice written on the ground
in this woman's presence, and under the circumstances she
most assuredly would have read what He wrote. We do
not know what *words* He wrote, but whatever the words,
the message they contained was the Word of God. The
woman was enlightened, the words of Jesus brought knowledge, understanding, and faith to her heart, and she acknowledged Him as *LORD.* "Wherefore I give you to understand, that no man speaking by the Spirit of God calleth
Jesus accursed: *and that no man (or woman) can say that*

Jesus is the Lord, BUT BY THE HOLY GHOST" (I Cor.
12:3). (This does not mean that a person cannot speak
those *words*—but when the Bible speaks of *confessing* Jesus
as Lord it means *from the heart*, in faith.)

*"Jesus said unto her, Neither do I condemn thee: Go,
and sin no more."* Please notice, Jesus did not say that this
woman had not sinned. He had come into the world to
seek and to save that which was lost, He had come into
the world to give His life a ransom for many and to pay
the sin-debt in full. Therefore He said to her, "I do not
pronounce judgment upon you, I do not condemn you. But
I DO say, *sin no more!"* There is no doubt in my mind
that this woman was saved as a result of her encounter
with Jesus, and I expect to meet her in that great resurrection morning.

Jesus the Light of the World

Verse 12: *"Then spake Jesus again unto them, saying,
I am the light of the world: he that followeth me shall
not walk in darkness, but shall have the light of life."*

"Then spake Jesus again . . . ." This takes us back to
verse 2, where our Lord was sitting in the temple and teaching the people when He was interrupted by the Pharisees
who brought the woman to Him. When the case was settled and the accusers were gone, He resumed His teaching.

"I am the light of the world." The feast of tabernacles
had just ended (ch. 7), recalling the life in the wilderness
and God's marvelous care of His children on that journey
(Lev. 23). The rock that gave forth water under Moses'
rod and the pillar of fire that led them by night were two
marks of God's special grace. On the last day of the feast,
referring to the carrying of water from the pool of Siloam,
Jesus had declared that He was the *living water.* In chapter 6, verses 31 through 35, with reference to the manna
with which God had fed the Israelites on their wilderness
journey, Jesus declared Himself to be the *living bread.*

NOW, with reference to the pillar of fire which had led
them, He declares that He is *the true Light* that guides
men through the wilderness of a sinful world, to the Paradise of God. Those who follow Jesus possess *"the light of
life."* Since Christ is the light of life, and since light *dis-
penses* life, the believer who lives in Christ and partakes
of His life automatically becomes "light in the Lord."

"For ye were sometimes darkness, but now are ye light
in the Lord: walk as children of light" (Eph. 5:8).

"Ye are all the children of light, and the children of
the day: we are not of the night, nor of darkness" (I Thess.
5:5).

Jesus is the living bread to nourish our inner man, He
is the water of life to quench the thirst of the inner man,
and He is just as truly *the LIGHT of life* to illumine the
walk of those who follow Him:

"If we walk in the light, as He is in the light, we have
fellowship one with another, and the blood of Jesus Christ
His Son cleanseth us from all sin" (I John 1:7).

"Darkness" in the New Testament denotes *sin,* as in
I John 1:6: "If we say that we have fellowship with Him,
and walk in darkness, we lie, and do not the truth." It
also denotes *ignorance and unbelief,* as in I Thessalonians
5:4: *"But YE, brethren, are not in darkness,* that that day
should overtake you as a thief." The woman whom Jesus
had just saved had been living in darkness—she was guilty
of the sin of adultery, and she was ignorant concerning
God's love and salvation by grace. Therefore Jesus said to
the people, "The person who believes in me, receives my
words, receives ME, the light of the world, shall be delivered from darkness and shall walk in paths of light. The
person who receives me as the light of the world will walk
in the light."

Jesus proclaimed Himself *"the light of the WORLD"*—
not just light for a few, but to all mankind who will follow
Him. There is enough light for everyone. Those who believe on Him will benefit from that light, those who *refuse*

to believe will abide in darkness:

"If our Gospel be hid, it is hid to them that are lost: in whom the god of this world hath blinded the minds of them which believe not, lest the light of the glorious Gospel of Christ, who is the image of God, should shine unto them. For we preach not ourselves, but Christ Jesus the Lord; and ourselves your servants for Jesus' sake. For God, who commanded the light to shine out of darkness, hath shined in our hearts, to give the light of the knowledge of the glory of God in the face of Jesus Christ" (II Cor. 4:3—6).

"Ye are a chosen generation, a royal priesthood, an holy nation, a peculiar people; that ye should shew forth the praises of Him who hath called you out of darkness into His marvellous light" (I Pet. 2:9).

Verse 13: *"The Pharisees therefore said unto Him, Thou bearest record of thyself; thy record is not true."*

It is not likely that the "Pharisees" in this verse are the same as those who brought the woman to Jesus. There were many Pharisees, they were a powerful religious group, and no doubt these were part of the crowd who attended the early morning Bible class where Jesus was teaching.

"Thou bearest record of thyself; thy record is not true." The meaning of this statement is simply, "You are a false witness." These people were *willingly ignorant* concerning the witness God had given—at the birth of Jesus, again at His baptism, through the miracles He wrought, and in other ways, such as Old Testament prophecies. They refused to accept the testimony God had given, they refused to let the light break into the darkness of their closed minds.

Verse 14: *"Jesus answered and said unto them, Though I bear record of myself, yet my record is true: for I know whence I came, and whither I go; but ye cannot tell whence I come, and whither I go."*

The miracles Jesus had performed certainly should have shown these skeptics that His testimony was not that of

an ordinary witness. They should have believed Him "for
the work's sake."

"I know whence I came." Jesus was speaking of His
pre-existence in the beginning with the Father. He came
forth *from* the Father on a divine mission, and He would
return to the glory He had *with* the Father before the world
began. Since this was true, His testimony was worthy and
should be received by man.

Notice the change of tense from *"I came"* to *"I come."*
"I *came"* refers to His own knowledge of His Incarnation.
"I *come"* accommodates the ignorance of His listeners and
refers to His immediate presence with them. His enemies
need not necessarily have known the former—His pre-existence, His Incarnation; but they certainly should have recognized present evidences—His miracles, His teaching. Therefore they could have acknowledged that He spoke with authority, the authority of God, who had sent Him. But they
refused to see beyond the natural, they were willingly ignorant, blinded by their father the devil, the god of this age.

Verse 15:   *"Ye judge after the flesh; I judge no man."*

Man looks on the outward appearance; God looks on the
inner man. The Pharisees judged everything from the standpoint of the flesh, they judged by the principles of this
world. All they knew about Jesus was what they had *seen,*
and they had evidently forgotten the words of their prophet
Isaiah, that Messiah would grow up as a tender plant out
of dry ground—meek, lowly, humble, coming as a lamb,
not as a great worldly king or political power. These people judged everything by false standards. Their minds and
hearts were filled with prejudice against Jesus; they had
convinced themselves that He was an impostor, a blasphemer, and that He should be put to death.

"I judge no man." Here Jesus set Himself in direct
contrast with the Pharisees. They had judged *and condemned* Him, but in His present mission and ministry He
judged no man. He came as the Lamb of God—not to

judge, but to seek and to save that which was lost. However, those who refuse to believe on Him as *Saviour* will one day stand before Him as Judge, for He *will* "judge the quick and the dead at His appearing and His kingdom" (II Tim. 4:1). On one occasion (Luke 9:51—56) the disciples asked Jesus if they should call down fire from heaven and consume their enemies, and He rebuked them: "Ye know not what manner of spirit ye are of. For the Son of man is not come to destroy men's lives, but to save them." Yes, He came to seek and to save even these Pharisees who were His bitter enemies, but they refused to hear Him.

Verse 16: *"And yet if I judge, my judgment is true: for I am not alone, but I and the Father that sent me."*

Although the mission of Jesus at that time was not to judge men, He was *qualified* to judge and His judgment would have been perfect, righteous, and trustworthy because He was God in flesh. This bears out the same thought declared in chapter 5, verse 19: "Then answered Jesus and said unto them, Verily, verily, I say unto you, The Son can do nothing of Himself, but what He seeth the Father do: for what things soever He doeth, these also doeth the Son likewise."

In John 5:30 Jesus said, "I can of mine own self do nothing: as I hear, I judge: and my judgment is just; because I seek not mine own will, but the will of the Father which hath sent me."

Our present verse declares again the paramount truth of the inseparable, eternal union between God the Father and God the Son. Actually, Jesus said, "As the Son of man I judge *no man.* On the contrary, I *save* all who will hear my words. But *you* will not hear me because you abide in darkness. However, if I *should* judge, I am qualified to judge and my judgment would be trustworthy, righteous, and just; because whatever I do, I do only what the *Father* does. I and my Father are one."

Verse 17: *"It is also written in your law, that the testi-*

mony of two men is true."

When Jesus said, *"YOUR law"* He was not speaking disrespectfully of the Law of Moses. In Matthew 5:17 He assured the people that He had not come to destroy the law, but to fulfill it, and according to Romans 10:4 He did exactly that: "For Christ is the *end* of the law for right-eousness to every one that believeth." But the Jews honored the Law of Moses, they acknowledged Moses as God's prophet and were proud to be known as his followers. They were continually reminding Jesus that He had broken the law when He healed on the Sabbath, and here He simply reminded them that *according* to the Law of Moses which they stressed so fervently, the testimony of two witnesses was to be recognized and accepted:

"At the mouth of two witnesses, or three witnesses, shall he that is worthy of death be put to death; but at the mouth of ONE witness he shall not be put to death. . .
One witness shall not rise up against a man for any iniq-uity, or for any sin, in any sin that he sinneth: at the mouth of *two* witnesses, or at the mouth of *three* witnesses, shall the matter be established" (Deut. 17:6; 19:15). The law said that the testimony of two witnesses was trust-worthy, therefore Jesus was bidding them observe that there were two Witnesses to His divine mission. GOD had testi-fied as to who Jesus was and had honored both His words and His works. Jesus Himself had declared that He was in the Father and the Father in Him, and that He worked and spoke as the Father taught Him. Therefore the "two witnesses" were in evidence, and Jesus was undoubtedly contrasting the testimony of Himself and God the Father with the testimony of ordinary men. I John 5:9 plainly tells us, "If we receive the witness of *men,* the witness of *God* is greater." The Pharisees were willing to receive the witness of ordinary men, but they would not receive the witness of God the Father and God the Son.

Verse 18:   *"I am one that bear witness of myself, and*

the Father that sent me beareth witness of me."

"I . . . bear witness of myself *. . . the Father . . .* beareth witness of me." Jesus the eternal Son testified of Himself—and *proved* His testimony by the things He did. God the Father witnessed concerning the Son—on four occasions He gave audible witness to the divine nature and mission of Jesus here on earth. God also gave testimony through the prophets concerning Jesus. In Genesis 3:15 God promised the seed of the woman, and the Old Testament prophets consistently declared that He would come.

We are told that it is almost impossible to translate the Greek language of this verse into English and still retain the full meaning. The Greek actually reads, *"I, the great I AM,* am the One witnessing about myself; and Jehovah my Father who sent me also witnesses of me." Jesus did not distinguish Himself from Jehovah God in respect to His divine, eternal BEING, but in respect to His *office.* When He said, "Jehovah the Father who sent me" He had reference to the official mission He had been sent into the world to perform—i. e., He was set forth to be a propitiation for sin.

The Jews were well acquainted with the reference to the great "I AM." They knew that "I AM" was Jehovah God of the Old Testament, the God of Israel. Jesus was God in flesh, therefore the great *"I AM"* in flesh testified, *God the Father* in heaven testified, the *prophets* throughout the Old Testament testified concerning Christ's divine nature and His divine mission on earth. If the Jews really *believed* the Law of Moses as they claimed to believe, they should have readily received their Messiah of whom Moses witnessed.

Verse 19: *"Then said they unto Him, Where is thy Father? Jesus answered, Ye neither know me, nor my Father: if ye had known me, ye should have known my Father also."*

"Where is thy Father?" was not a sincere question. It was asked in sarcasm, in a sneering, jeering manner. You

will notice that the Jews did not ask Jesus, *"WHO is thy Father?"* but *"WHERE is thy Father?"* I imagine they looked around as if searching for someone, expecting someone to step forward and stand by His side to testify in His behalf. Since they refused to believe that Jesus was the divine Son of God, they did not ask WHO His Father was. Their attitude said, "You claim to have two witnesses— yourself and your Father. We see YOU, now let us see your FATHER."

When Jesus was on the cross these Jews taunted Him, "IF you are the Son of God, save yourself and us! IF you are the Son of God, come down from the cross and we will believe!" They were continually asking Jesus to *show* them, give them evidence for the natural eye. The world cries out, *"SHOW us,* and we will believe." But faith says, *"BELIEVE*—and you will *see* the glory of God."

"Jesus answered, Ye neither know me, NOR my Father: If ye had known me, ye should have known my Father also." Those who ignore Jesus, both in the reality of His Person and in the work that He did, are ignorant of God the Father. It is *through the Son* that God the Father reveals Himself to man (John 1:18). To confess God as Father and yet reject Jesus the Son is to be spiritually blind and grossly ignorant. He who knows the Father *in reality* also knows the Son, and until he knows the Son he cannot know the Father. This was made very clear in verse 23 of chapter 5: "All men should honour the Son, even as they honour the Father. *He that honoureth not the Son honoureth not the Father which hath sent Him."*

"If ye had known me, ye should have known my Father also." Those who know God *in truth* know Him because *the Son* has made the Father known to them. Apart from the Son there is no salvation. It is in the only begotten Son that the Father is well pleased, and we can know the Father only as we know the Son, for *Christ IS Christianity.*

Verse 20: *"These words spake Jesus in the treasury, as*

He taught in the temple: and no man laid hands on Him; for His hour was not yet come."

This verse makes it plain that Jesus did not deliver the message of His messiahship in a secluded spot, but publicly and openly, in one of the most prominent places in the temple—*"the treasury."* This was the part of the temple where the sacred offerings were kept, and it was therefore frequented often, and by many people.

"And no man laid hands on Him." They *wanted* to! They wanted to close His mouth and stop His testimony—but they were divinely restrained. According to God's eternal blueprint, there was a definite and foreordained time when Jesus would surrender to His enemies; but until that time came, they could not touch Him! In Luke 22:53, when Judas came to Gethsemane and betrayed Jesus with a kiss, Jesus said to the chief priests, elders, and soldiers, "When I was daily with you in the temple, ye stretched forth no hands against me: but *this is YOUR hour, and the power of darkness."* When the moment arrived for Him to be taken by His enemies, arrested, condemned, and crucified, He surrendered to them; but until that very moment they could not take Him because He was divinely protected.

I am not a fatalist, but I firmly believe that it is impossible for Satan to touch a child of God without God's permission. Believers are led by the Spirit, protected by divine restraint, and Satan cannot bring harm to them unless God permits it. How precious to the Christian is Romans 8:28: "We know that ALL things work together for good to them that love God, to them who are the called according to His purpose!" *Until the hour comes for a Christian to be tried, tested, suffer, or die, he cannot be touched by the enemy.*

Verse 21: *"Then said Jesus again unto them, I go my way, and ye shall seek me, and shall die in your sins: whither I go, ye cannot come."*

When Jesus said, *"I go my way"* He meant that His

mission was almost over, the work He had come to do was
almost finished.   He would soon leave this world and return to the Father in heaven.   His statement should have
caused the Jews to inquire further concerning His identity
and His divine nature.   Certainly after His repeated declar-
ations that He had been with the Father in the beginning,
that He and the Father were one, and that He did nothing
independently of the Father, they should have realized that
His statements in this verse were unusual indeed.

"Ye shall seek me, and shall die in your sins."   Yes,
after His crucifixion some of these very people would seek
Him—but it would be too late.   Too late they would discover that He was the Messiah, the One who had come to
save them; but *for them* the door of mercy would be closed.
They would seek in vain, because they had not known the
time of their visitation (Luke 19:44).   The Gospel was "to
the Jew first" (Rom. 1:16).   The Jews were exposed to the
Word in flesh, but their minds and hearts were closed to
the Gospel, the god of this age had blinded them to spiritual things, and they rejected their Messiah.   Because of
this, they would *"die in their sins."*

"Whither I go, ye cannot come"—meaning heaven.   The
wicked cannot enter heaven.   All who come to God must
believe on the Lord Jesus Christ and receive Him as personal Saviour; all who *refuse to believe* stand condemned
ALREADY (John 3:18).

The statement in this verse was made primarily to the
nation Israel.   No nation on earth has been so miserable,
so unsettled, so persecuted, as the Jewish people have been.
They are still expecting their Messiah.   They look for Him,
they hunger for Him, but they cannot find Him—and they
will not find Him until He returns the second time and they
see the scars in His hands and feet.   The Jews who find
Him *before* that time will find Him through faith in His
shed blood and finished work!

The fact that Jesus told these Jews that they would die
in their sins did not mean that they were *too sinful* to be

saved—indeed not. He simply meant that the Jews *as a nation* would be hardened in unbelief, and even though many of them would be saved individually, the nation as such would die in sin. The statement Jesus made here was, in a sense, prophetic. For further light on this, please study Acts 28:25—27 and Romans 11:7—12.

Even today many seek the Lord too late. Isaiah cried out, warning that we should seek the Lord while He may be found and call upon Him while He is near. The Apostle Paul warned that TODAY is the day of salvation, NOW is the accepted time. A very solemn warning is found in Proverbs 1:22—33. Read it. It has been quoted in these pages, but it will do you good to read it again. Also study Matthew 25:11,12; Luke chapter 13; Hebrews 6:1—8; 11: 26—31.

It is dangerous to be *exposed* to the Gospel, to recognize the need of a Saviour, and then *reject* the message of salvation. If you are not saved, dear reader, if you acknowledge your need of a Saviour and you hear the call of the Spirit, remember TODAY is the day of salvation, NOW is the accepted time. Seek ye the Lord while He may be found; no man can come to Jesus except the Father draw Him!

"Ye shall seek me . . . Whither I go, ye cannot come" is an expression found in almost the same words three times in the Gospel of John. In our present verse and in chapter 7 verse 34, Jesus was speaking to the unbelieving scribes and Pharisees. When He used the same words in chapter 13 verse 33 He was speaking to His disciples. When He spoke to the unconverted religious leaders He added, *"Ye shall die in your sins";* but when He spoke to the disciples He was preparing them for the temporary separation which would occur by way of His ascension. He would be taken from them, and *at that particular time* they could not follow Him.

Verse 22: *"Then said the Jews, Will He kill Himself? because He saith, Whither I go, ye cannot come."*

The enemies of Jesus were greatly disturbed by His statement in the previous verse. In chapter 7 verse 34 they
wondered if He meant that He was turning to the *Gentile*
world since the Jews had rejected His message; but now
they began to think along another line. They wondered if
He planned to take His own life, thereby departing this
world for another. He had made it clear that He knew they
were planning to destroy Him, and possibly they thought
He meant to beat them to their wicked scheme by taking
His own life. History tells us that when Titus the Roman
overran Jerusalem in 70 A. D., many of the Jews did take
their own lives rather than face the horrible death in store
for them at the hands of the enemy.

Verse 23: *"And He said unto them, Ye are from beneath;
I am from above: ye are of this world; I am not of this
world."*

Jesus and His enemies had nothing in common. There
was no harmony, no fellowship. The Pharisees lived,
planned, and thought only in terms of this world, in terms
of the flesh. Jesus was a citizen of another world, He came
from the Father in heaven, He was in the world to do the
work the Father sent Him to do; and when He had finished that work He would return to His former glory. But
since the Jews loved the things of the world and thought
only in terms of the world, they could not go where He was
going. They refused to believe on Him as the Lamb of
God who came to take away the sin of the world, and they
would therefore *die* in their sins.

When Jesus used the terms *"from beneath"* and *"from
above"* He contrasted earth and heaven: "If ye then be
risen with Christ, seek those things which are above, where
Christ sitteth on the right hand of God. Set your affection
on things above, not on things on the earth. For ye are
dead, and your life is hid with Christ in God" (Col. 3:1—3).

"Ye are of this world." In I John 2:15—11 we are commanded, "Love NOT the world, neither the things that are

IN the world. *If any man love the world, the love of the Father is not in him. For all that is in the world, the lust of the flesh, and the lust of the eyes, and the pride of life, is not of the Father, but is of the world.* And the world passeth away, and the lust thereof: but he that doeth the will of God abideth for ever."

"I am NOT of this world." Neither are true *believers* of this world. Our citizenship is in heaven (Eph. 2:6; Phil. 3:20). Please read John 15:19; 17:16; and I John 4:5,6.

Verse 24: *"I said therefore unto you, that ye shall die in your sins: for if ye believe not that I am He, ye shall die in your sins."*

Jesus clearly tells *why* He said, "Ye shall die in your sins": *"YE BELIEVE NOT that I am He."* Greek scholars tell us that the pronoun "He" is not in the original text. Therefore, Jesus said to the Jews, *"Ye believe not that I AM."* They well knew that "I AM" was Jehovah God, and that by this declaration Jesus was telling them that He was God in flesh. But they did not believe.

The *sin of unbelief* brought misery and destruction upon the Jews: "He that believeth on Him is not condemned: but he that believeth not is condemned already, because he hath not believed in the name of the only begotten Son of God. . . He that believeth on the Son hath everlasting life: and he that believeth not the Son shall not see life; but the wrath of God abideth on him" (John 3:18,36). The sin of unbelief is the most insulting sin man can commit against a holy God, because it makes God a liar: "He that believeth on the Son of God hath the witness in himself: *he that believeth NOT God hath made Him a liar;* because he believeth not the record that God gave of His Son" (I John 5:10).

Many people today say nice things about Jesus: they speak of Him as a great teacher, the founder of a great religion. It is true that He was a great teacher, but being a great teacher is not sufficient for salvation. He was *not* the founder of a great religion—*He was Christianity, GOD IN FLESH*, and we must believe on Him "as the Scripture hath said." He is still saying to unbelievers, "You must believe that I AM, *or ye shall die in your sins!*"

Verse 25: *"Then said they unto Him, Who art thou? And Jesus saith unto them, Even the same that I said unto you from the beginning."*

Malice and anger were behind their question here. These men knew who Jesus claimed to be; on several occasions they had heard Him declare that He came *from* God and would return *to* God. But they were hoping to lead Him to make some new declaration which could be used against Him, so they tauntingly asked, *"Who are YOU* to say such things about us—the religious leaders, children of Abraham and disciples of Moses?"

Jesus replied, *"Even the same that I said unto you from the beginning."* He gave them no new declaration. He did not need to repeat anything He had said, for when He spoke, His words were "Thus saith the LORD." So He simply said, "Why do you ask me again who I am? I have *told* you who I am, and if you did not believe me then, you would not believe me if I repeated it now."

"The beginning" here refers to the beginning of the Lord's earthly ministry, not to the beginning of all things. (See also John 6:64; 15:27; 16:4.)

Verses 26 and 27: *"I have many things to say and to judge of you: but He that sent me is true; and I speak to the world those things which I have heard of Him. They understood not that He spake to them of the Father."*

What Jesus said here was simply this: "I have a perfect right to say what I have said to you, and I might say *many other things* to you. I am not an ordinary prophet; I am from God the Father—yea, I am God in flesh." There were many other judgments He could have pronounced upon them, but He did not do so at that time. He would, how-

ever, have them know that what He said was *true* because
He spoke only the words given to Him by the Father. They
were not words of His own choosing, but the Word of the
living God who had sent Him and who dwelt in Him. But
the scribes and Pharisees were in such complete spiritual
darkness that they could not understand that Jesus spoke
to them of the *heavenly* Father, the God of their fathers,
the same God whom they claimed to reverence and worship.
They thought He referred to some earthly group who had
sent Him to speak to them.

Verse 28: *"Then said Jesus unto them, When ye have
lifted up the Son of man, then shall ye know that I am He,
and that I do nothing of myself; but as my Father hath
taught me, I speak these things."*

Jesus entered His public ministry speaking as no man
had ever spoken. He wrought miracles beyond what any
ordinary man could have done. But in spite of all that
He said and did, in spite of all that He had proved to be,
the majority of the Jews still refused to believe on Him,
they refused to believe that He was sent from God, the Son
of God, Messiah and Saviour. Their object in following
Him day by day and continually watching Him was that
they might find something by which they could accuse Him,
arrest Him, convict Him, and put Him to death. Jesus
knew their hearts, and He also knew what lay ahead—He
knew *all* things. Therefore He said to them, "When you
have nailed me to the cross and lifted me between heaven
and earth, *you will know who I am!"*

What *happened* when they lifted Jesus up on the cross?
How did God tell these people that this was His only begotten Son—not an impostor, not an ordinary prophet, not
the deceiver they claimed Him to be?

In Matthew 27:35—54 we find the record: "And they
crucified Him, and parted His garments, casting lots: that
it might be fulfilled which was spoken by the prophet,
They parted my garments among them, and upon my vesture

did they cast lots. And sitting down they watched Him there; and set up over His head His accusation written, THIS IS JESUS THE KING OF THE JEWS. Then were there two thieves crucified with Him, one on the right hand, and another on the left. And they that passed by reviled Him, wagging their heads, and saying, Thou that destroyest the temple, and buildest it in three days, save thyself. If thou be the Son of God, come down from the cross. Likewise also the chief priests mocking Him, with the scribes and elders, said, He saved others; Himself He cannot save. If He be the King of Israel, let Him now come down from the cross, and we will believe Him. *He trusted in God; let Him deliver Him now, if He will have Him: for He said, I am the Son of God."*

Up to this point, nothing of an alarming nature had happened; but now God began to tell the people who Jesus was:

"Now from the sixth hour there was darkness over all the land unto the ninth hour." At *high noon,* darkness engulfed the whole world! The Man on the middle cross had said, "I am the light of the world . . . When you lift me up on the cross, God will *tell* you who I am!" Now God had turned out the lights of the universe, and by so doing He wrote "Finished!" across physical existence, for without *light,* man could not live.

"And about the ninth hour Jesus cried with a loud voice, saying . . . My God, my God, why hast thou forsaken me? . . . Jesus, when He had cried again with a loud voice, yielded up the ghost. *AND, BEHOLD, THE VEIL OF THE TEMPLE WAS RENT IN TWAIN FROM THE TOP TO THE BOTTOM."* This Man on the middle cross had claimed to be Messiah, God in flesh. He had said to these people, "I am your Saviour, your Redeemer, your High Priest. I am the ONE Sacrifice, the Lamb without spot or blemish. I am the Way, the Truth, the Life." But they said, "You are an impostor! We know who you are. We know your father, we know your mother, we know that you are the product of fornication." They accused Him of everything that was common, ungodly, and insulting. But when they lifted Him up on the cross, the veil in the temple was rent in twain from top to bottom, the veil that separated the holy of holies from the outer court. The holy of holies now lay naked and open to all. When the veil of the temple was rent in twain, God wrote "Finished!" across the religion of the Jews.

But God said more: When Jesus died on the cross, "the earth did quake, and the rocks rent; *and the graves were opened; AND MANY BODIES OF THE SAINTS WHICH SLEPT AROSE, AND CAME OUT OF THE GRAVES after His resurrection,* and went into the holy city, and appeared unto many."

Jesus had said, "I am the resurrection, and the life: he that believeth in me, though he were dead, yet shall he live: and whosoever liveth and believeth in me shall never die"—but they did not believe Him! They refused to receive Him as the resurrection and the life; but when He rose from the dead, many bodies of saints arose, bodies that had been in the grave for many years, and went into Jerusalem and appeared to many of the people, living testimony that Jesus was the resurrection and the life.

Jesus had said, "When ye have lifted up the Son of man, then shall ye know that I am He, and that I do nothing of myself; but as my Father hath taught me, I speak these things." And when He died on the cross, God turned out the lights in the entire universe, writing "Finished" across physical existence, because without the sunlight life could not exist. When Jesus died on the cross, God split the veil in the temple from top to bottom, writing "Finished" across Judaism, for without the veil the Jews could not worship. When Jesus rose from the dead, the bodies of many of the saints rose with Him and walked into Jerusalem, thus testifying to all that Jesus was truly the resurrection and the life. Yes, God did testify when wicked men lifted Jesus on the cross. He told them who Jesus was. Some believed;

others did not.

The same is true today. Regardless of what God might do, regardless of what miracles He might perform, there are some who would refuse to believe. You may rest assured that all who are not convinced through His Word *will BE convinced* when they stand before God and hear Him say, "Depart, I never knew you."

It is always *"the Son of man"* who is lifted up. On the cross as the Son of man, Jesus displayed to the world His highest act of self-renunciation and gave the clearest proof that He was all that He claimed to be. He was God in flesh, yet He was the Son of man, obedient unto death, even the death of the cross. "Wherefore God also hath highly exalted Him, and given Him a name which is above every name: that at the name of Jesus every knee should bow, of things in heaven, and things in earth, and things under the earth; and that every tongue should confess that Jesus Christ is Lord, to the glory of God the Father" (Phil. 2:9—11).

Verse 29: *"And He that sent me is with me: the Father hath not left me alone; for I do always those things that please Him."*

Here again is expressed the unity of Father and Son. The Father's constant presence with the Son was based on the fact of the perfect doing of the will of God by Jesus the Son of man.

Only Jesus could have truthfully said, *"I do always those things that please Him."* Such words express the spotless perfection and the divine holiness of the Son of God, and His testimony must be accepted by finite man in faith. No mortal could ever justifiably say, "I do always those things that please God," for when we have done our utmost we must confess that we have fallen far short of doing the complete will of God!

Verse 30: *"As He spake these words, many believed on Him."*

"These words" indicate the entire discourse of Jesus at this time, beginning with verse 12. No doubt there was much in His teaching that reminded the people of prophesies from the Old Testament, and thus *"many believed on Him,"* but only with intellectual belief. Their hearts were unchanged, they did not believe on Him as Saviour and Lord. This is proved by their later actions, up to the time of His crucifixion. It is not believing *about* Jesus that makes men sons of God; it is believing ON Him, trusting from the heart: "For with the heart man believeth unto righteousness; and with the mouth confession is made unto salvation" (Rom. 10:10).

Verse 31: *"Then said Jesus to those Jews which believed on Him, If ye continue in my Word, then are ye my disciples indeed."*

Faith without works is dead. Discipleship depends upon permanent application of the Word. Passing impulses and emotion do not make true Christians.

"If ye continue in my Word" does not mean that these people had *accepted* the Word, at least not in the terms of "except ye eat my flesh and drink my blood," the actual appropriation of the Word. What Jesus was saying here is simply this: "If you receive me in truth, you will take a firm stand and *continue* in the Word which you have received." The same truth is expressed in many other places in the New Testament, as in Romans 8:1 where Paul said, "There is therefore now no condemnation to them which are in Christ Jesus, *who walk not after the flesh, but after the Spirit."* You will notice that Paul did not say, "IF they walk not after the flesh," but *"WHO WALK NOT after the flesh."* Since Christ is in the believer, the believer walks in the Spirit. We are children of light and we *walk* in the light because Christ abides within. The proof of true faith, according to our present verse, is *walking* in faith, *abiding in the Word.*

Ignorance Is the Mother of Slavery

Verse 32: *"And ye shall know the truth, and the truth shall make you free."*

What did Jesus mean when He said, *"Ye shall know the truth"*? He meant the whole *doctrine of truth* concerning *Himself*—His eternal existence with the Father, the fact that He had life in Himself, His nature as very God, yet very man, and the truth concerning His mission on earth.

"The truth shall make you free." Acceptance of the Word of God breaks the shackles of sin, the shackles of human tradition, and the shackles of ecclesiastical and religious bondage. Truth also sets us free from the fear that has torment (I John 4:18). These scribes and Pharisees were bound in spiritual slavery—they were in bondage to the traditions of men and the religion of their fathers. In Luke 4:18 Jesus said, "The Spirit of the Lord is upon me, because He hath anointed me to preach the Gospel to the poor; He hath sent me to heal the brokenhearted, *to preach deliverance to the captives,* and recovering of sight to the blind, to set at liberty them that are bruised." In other words, He had come to declare the truth that would set men free if they would only hear and believe His words.

"The truth" sets us free from condemnation and delivers us from death: "Verily, verily, I say unto you, He that heareth my Word, and believeth on Him that sent me, hath everlasting life, and shall not come into condemnation; but is passed from death unto life" (John 5:24).

Verse 33: *"They answered Him, We be Abraham's seed, and were never in bondage to any man: how sayest thou, Ye shall be made free?"*

The Pharisees demonstrated the fact that *pride* blinds the mind of man to the truth of God. It is true that they were Abraham's seed, his blood ran in their veins—but the faith of Abraham was not in their hearts.

"We . . . were never in bondage to any man." Had they forgotten the Egyptian bondage? the Babylonian bondage? At *that very moment* they were in bondage to the Romans! That was why they were looking for Messiah to come as an outstanding military or political leader; they longed to be free of the power of Rome. It was to these people that John the Baptist preached, "Think not to say within yourselves, *We have Abraham to our father:* for I say unto you, that God is able of these stones to raise up children unto Abraham" (Matt. 3:9). In connection with this, please read Isaiah 41:8 and Galatians 3:29.

The Jews were blinded to their *need* of spiritual blessings. They considered themselves custodians of divine truth, free-born sons of Abraham, and *pride closed their minds* to The Truth which would have made them free!

"How sayest thou, Ye shall be made free?" This question was asked in anger and resentment, but it was also a question of curiosity. They remembered the glorious kingdom of Messiah which their prophets had foretold, and it could be that they were indirectly asking if Jesus would at that time restore the kingdom to Israel. Would He really set them free from the Romans? The Jews were always ready to give a carnal interpretation to spiritual language used by Jesus, but when He spoke of the bondage of sin and told them that the truth would set them free, His words were strange to them, words that were beyond their understanding because they were carnal in their thinking. Paul said, "To be carnally minded is death; but to be spiritually minded is life and peace. Because the carnal mind is enmity against God: for it is not subject to the law of God, neither indeed can be" (Rom. 8:6,7).

Verses 34 and 35: *"Jesus answered them, Verily, verily, I say unto you, Whosoever committeth sin is the servant of sin. And the servant abideth not in the house for ever: but the Son abideth ever."*

Here we find another "double verily," indicating the very

important truth concerning the kind of liberty Jesus was speaking of. He illustrated this freedom by showing them the kind of slavery from which He would *deliver* them if they would only receive the truth. He could set them free from sin, He could free their darkened minds and their unbelieving hearts.

"Whosoever committeth sin is the servant of sin." The person who lives in habitual sin, wilful sin being the habit of life, is acknowledged as the servant (or slave) of sin. In Romans 6:16−23 Paul said, "Know ye not, that to whom ye yield yourselves servants to obey, his servants ye are to whom ye obey; whether of sin unto death, or of obedience unto righteousness? But God be thanked, that *ye were the servants of sin, but ye have obeyed from the heart that form of doctrine which was delivered you. Being then made free from sin, ye became the servants of righteousness.* I speak after the manner of men because of the infirmity of your flesh: for as ye have yielded your members *servants to uncleanness and to iniquity unto iniquity;* even so now yield your members *servants to righteousness unto holiness.* For when ye were the *servants of sin,* ye were *free from righteousness.* What fruit had ye then in those things whereof ye are now ashamed? for the end of those things is death. But now being made *free from sin,* and become *servants to God,* ye have your fruit unto holiness, and the end everlasting life. For the wages of sin is death; but the gift of God is eternal life through Jesus Christ our Lord."

II Peter 2:19 tells us that "of whom a man is overcome, of the same is he brought in bondage."

"The servant abideth not in the house for ever"(notice the contrast here): *"but the SON abideth ever."* A servant (slave) had no guaranteed privileges or rights. He was the property of another, the creature of the will and pleasure of the one who owned him. There was no point of common interest between the slave and his master. He could be sold, he could be disowned and sent away, he could even be put to death if his master so willed. The son, on the

other hand, had his own particular place in the home and could abide there always. He was second only to the father, the head of the house. He was heir of all, the object of love, care, and pride.

Jesus used this illustration, contrasting son and slave, in order to show the Jews that *they* were slaves to the system under which they were living, they were in bondage to the ceremonial laws and the traditions of the Pharisees. As servants and slaves, they could be cast out of God's favor at any moment, but if they would only hear the Lord Jesus, the Messiah who would set them free from the bondage of sin, they would no longer be servants, but sons, and would abide in God's house and in His favor throughout all eternity.

Certainly the Jews were familiar with the Old Testament account of Hagar and Ishmael who as bondservants were cast out of Abraham's house, while Isaac, son of promise and rightful heir, remained. (Read the account in Genesis chapter 16, and 21:9—21.) Jesus wanted the Jews to be like Isaac and accept the place and privilege of sons forever. He wanted them to find liberty in His Word and in Him, their true Messiah.

Under the Mosaic system the priests were servants, they stood daily offering sacrifices; but Christ was the Son who came to offer ONE sacrifice, for all, forever, never to be repeated. The Jewish priests could not set men free, and many times they offered the same sacrifice for the same sin over and over again (Hebrews, chapter 10). But Jesus the Son had power to set men free. He invited them to hear the truth, believe the truth, and be set free *eternally*.

Paul gives more light on this in Hebrews 3:1—6: "Wherefore, holy brethren, partakers of the heavenly calling, consider the Apostle and High Priest of our profession, Christ Jesus; who was faithful to Him that appointed Him, as also Moses was faithful in all His house. For this Man was counted worthy of more glory than Moses, inasmuch as he who hath builded the house hath more honour than the

house.   For every house is builded by some man; but He
that built all things is God. And *Moses verily was faithful
in all His house, as a SERVANT*, for a testimony of those
things which were to be spoken after; *but Christ as a SON
over His own house*; whose house are we, if we hold fast
the confidence and the rejoicing of the hope firm unto the
end."

Verse 36:   *"If the Son therefore shall make you free, ye
shall be free indeed."*

Here is explained what Jesus meant by freedom.   He
spoke of *freedom from SIN*—freedom from its power, its
guilt, and its consequences.   He was trying to show the
Jews that if they would receive Him He would deliver them
from the burden of sin and set them *"free indeed"*—(which
means "truly free").   If the Son of God makes men free,
they are free in the fullest sense of the meaning of freedom.

Jesus always made it clear that He was not speaking of
civil liberty, but of liberty for the inner man.   Political
freedom is worthless if we are not children of God by faith
in Jesus Christ.   The only people on earth who are *really
free* are those who are born of the Holy Spirit, washed in
the blood of Jesus, and saved by the grace of God—but
JESUS is the only one who can give this liberty.   It cannot
be earned, it cannot be bought.   It must be received by
faith from the Lord Jesus Christ. Have YOU received Him
as YOUR Saviour?   Have you asked Him to set YOU free?
If not, do it now!

Verse 37:   *"I know that ye are Abraham's seed; but ye
seek to kill me, because my Word hath no place in you."*

In verse 33 the Jews said, "We be Abraham's seed, and
were never in bondage to any man."   Jesus showed them
the *nature* of their bondage and offered them true liberty.
Now He answers them concerning their relationship to Abraham: *"I know that ye are Abraham's seed."*   They were
carnal descendants of Abraham, and He readily admitted
this fact.   *"But ye seek to kill me."*   Being related to Abra-

ham from the standpoint of the flesh had not helped them, because they were seeking to kill the Messiah, the One who came to fulfill the promises Jehovah God had made to Abraham. They were Abraham's descendants only from the standpoint of the flesh; they were not related to him in spirit, else they would not have been plotting the death of their Messiah. Here Jesus again displayed His perfect knowledge of all the plans and the full program of His enemies. Had they not been so blinded by pride and their carnal nature, they should have seen His omniscience and recognized Him as more than man.

"My Word hath no place in you." These Jews had heard John the Baptist announce the coming King, the Messiah. They had listened to the words of Jesus ever since He entered His public ministry; but even though they had heard the Word with their ears it had not found its way into their hearts. *"Abraham believed God"* (Rom. 4:3), but these people who claimed to be his descendants did not believe God's Son (God in flesh); therefore they were not related to Abraham spiritually.

There are tens of thousands *today* who attend church every Sunday, they hear the Word—and from an *intellectual* standpoint they *believe;* but with the heart of faith they reject the message of the Word. Oh, yes, they believe there IS a God, they believe Jesus was a great person, a great teacher who worked wonderful miracles; but they do not believe on Him as their own personal Saviour and Lord; therefore they are not born again children of God.

In this verse, Jesus attaches great significance to the *Word.* No wonder Satan, through liberals and modernists, is attempting more than ever to discredit the Word of God and destroy the verbally inspired Scriptures! If he could destroy the Word of God he would undermine Christianity—but praise God, "For ever, O Lord, thy Word is settled in heaven" (Psalm 119:89).

Verse 38: *"I speak that which I have seen with my Father: and ye do that which ye have seen with your father."*

"That which I have seen with my Father" refers to Christ's eternal position in the Godhead—second Person of the Trinity, with God in the beginning. He was born *JE-SUS, Saviour;* but God's Christ was in the beginning with God; He did not *"begin* to live" as Christ, He WAS in the beginning, before *anything* was. Thus He points to the fact of His eternal existence.   The words He spoke were the words His Father had sent Him into the world to declare.

"Ye do that which ye have seen with YOUR father (the devil)."   It was Satan who had put it into the minds of the Jews to destroy Jesus, and here Jesus let them know that He was acquainted with their plan and knew that they were listening to the devil's suggestions.

Verses 39 and 40: *"They answered and said unto Him, Abraham is our father. Jesus saith unto them, If ye were Abraham's children, ye would do the works of Abraham. But now ye seek to kill me, a Man that hath told you the truth, which I have heard of God: this did not Abraham."*

Evidently the Jews *understood* that Jesus was speaking of the devil as their father, because they immediately declared, *"ABRAHAM is our father!"*   Jesus replied, *"If ye were Abraham's children, ye would do the WORKS of Abraham.*   If you were children of Abraham according to faith, you would not be planning to put me to death; you would be doing what Abraham did."

To *"work the works of Abraham"* would of course point them back to Genesis 12:1—3 where God told Abraham, "Get thee out of thy country, and from thy kindred, and from thy father's house, unto a land that I will shew thee: and I will make of thee a great nation, and I will bless thee, and make thy name great; and thou shalt be a blessing: and I will bless them that bless thee, and curse him that curseth thee: and in thee shall all families of the earth be blessed."

Then in Hebrews 11:8—10 we read, *"By faith* Abraham, when he was called to go out into a place which he should after receive for an inheritance, *obeyed; and he went out, NOT KNOWING WHITHER HE WENT.* By faith he sojourned in the land of promise, as in a strange country, dwelling in tabernacles with Isaac and Jacob, the heirs with him of the same promise: FOR HE LOOKED FOR A CITY WHICH HATH FOUNDATIONS, WHOSE BUILD-ER AND MAKER IS GOD.''

Yet these Jews, claiming to be the seed of Abraham, re-fused to hear and obey the words of Jesus—the words of GOD—thus denying the faith of Abraham and testifying that they were children of Satan. Ancestry will not save us, it matters not if we are descendants of preachers, Bible teach-ers, missionaries. Each individual must give an account of himself to God (Rom. 14:12). The very fact that these Jews were plotting and planning to crucify Jesus proved that they were not Abraham's children in spirit and faith. Paul said, "He is not a Jew, which is one outwardly; neither is that circumcision, which is outward in the flesh: but he is a Jew, which is one inwardly; and circumcision is that of the heart, in the spirit, and not in the letter; whose praise is not of men, but of God" (Rom. 2:28,29).

Fleshly relationship, ecclesiastical standing, church mem-bership and education profit nothing apart from the saving grace of God and the cleansing blood of Jesus Christ. What shall a man profit, though descended from many generations of church people, though he himself be a church member living a "good" life, if he never personally receives the Lord Jesus Christ as Saviour? For no man cometh unto the Father but by HIM (John 14:6).

There is a singular statement in verse 40: Jesus refers to Himself as *"a man"*—an expression He uses nowhere else in the Gospels. In other places, when pointing to His human nature, He referred to Himself as "the *Son* of man," but not as simply "a man." There IS a Man in heaven now, our compassionate and faithful High Priest, the only Mediator between God and man: "For there is one God, and one Mediator between God and men, the Man Christ

Jesus" (I Tim. 2:5).

"This did not Abraham." This means that the conduct of these Jews was exactly opposite what Abraham would have done had he been living then—and as we read of the life of Abraham and compare it with the conduct of this group, we see that they did exactly the opposite of what Abraham did.

Verse 41: *"Ye do the deeds of your father. Then said they to Him, We be not born of fornication; we have one Father, even God."*

"Ye do the deeds of your father." There is no mistaking what Jesus meant here. He spelled out to these men that they were doing the deeds of Satan because Satan was their *father.* Their plans and actions *proved* that they were children of the devil rather than children of Abraham.

"WE be not born of fornication!" The Jews did not misunderstand our Lord's statement. He was speaking to them as a nation, not as individuals. The question was, Who was their *spiritual* father? From whom did they get their spiritual character? They immediately said, "We are not heathen idolaters, we are from Abraham." Idolatry was called "fornication" because it was unfaithfulness to the covenant of God. This is made clear in the Old Testament. Also, their words could have had a twofold meaning, and in a subtle way they could have been reminding Jesus that insofar as *they* were concerned, *HE* had been conceived out of wedlock, born of fornication. In other words, they were saying, "WE *know* who OUR father is, but YOU are the product of fornication. So who are YOU to tell us that we are children of the devil?"

"We have one Father, even God." It is true that in the Old Testament God is called the Father of Israel (Deut. 32:6; I Chron. 29:10; Isa. 63:16; 64:8; Mal. 1:6); but this refers to Him as the Father of the *nation* Israel, not as the Father of individual Jews.

Verse 42: *"Jesus said unto them, If God were your Fa-*

ther, ye would love me: for I proceeded forth and came from
God; neither came I of myself, but He sent me."

According to the words of Jesus here, there is one sure
way we can know if we are born of God: *"If God were*
your Father, YE WOULD LOVE ME." In connection with
this please read I John 4:7—21. These Jews were the children of Abraham by natural heritage, they were the children
of God by covenant and nationality, but they were NOT
God's children by saving grace, born of His Spirit; for if
this were true, *they would show their sonship by loving the*
Son of God, even Jesus Himself. Do YOU love Christ? Do
you honor Him as the only begotten of the Father—crucified, buried, risen, ascended, coming again? If you do not
love Christ you do not know God: "Whosoever transgresseth,
and abideth not in the doctrine of Christ, hath not God.
He that abideth in the doctrine of Christ, he hath both the
Father and the Son" (II John 9).

They are ministers of *Satan* who teach that God is the
Father of all, full of love, mercy, and compassion, and that
no person will be lost. Such doctrine is man-made, not
divinely inspired. The Fatherhood of God and the brotherhood of man is not taught in the Bible. It is true that God
is love, it is true that He is a God of mercy, longsuffering,
not willing that any should perish; but those who will not
perish are those who have exercised personal faith in the
finished work of the Lord Jesus Christ. God is the Father
of all who believe on Jesus and trust Him as Saviour. The
devil is the father of all who refuse to believe on Jesus and
trust Him (John 8:44).

In our present verse Jesus clearly declared His divine
nature, His divinely appointed mission, and His ministry
on earth. He *"proceeded forth and came from God,"* He
was in the beginning *with* God, the Eternal Son from everlasting to everlasting. He did not come into this world
independently or without commission. He was divinely
appointed by Jehovah God, He came as the Father's last

Messenger to lost mankind; and if these Jews really did love God, they would love His Messenger. A true child of God loves the things of God, and first and foremost a true believer will love God's only begotten Son who is the brightness of God's glory and "the express image of His Person" (Heb. 1:3). Those who do not love the Son do not love the Father, they are not children of God:

"Whosoever believeth that Jesus is the Christ is born of God: and every one that loveth Him that begat loveth Him also that is begotten of Him" (I John 5:1).

Verse 43: *"Why do ye not understand my speech? even because ye cannot hear my word."*

Notice in this verse *"speech"* and *"word."* When Jesus referred to His *speech* He meant His manner of speaking, His way of expressing Himself and presenting the truth *concerning* Himself. When He spoke of His *word* He meant His *doctrine* (or the matter of substance of speech). He was the WORD in flesh, and the words He spoke were spirit and life. But the Jews did not *hear* the words of Jesus because they did not have a *will* to hear. They were continually seeking something by which they could accuse Him, they deliberately misinterpreted what He said, they refused His teaching, and instead of accepting His words as the Word of God they twisted His expressions and language to accuse Him of blasphemy! When He declared, *"I am the bread of life,"* they asked, "How can this man give us His flesh to eat?" thus misinterpreting His words and making them refer to literal bread. When He told them the truth would set them free, they immediately turned their thoughts to political freedom, deliverance from Roman rule. When He spoke of their father, they twisted the words and made them apply to Abraham. They could not hear the words of Jesus because they would not surrender their stubborn wills to the Holy Spirit (the only One who can open the mind and heart of man to receive the Word of God that brings salvation). "For what man knoweth the things of a man, save the spirit of man which is in him? even so the things of God knoweth no man, but the Spirit of God. Now we have received, not the spirit of the world, but the spirit which is of God; that we might know the things that are freely given to us of God" (I Cor. 2:11,12).

There Is a Personal Devil

Verse 44: *"Ye are of your father the devil, and the lusts of your father ye will do. He was a murderer from the beginning, and abode not in the truth, because there is no truth in him. When he speaketh a lie, he speaketh of his own: for he is a liar, and the father of it."*

"Ye are of your father the devil." If God were not their father (and it was evident that He was not) there was but one alternative. There is no middle ground with God, and Jesus plainly expressed this fact—nor did He "sugar-coat" His words. I wonder what would happen today if a pastor in a liberal church should step into the pulpit on Sunday morning and announce that all who follow the world—sin, lust, lying, gambling, adultery—are of their father, the devil? I wonder if there would not be some more "fanatics" burned at the stake? *Jesus* gave His messages plainly, sternly, and (on occasion) in language that was rough and rugged!

How is Satan the father of the wicked? He does not have power to create—*man was created by God and in God's own image.* Nor does Satan have power to create the wicked in the same sense that God creates the ungodly into "a new man in Christ Jesus." The devil simply takes the unregenerated man who is "born in sin," works on his mind and his sinful nature, and by getting him under his influence leads him into unbelief and wickedness. In this sense, he is the father of the wicked.

"The lusts of your father ye will do." Strong emphasis is placed on the pronoun "YE." That is, *"YE have a will, a heart, and a mind* to do the things Satan suggests; you are naturally his children. You do the things that are pe-

culiarly characteristic of him, things he suggests, and therefore you are his children."

"He was a murderer from the beginning." When Satan
tempted Eve, she and Adam sinned, and they died spiritually.   Therefore, Satan not only murdered *one* man—he
killed the whole human race, for "in Adam all die" (I Cor.
15:22). Satan is definitely a murderer.

The *"beginning"* here is not the beginning of creation,
but the beginning of Satan as we know him today.   We
find the origin of the devil in Ezekiel 28:11—15:

"Moreover the word of the Lord came unto me, saying,
Son of man, take up a lamentation upon the king of Tyrus,
and say unto him, Thus saith the Lord God: Thou sealest
up the sum, full of wisdom, and perfect in beauty.   Thou
hast been in Eden the garden of God; every precious stone
was thy covering, the sardius, topaz, and the diamond, the
beryl, the onyx, and the jasper, the sapphire, the emerald,
and the carbuncle, and gold: the workmanship of thy tab-
rets and of thy pipes was prepared in thee in the day that
thou wast created.   Thou art the anointed cherub that covereth; and I have set thee so: thou wast upon the holy
mountain of God; thou hast walked up and down in the
midst of the stones of fire.   *Thou wast perfect in thy ways
from the day that thou wast created, till iniquity was found
in thee."*

The creature whom we know as Satan was not *created*
a devil, liar, and murderer—quite the opposite: he was
"the anointed cherub that covereth."

You will notice that the person described in the passage
just quoted from Ezekiel could not have been an ordinary
man or an earthly king: "Thou sealest up the sum, *full of
wisdom, and perfect in beauty."*   This could not be said
of ordinary men.   *"Thou hast been in Eden the garden of
God."*   Adam and Eve were the only members of the human
race who ever walked in Eden.   *"Every precious stone was
thy covering."*   This person was honored, he enjoyed a
place of dignity in the heavens.   And we especially note

that he was *"created."* This proves beyond any shadow of doubt that this was not a man like Adam, Abraham, or Moses, because Adam was the only *created* man: *all other human kind have been BORN.*

This "anointed cherub that covereth" was appointed "high sheriff" of God's throne, he had access to the very throne of Jehovah, and he "walked up and down in the stones of fire"; he was in "the holy mountain of God"—the very place where God's throne is, where the "stones of fire" blaze out to the glory of God. He was "perfect" in his ways "until *iniquity* was found in (him)." The day iniquity was born in his heart and displayed through his actions was the day the "anointed cherub" became the devil, a murderer and the father of lies!

What was the "iniquity" that was found in the heart of this personality? It was *pride* that brought about his fall. Isaiah describes this in Isaiah 14:12—15:

"How art thou fallen from heaven, O Lucifer, son of the morning! How art thou cut down to the ground, which didst weaken the nations! For thou hast said in thine heart, I will ascend into heaven, I will exalt my throne above the stars of God: I will sit also upon the mount of the congregation, in the sides of the north: I will ascend above the heights of the clouds; I will be like the most High. Yet thou shalt be brought down to hell, to the sides of the pit."

Notice the frequent use of "I" in this passage. The "anointed cherub" was no longer willing to be in subordination to God. He wanted to exalt himself above God's throne, so he "brainwashed" some of the angels and led them to believe that they could *overthrow* God and take the throne of heaven. However, the Creator is greater than the created; and when rebellion broke out, God threw Lucifer and the fallen angels out of heaven. Jude tells us that "the angels which kept not their first estate, but left their own habitation, He hath reserved in everlasting chains under darkness unto the judgment of the great day" (Jude 6). In Revelation 20:10 we read of Satan's final doom:

"And the devil that deceived them was cast into the lake of fire and brimstone, where the beast and the false prophet are, and shall be tormented day and night for ever and ever." Many Bible scholars believe it was when Satan was cast down from heaven that the earth became "without form, and void," as described in Genesis 1:2.

Satan was not always Satan, he was not always a liar and the father of lies, but he *"abode not in truth."* He originally lived in truth and righteousness, but he *fell away* from truth and became the loathesome creature we know as Satan. *"Truth"* here stands for God, His Word, righteousness, holiness, true doctrine. It also stands for conformity to the mind of Jehovah God, who IS truth. The devil is a *being,* a *personality.* Just as truly as *Jesus* is a Person, *Satan* is a person—but one in whom there is no truth.

"There is no truth in him." Jesus did not say that truth was *never IN* Satan, but that he "abode not" in truth. In other words, he *"stood* not" in truth. He fell from his first estate—and he did it of his own free will.

"When he speaketh a lie, he speaketh of his own." This is the same thought as that of Matthew 12:34: ". . . how can ye, being evil, speak good things? for out of the abundance of the heart the mouth speaketh." Satan speaks of those things that fill his heart—lying, murder, lust, unrighteousness, ungodliness.

"For he is a liar and the father of it." I believe Jesus referred here to the great lie in the Garden of Eden, when Satan came to Eve and asked, *"Hath God said,* Ye shall not eat of every tree of the garden?" God had clearly spelled out to Adam that the day he ate of the forbidden fruit he would surely die, but Satan said to Eve, *"Ye shall NOT surely die"* (Gen. 3:1—4). Here Satan spoke the great original lie and became the father of lies, because that is where the real trouble began. When Satan speaks a lie he speaks of his own will, nature, and character; therefore, those who are liars, those who *live* a lie, are children of

the devil.

Verse 45: *"And because I tell you the truth, ye believe me not."*

Here is a marked contrast: Jesus speaks truth because *He IS truth* (John 14:6; 17:17); the devil *cannot* speak truth because *"there is no truth IN him."* In other words, Jesus said to the Jews, "You are willing to listen to The Lie, but you do not have a will to hear The Truth." There are people today who will pay a minister—and pay him well—to preach lies; but if that same minister should preach the truth in all of its purity and power they would refuse to pay his salary! True ministers of the Gospel know that mankind in general does not want pure, unadulterated truth, and he who preaches the Word of God without fear, favor, or compromise will suffer persecution and be rejected by the majority of those who hear him. Jesus made this clear in John 15:20 when He said to His disciples, "Remember the word that I said unto you, The servant is not greater than his lord. If they have persecuted me, they will also persecute you; if they have kept my saying, they will keep your's also." If they persecuted Jesus and refused to hear Him, they will refuse to hear a true minister today.

Verse 46: *"Which of you convinceth me of sin? And if I say the truth, why do ye not believe me?"*

No mortal ever lived who could ask, *"Which of you convinceth me of sin?"* and not be answered by his enemies, but not one person could bring an accusation against Jesus. No other man ever lived without sin, but Jesus was holy, harmless, undefiled—yea, *He was the righteousness of God in flesh.* Not able to bring accusation against Him, their very silence confessed that He was sinless; and since this was true, *why did they not BELIEVE Him?* In the next verse Jesus answers that question:

Verse 47: *"He that is of God heareth God's words: ye therefore hear them not, because ye are not of God."*

The enemies of Jesus could not accuse Him of sin because He had committed no sin. Therefore they had no legitimate reason for refusing to hear and believe what He said. Jesus supplied the answer to His question, and by that answer proved their wickedness and that they were children of the devil. The born again child of God is willing to hear the *Word* of God with pleasure, he is willing to *walk* in the Word. If the Jews had been children of God they would have heard the Word, they would have received Jesus as their Messiah; but they were neither children of God nor the spiritual children of Abraham.

In John 10:27, in His discourse on the Good Shepherd, Jesus said, "My sheep hear my voice, and I know them, and they follow me." The truly born again person knows the Saviour's voice and recognizes the Word of God. If you do not recognize the preaching of a liberal or a modernist, I am afraid you have never been saved. The Word of God clearly teaches that born again people possess the Holy Spirit, who leads into all truth. The Holy Spirit will reveal the false prophet: "Ye have an unction from the Holy One, and ye know all things. . . But the anointing which ye have received of Him abideth in you, and ye need not that any man teach you: but as the same anointing teacheth you of all things, and is truth, and is no lie, and even as it hath taught you, ye shall abide in Him" (I John 2:20,27).

We will never fully understand ALL Scripture, but we can understand enough to be born again, to walk in the straight and narrow way and serve God with heart, soul, and body! Those things that we do *not* understand prove that the Bible is not an ordinary book, and what God wants us to know is revealed to us: "The secret things belong unto the Lord our God: *but those things which are revealed belong unto us and to our children for ever,* that we may do all the words of this law" (Deut. 29:29).

Verse 48: *"Then answered the Jews, and said unto Him, Say we not well that thou art a Samaritan, and hast a devil?"*

If these Jews did not commit the unpardonable sin on this occasion, they certainly came very close to it! When they called Jesus a Samaritan they were declaring that He was a half-breed, little better than a heathen and certainly not a pure Jew. To call Him a Samaritan was to slander Him with as ugly a term as they knew how to use.

When they said, *"Thou . . . hast a devil"* they were repeating practically the same thing they said in chapter 7 verse 20. They meant that Jesus was mad (crazy), and that He was demon-possessed to the extent that He was speaking under the power and influence of demons, and not by the power of God as He claimed. In Matthew 12:22—32 such conduct on the part of the Pharisees caused them to commit the unpardonable sin. On that particular occasion Jesus healed a man who was blind and dumb, and the Pharisees gave credit to Beelzebub, prince of demons. Jesus then said to them, ". . . I say unto you, All manner of sin and blasphemy shall be forgiven unto men: but the blasphemy against the Holy Ghost shall not be forgiven unto men. And whosoever speaketh a word against the Son of man, it shall be forgiven him: but whosoever speaketh against the Holy Ghost, it shall not be forgiven him, neither in this world, neither in the world to come" (Matt. 12:31,32).

Since Jesus received such treatment at the hands of unbelieving Jews, we need not be surprised today when unbelievers slander *us* through names and insulting remarks. We are children of God, and when the enemies of the cross reproach us the reproaches fall on Jesus. We should rejoice that we are counted worthy to suffer reproach, to be persecuted and slandered for His name's sake.

Verse 49: *"Jesus answered, I have not a devil; but I honour my Father, and ye do dishonour me."*

To dishonor the Son was to dishonor the Father also, because the Father had sent Him into the world, He was working the works the Father gave Him to do, He was speaking the words the Father gave Him to speak. Remember, in chapter 5 verse 23 Jesus told these people, "All men should honour the Son, even as they honour the Father. *He that honoureth not the Son honoureth not the Father which hath sent Him.*"

Verse 50:   *"And I seek not mine own glory: there is One that seeketh and judgeth."*

Jesus had not come into the world to seek glory for Himself, but rather to glorify the Father in heaven. He had not come to seek an earthly kingdom, but to declare the love of God and make known the good news of the Gospel. He had not come to seek honor from men, therefore their accusations did not make Him guilty and the dishonor they heaped upon Him did not hurt Him.

"There is One that seeketh and judgeth."   God seeks men who will glorify Jesus, and He judges the conduct of those who dishonor and slander the name of His only begotten Son.   There is a comforting truth in Ecclesiastes 5:8: "If thou seest the oppression of the poor, and violent perverting of judgment and justice in a province, marvel not at the matter; for He that is higher than the highest regardeth; and there be higher than they."

Believers find comfort and joy in the fact that there is One, even God, who sees all and knows all, and who will *judge* all in that last day. If we suffer for Christ's sake we will be rewarded. Paul said in Romans 8:18, "I reckon that the sufferings of this present time are not worthy to be compared with the glory which shall be revealed in us."

Verse 51:   *"Verily, verily, I say unto you, If a man keep my saying, he shall never see death."*

Another "double verily," calling attention to a tremendous message with a divine promise to all who hear the Word, receive it, and keep the sayings of the Lord Jesus Christ.

In Deuteronomy 30:15—19 Moses said to the rebellious Israelites, "See, I have set before thee this day life and good, and death and evil; in that I command thee this day to love the Lord thy God, to walk in His ways, and to keep His commandments and His statutes and His judgments, that thou mayest live and multiply: and the Lord thy God shall bless thee in the land whither thou goest to possess it.

"But if thine heart turn away, so that thou wilt not hear, but shalt be drawn away, and worship other gods, and serve them; I denounce unto you this day, that ye shall surely perish, and that ye shall not prolong your days upon the land, whither thou passest over Jordan to go to possess it. I call heaven and earth to record this day against you, that I have set before you life and death, blessing and cursing: therefore choose life, that both thou and thy seed may live."

In our present Scripture Jesus, like Moses, gave the Jews the divine truth of life and death: *"Hear my sayings, keep my sayings, and you will escape death;* but if you *refuse* to receive my sayings, you will face *eternal* death in outer darkness, where there is weeping, wailing, and gnashing of teeth!"

The *sayings* of Jesus here included much more than the words He had spoken at that particular time; they embraced *the entire doctrine of the Gospel.* When He said, *"shall never see death"* He did not mean that the person who receives Him will never die *physically.* There will of course be some who will not die—saints who are living at the Rapture will be caught up to meet Jesus in the air (I Thess. 4:13—18; I Cor. 15:51—54). Jesus was speaking here of *spiritual* death. All who hear the Word of God and receive Jesus on the terms of the Gospel will be delivered from condemnation of sin, and will therefore be delivered from spiritual death. Since the day Adam deliberately disobeyed God and died spiritually as a *result* of that disobedience, men (good and bad) have died. It is *appointed* unto man to die. *Physical death* is the wages of sin, along with eternal damnation in the lake of fire; but *believers are saved*

from eternal damnation and delivered from the sting and
the fear of death.

In connection with this, study Hebrews 2:9—15. Those
verses tell us that Jesus by the grace of God tasted death
for every man and destroyed him who had the power of
death. I thank God that the devil has no power to destroy
me physically or spiritually. It is true that in the flesh we
groan, in the flesh we are often troubled, but we do not
fear because the born again child of God knows that Jesus
conquered the world, the flesh, the devil, death, hell, and
the grave, and we have His promise that we are more than
conquerors through Him. (Study Romans 8:31—39.)

Verses 52 and 53: *"Then said the Jews unto Him, Now
we know that thou hast a devil. Abraham is dead, and
the prophets; and thou sayest, If a man keep my saying,
he shall never taste of death. Art thou greater than our
father Abraham, which is dead? and the prophets are dead:
whom makest thou thyself?"*

In other words, the Jews said, *"NOW we KNOW for
sure that you are crazy!* Only an insane person would talk
like that. Abraham is dead, the holy prophets—Moses,
Isaiah, Jeremiah—all are dead; and now you say that if we
keep your sayings we shall never *see* death. What you are
actually saying is that you are greater than Abraham, Isaac,
Jacob, and the prophets who are dead and in their graves
these many years. Instead of *receiving* your words, we
know BY those words that you are beside yourself. You
are insane."

Then they asked a question which proved that Jesus had
succeeded in arousing their curiosity, though I doubt their
sincerity. They asked, "Who ARE you, anyway? Do you
really think you are greater than Abraham?" These people
who professed so strongly to believe in the patriarchs and
prophets, who claimed to honor Moses and the Law of
Moses, were blinded to the One of whom the patriarchs
and prophets spoke—their Messiah and Redeemer.

Verse 54: *"Jesus answered, If I honour myself, my honour is nothing: it is my Father that honoureth me; of whom ye say, that He is your God."*

Jesus made it plain that He was not seeking glory and honor from men. It was the God whom they *claimed to know* who had honored Him and given Him the words He spoke to them, and He sought no honor independently of the God whom He had come into the world to glorify.

"It is my Father that honoureth me." Here Jesus pointed to the miracles, the mighty works, and all of the signs and wonders He had wrought during His earthly ministry. In John 5:36 He said, "I have greater witness than that of John: *for the works which the Father hath given me to finish, the same works that I do, bear witness of me, that the Father hath sent me."* Also in John 14:10,11 He said, "Believest thou not that I am in the Father, and the Father in me? The words that I speak unto you I speak not of myself: but the Father that dwelleth in me, He doeth the works. Believe me that I am in the Father, and the Father in me: *or else believe me for the very works' sake."*

Verse 55: *"Yet ye have not known Him; but I know Him: and if I should say, I know Him not, I shall be a liar like unto you: but I know Him, and keep His saying."*

These words of Jesus are quite understandable, but they are also words that cut to a depth beyond our imagination! The Jews had professed to know God, but Jesus plainly declares, *"Ye have NOT known Him."*

He continued with such boldness as few (if any) men would dare demonstrate in the pulpit today: *"But I know Him . . . If I should say, I know Him not, I SHALL BE A LIAR LIKE UNTO YOU!"* They professed with their lips to know God, but their words and their works denied that they knew either His will, His purpose, or His character.

But JESUS knew the Father. He had been with Him through all eternity, He proceeded *from* Him, He was commissioned BY Him. He knew the Father so perfectly and completely that if He should say He did not know Him He would be a liar just as *they* were. It is not wrong for ministers of the Gospel to speak in plain words and understandable language. Take the following Scriptures for example:

Jeremiah 22:5: "If ye will not hear these words, *I swear by myself, saith the Lord,* that this house shall become a desolation."

Hebrews 6:13: "For when God made promise to Abraham, *because He could swear by no greater, He sware by Himself.*"

Ezekiel 33:11: "*As I live, saith the Lord God,* I have no pleasure in the death of the wicked; but that the wicked turn from his way and live: turn ye, turn ye from your evil ways; for why will ye die, O house of Israel?"

Verse 56: *"Your father Abraham rejoiced to see my day: and he saw it, and was glad."*

Yes, Abraham DID see the day of Jesus. By faith he saw that day afar off, and he rejoiced because he knew that God would keep His promise (Gen. 12:1−3). It was through the seed of Abraham that the Messiah came.

Notice, Jesus did not say, "Abraham saw ME," but *"Abraham saw MY DAY."* Abraham did see the day of Jesus in that God told him there was to be such a day, and even though Abraham saw that day only through the eye of faith, *he rejoiced* because he knew that every promise God made to His people would be kept. "For what saith the Scripture? *Abraham believed God, and it was counted unto him for righteousness*" (Rom. 4:3).

Verse 57: *"Then said the Jews unto Him, Thou art not yet fifty years old, and hast thou seen Abraham?"*

Again the Jews misinterpreted the Lord's words. They thought He was telling them that Abraham saw HIM, a Man, in a body. They had read the fifty-third chapter of

Isaiah, but they did not recognize their Messiah, the Lamb of God who would come to offer the one sacrifice never to be repeated, the sacrifice of His own blood on a rugged cross.

"Thou art not yet fifty years old." Blinded by the god of this age, these carnally-minded men could not recognize that as the Son of God (which Jesus had repeatedly claimed to be), as very God in flesh, He was from everlasting to everlasting. He was with God *in the beginning,* and His existence could not be measured in years! They had no faith in His words, and apart from faith it is impossible to please God. God deals in faith, He honors faith and blesses men according to their faith.

Verse 58: *"Jesus said unto them, Verily, verily, I say unto you, Before Abraham was, I am."*

The Jews readily understood who "I AM" was. They knew Jesus was openly declaring that He existed before *Abraham* existed, that He was the great I AM, eternal God, the God of Abraham, Isaac, and Jacob. Jesus was declaring here, "Before Abraham was born, I was one with the Father in eternity!" He did not say, "Before Abraham was, I *was."* He could have said that and it would have been true; but He was making a divine declaration to His enemies, those who refused to receive Him as Messiah, very God in flesh. So what He said was, "Before Abraham *was, I AM."* He had no beginning, He was *IN the beginning.* He did not *begin* to live, for as the Father had life in Himself, so the Son had life in *Himself.* There was never a time when the Godhead was not—Father, Son, and Holy Ghost, *eternal.*

In the declaration of eternal truth here spoken by Jesus, we see *the Creator IN the creature.* This Man upon whom they were looking was the tabernacle in which the Creator abode. God was IN CHRIST as He stood there speaking to the Jews. This One was made of the seed of Abraham, and before Abraham was (and in order that Abraham might

BE) this One WAS.   Divinity knows no past or future;
Divinity knows only the eternal present.   God is not "I
was," nor "I will be," but "I AM."   Jesus said to Thomas,
"I AM the Way."   He has always been the Way, He al-
ways will be the Way.   He was the Way in the Garden of
Eden, He was the Way throughout the Old Testament era,
He is the Way today and will be the Way until the con-
summation of all things—and then He will be the glorified
One in the eternal ages when all things are made new.

Christ is the Father's object of eternal glory, the One
upon whom all eternal glory will be bestowed throughout
the ceaseless ages of eternity.   He is the Pearl of great price,
the Jewel of jewels, the One to whom God will direct all
glory and praise in the eternities that lie ahead—and rightly
so, because Jesus paid the sin-debt, the creature in whom
the Creator dwelt conquered the world, the flesh, the devil,
death, hell, and the grave.   He ascended, and is now seated
at the right hand of the Majesty, to make intercession for
all who will come to God by Him.   Therefore He is worthy
of all praise, glory, honor, adoration, and worship—now and
throughout all the ceaseless ages of eternity.

Verse 59:   *"Then took they up stones to cast at Him:
but Jesus hid Himself, and went out of the temple, going
through the midst of them, and so passed by."*

From this we know that the Jews knew *exactly* what
Jesus had said to them.   They understood that He had just
announced Himself as God in flesh, that He had boldly
claimed to be greater than Abraham because He was the
great I AM.   But they did not believe Him and they considered what He said to be the height of blasphemy.   According to their law and their religion, therefore, such an
one should be stoned, and in a rage of anger they took up
stones to stone Him to death!

"But Jesus hid Himself, and went out of the temple."
It was not yet the appointed time for Him to die.   He came
to be lifted up on a cross, not to be stoned to death.   So

He withdrew—apparently a miraculous withdrawal, for He passed *"through the midst of them"* without being seen. Because of His omnipotence and His omniscience, He could walk through a crowd without being detected. The two disciples who walked with Him on the road to Emmaus saw Him—and yet they did not see Him. Luke 24:16 tells us that "their eyes were holden that they should not know Him." (See also Luke 4:30.)

Those of us who are witnesses for Jesus should take courage when we are laughed at, criticized, persecuted. Most of us do not know the *meaning* of persecution—but if we think we are persecuted, if we entertain the idea that the ministry should be easy, we should re-read verses 12 through 59 of this chapter. Ten times in those verses the enemies of Jesus interrupted Him, contradicted Him, mocked Him, reviled Him—but He kept His dignity; and even though He endured "such contradiction of sinners" He came into the world to present Himself to them in love, and to give His life for them.

The fact that His enemies could not answer Him, they could not silence Him, nor could they destroy Him, is evidence that the words He spoke were the words of God. His doctrine was God's truth. He was the Man Christ Jesus, but He was also *God the Creator IN the creature.*

CHAPTER IX

1. And as Jesus passed by, he saw a man which was blind from his birth.

2. And his disciples asked him, saying, Master, who did sin, this man, or his parents, that he was born blind?

3. Jesus answered, Neither hath this man sinned, nor his parents: but that the works of God should be made manifest in him.

4. I must work the works of him that sent me, while it is day: the night cometh, when no man can work.

5. As long as I am in the world, I am the light of the world.

6. When he had thus spoken, he spat on the ground, and made clay of the spittle, and he anointed the eyes of the blind man with the clay,

7. And said unto him, Go, wash in the pool of Siloam, (which is by interpretation, Sent.) He went his way therefore, and washed, and came seeing.

8. The neighbours therefore, and they which before had seen him that he was blind, said, Is not this he that sat and begged?

9. Some said, This is he: others said, He is like him: but he said, I am he.

10. Therefore said they unto him, How were thine eyes opened?

11. He answered and said, A man that is called Jesus made clay, and anointed mine eyes, and said unto me, Go to the pool of Siloam, and wash: and I went and washed, and I received sight.

12. Then said they unto him, Where is he? He said, I know not.

13. They brought to the Pharisees him that aforetime was blind.

14. And it was the sabbath day when Jesus made the clay, and opened his eyes.

15. Then again the Pharisees also asked him how he had received his sight. He said unto them, He put clay upon mine eyes, and I washed, and do see.

16. Therefore said some of the Pharisees, This man is not of God, because he keepeth not the sabbath day. Others said, How can a man that is a sinner do such miracles? And there was a division among them.

17. They say unto the blind man again, What sayest thou of him, that he hath opened thine eyes? He said, He is a prophet.

18. But the Jews did not believe concerning him, that he had been blind, and received his sight, until they called the parents of him that had received his sight.

19. And they asked them, saying, Is this your son, who ye say was born blind? how then doth he now see?

20. His parents answered them and said, We know that this is our son, and that he was born blind:

21. But by what means he now seeth, we know not; or who hath opened his eyes, we know not: he is of age; ask him: he shall speak for himself.

22. These words spake his parents, because they feared the Jews: for the Jews had agreed already, that if any man did confess that he was Christ, he should be put out of the synagogue.

23. Therefore said his parents, He is of age; ask him.

24. Then again called they the man that was blind, and said unto him, Give God the praise: we know that this man is a sinner.

25. He answered and said, Whether he be a sinner or no, I know not: one thing I know, that, whereas I was blind, now I see.

26. Then said they to him again, What did he to thee? how opened he thine eyes?

27. He answered them, I have told you already, and ye did not hear: wherefore would ye hear it again? will ye also be his disciples?

28. Then they reviled him, and said, Thou art his disciple; but we are Moses' disciples.

29. We know that God spake unto Moses: as for this fellow, we know not from whence he is.

30. The man answered and said unto them, Why herein is a marvellous thing, that ye know not from whence he is, and yet he hath opened mine eyes.

31. Now we know that God heareth not sinners: but if any man be a worshipper of God, and doeth his will, him he heareth.

32. Since the world began was it not heard that any man opened the eyes of one that was born blind.

33. If this man were not of God, he could do nothing.

34. They answered and said unto him, Thou wast altogether born in sins, and dost thou teach us? And they cast him out.

35. Jesus heard that they had cast him out; and when he had found him, he said unto him, Dost thou believe on the Son of God?

36. He answered and said, Who is he, Lord, that I might believe on him?

37. And Jesus said unto him, Thou hast both seen him, and it is he that talketh with thee.

38. And he said, Lord, I believe. And he worshipped him.

39. And Jesus said, For judgment I am come into this world, that

they which see not might see; and that they which see might be made blind.

40. And some of the Pharisees which were with him heard these words, and said unto him, Are we blind also?

41. Jesus said unto them, If ye were blind, ye should have no sin: but now ye say, We see; therefore your sin remaineth.

There are several outstanding things about the miracle which occupies this entire chapter of John's Gospel. Only John the Beloved records this miracle and, like each of the other miracles in his Gospel, it is described carefully, with every detail pointed out. This is one of the four recorded miracles wrought by Jesus in Judaea, near the city of Jerusalem. John records eight of the miracles of Jesus—four in Galilee (the first at the marriage supper at Cana, then the healing of the nobleman's son, the feeding of the five thousand, and Jesus' walking on the water); and four miracles wrought in *Judaea* (the purification of the temple, the healing of the impotent man, restoration of sight to the blind, and the raising of Lazarus). Each of these miracles presents a clear, vivid picture of spiritual things.

The miracle recorded here was one of the miracles the Jews were taught to expect in the time of their Messiah: "In that day shall the deaf hear the words of the book, and the eyes of the blind shall see out of obscurity, and out of darkness" (Isa. 29:18).

This was also one of the miracles denoting that Messiah had come: "Now when John had heard in the prison the works of Christ, he sent two of his disciples, and said unto Him, Art thou He that should come, or do we look for another? Jesus answered and said unto them, Go and shew John again those things which ye do hear and see: The blind receive their sight, and the lame walk, the lepers are cleansed, and the deaf hear, the dead are raised up, and the poor have the Gospel preached to them" (Matt. 11:2—5).

This miracle was wrought in a place so public, with so many people present, that it could not be denied; and the man upon whom it was wrought was so well known by everyone that it could not be ignored. The Jews were forced to face it.

Verse 1:   *"And as Jesus passed by, He saw a man which was blind from his birth."*

The Scripture does not tell us where this man was. Perhaps, like the lame man whom Peter and John encountered in Acts 3, he was sitting near the temple gate, since those who went into the house of worship would be more likely to give alms than those in other places. In the religion of the Jews, the law took care of the blind: "Thou shalt not curse the deaf, nor put a stumblingblock before the blind, but shalt fear thy God: I am the Lord" (Lev. 19:14). Also in Deuteronomy 27:18 we read, "Cursed be he that maketh the blind to wander out of the way."

It is interesting that this blind man did not beg for healing, he did not cry out as did blind Bartimaeus (Mark 10: 46,47). The Word tells us that *"as Jesus passed by, HE SAW a man which was blind from his birth."* The Lord's eyes were all-seeing, He never missed a poor, needy soul. He saw the blind man and healed him unasked, as was true in the case of the impotent man in John 5 who had been paralyzed for so long a time.

More miracles on blind persons are recorded than any other form of human sickness. We read where He healed one deaf and dumb man, once where He healed a man of palsy, one of dropsy, two references where He healed lepers, two cases where He healed persons ill of a fever, three times where He raised dead persons to life, and *four cases* (possibly five) of blindness healed. (In connection with this please study Isaiah 32:3; 35:5; and 42:7.)

Verse 2:   *"And His disciples asked Him, saying, Master, who did sin, this man, or his parents, that he was born blind?"*

"His disciples asked Him" shows that Jesus was surrounded by His usual followers, and this would seem to

indicate a break between the last part of chapter 8 and the event recorded here. In the last verse of chapter 8, Jesus by divine power hid Himself and moved through the midst of His enemies without being seen, and it does not seem reasonable that He would be immediately surrounded by His disciples again. So there was probably a break, a lapse of time, between the events in chapter 8 and those in this chapter.

"Master, who did sin, this man, or his parents?" Here the disciples were probably thinking of Exodus 20:5 where God said, ". . . I the Lord thy God am a jealous God, visiting the iniquity of the fathers upon the children unto the third and fourth generation of them that hate me." They had forgotten the truth of Ezekiel 18:20: "The soul that sinneth, it shall die. The son shall not bear the iniquity of the father, neither shall the father bear the iniquity of the son: the righteousness of the righteous shall be upon him, and the wickedness of the wicked shall be upon him."

Mankind is prone to think that all bodily suffering and sickness are the direct results of sin in the life of an individual, and even if judgment is not *openly declared* it is assumed that the sick person has committed some outstanding sin or is a very wicked person. The friends of Job were guilty of this sin of judging, and in Acts 28, when Paul was shipwrecked on the Island of Melita and was bitten by a viper, the people said, "No doubt this man is a murderer, whom, though he hath escaped the sea, yet vengeance suffereth not to live." But Paul shook off the viper and was unharmed by its venemous bite. THEN we are told, "Howbeit they looked when he should have swollen, or fallen down dead suddenly: but after they had looked a great while, and saw no harm come to him, *they changed their minds, and said that he was a God!"* Read the story in Acts 28:1—6. This line of thinking appears to be the cause of the disciples asking Jesus who had sinned—the blind man, or his parents. (Please study also the words of Jesus as recorded in Luke 13:1—5.)

The word translated *"Master"* in our present verse is
the same Greek word rendered "Rabbi" in John 1:38,49;
3:2,26; and 6:25.   There is no explanation given as to why
it was rendered "Master" here and "Rabbi" in the other
five verses.

Verse 3:   *"Jesus answered, Neither hath this man sinned,
nor his parents: but that the works of God should be made
manifest in him."*

This does not mean that the man and his parents had
never committed sin, *"for ALL have sinned* and come short
of the glory of God" (Rom. 3:23); but Jesus simply means
that the *blindness* of this young man was not caused by
sins committed by either his parents or himself.   Neither
does this verse teach that the sins of the parents do not
cause the children to suffer.   We know that in many instances the sins of parents DO bring suffering on the children in various ways.   Present day periodicals and medical
publications make no secret of the fact that mothers who
are dope addicts are likely to give birth to children who
are addicted to dope even at the time of their birth.   It is
believed that mothers who are heavy drinkers, and even
those who are users of tobacco, give their offspring a *degree*
of those habits in their prenatal bloodstream!   There are
many other ways in which children can suffer because of
the sins of their parents, but in *this* case the son's blindness was not due to sin on the part of his immediate family.

*"But that the works of God should be made manifest in
him."*   The truth declared here must be accepted by faith.
The statement is clear: This man's blindness was ordained
of God *that this miracle might show forth the power Jesus
possessed,* to show the people that He was all He claimed
to be—that He was *from* God, the *Son of God,* yea, *very
God in flesh.*   These words shed light on the question of
why God allowed evil to come into His creation.   He allowed Satan and evil to come in order that He might show
His mercy, compassion, and saving grace.   If man had never

sinned, God would not have had opportunity to show the exceeding riches of His grace in His kindness toward us through Christ Jesus our Lord (Eph. 2:1—10). Allowing Satan to enter the Garden of Eden (thus permitting evil to enter the world) made possible God's works of mercy and grace, and His unknowable wisdom in providing salvation for sinners—salvation that has been manifested to all. Redeeming the sinner, redeeming the Church (the body of Christ) was "to the intent that now unto the principalities and powers in heavenly places might be known by the Church the manifold wisdom of God, according to the eternal purpose which He purposed in Christ Jesus our Lord" (Eph. 3:10,11). Because man fell, we have the message of God's love, compassion, saving grace—and the cross. Adam was innocent, but innocence is negative. *Believers* are not innocent. Believers are *righteous,* because when we believe on Jesus, God *imputes* righteousness to us. *Christ is our righteousness;* therefore it is more glorious to be a son of God through the miracle of the new birth than to be as Adam was in the Garden of Eden. Believers are sons of God *by redemption* as well as by creation.

I will never fully understand Romans 8:28, but I believe every word of it: "We know that all things work together for good to them that love God, to them who are the called according to His purpose." Romans 9:17 is another verse that I accept by faith: "For the Scripture saith unto Pharaoh, Even for this same purpose have I raised thee up, that I might shew my power in thee, and that my name might be declared throughout all the earth."

There are no accidents with God. He allows nothing to happen without a reason, and He always works things out to His eternal glory and (in the end) *to the benefit of all mankind.*

Consider this: If a sinner should suddenly be lifted out of hell and placed in the middle of heaven, heaven would be hell to that sinner because in order for a sinner to enjoy heaven he must be saved by God's grace, the *inner man* must be changed. Heaven is a prepared place for prepared people, and the person who does not love the Word of God, the people of God, and the things of God would not be at home in heaven. God has prepared a place of holiness, righteousness, purity; therefore if a sinner should suddenly be snatched out of hell and placed in Paradise, Paradise would immediately become hell to that person who had not been born of the Spirit, saved by God's grace. To enter and enjoy heaven we must be made new creations in Christ Jesus (II Cor. 5:17).

Why was this man born blind? *"That the works of God should be made manifest in him."* *Why* did Adam fall? That God might give us the last Adam, the Lord Jesus Christ, that man might be saved. *Why* is evil permitted in the world today? That God may be glorified in saving us *from* evil and imputing unto us righteousness, holiness, and godliness. *Why* does the body of man (even the body of a true believer) get sick and die? That God might be glorified in raising that body from the dead, giving immortality to mortals, and giving us a body like the glorious body of Jesus (I John 3:1,2).

Verse 4: *"I must work the works of Him that sent me, while it is day: the night cometh, when no man can work."*

"Works" connects this verse with the preceding verse. Jesus said to His disciples, "The healing of this man who was born blind is one of the great works my Father appointed me to do. While it is day I must *do* the works appointed unto me. The blindness of this man was ordained of God that I might show forth my divine power in healing him."

"While it is day" refers to the earthly ministry of Jesus, and to His bodily presence with His disciples. It was a time of unusual blessing for those who walked in the sunlight of His love and the brightness of His divine Person. When He finished His public ministry and was taken up out of their sight, the absence of His visible presence be-

came night, because even though they had the *promise* of the Comforter, they did not fully understand the days that would follow the Lord's ascension, and undoubtedly they knew some dark, disappointing moments.

We are not to understand by this statement, however, that after Jesus left the earth there was no more light for believers. In I John 1:7 we read, "If we walk in the light, as He is in the light, we have fellowship one with another, and the blood of Jesus Christ His Son cleanseth us from all sin." Believers *do* enjoy spiritual light, *the Church* walks in the light; but the disciples were left in a period of night when Jesus was arrested, tried, condemned, crucified, and taken up to heaven after His resurrection.

In Romans 13:12 we read, "The night is far spent, the day is at hand: let us therefore cast off the works of darkness, and let us put on the armour of light." In this passage Paul speaks of Christ's bodily absence as "night," and then refers to His coming again in the Rapture as the "day" —which will be a bright one indeed for believers!

There could also be a prophetic reference in verse four, referring to the blindness that would come upon Israel as described by Paul in the eleventh chapter of Romans. (Please study that chapter in its entirety.) It is true that Israel *as a nation* walks in darkness today even though the Jewish people are returning to their new state of Israel. They are returning in spiritual darkness, they are still expecting the coming of their Messiah. A few individual Jews have been born again and walk in the light; but as a nation Israel gropes in darkness—and will do so until that day when Jesus comes again. At that time they will see Him, they will see the prints of the nails in His hands, they will then recognize Him and receive Him as Messiah. That will be a day of glorious light for Israel!

Verse 5: *"As long as I am in the world, I am the light of the world."*

Here Jesus declared His purpose in coming *into* the world,

and also His position while He walked among men. He came into the world to be the LIGHT, the spiritual guide, to deliver men from darkness and put the light of God within. Jesus was about to heal a blind man on the Sabbath; He knew the Jews would disapprove of what He was doing, and He defended His actions by saying to His disciples, "As long as I am IN the world I will be The LIGHT of the world and will deliver men's souls from sin and their bodies from disease. While it is day I must do the works of Him who sent me. I must use every opportunity—not only six days, but also on the Sabbath—to do good works while I am here on earth."

Verses 6 and 7: *"When He had thus spoken, He spat on the ground, and made clay of the spittle, and He anointed the eyes of the blind man with the clay, and said unto him, Go, wash in the pool of Siloam, (which is by interpretation, Sent.) He went his way therefore, and washed, and came seeing."*

Spittle is mentioned three times in connection with miracles wrought by Jesus—here in verse 6, and twice in the Gospel of Mark:

"And they bring unto Him one that was deaf, and had an impediment in his speech; and they beseech Him to put His hand upon him. And He took him aside from the multitude, and put His fingers into his ears, *and He spit,* and touched his tongue; and looking up to heaven, He sighed, and saith unto him, Ephphatha, that is, Be opened. And straightway his ears were opened, and the string of his tongue was loosed, and he spake plain" (Mark 7:32—35).

"And He cometh to Bethsaida; and they bring a blind man unto Him, and besought Him to touch Him. And He took the blind man by the hand, and led Him out of the town; and when He had spit on his eyes, and put His hands upon him, He asked him if he saw ought. And he looked up, and said, I see men as trees, walking. After that He put His hands again upon his eyes, and made him look up:

and he was restored, and saw every man clearly" (Mark 8:22—25).

In each of these instances, you will note that our Lord performed the miracle in a different manner. We do not know why He made clay of the spittle and anointed the eyes of the man in our present verse. Certainly He could have spoken a word and the man would have been healed; or He could have healed him simply by looking upon him. But on this particular occasion, for reasons known only to Himself and the heavenly Father, He spat on the ground, made clay of the spittle, anointed the man's eyes, and then gave him instructions as to what he should do. We know that neither the clay nor the spittle opened the man's eyes. *He was healed by obeying the WORD.*

The same was true in many instances in the Old Testament. When the Israelites were bitten by serpents in the wilderness, God told Moses to make a serpent of brass, lift it up on a pole, and tell the people to look upon the serpent and be healed. Those who obeyed the Word were healed, those who refused to obey the Word *died.* There was no healing power in either the serpent or the brass from which it was made, but *obedience to the WORD* brought healing (Num. 21:6—9).

When the Israelites thirsted on their journey, God did not tell Moses to dig a well; He told him to *strike a rock.* Moses obeyed, and water gushed from the rock (Ex. 17:6).

When the walls of Jericho seemed immune to destruction, God destroyed them—not with a hydrogen bomb, but by blasts on ram's horns (Josh. 6:1—20).

God's man slew a thousand of the enemy—not with spears or bayonets, but with the jawbone of an ass (Judges 15:15,16).

God healed the salt water with salt (II Kings 2:19—21), and made bitter water sweet by simply commanding Moses to cast a tree into the water (Ex. 15:23—25). A shepherd boy slew a giant with a slingshot and a stone from the bed of a brook (I Sam. 17:40,49,50).

God's ways are not our ways, and we have no right to question what He does. In the case of the man who had been blind since birth, Jesus could have spoken the word and sight would have been his instantly; but He made clay and with that clay anointed the man's eyes. By the laws of nature, if *we* rubbed clay in someone's eyes it would blind him; but Jesus used that which would normally blind a man, and brought about the miracle of opening his eyes. The man did not ask HOW his eyes were healed; he simply believed the miracle.   In like manner, we need not ask HOW the blood of Jesus cleanses us from sin; we simply need to *believe* and experience the miracle. The cross is a stumbling block to those who refuse to come to God by faith in the finished work of Jesus; but to those who come to God, the cross is the power of God unto salvation.

"Go, wash in the pool of Siloam." You will notice that up to this point the blind man had done nothing to obtain healing. *Jesus SAW the man, He desired* to heal him, He approached him, He made clay and anointed his eyes. THEN He gave the man instructions to go wash in the pool of Siloam.   This command would remind any religious Jew of the similar instructions Elisha gave Naaman the leper: "Go and wash in Jordan seven times, and thy flesh shall come again to thee, and thou shalt be clean" (II Kings 5:10).

I assure you that if the blind man had not obeyed when Jesus said, "Go," he would have remained blind as long as he lived. The water in the pool of Siloam possessed no healing power; it was obedience to the WORD that brought healing. Jesus commanded this man, *"Go."*   Today He invites us, *"Come."*

"Come unto me, all ye that labour and are heavy laden, and I will give you rest" (Matt. 11:28).

"Him that cometh to me I will in no wise cast out" (John 6:37b).

"The Spirit and the bride say, Come. And let him that heareth say, Come. And let him that is athirst come. And *whosoever will, let him take the water of life freely"* (Rev. 22:17).

Please note, Jesus did not say to this blind man, "Go and wash in the water of your choice." He did not say, "Go and wash wherever you think best." Nor did He instruct the man to "Go to the *nearest* water and wash." He gave the man specific directions and instructions: "Go wash in *the pool of Siloam"*—and if the man had decided that he did not choose to wash in the pool of Siloam but had rather travel to *the river Jordan* and wash, he would not have received his sight.

We receive nothing from God unless we obey the Word. If we hope to receive His blessings, we must *claim* those blessings according to directions given in the Word. We are not saved according to our own plan or program, nor by what men may say. We are saved according to the plan and program blueprinted by Almighty God.

In the parenthetical statement in verse 7, we learn that *"Siloam is by interpretation 'SENT.' "* The pool of Siloam is first mentioned in Nehemiah 3:15 (Siloah), and again in Isaiah 8:6 (Shiloah).

The question naturally arises, Why did John insert the parenthesis in this verse, especially naming the pool? The only reasonable answer insofar as I can see is that all devout Jews would understand the expression "Sent One" to point to their Messiah whom God had sent. Jesus the great Healer of soul, spirit, and body, the "Sent One" from God, was the "Siloam" (the fountain) of all spiritual blessings and of all temporal blessings as well, for "every good gift and every perfect gift is from above, and cometh down from the Father of lights, with whom is no variableness, neither shadow of turning" (James 1:17).

"He went . . . and washed, and came seeing." We are not told whether someone *led* this young man to the pool of Siloam, or if he went alone. Since he had lived all of his life in that community it is not unreasonable to think that he went there alone, perhaps had been there many

times before. The important thing is that when Jesus instructed him to go and wash, he obeyed without question and without asking mortal help.

There is no doubt in my mind that this man was healed the moment he applied water to his eyes and washed away the clay. The Scripture tells us that he washed and *"came seeing."* The fact that the man could even *walk* after gaining his vision was a miracle within itself! Today, if the miracle of modern surgery restores a person's eyesight, it is many days before the full force of the sunlight is allowed to break in upon the enlightened eyes. But notice that *this* man was *instantly* healed, his sight was *instantly* given to him—*and Jesus did not put colored glasses on him!* When God works a miracle the results are one hundred percent successful.

The same is true in our salvation. When God saves us He does not *partially* save us, He does not just "patch us up." No, He makes us *new creations* in Christ, "old things are passed away; *behold, ALL things are become new"* (II Cor. 5:17).

Verse 8: *"The neighbours therefore, and they which before had seen him that he was blind, said, Is not this he that sat and begged?"*

The mention of the man's *"neighbours"* would indicate that he returned to his own house as soon as his eyes were opened—which would be a natural and understandable thing for him to do. His "neighbours" must mean those who lived near him, and *"they which before had seen him that he was blind"* were the people who were accustomed to seeing him begging in the city. In those days, as today, blind beggars were found on the main thoroughfares near public buildings where the greatest number of people would see them. Since this man had been blind all of his life, I do not doubt that he had become a familiar sight to literally hundreds of people who had grown accustomed to seeing him begging.

The people asked of each other, *"Is not this he that sat and begged?"* This removes any doubt that this man was poor, belonging to the most humble class of Jews. It is true that *today* many blind persons are well educated and have found a way by which they can be self-supporting and live in comfortable circumstances; but in that day most blind people were more likely to be poverty stricken and dependent upon charity.

Verse 9: *"Some said, This is he: others said, He is like him: but he said, I am he."*

Some who saw this man immediately recognized him as the blind beggar whom they were so accustomed to seeing, and even though his eyes were now opened they definitely identified him as their neighbor who had been blind.

"Others said, He is LIKE him." Those who made this statement were more than likely the people who lived in and near Jerusalem who had *seen* the blind man—perhaps time after time—but still did not know him well enough to be sure of his identity. After all, the miracle that had been wrought on this man had changed his appearance; there can be no doubt of that. Look into the face of a person who has never seen the light of day, a person whose eyes are totally unsighted. Now imagine that face transformed with the joy and wonder of clear, sighted eyes—and it will be easy to understand that this man was so transformed by the miracle that those who had seen him on repeated occasions could not positively identify him as the blind beggar with whom they were reasonably familiar.

There is a tremendous spiritual lesson here. When a poor, sin-blinded unbeliever is converted, born again through the miracle wrought by the Holy Spirit, his mind is opened and there is a very noticeable change in that person—yes, even in his appearance. It is true that born again Christians live in the same old tabernacle of flesh, but when one is born of the Spirit his entire manner and way of life will be changed.

Notice that there was no doubt in the mind of the man who had been healed. He gave a positive, clear-cut testimony: *"I AM HE."* He heard his neighbors and acquaintances discussing him, asking questions and expressing doubt as to his identity; so he made it clear that he was the man whom they had known as a blind beggar.

Verse 10:   *"Therefore said they unto him, How were thine eyes opened?"*

This question came from the group who gathered around the blind man when he returned from the pool of Siloam after his eyes were opened. Some were his neighbors, and others in the group could have been strangers who heard of the miracle and wanted to see this man whose eyes had been so miraculously opened. Such wonders would certainly attract all who heard about it. They gathered around him and asked, *"How* were thine eyes opened?"

Verse 11:   *"He answered and said, A Man that is called Jesus made clay, and anointed mine eyes, and said unto me, Go to the pool of Siloam, and wash: and I went and washed, and I received sight."*

The man gave a simple, understandable account of the facts in the case. How he knew the Lord's name was *Jesus,* we can only guess. Perhaps one of the people who witnessed the miracle told him it was Jesus who healed him. At any rate, the beggar recognized the Lord simply as "a Man called Jesus," and no more. This is evidenced in verse 35 when Jesus asked him, "Dost thou believe on the Son of God?" The man replied, *"Who IS He, Lord,* that I might believe on Him?" When he confessed here that a Man named Jesus performed the miracle that opened his eyes, he did not at that time *know* that Jesus was the Son of God, Saviour of sinners; but he accurately gave each fact of the miracle—"A Man called Jesus put clay on my eyes, told me to go and wash in the pool of Siloam. I went, I washed as He commanded, and I received my sight."

Verse 12: *"Then said they unto him, Where is He? He said, I know not."*

The desire to see Jesus was natural, but it is not probable that those who asked, *"Where IS He?"* intended to worship Him or praise His name for the wonderful miracle He had just wrought. They were no doubt His enemies, and they wanted to lay hands on Him and bring Him before the rulers to have Him condemned to death.

The answer the man gave certainly seems to indicate that he did not return to the place where he had begged for alms, but after his eyes were opened he had gone home to tell his loved ones. If he had returned to the place where Jesus healed him he would probably have told his inquirers that Jesus had been there only a short time before and therefore could not be very far away. These people seemed to think that the worker of such a miracle would not be very far from the subject of the miracle. They were judging Jesus by human standards and did not understand that He always *avoided* publicity rather than seeking it.

Verse 13: *"They brought to the Pharisees him that aforetime was blind."*

"They" who brought this young man to the Pharisees must have been the people who lived in the same neighborhood with him. They thought a miracle as marvelous as this sudden healing of a man born blind demanded further investigation; so they brought him before the "great council," or the Sanhedrin, no doubt the same body of men before whom our Lord testified and made His defense in chapter 5. There was no *other* group in the religious realm in Jerusalem who could excommunicate a person, and these men *did* cast this young man out of the synagogue. (See verse 34.)

Verse 14: *"And it was the sabbath day when Jesus made the clay, and opened his eyes."*

That the clay was made on the Sabbath is pointed out

for two reasons: First, to prove that Jesus was Lord of the Sabbath as well as of all other days. He had come to fulfill days, ceremonies, feasts—in short, He had come to fulfill the entire *old economy* that the *new* dispensation might bring life through the Spirit. In the second place, it emphasizes the bitter hatred and enmity of the Jews against the Lord Jesus Christ, whom they looked upon as a lawbreaker and a desecrater of their holy Sabbath.

In *performing* miracles on the Sabbath, Jesus was teaching the Jews the true meaning of the Sabbath, showing them that works of mercy and deeds of love are to be performed even on that day. Works of mercy, pity, and charity are always seasonable, and should be done to the glory of God and in the name of Jesus.

Verse 15: *"Then again the Pharisees also asked him how he had received his sight. He said unto them, He put clay upon mine eyes, and I washed, and do see."*

"Again the PHARISEES asked him." This was the same question the *neighbors* had asked him. They knew he had been born blind, they knew his eyes were now miraculously open, and they wanted to know how this came about. The Pharisees, since they were the religious leaders of that day, should have been far more interested in the completeness and effectiveness of the healing, than in how it had been accomplished. The paramount question about a sinner's salvation is not the mode (or manner) in which it has been effected, but whether or not the person professing salvation has been truly saved. Has the work of regeneration really been done in the heart? Some of the most far-reaching religious disputes among men do not concern the fact that the Holy Spirit has renewed the heart, but the *way in which it was done!* We know there is only one way of salvation— by grace through faith; but some groups declare that they are *the sole custodians* of the way, and some even argue about the position or posture of the body when one is saved. Others contend that a person cannot be saved except in

church. It matters not whether one is in a temple, in a church bowing at an altar, riding down the highway in an automobile, flying in an airplane, or lying on a bed in the darkness of the night or wee hours of the morning. Anyone can be saved wherever he may be if he feels the need of the Saviour, repents, and calls on His name in faith believing!

The man boldly gave the Pharisees the same answer he had given his neighbors, except he did not mention the name of Jesus. He used the pronoun "He," thus indicating that he knew the Pharisees would understand he was speaking of Jesus.

The testimony and simple, straightforward boldness of this poor beggar are not to be passed over lightly. He did not hesitate to stand up before them and testify concerning this Jesus whom they hated. He faced severe persecution, he knew that *even his own parents* would not testify in his behalf because it had been agreed (v. 22) that anyone who confessed the Christ would be put out of the synagogue. He was so thankful for his eyesight, it made little difference to him what consequences might follow.

The command of the Lord God is, *"Let the redeemed of the Lord say so!"* (Psalm 107:2). We should never be ashamed of Jesus, ashamed to tell out the good news of salvation and let men know that the Gospel has come into our own lives.

Verse 16: *"Therefore said some of the Pharisees, This man is not of God, because He keepeth not the sabbath day. Others said, How can a man that is a sinner do such miracles? And there was a division among them."*

Here we see two classes of Pharisees—one group made up of the bigoted enemies of the Lord Jesus Christ, ready to pounce upon anything by which they could accuse Him of being a heretic and an enemy to the religion of their fathers. They said, "This Man is not of God. He is a wicked Man because He keepeth not the Sabbath day."

They were inferring that a man sent from God, a *prophet* of God, would not work on the Sabbath—and in this they displayed their ignorance of things truly spiritual.

The other group of Pharisees was made up of a small minority who had watched Jesus, they had listened to His wonderful words of life and witnessed His miracles. *They* asked, "How can a man *not* sent from God, a man who is wicked and ungodly, do such an astonishing thing as opening the eyes of a man who had never seen the light of day?" This was practically the same confession Nicodemus made when he first came to Jesus by night, confessing, "No man can do these miracles that thou doest, except God be with him." The majority of the Pharisees were against Him, but there was a minority who, like Nicodemus (and possibly Gamaliel) were reasonable enough to see that no ordinary man could perform the miracles Jesus had wrought.

"There was a division among them." We find these words three times in the Gospel of John—here, and in chapter 7 verse 43, and chapter 10 verse 19. You will notice that this small minority did not openly say what they really *wanted* to say—that is, they did not make a dogmatic assertion. They asked a question, indicating their fear of what the majority group would say. Thus, although one group wanted to destroy Jesus and the other group wanted to save Him, *neither* group was bold and dogmatic in their statements. The majority of the Pharisees feared the mob of the common people, and the minority feared the Sanhedrin and the rulers in the synagogue.

Even today, in large assemblies where men meet to consider religious questions, there are always some who are God-fearing believers, willing to support the truth; but they sit among *enemies,* and many times they do not speak all that is in their hearts. *Gamaliel* sat in such an assembly. (Read Acts 5:34—39.) We should not stay away from church just because we are outnumbered. If there is an opportunity to defend the truth we should defend it, whether that defense be against few or many. We should be strong in the Lord and in the power of His might. In Acts 4:20 the disciples said, "We cannot but speak the things which we have seen and heard."

We cannot truthfully say that all divisions are evil, nor is all concord and unity necessarily *good*. We must be led by the Spirit in all things; we must "*try* the spirits whether they are of God" (I John 4:1).

Verse 17: *"They say unto the blind man again, What sayest thou of Him, that He hath opened thine eyes? He said, He is a prophet."*

It is most interesting that these supposedly learned, dignified, proud religionists stooped to ask a poor beggar, "What do you think about this Person? Who do you think He is? According to your testimony He wrought this cure on you, so tell us what you really think about Him."

The question the Pharisees asked did not pertain to the greatness or *quality* of the miracle, but to the Person who performed it. They were still trying to get the man who had been healed to say something about Jesus that would open the door for them to condemn Him.

"He said, HE IS A PROPHET." A prophet is not always someone who foretells things to come. The Bible use of the word has a much wider meaning. Prophets in the Old Testament were not all foretellers of things to come; many of them were men who preached warning and worked miracles. It was in this sense that the blind man called the Lord Jesus a "prophet"—not so much because of what He *said*, but because of what He *did*.

Most of the Jews accepted Jesus as a prophet—but no more than that. The multitude that followed Him into Jerusalem said, "This is Jesus the prophet of Nazareth of Galilee" (Matt. 21:11). In Matthew 21:46 we read that when the Pharisees sought to lay hands on Jesus, "they feared the multitude, because they took Him for a prophet, "or as one of the prophets." When Jesus raised the son of the widow of Nain, "there came a fear on all: and they glorified God, saying, That a great prophet is risen up among us" (Luke 7:16). The two disciples on the way to Emmaus spoke of Him as "a prophet mighty in deed and word before God and all the people" (Luke 24:19). The beggar in our present verse did not testify that Jesus was "THE Prophet" (the Messiah) promised by Moses. He only said "a prophet"—but even this statement required courage on his part and signified *the beginning of faith in his heart.* It was a declaration of his belief that Jesus was a Prophet especially raised by God and endued with power, as were Elijah and Moses.

Bible scholars say that according to a Jewish maxim, a prophet might dispense with the observance of the Sabbath in order to perform a mission of mercy, and it is entirely possible that the healed man knew this. At any rate, his proclaiming Jesus as a prophet dealt a serious blow to the Pharisees. Many things *were* allowed a true prophet sent to the people under God's call and commission. They were given special privileges relating to the observance of the ceremonial laws. (We see this in the lives of David and Elijah.) Therefore the answer this young man gave the Pharisees carried much weight, and they knew it.

Verse 18:   *"But the Jews did not believe concerning him, that he had been blind, and received his sight, until they called the parents of him that had received his sight."*

Here, as in many other places, we see the extraordinary unbelief of the Jews and their determination to close their eyes against the light. They had abundant opportunity to believe, they had walked and talked with Jesus, they were exposed to His teachings, they had witnessed His miracles; but they refused to believe. The thing that makes agnostics and infidels of men is the want of *will to believe* the simple Gospel, not want of *reasons* for believing. They are willfully blind, willfully ignorant, and (I say this with fear and trembling and in utmost reverence) God cannot help any man *unless that man has a will to believe.*

Our present verse tells us that the Jews (the religious leaders, primarily the Pharisees) did not believe *"until they called the parents of him that had received his sight." "Until"* does not indicate a matter of conclusion on their part after they talked with the man's parents. The context shows that they were unbelievers *before* they called the parents and they *remained* unbelievers even after the parents gave testimony that their son had been blind and could now see. The fact that the parents were called simply means that they were summoned to appear before the council of the Sanhedrin, just as witnesses today are summoned to appear in our courts.

Verse 19: *"And they asked them, saying, Is this your son, who ye say was born blind? How then doth he now see?"*

Paul tells us that the Lord "taketh the wise in their own craftiness" (I Cor. 3:19). In other words, Satan's schemes sometimes backfire—and such was the case here. The enemies of Jesus did not help their cause by calling in the parents of the healed man. On the contrary, they brought before the public eye two of the best witnesses the man could possibly have had concerning his identity.

Notice the way the Pharisees phrased their question: "Is this your son, *who ye SAY* was born blind?"—insinuating that they thought the parents were acting deceitfully, plotting against them on behalf of Jesus by sending out a report that their son had been born blind. From the language used here it would certainly seem that the Pharisees believed the parents to be lying about their son. And then they asked, *"How then doth he now SEE?"*

Verses 20—22: *"His parents answered them and said, We know that this is our son, and that he was born blind: But by what means he now seeth, we know not; or who hath opened his eyes, we know not: he is of age; ask him: he shall speak for himself. These words spake his parents, because they feared the Jews: for the Jews had agreed already, that if any man did confess that He was Christ, he should be put out of the synagogue."*

The parents made a clear declaration, one that the Pharisees could not contradict: "We KNOW that this is *our son."* (Certainly this is reasonable. The parents could not be mistaken about a child who had been born into their own home.) "We KNOW . . . that he was *born blind!"* This statement, too, was beyond contradiction. The man was their child, and they could not possibly be mistaken about their baby having been born blind.

"But by what means he now seeth . . . or who hath opened his eyes, we know not." I cannot believe that this man had not told his parents who opened his eyes. It would only have been natural for him to want them to be the first to know of his healing. This statement made by the parents plainly shows their determination to have no more to do with the case than was absolutely necessary. The reason for their attitude is clearly given in verse 22. They said to the Pharisees, *"He is of age; ask HIM."*

"These words spake his parents, because they feared the Jews." Fear of the Jews is mentioned four times in the Gospel of John: We find it in our present verse, in chapter 7 verse 13, in chapter 12 verse 42, and in chapter 19 verse 38. The fact that *"the Jews had agreed already"* proves that their minds were made up, and no matter what Jesus said or did, they would not believe.

"If any man did confess that He was Christ, he should be put out of the synagogue." It was a serious thing indeed for a Jew to be put out of the synagogue. Such action was equivalent to being cut off from all relatives and from all communion with other Jews. In other words, it meant *total excommunication.* Even today, if a Jew becomes a Christian, he is disowned—by his own family, as well as by other orthodox Jews. According to the testimony of converted Jews with whom I have talked, a Jewish family actually holds a public funeral for a member of that family

who becomes a believer. In the days of Jesus' earthly ministry, it was a grave thing to risk being turned out of the synagogue.

It seems to me that the parents of this man would have been so happy to have their son healed, they would have gladly testified that Jesus had opened their boy's eyes. If they had boldly witnessed for Jesus, their home could have become a great revival center; but instead of witnessing as they should have done, for fear of the Jews they denied knowledge of who had healed their boy.

Verse 23:   *"Therefore said his parents, He is of age; ask him."*

In those days a young man was declared *"of age"* when he was thirty years old. The parents of this man did not want to be suspected of favoring or defending the One who had healed him. They therefore referred all questions to him personally and declined to offer any opinion concerning the *means* of the miracle, or the identity of the Man who had wrought it.

Verse 24:   *"Then again called they the man that was blind, and said unto him, Give God the praise: we know that this Man is a sinner."*

The man who was healed of blindness was summoned to appear before the Sanhedrin for the *second* time. It could be that he had been asked to leave while his parents were questioned; but when they refused to testify concerning the Person who had healed him, there was no alternative but to recall the son and question him again.

In their cross-examination the Pharisees said to him, *"Give GOD the praise. WE know that this Man is a sinner!"* The personal pronoun "we" is very emphatic in the Greek—that is, *"WE who are the learned men in Israel* ought to know best." After all, this was but a poor, ignorant beggar, a man who until now had never seen the light of day and had made his living by begging on the streets of the city. He had never attended the schools of religion, he was not versed in their traditions, and these learned men felt that they knew more than this beggar and they expected him to do what they *told* him to do. Therefore they commanded him, "Give *God* the honor and glory for your healing, because this Sabbath-breaker, this sinner, could not have opened your eyes."

Verse 25: *"He answered and said, Whether He be a sinner or no, I know not: one thing I know, that, whereas I was blind, now I see."*

The man's answer to the Sanhedrin was simple, but clear and positive: he could not tell them whether or not Jesus was a sinner, but one thing he DID know for certain: He declared, *"Whereas I was BLIND, now I see!"* The main point of his testimony was *the REALITY of the miracle.* He KNEW he had been blind from birth, he knew that he NOW COULD SEE, and that was the all-important thing to him. He did not at that time say anything about the character of Jesus, he did not know whether He was a sinner or not; but he knew that he must believe his own senses, and his own senses testified to him that he was now seeing, whereas he had been blind since the day he was born. Therefore, the fact of his sight he doubted not. He could answer clearly concerning the *accomplished fact* of his healing.

I believe the testimony in verse 25 declares a truth concerning salvation. I believe it is impossible for a person to be saved and not *know* it. All sinners are spiritually *blind;* and when one is born again *his spiritual eyes are opened.* Paul said, "If our Gospel be hid, it is hid to them that are lost: *in whom the god of this world hath blinded the minds of them which believe not,* lest the light of the glorious Gospel of Christ, who is the image of God, should shine unto them" (II Cor. 4:3,4). To receive Jesus is to have the blinded mind opened and the inner man healed. There are many things about salvation that we cannot know, understand, or explain; but we CAN know that whereas we were *lost*—miserable and in sin—we have undergone a complete change of heart, mind, and spirit. Everything about us is different because we are new creations in Christ—*and we KNOW it!*

Paul declared, *". . . I KNOW whom I have believed,* and am persuaded that He is able to keep that which I have committed unto Him against that day" (II Tim. 1:12).

John testified, *"We KNOW that we have passed from death unto life . . ."* (I John 3:14a).

In I John 5:10—13 we read, *"He that believeth on the Son of God hath the witness in HIMSELF:* he that believeth not God hath made Him a liar; because he believeth not the record that God gave of His Son. And this is the record, that God hath given to us eternal life, and this life is in His Son. He that hath the Son hath life; and he that hath not the Son of God hath not life. *These things have I written unto you that believe on the name of the Son of God; THAT YE MAY KNOW that ye have eternal life, and that ye may believe on the name of the Son of God."*

True faith looks only to the *result,* and does not worry about the manner in which the result is brought about. On the contrary, *unbelief* refuses to look at result alone, but excuses itself by asking questions about the *manner* that obtained the result. "Without faith it is impossible to please Him: for he that cometh to God must believe that He is, and that He is a rewarder of them that diligently seek Him" (Heb. 11:6).

Dear friend, if YOU do not know you are born again just as surely as you know you are breathing, I beg you to bow your head and tell Jesus you want to be saved. Ask forgiveness for your sins, receive Jesus, and God will save you this very moment. *Bible salvation* produces assurance— we KNOW that we have passed from death unto life, we KNOW that whereas we were blind, groping in the darkness of sin, *NOW we see,* and we walk in the light because we are children of light.

Verse 26:   *"Then said they to him again, What did He to thee?   How opened He thine eyes?"*

When the enemies of Jesus renewed their examination of this man they questioned him concerning the *manner* of the opening of his eyes.   Previously they had examined him concerning WHO opened his eyes, and now they want to know HOW his eyes were opened.   (They would have been better off had they dropped the subject, for in continuing their reckless cross-examination of the man they were put to shame, as we will see in the ensuing verses.)

The devil defeats his own diabolical purpose when he brings persecution against believers—especially weak believers and newborn babes in Christ.   Believers learn important lessons under pressure, persecution, attacks from Satan—lessons they would never have known *had they not been persecuted.*   The Church *grows* under such circumstances.   It has been said that the blood of martyrs is the seed of the Church, and one sad thing today is that true believers are not speaking out as they should.   If they *were,* there would be more persecution aimed at the Church. Most Christians today know nothing of suffering for Christ's sake.

Verse 27:   *"He answered them, I have told you already, and ye did not hear: wherefore would ye hear it again? Will ye also be His disciples?"*

Here the young man's reply indicates growing impatience. He sees no point in their repetition of the same questions. Can it be that they are trying to make him deny the fact that he can *see?*   Are they trying to make him disbelieve his own senses?   His answer here implies, "I have already told you *exactly* what happened, and I have nothing to add to that testimony.   You did not believe what I told you, so why should I say the same thing again?   Would you like to hear a *repetition* of the same testimony?   I refuse to change it—there is nothing to add to it, and I refuse to take anything away from it.   If you did not believe me the first time, would you believe me if I repeated the same testimony?"

"Would ye" and *"will ye"* are the same words in the
Greek.   The real meaning is "Do ye *will?* Do ye have
a will to hear? Are you willing now to believe on Him?"
Undoubtedly the question was asked in ridicule or sarcasm.
It does not seem reasonable that the man asked such a
question in a serious manner, considering the long-drawn-out
examination these men had just imposed upon him.   It
seems to me that the beggar was saying, "From your repeated questions, you indicate that you yourselves would
like to become His disciples. *Is that really what you want?"*

Verses 28 and 29:   *"Then they reviled him, and said,
Thou art His disciple; but we are Moses' disciples. We
know that God spake unto Moses: as for this fellow, we
know not from whence He is."*

The Pharisees were insulted by the intimation that they
would become disciples of Jesus! *They,* of all men—wise,
learned, students of the law, teachers and leaders in Israel,
would never become followers of this impostor! They declared, *"WE* are disciples of *Moses,* we are children of
Abraham! Only poor ignorant people like yourself would
follow this fellow."   They spoke of Moses as though he
had been an enemy to Jesus, whereas Moses prophesied
concerning the Messiah and looked forward to the day when
He should come.   They needed to re-read Deuteronomy
18:15—19.

"As for this fellow, we know not from whence He is."
In other words, they said, "We *know* God sent Moses and
commissioned him to be our law-giver and a teacher in
Israel.   We are pleasing God when we follow Moses because
Moses was God's prophet.   But we do not know who com-
missioned this Jesus whom you say healed your blindness;
we do not know who gave Him authority to teach or preach.
But we KNOW who Moses was, therefore we follow him."

("From whence He came" in this instance does not refer
to a geographical location, but to the authority under which

Jesus preached and wrought His miracles.) It was firmly implanted in the Jewish mind that *"God spake unto MO-SES,"* but they refused to believe that God had spoken to or through the Lord Jesus Christ.

Verse 30: *"The man answered and said unto them, Why herein is a marvellous thing, that ye know not from whence He is, and yet He hath opened mine eyes."*

The pronoun *"ye"* is very strong here, meaning "YOU Pharisees, you who are rulers and learned people professing to be well versed in religion. YOU should know that no ordinary man could open the eyes of one born blind. Such a thing has never occurred before and therefore you should recognize this Man as from God. He is a prophet, and yet you will not confess this truth, you have no will to believe it."

Verse 31: *"Now we know that God heareth not sinners: but if any man be a worshipper of God, and doeth His will, him He heareth."*

Thus the healed man continued his simple line of reasoning. It was an admitted principle among the Jews that God did not hear a wicked man's prayer, nor did He give him power to perform great miracles. Those who worked miracles were enabled by God to perform such works, they were men who feared God and followed His will. The Pharisees knew this, they knew God did not look on impenitent sinners with favor. Thus the young man's simple reasoning was supported by the Jews' own doctrine. *"God heareth not sinners"* applies to those who do not acknowledge their sin nor feel the need for forgiveness. That God will not hear impenitent sinners is taught in such texts as Job 35:12; Psalm 18:41; Proverbs 1:28; 28:9; Isaiah 1:15; Jeremiah 11:11; 14:12; Ezekiel 8:18; Micah 3:4; Zechariah 7:13.

This does not mean that God does not hear a convicted, penitent sinner when he cries out for mercy and pardon. Both the Old and the New Testaments clearly teach that

God *does* hear sinners who are of a broken and a contrite heart. (Study Psalm 34:18; 51:17; Isaiah 1:18; I John 1:9; Romans 10:13.)

"A worshipper of God" means much more than outward worship such as saying prayers and worshipping God in the sanctuary. It refers to a God-fearing person, one who honors God and *"doeth His will."* Elijah was such a man. God heard Elijah on Mount Carmel, answered his prayer, and a great miracle was wrought; but the worshippers of Baal did not receive an answer to their prayers. Read the account in I Kings 18:17—40.

The healed beggar had not yet known or believed that Jesus was very God, Messiah and Saviour of sinners. He believed Him to be a righteous man, one whom God would hear when He prayed; but he did not as yet see Him as One who worked miracles by His own power. He did not recognize Him as God in flesh, but his faith was growing. If a person desires to know the truth, God will make it possible for that person to hear and know the truth.

Verse 32: *"Since the world began was it not heard that any man opened the eyes of one that was born blind."*

Verses 32 and 33 give the conclusion of the argument of the man who had been blind from his birth until the moment Jesus opened his eyes. For the eyes of one born blind to be opened and made to see clearly, was a work beyond the power of any ordinary man. Such had not been heard of since the world began. Therefore the man knew this was the work of Almighty God. In other words he said to the Pharisees, "This Man Jesus has worked a work not possible to any save God. You have witnessed the evidence of this miracle, you have seen it proved that He is sent from God and empowered by God—otherwise He could not have opened my eyes."

"Since the world began" in the Greek reads "from the AGE of the world," meaning from the beginning. We find the same truth set forth in Acts 3:21; 15:18; and Ephesians

3:9.

This man who had never attended a theological school was more learned than the Pharisees in things of the Spirit and judged divine things more correctly than did the entire council of the Pharisees. Nor are we always led correctly by those in authority today, such as bishops and other religious rulers. Many times the Spirit reveals things to laymen, and often the ordinary church member has a deeper insight into the things of God than do some of the outstanding men in the field of religion.

Verse 33: *"If this Man were not of God, He could do nothing."*

Considering what the Pharisees said to this man in the following verse, this statement evidently made them furious. In verse 24 they had told him that Jesus was a sinner; and now he refutes their claim by boldly declaring that if "this Man were not *of God,* He could do nothing." This so increased their anger that they in return hurled insults at him.

Verse 34: *"They answered and said unto him, Thou wast altogether born in sins, and dost thou teach us? And they cast him out."*

The Pharisees knew that this man's argument was unanswerable; therefore they turned on him and began to abuse and ridicule him. They said, *"Who are YOU?* You are a miserable wicked creature, born in sin and suffering all of your life *because* of sin. Yet you presume to teach US, the religious leaders in Israel! Do you think you know more about spiritual things than WE know?"

"And they CAST HIM OUT." This means much more than casting this young man out of the room where the meeting was being held. It means that they cast him out of the synagogue, a formal excommunication from the commonwealth of Israel—religiously, politically, socially. This was the most humiliating thing that could happen to a Jew.

When men of authority and high standing begin to abuse

those who are of much *lesser* power and authority, such abuse testifies that they are losing the battle and therefore they grow angry and impatient. Pure truth can wait, pure truth can afford to be *patient;* but error cannot wait, error cannot afford to be patient. The Pharisees could not answer this man's argument, therefore they tried to silence him through intimidation and slander. A Jew's fear and dread of excommunication from the commonwealth of Israel was second only to his fear of physical death.

There are instances *today* when sincere young ministers have been expelled from theological institutions simply because they did not fit in with the "program." But thank God, big churches, denominations, theological schools and religious assemblies cannot excommunicate us from life eternal! Christ, the author of eternal life, was excommunicated. He was not only banished, He was nailed to a cross. We should rejoice when we are counted worthy to be persecuted for His sake. Paul told young Timothy, "Yea, and all that will live godly in Christ Jesus shall suffer persecution" (II Tim. 3:12). Jesus said to His disciples, "In the world ye shall have tribulation: but be of good cheer; I have overcome the world" (John 16:33). It is an honor to be excommunicated from any religious assembly or school that denies the verbal inspiration of the Scriptures, the deity of Christ, or any other fundamentals of the faith.

Verses 35 and 36: *"Jesus heard that they had cast him out; and when He had found him, He said unto him, Dost thou believe on the Son of God? He answered and said, Who is He, Lord, that I might believe on Him?"*

There was probably an interval of time between verse 34 and verse 35. It does not seem reasonable that the events recorded in the present and following verses (and the first part of chapter 10) would take place the same day Jesus healed the blind man.

"Jesus heard that they had cast him out." Of course Jesus knew all about this man's persecution even *before it*

happened, but He did nothing about it until it was publicly reported throughout Jerusalem.

"And when He had found him . . . ." When the Jews cast him out of the temple, the *Lord of the temple* was waiting to receive him—and He will do the same for any believer today who is called upon to suffer for Christ's sake! He is a very present help in time of trouble, ready at all times to speak words of consolation, comfort, and peace to a suffering believer.

"He said unto him, Dost thou believe on the Son of God?" This is one of the few places in the Gospels where Jesus referred to Himself as *"the Son of God."* (See also John 3:18; 5:25; 10:36; and 11:4.)

The Greek word translated *"thou"* is very emphatic in this verse. What Jesus actually said to the healed man was, "Many others are unbelieving. Dost *thou* believe? The masses refuse to believe that I am the Son of God—*WILL YOU believe?* Do you have *a WILL to believe?"* The man had already confessed that Jesus was a prophet, and here Jesus gave him the opportunity to take the step of saving faith: "Whosoever believeth that Jesus is the Christ is born of God . . ." (I John 5:1).

This man *did* have a will to believe. He asked, *"Who IS He, Lord, that I might believe on Him?"* When a person begins to inquire about the Lord Jesus Christ, that person is well on the way to redemption. The question of questions is, "What think ye of Christ? Whose Son is He?" This young man's expression was one of longing, and the soul that longs to know Jesus *will come to know Him.*

Verse 37: *"And Jesus said unto him, Thou hast both seen Him, and it is He that talketh with thee."*

In only one other instance (when He was dealing with the Samaritan woman at Jacob's well) did Jesus so clearly and unmistakably declare His divinity and messiahship. He knew the heart of this man, He knew that the question came from a sincere longing to exercise true faith in the

Lord Jesus Christ.

"The meek will He guide in judgment: and the meek will He teach His way" (Psalm 25:9).

". . . Thou hast hid these things from the wise and prudent, and hast revealed them unto babes" (Matt. 11:25).

"Blessed are they which are persecuted for righteousness' sake: for their's is the kingdom of heaven. Blessed are ye, when men shall revile you, and persecute you, and shall say all manner of evil against you falsely, for my sake. Rejoice, and be exceeding glad: for great is your reward in heaven: for so persecuted they the prophets which were before you" (Matt. 5:10—12).

"For ye see your calling, brethren, how that not many wise men after the flesh, not many mighty, not many noble, are called: but God hath chosen the foolish things of the world to confound the wise; and God hath chosen the weak things of the world to confound the things which are mighty; and base things of the world, and things which are despised, hath God chosen, yea, and things which are not, to bring to nought things that are: that no flesh should glory in His presence. But of Him are ye in Christ Jesus, who of God is made unto us wisdom, and righteousness, and sanctification, and redemption: That, according as it is written, He that glorieth, let him glory in the Lord" (I Cor. 1:26—31).

Verse 38: *"And he said, Lord, I believe. And he worshipped Him."*

The Holy Spirit was working on this man's heart, and the more he thought about the miracle of healing that had given sight to his blinded eyes, the more he was convinced that the Person who had wrought that miracle was the Messiah, the Christ of God. He had heard and obeyed the words of Jesus—and received the healing of his eyes. Faith comes by hearing, and hearing by the Word. He said, *"Lord, I BELIEVE. And he worshipped Him!"*

This statement was more than a display of respect and

reverence toward Jesus. This individual knew that he was in the presence of the Son of God—yea, very God in flesh. Jesus did not rebuke him, but *accepted* his worship, thereby testifying that He was truly the Son of God, because *only God* is worthy of worship—and no true prophet ever allowed men to fall at his feet and worship him. (Read Acts 10:25, 26; 14:8—18; Revelation 19:10 and 22:9.)

In studying the miracles of Jesus we find that very few worshipped Him after they were healed and blessed by Him. In Luke 17:12—19 we read of the ten lepers whom Jesus healed, "and *ONE of them,* when he saw that he was healed, turned back, and with a loud voice glorified God, and fell down on his face at His feet, giving Him thanks ...And Jesus answering said, *Were there not TEN cleansed?* but where are the NINE? *There are not found that re-turned to give glory to God, save this stranger.* And He said unto him, Arise, go thy way: thy faith hath made thee whole."

Verse 39: *"And Jesus said, For judgment I am come into this world, that they which see not might see; and that they which see might be made blind."*

John 3:17 told us that "God sent not His Son into the world to condemn the world; but that the world through Him might be saved." In John 12:47 Jesus said, "If any man hear my words, and believe not, I judge him not: for I came not to judge the world, but to save the world." Yet there is no contradiction between those two passages and the statement in our present verse. It is true that Jesus did not come into the world to be a Judge *at that time;* He came to seek and to save the lost, to take away sin. But even though at that time He had not come to judge, He had come to *produce* a judgment, to bring about a distinction (a division) between men. He came—the Light of the world—to be the cause of light breaking on minds that had a will to know Him and believe on Him as Messiah. His coming into the world was the cause of light breaking in on minds which, *before* He came, sat in darkness. When He came, *those who believed* saw the light. *Until* He came, it was not possible for them to see. This is similar to what Simeon said in Luke 2:34,35: ". . . *that the thoughts of many hearts may be revealed."*

Poor fishermen and humble, ordinary people had light revealed to them that never *could* have been revealed had not Jesus come into the world. On the other hand, the self-righteous Pharisees, proud of their lineage and boasting that they were Abraham's seed, were given over to judicial blindness *because they rejected Jesus* (Matt. 11:25). Rejected light becomes darkness; thus those who once saw, became utterly blind. The Gospel, when received, brings light and salvation, but when rejected, the same Gospel automatically causes blindness to engulf the mind and heart of the person who rejects it. Those who reject the truth will automatically follow error. There is no such thing as "spiritual neutrality." Believe on Jesus and we are set free. Reject Him, and we surrender to bondage, darkness, despair, and damnation:

"This then is the message which we have heard of Him, and declare unto you, that *God is light, and in Him is no darkness at all. If we say that we have fellowship with Him, and walk in darkness, we lie, and do not the truth: But if we walk in the light, as HE is in the light,* we have fellowship one with another, and the blood of Jesus Christ His Son cleanseth us from all sin" (I John 1:5—7).

In our present verse, the statement *"that they which see might be made blind"* in the Greek reads "that they which see *might BECOME blind."*

"Judgment" on this occasion is not used in an active sense, as when God will judge the quick and the dead at the end of time. It is a work of discrimination which was one consequence (not purpose) of Christ's coming into the world. When the Lord Jesus Christ came into the world, all men automatically divided themselves into two classes: they showed themselves to belong to darkness, or to light.

They *received* the light, or they *rejected* it. Those who were "blind"—the simple, ignorant people like the man whom Jesus had just healed, saw *because they had a WILL to see;* but those who professed to have sight, the proud, presumptuous, religious leaders who thought they were spiritually clear-sighted, were found to be *utterly BLIND.*

Verse 40: *"And some of the Pharisees which were with Him heard these words, and said to Him, Are we blind also?"*

Rest assured that this was not a sincere, anxious inquiry concerning their spiritual status. They were really asking, "Do you mean to say that we, learned doctors of the law, are blind? that we do not understand the things of Moses the prophet?" ("Behold, thou art called a Jew, and restest in the law, and makest thy boast of God"—Rom. 2:17). In their own estimation, these proud, self-righteous people were *custodians of the light,* and jested at the thought that anyone could call them *blind!*

Verse 41: *"Jesus said unto them, If ye were blind, ye should have no sin: but now ye say, We see; therefore your sin remaineth."*

Jesus gave His enemies a remarkable answer! He said to them, "You would be far better off if you WERE blind! If you recognized your blindness and confessed it, if you came to the light, you would not be guilty of the sin that will damn you, the sin of unbelief. This poor beggar has openly confessed that I am Messiah, the Son of God, but *you* refuse to believe. *Therefore your sin remaineth,* the greatest sin man can commit against a holy God."

Our Lord did not mean that ignorance makes men free from guilt. He meant that one who is an out-and-out sinner, guilty and deserving hell, is much easier to reach with the Gospel than are those who are "religious but lost." The hardest person to reach with the Gospel is the self-confident, self-righteous moral person who is trusting in good works, upright living—or perhaps in the fact that he comes through a line of ministers, missionaries, and leaders in the church. Such a one will testify that he has always been "good," he has never been out in sin, and therefore does not need what he terms a "slaughterhouse religion." It is almost impossible to break in upon such people with the Gospel and make them realize that they are lost and stand in need of the Saviour. Churches in America today are literally filled with people who have "joined" the church, they have been baptized by one method or another, they attend services, give of their income and of their time—but they have never had a personal experience with Jesus! Salvation is not by living, giving, doing or NOT doing; it is by receiving Jesus: "As many as received Him, to them gave He power to become the sons of God, even to them that believe on His name: Which were born, not of blood, nor of the will of the flesh, nor of the will of man, but of God" (John 1:12,13).

Better had one been born in the darkest jungles of earth and never heard the Gospel, than to be exposed to the truth and *reject* it. It would be better to live and die without ever seeing a Bible or hearing the name of Jesus, than to live in America—land of the open Bible, a land with churches on almost every corner—and reject the blood-bought salvation of the cross of Jesus! Men will be judged according to the light they *rejected,* according to the truth to which they were exposed but refused to receive. "For unto whomsoever much is given, of him shall be much required . . ." (Luke 12:48).

This miracle, the opening of the eyes of a man blind from birth, has great spiritual significance because it presents a beautiful picture of the illumination of the heart and spirit in the salvation of a sinner. All unbelievers are blind (II Cor. 4:3,4), but when one believes on the Lord Jesus Christ—the Light of the world—he then walks in the light because he has become a *child* of light.

It is most interesting to me that the Scripture gives no further information about the man who was healed of his blindness—further proof that the Bible is verbally inspired, for if ordinary men had written this account, they would certainly have followed it with further references. The healed man would have been called upon to testify at great rallies and would have been used on many occasions as an example; but this was not true in the ministry of Jesus. *Many* believed and were healed whose names are not recorded in the Word of God: "And there are also many other things which Jesus did, the which, if they should be written every one, *I suppose that even the world itself could not contain the books that should be written.* Amen" (John 21:25).

The born again Christian can say with this man who was healed of blindness, "One thing I KNOW, that, whereas I was blind, NOW I SEE!" Whereas we were dead in trespasses and sins, NOW we are alive unto God. Whereas we were bound by Satan, the truth has made us free. Dear reader, if you do not know that you are born again just as surely as this man knew he had received his physical sight, I urge you to find some quiet place and get on your knees before an open Bible, put your faith in the finished work of Jesus and let Him come into your heart this moment. Then you, too, can say, "Whereas I was blind, NOW I see!"

CHAPTER X

1. Verily, verily, I say unto you, He that entereth not by the door into the sheepfold, but climbeth up some other way, the same is a thief and a robber.

2. But he that entereth in by the door is the shepherd of the sheep.

3. To him the porter openeth; and the sheep hear his voice: and he calleth his own sheep by name, and leadeth them out.

4. And when he putteth forth his own sheep, he goeth before them, and the sheep follow him: for they know his voice.

5. And a stranger will they not follow, but will flee from him: for they know not the voice of strangers.

6. This parable spake Jesus unto them: but they understood not what things they were which he spake unto them.

7. Then said Jesus unto them again, Verily, verily, I say unto you, I am the door of the sheep.

8. All that ever came before me are thieves and robbers: but the sheep did not hear them.

9. I am the door: by me if any man enter in, he shall be saved, and shall go in and out, and find pasture.

10. The thief cometh not, but for to steal, and to kill, and to destroy: I am come that they might have life, and that they might have it more abundantly.

11. I am the good shepherd: the good shepherd giveth his life for the sheep.

12. But he that is an hireling, and not the shepherd, whose own the sheep are not, seeth the wolf coming, and leaveth the sheep, and fleeth: and the wolf catcheth them, and scattereth the sheep.

13. The hireling fleeth, because he is an hireling, and careth not for the sheep.

14. I am the good shepherd, and know my sheep, and am known of mine.

15. As the Father knoweth me, even so know I the Father: and I lay down my life for the sheep.

16. And other sheep I have, which are not of this fold: them also I must bring, and they shall hear my voice; and there shall be one fold, and one shepherd.

17. Therefore doth my Father love me, because I lay down my life,

that I might take it again.

18. No man taketh it from me, but I lay it down of myself. I have power to lay it down, and I have power to take it again. This commandment have I received of my Father.

19. There was a division therefore again among the Jews for these sayings.

20. And many of them said, He hath a devil, and is mad; why hear ye him?

21. Others said, These are not the words of him that hath a devil. Can a devil open the eyes of the blind?

22. And it was at Jerusalem the feast of the dedication, and it was winter.

23. And Jesus walked in the temple in Solomon's porch.

24. Then came the Jews round about him, and said unto him, How long dost thou make us to doubt? If thou be the Christ, tell us plainly.

25. Jesus answered them, I told you, and ye believed not: the works that I do in my Father's name, they bear witness of me.

26. But ye believe not, because ye are not of my sheep, as I said unto you.

27. My sheep hear my voice, and I know them, and they follow me:

28. And I give unto them eternal life; and they shall never perish, neither shall any man pluck them out of my hand.

29. My Father, which gave them me, is greater than all; and no man is able to pluck them out of my Father's hand.

30. I and my Father are one.

31. Then the Jews took up stones again to stone him.

32. Jesus answered them, Many good works have I shewed you from my Father; for which of those works do ye stone me?

33. The Jews answered him, saying, For a good work we stone thee not; but for blasphemy; and because that thou, being a man, makest thyself God.

34. Jesus answered them, Is it not written in your law, I said, Ye are gods?

35. If he called them gods, unto whom the word of God came, and the scripture cannot be broken;

36. Say ye of him, whom the Father hath sanctified, and sent into the world, Thou blasphemest; because I said, I am the Son of God?

37. If I do not the works of my Father, believe me not.

38. But if I do, though ye believe not me, believe the works: that ye may know, and believe, that the Father is in me, and I in him.

39. Therefore they sought again to take him: but he escaped out of their hand,

40. And went away again beyond Jordan into the place where John

at first baptized; and there he abode.

41. And many resorted unto him, and said, John did no miracle: but all things that John spake of this man were true.

42. And many believed on him there.

I would like to point out three things about the first nine verses of this chapter:

1. The passage here is closely connected with the preceding chapter; in fact, Jesus continues His remarks to the hostile Pharisees because of their conduct toward the man born blind. The opening sentence of chapter 10 should be read as a continuation of the closing verse in chapter 9, without a break or separation. Thus we would read, "If ye were blind, ye should have no sin: but now ye say, We see; therefore your sin remaineth. Verily, verily, I say unto you . . . ."

2. We find a parable in this passage—and like all the parables of Jesus, it sets forth one primary lesson. Keeping this in mind, we must be careful not to go "overboard" on every little detail; we must not stretch the truth or mishandle the Word in order to attach a spiritual meaning to every little part of the picture presented in this parable. In this particular passage, the general lesson is that Christ points out the resemblance between the Church and a sheepfold. The Church is the fold into which God calls and assembles all of His people. Jesus portrays Himself as the DOOR to the fold, and there is *no other entrance* into the true Church. Whosoever enters must enter through the Lord Jesus Christ. He has always been the Way—yes, even since the Garden of Eden. The Old Testament believers looked *forward* to the coming of the Lamb, the New Testament believer looks *back* to Calvary where Jesus paid the sin-debt.

3. His object in giving this parable to His enemies was to show them just how unfit they were to be leaders and teachers in Israel. They did not understand the true mean-

ing and work of God's undershepherds and therefore they had not taken up their office in the right spirit.

You will also notice that in the first nine verses of this chapter, Jesus refers to Himself as "the Door"—and only as the Door.   It is not until verse 11 that He refers to Himself as the Good Shepherd.

Christ's Discourse
on the Qualifications of a Good Shepherd

Verse 1: *"Verily, verily, I say unto you, He that entereth not by the door into the sheepfold, but climbeth up some other way, the same is a thief and a robber."*

Here another "double verily" prefaces an outstanding truth.   Jesus uses a very down-to-earth illustration, one which appealed to the everyday experience of His hearers. He was speaking to men who were familiar with sheep and the sheepfold, and they well knew that anyone who tried to enter the sheepfold by climbing over the wall (instead of entering through the door) would be suspected of being a thief.   The shepherd of a flock always entered by the door, *never* by climbing over the fence.

The Pharisees claimed to be spiritual leaders, teachers, and custodians of the law of God—but they had not been appointed as such by the Lord Jesus; they had entered the office by means other than spiritual or divine authority, and were therefore spiritual thieves and robbers.   Instead of *helping* souls to be saved, they were *robbing* them of the very opportunity of salvation because they were teaching traditions of men.   The true pastor and teacher in the Church is appointed, ordained, and commissioned of God and led by the Spirit.   There are many today who have entered the ministry by ways other than through the Door. They have taken up the ministry—not by divine appointment—but by choice of a "profession" or for some other reason.

"The sheepfold" here is the true Church, and those who

would enter must enter by the Door, the Lord Jesus Christ. He is the way, the truth, and the life; no man cometh to the Father but by Him. The person is a spiritual thief and robber who attempts to enter heaven through church membership, water baptism, good living, liberal giving, observing the Golden Rule, attempting to keep the Law of Moses, or by any *other* way except by and through the finished work of Him who is *The DOOR.* Such a person would stick a gun in the face of Jesus and steal that which He alone could (and did) purchase—*salvation by grace through faith in His shed blood!*

Keeping sheep was common in Palestine, and the people to whom Jesus spoke this parable understood His references better than most of us would understand them. Shepherds, sheepfolds, thieves who climbed over the wall instead of entering by the door, were terms familiar to the Jews, and they understood perfectly what Jesus was saying. (Study the entire twenty-third chapter of Jeremiah, the entire thirty-fourth chapter of Ezekiel, and the eleventh chapter of Zechariah.)

Yes, the members of the Sanhedrin knew well the habits of the shepherd and the rules pertaining to the sheepfold. We are instructed to be "wise as serpents and harmless as doves," and Jesus was just that. If He had looked into the faces of these teachers and leaders in Israel and said, "YOU are thieves and robbers!" they would have pounced upon Him in their rage; but through the simple, plain teaching of the parable, He indirectly pointed them out as spiritual thieves and robbers—and I believe they understood His meaning.

There are times when God's ministers need to cry aloud and spare not; preach the Word in season, out of season; reprove, rebuke, exhort. On many occasions Jesus *did* rebuke sternly. One will never read more scorching, cutting words than those spoken by Him in Matthew 23. The pure, unadulterated Word of God cuts—it is sharper than a two-edged sword, and God's ministers are commanded to *preach* the Word. We have entirely too much sugar-coated, chocolate-covered preaching today. We need more hell-fire and brimstone across the pulpit, and less compromise.

When we study the earthly ministry of Jesus we find that false teachers were most offensive to Him. He sharply rebuked false prophets and false shepherds. This is as it should be, for a false teacher is the most dangerous person on earth. Bank robbers deprive men of money, burglars who break into homes and steal clothes, jewels, and other personal property steal that which can be replaced; but a *spiritual robber,* a teacher of error, robs men of the right to eternal life, and those who follow such a teacher will have taken from them the dearest thing man could ever possess! In Matthew 16:26 the Lord Himself asked, *"What is a man profited, if he shall gain the whole world, and lose his own soul? or what shall a man give in exchange for his soul?"*

The Greek word rendered *"thief"* in this verse means "secret fraud and dishonesty," and the Greek word here translated *"robber"* implies more than open violence. There are many kinds of false teachers. Some are boisterous, bold, bragging about their liberalism. These take great pride in denying the virgin birth, the verbal inspiration of the Scriptures. Others are subtle; they come in sheep's clothing but inwardly they are ravening wolves. These are the most dangerous. There are educated preachers in pulpits across this land today who preach just enough truth to lead men into error. They say nice things about Jesus, they speak of Him in glowing terms as a great teacher, even a worker of great miracles; but when they are pinned down for a declaration of what they really believe, they can only confess that they believe Jesus to have been a great man—and that is true. He WAS a great Man, but He was more: HE WAS GOD IN FLESH—and this the liberals and modernists will deny.

"There is a way that seemeth right unto a man, but the end thereof are the ways of death" (Prov. 16:25). There is a *way* (singular) that seemeth right to *a man* (an individual). Many individuals today have manufactured their own ways, interpreting Scripture to fit their own ideas and doctrines, and this should not be. We are to study and rightly divide the Word. We are not to warp, twist, add to or take from the Word of God in order to make it fit our desires or our own personal "religion." Notice, the verse just quoted from Proverbs says, "There is a way that seemeth right unto a man, but the *end* thereof are the WAYS (plural) *of death.*" All "ways" are ways of death; there is only ONE way of life, and Jesus is that WAY. There is no other door through which we can enter heaven. "Neither is there salvation in any other: for there is none other name under heaven given among men, whereby we must be saved" (Acts 4:12). Any minister who preaches any other doctrine is a thief and a robber, and he will suffer the damnations of hell.

Verse 2: *"But he that entereth in by the door is the shepherd of the sheep."*

The true shepherd of the flock—he who has been commissioned to care for the sheep—has a perfect right to enter into the sheepfold by the door, and is not afraid to be seen doing so.

In this verse, Jesus is not speaking of Himself, but of God's *undershepherds.* He speaks of Himself later, in verse 11, but in this verse He is the *Door* by which others enter. A true minister of the Gospel enters the Church by the Door, the Lord Jesus Christ—and because he enters by the Door he is a *true shepherd,* one who loves and cares for the flock. Those who enter the ministry through personal ambition, for love of ease, or for any other reason except to bring men to Jesus, are thieves and robbers. True shepherds are God-appointed.

Verse 3: *"To him the porter openeth; and the sheep hear his voice: and he calleth his own sheep by name, and leadeth them out."*

Here we see four characteristics of a true shepherd— characteristics not possessed by a thief or a robber:

1. *"To him the porter openeth."* The true shepherd is known by the porter. He enters by the door, he does not try to climb over the wall.
2. *"The sheep hear his voice."* The sheep recognize the voice of the true shepherd, they listen to him, they obey what he says.
3. *"He calleth his own sheep by name."* The true shepherd knows the members of his flock individually.
4. *"He . . . leadeth them out."* The true shepherd leads the sheep to good pasture; he wants good food for them, that they may *grow* and be healthy and strong.

The Eastern sheepfold was an enclosure of high, strong walls, and had a porter (or gate keeper) on guard at night because the sheep could not be safely left alone. It was the porter's duty to guard the sheep until morning and then open the gate to the true shepherds, who passed into the enclosure again to claim their sheep. The shepherds knew each sheep in their flock; they often had a name for each sheep, and the sheep *knew* their names.

Shepherds in the east *lead* their sheep, they do not drive them. When I visited Palestine I saw shepherds grazing their flocks at the foot of Mt. Nebo, and when the sun began to set they called to the sheep which were grazing in the valley, all flocks mixing and mingling together as they fed. But when each shepherd gave his own peculiar call, the sheep of his fold followed him, leaving the combined flocks and following the voice of the shepherd they knew. No wonder David said, "The LORD is MY Shepherd . . . He leadeth me."

"To him the Porter openeth." There are various interpretations and opinions as to who *"the Porter"* is. Personally, I do not think it abuses Scripture to say that the Porter is JESUS. I believe the true meaning here is that a true shepherd not only enters by the legitimate way

(through the Door), but also every facility is made for his entrance—that is, he is divinely appointed, anointed, commissioned, and sent; and *He who appoints also OPENS THE DOOR.* In Revelation 3:8 we read, "I know thy works: behold, *I have set before thee an open door, and no man can shut it:* for thou hast a little strength, and hast kept my Word, and hast not denied my name."

Verse 4: *"And when he putteth forth his own sheep, he goeth before them, and the sheep follow him: for they know his voice."*

This verse continues the description of the true and faithful shepherd. When the true shepherd leads his sheep from the fold to the pasture, he walks before them and leads them "into *green* pastures."

In Bible lands the shepherds always *go before* the sheep; they never *drive* them. Thus the shepherd never requires his sheep to go where he has not gone before them. The same is true of our Good Shepherd, the Lord Jesus Christ. HE walked this earthly journey before He asked us to follow in His steps. He was made in all things like unto His brethren, "that He might be a merciful and faithful High Priest in things pertaining to God, to make reconciliation for the sins of the people" (Heb. 2:17). Jesus was tempted in all points as we are, yet He was without sin. He *overcame* the world, the flesh, the devil, death, hell, and the grave—and He will never ask us to walk one step more than He walked before us!

"The sheep follow him: for they know his voice." All born again believers have within them the Holy Spirit, and therefore a born again believer will hear the voice of a true shepherd. When truth is preached from the pulpit, the child of God *recognizes* that truth, for "the Spirit Himself beareth witness with our spirit, that we are the children of God" (Rom. 8:16). If you, dear reader, cannot discern the voice of a true shepherd, if you cannot differentiate between truth and error, I am afraid you have never been

born again!

Verse 5: *"And a stranger will they not follow, but will
flee from him: for they know not the voice of strangers."*

In this verse Jesus brings to conclusion His presentation
of a true shepherd and his flock. The Jews knew that
sheep were accustomed to the voice of *one shepherd* and
would not obey the call of a stranger. On the contrary,
they would be *frightened* by a strange voice. The same is
true in the life of a believer. Since the Holy Spirit abides
within the heart of every child of God, the born again believer will not obey the voice of a false shepherd. Remember, "He leadeth me in paths of *righteousness"*—not in
paths of error. The Holy Spirit will reveal the false teacher: "Ye have an unction from the Holy One, and ye know
all things" (I John 2:20).

In spite of the fact that sheep are said to be the most
stupid of animals, they have some remarkable characteristics—for instance, they have a singular faculty to hear
and recognize the voice of their shepherd, *and they follow
ONLY the voice they know.* A tiny, day-old lamb among
thousands of sheep will recognize the voice of its own mother. In the same way, believers know the voice of God,
the voice of the true undershepherd as God speaks through
him. Born again, blood-washed children of God do not go
astray after error.

Fellow believer, if you are attending a modernistic church
where a liberal gospel is preached, denying the virgin birth,
the verbal inspiration of the Bible, the blood atonement,
the return of Jesus—or any other fundamental doctrine of
"the faith which was once delivered unto the saints" (Jude
3), you should *get out of that church!* You should not
expose yourself to error, and it is gross sin to support a
minister or a church where error is preached (II John 7—11).
No thinking person would trust his business affairs to a
lawyer who was known to be dishonest, nor would he use
the services of a doctor who was a known "quack." We

should be a million times more careful of things concerning the welfare of our soul than we are in matters of this life.

No doubt some of you are saying, "My minister is a *liberal,* but he does preach *some* Gospel; therefore I take the good and leave the bad." But JESUS said His sheep would *FLEE FROM the voice of strangers.* It is not enough to weed out error and take what little good there may be. God's Word commands us to "have no fellowship with the unfruitful works of darkness, but rather reprove them" (Eph. 5:11). We are also commanded, "Come out from among them, and be ye separate . . . and touch not the unclean thing . . ." (II Cor. 6:17). We are to flee from teachers of error as we would flee from any other deadly disease or danger, for "their word will eat as doth a canker" (II Tim. 2:17).

To the Galatian Christians Paul wrote, "I marvel that ye are so soon removed from Him that called you into the grace of Christ unto another gospel: which is not another; but there be some that trouble you, and would pervert the Gospel of Christ. But though we, or an angel from heaven, preach any other gospel unto you than that which we have preached unto you, *let him be accursed.* As we said before, so say I now again, *If any man preach any other gospel unto you than that ye have received, let him be accursed"* (Gal. 1:6—9).

Verse 6: *"This parable spake Jesus unto them: but they understood not what things they were which He spake unto them."*

The Scripture makes it plain that this is a parable. (The Greek word used suggests an allegory or figurative picture.) Even though the Pharisees lived in the midst of the things of which Jesus spoke and were well acquainted with the characteristics of everything He mentioned, *"they under-stood not what things they were which He spake unto them."* Why? Because they were willfully ignorant—proud, filled with their own self-righteousness. They did not see themselves as they really were—thieves and robbers (spiritually speaking), even while they claimed to be pastors and teachers. They were leading souls to damnation, not to salvation. They could not see their own lack of qualifications for teachers and leaders, and their actions proved that they were not God-appointed shepherds of the flock. They had evidently forgotten Ezekiel 34; otherwise they would have clearly understood the parable Jesus had just given them. (Please study Ezekiel, chapter 34, in connection with this.)

Verse 7: *"Then said Jesus unto them again, Verily, verily, I say unto you, I am the door of the sheep."*

Even though our Lord knew the hearts and minds of these people, He patiently explained the meaning of the parable He had just given. Men have always been slow to hear—and slower to *believe.* We can learn a lesson in patience here; we should keep on telling the old, old story over and over again, repeating the message of saving grace, knowing that the Word will be used to the glory of God: "So shall my Word be that goeth forth . . . It shall not return unto me void, but it shall accomplish that which I please, and it shall prosper in the thing whereto I sent it" (Isa. 55:11).

"I AM THE DOOR of the sheep." The full import of this statement, preceded by a "double verily," cannot be overemphasized: Jesus, *and HE ALONE,* is the Door through which *all* must enter if they would come into God's fold. Shepherd and sheep—pastor, teacher, evangelist, missionary, layman—all must enter by and through Jesus Christ.

It is most interesting to notice the beautiful, meaningful figures under which Jesus presented Himself and His office to Israel in John's Gospel—i. e., "the Bread of Life . . . the Living Water . . . the Light of the world . . . the Door . . . the Good Shepherd"—and the Jews *should* have understood the meaning of each and every one of these figures as Jesus offered Himself to them as their Messiah. His offering of Himself as the Door—the ONLY Door—into the fold corresponds to His warning in the Sermon on the Mount when He declared, "Enter ye in at the strait gate: for wide is the gate, and broad is the way, that leadeth to destruction, and many there be which go in thereat: because strait is the gate, and narrow is the way, which leadeth unto life, and few there be that find it" (Matt. 7:13,14).

Verse 8: *"All that ever came before me are thieves and robbers: but the sheep did not hear them."*

The present tense of the verb ("are") indicates that Jesus was not speaking of the prophets or anyone who came "before" Him from the standpoint of time or place. Therefore we must interpret the *"before me"* in *another sense* than that of time or place. I believe that what Jesus said was meant for the very Pharisees to whom He was talking. The meaning would be those who came before Him *in honor or authority,* those who did not put Him first, but claimed honor for themselves instead of honor for Jesus, those who had misled the people, serving their own ends instead of serving God and His truth.

These so-called spiritual leaders of Israel who shut up the kingdom of heaven to others, were "thieves and robbers" because they neither went in themselves nor suffered them that were entering to go in (Matt. 23:13).

"The sheep did not hear them." The *"sheep"* refers to born again believers, God-fearing people such as Simeon, Anna, and others who were looking for Messiah and had not ceased to have faith that He would come—and when He DID come they recognized Him as the Christ of God:

"And behold, there was a man in Jerusalem, whose name was *Simeon; and the same man was just and devout, waiting for the consolation of Israel: and the Holy Ghost was upon him. And it was revealed unto him by the Holy Ghost, that he should not see death, before he had seen the Lord's Christ.* And he came by the Spirit into the temple: and when the parents brought in the child Jesus, to do for Him after the custom of the law, then took he Him up in his arms, and blessed God, and said, Lord, now lettest thou thy servant depart in peace, according to thy Word: *for mine eyes have seen thy salvation, which thou hast prepared before the face of all people; a light to lighten the Gentiles, and the glory of thy people Israel"* (Luke 2:25—32).

"And there was one Anna, a prophetess, the daughter of Phanuel, of the tribe of Aser: she was of a great age, and had lived with an husband seven years from her virginity; and she was a widow of about fourscore and four years, which departed not from the temple, but served God with fastings and prayers night and day. And she coming in that instant gave thanks likewise unto the Lord, and spake of Him to all them that looked for redemption in Jerusalem" (Luke 2:36—38).

A born again, blood-washed believer will not "hear" a false teacher. The Holy Spirit in the heart of a true believer will make known the error that is being taught. But we must remember that church members are not necessarily *sheep;* not all persons who join the church are saved. When Jesus spoke of "sheep" He had reference to the faithful members of the kingdom of God, those who recognized the voice of the shepherd.

Verse 9: *"I am the door: by me if any man enter in, he shall be saved, and shall go in and out, and find pasture."*

Four interesting things are implied in this verse:

1. All who come to Jesus shall be saved *individually.*

2. All who come to God through Jesus THE Door shall not only receive life, but shall also receive intimate fellowship and communion with God the Father.

3. All who come to God through Jesus shall "go in and out" (suggestive of both security and liberty) and shall be furnished with gifts to be used to bless other members of the New Testament Church.

4. All who come to God through Jesus shall find food, refreshment for soul and spirit—and HE is the only One
who can furnish that food.

We notice here that Jesus did not say if *only the learned
Pharisees* would enter in.   He said, "By me if ANY man
enter in, he shall be saved."   It is true that when Jesus
sent out the twelve He instructed them, "Go not into the
way of the Gentiles, and into any city of the Samaritans
enter ye not: *but go rather to the lost sheep of the house
of Israel*" (Matt. 10:5,6).   But now He invites any and all,
great and small, wicked or clean and upright, rich or poor,
wise or unwise, bond or free, white or colored, ANY who
will enter heaven by Jesus the Door shall be saved!   Certainly this completely destroys the doctrine of limited atonement—that some are elected to be saved and others are
NOT elected.

To *"go in and out"* signifies liberty such as we have
in our own home, expressing the marvelous communion
and happy fellowship the believer has with Christ.   Acts
1:21 speaks of "the time that the Lord Jesus *went in and
out among us.*"

In John 14:23 Jesus said, "If a man love me, he will
keep my words: and my Father will love him, *and we will
come unto him, and make our abode with him.*"

In Revelation 3:20 we read, "Behold, I stand at the
door, and knock: if any man hear my voice, and open
the door, *I will come in to him, and will sup with him,
and he with me.*"

To *"find pasture"* means food, comfort, refreshment—
which all who come to Jesus will receive.

To *"go in and out and find pasture"* points to the love
and protection Jesus has for each of His sheep.   The person who believes on Jesus becomes a *son,* not a *slave.*
He goes in and out enjoying liberty each day.   God does
not put a fence around His children.   They have liberty
and they are led and protected by the Good Shepherd.
This marvelous statement of our Lord's turns our thoughts

to the Twenty-Third Psalm, which is no doubt what He intended:

"The Lord is my Shepherd; I shall not want. He maketh me to lie down in green pastures: He leadeth me beside the still waters. He restoreth my soul: He leadeth me in the paths of righteousness for His name's sake. Yea, though I walk through the valley of the shadow of death, I will fear no evil: for thou art with me; thy rod and thy staff they comfort me. Thou preparest a table before me in the presence of mine enemies: thou anointest my head with oil; my cup runneth over. Surely goodness and mercy shall follow me all the days of my life: and I will dwell in the house of the Lord for ever" (Psalm 23).

The *"shepherd"* in verse 2 is the undershepherd (pastor) who has entered the Church through Jesus, the Door. I am sure you have noticed that throughout the passage, much stress is laid on "the *voice* of the shepherd," and on *hearing* that voice—(and in this instance the "voice" means the teaching of the true shepherd). He is the one who has entered by the Door, he is the one who speaks words which he hears through the voice of the Chief Shepherd, the Lord Jesus Christ. The true shepherd (the God-ordained minister) gives forth the Word of God, thus feeding his flock. But shepherd *and sheep* must enter the fold through the one DOOR, the Lord Jesus Christ.

It is worthy of our notice that a door serves two purposes: It allows *friends* to come in, and it keeps enemies *out*. The *door* is not a hole in the wall; the hole in the wall is the *doorWAY*. The *door* is the movable structure—glass, wood, or metal—which *closes* the doorway. It opens and closes, and when the *door* is open, the *doorway* is open; but when the door is closed it is impossible to enter through the doorway. Thus we see that Jesus is the DOOR, the One who will receive us if we believe on Him and trust Him; but if we refuse to believe, He is the Door that will close to keep us out of heaven. The same Door that allows us to enter, through faith in His finished work, will see to it that we do NOT enter if we refuse to believe on Him. He is the Door, the Way, the Truth, the Life. He will open the way to heaven to those who hear His Word and believe on Him. In Matthew 10:32,33 He said, *"Whosoever therefore shall confess me before men, him will I confess also before my Father which is in heaven. But whosoever shall deny me before men, him will I also deny before my Father which is in heaven."*

Christ Our Good Shepherd

Verse 10: *"The thief cometh not, but for to steal, and to kill, and to destroy: I am come that they might have life, and that they might have it more abundantly."*

In this and the verses that follow, the Lord drops the figure of Himself as the Door and presents Himself as the Good Shepherd. In this verse He contrasts the object of the false shepherd with His own object of coming into the world.

"The thief cometh not, but for to steal, and to kill, and to destroy." The background here is still that of the sheep-fold, which Jesus uses to show the difference between the false shepherd and Himself, the Good Shepherd. A thief does not enter the sheepfold in the interest of the flock, but in his *own* interest; he comes not to help, but to harm. These Pharisees were teachers in the religion of the Jews *to their own advantage.* They taught doctrine which ruined souls and led them astray instead of saving them. The same is true today. In many pulpits, "false shepherds" have entered the ministry to use it to their own ends, whereas all *true* shepherds are in the ministry because they entered by the Door, and such a minister has the good of his flock at heart. The Apostle Paul was that kind of minister. He said, *"I thank Christ Jesus our Lord, who hath enabled me, for that He counted me faithful, putting me into the ministry"* (I Tim. 1:12).

In contrast with these false shepherds (the thieves and robbers), Jesus presents *Himself* and His main purpose in leaving the bosom of the Father to come into the world: *"I am come that they might have life, and that they might have it more abundantly."* The thief comes to *take* life; Jesus came to *give* life—life abundant, which is the spiritual birthright of every believer.

"They" in the latter part of our present verse refers to the *"ANY man"* of verse 9—ANY man who will enter in by the Door.

"Abundantly" points to the marvelous grace of God, and what that grace affords. "For the grace of God *that bringeth salvation* hath appeared to all men, *teaching us* that, denying ungodliness and worldly lusts, we should live soberly, righteously, and godly, in this present world; *looking for that blessed hope,* and the glorious appearing of the great God and our Saviour Jesus Christ; who gave Himself for us, that He might redeem us from all iniquity, and purify unto Himself *a peculiar people,* zealous of good works" (Tit. 2:11—14).

Jesus came that men might see the way of life more clearly—and certainly the New Testament gives a much clearer picture of redemption, righteousness, justification, and sanctification than is given in the Old Testament. For example, *Job* cried out, "If a man die, shall he live again?" (Job 14:14). But we KNOW that we have passed from death unto life, *"we know that we dwell in Him, and He in us, because He hath given us of His Spirit"* (I John 4:13). The Gospel of the grace of God—faith in the finished work of Jesus—brings pardon, peace, and assurance which the Old Testament saint simply did not have. When *Jesus* came, light and life came (John 1:4—9).

To Timothy, his son in the ministry, Paul wrote: "God hath not given us the spirit of fear; but of power, and of love, and of a sound mind. Be not thou therefore ashamed of the testimony of our Lord, nor of me His prisoner: but be thou partaker of the afflictions of the Gospel according to the power of God; who hath saved us, and called us with an holy calling, not according to our works, but according to His own purpose and grace, which was given us in Christ Jesus before the world began, but is now made manifest by the appearing of our Saviour Jesus Christ, who hath abolished death, and hath brought life and immortality to light through the Gospel: whereunto I am appointed a preacher, and an apostle, and a teacher of the Gentiles. For the which cause I also suffer these things: nevertheless I am not ashamed: FOR I KNOW WHOM I HAVE BELIEVED, AND AM PERSUADED THAT HE IS ABLE TO KEEP THAT WHICH I HAVE COMMITTED UNTO HIM AGAINST THAT DAY" (II Tim. 1:7−12).

In Romans 5:15−21 we read, "But not as the offence, so also is the free gift. For if through the offence of one many be dead, *much more the grace of God, and the gift by grace, which is by one Man, Jesus Christ, hath abounded unto many.* And not as it was by one that sinned, so is the gift: for the judgment was by one to condemnation, but *the free gift is of many offences unto justification.* For if by one man's offence death reigned by one; *much more they which receive abundance of grace and of the gift of righteousness shall reign in life by One, Jesus Christ.* Therefore as by the offence of one judgment came upon all men to condemnation; *even so by the righteousness of One the free gift came upon all men unto justification of life.* For as by one man's disobedience many were made sinners, *so by the obedience of One shall many be made righteous.* Moreover the law entered, that the offence might abound. But where sin abounded, *grace did much more abound:* That as sin hath reigned unto death, *even so might GRACE reign through righteousness unto eternal life by Jesus Christ our Lord."*

Dear fellow believer, are YOU enjoying *your spiritual birthright,* or is the new birth the extent of your Christianity? If this be true, you are being cheated! Yield yourself unreservedly unto God—your body a living sacrifice, your members as instruments of righteousness, and *in all that you do* do all to the glory of God; and you will know joy unspeakable, unshakable assurance, and life abundant as you have never known it. Jesus came—not only to save us, but also to bless us far above anything we can think or ask; but He cannot bless a naughty, selfish child. We must yield our all to Him if we hope to enjoy our spiritual birthright.

Verse 11: *"I am the Good Shepherd: the Good Shepherd giveth His life for the sheep."*

In other words, Jesus said to the Jews, "To all who believe in me, I am exactly what a good shepherd is to the sheep of his fold. A good shepherd loves his sheep, he watches over and protects them—and if necessary, *he gives his LIFE* for them."

When I visited Palestine, a dear missionary who had spent thirty-five years in that land told me this story:

Shortly after his arrival in the Holy Land he visited one of the shepherds just at sunset, when the sheep were being led into the fold. Except for the common sheepfold in or near a town, most of the sheepfolds—in the fields or desert—are made of thorn bushes such as were used to fashion the crown of thorns for Jesus. The bushes are planted close together, they grow tall, and the thorns are so deadly it would be impossible for any animal or person to get through them without being horribly mutilated.

But there is a doorway in the wall of thorns, and through this doorway the shepherd entered, the sheep followed, then the shepherd circled around and came back to the entrance—but the missionary saw nothing with which the shepherd could close the doorway; so he asked, "Where is the door? What keeps out the predatory animals and thieves?"

The dear old shepherd sat down in the doorway, put his feet against one side of the entrance, leaned back against the other side, looked up at the missionary and replied, *"I* am the door! Before anything or anyone can harm one of my sheep, he must first pass over me."

As I listened to the missionary tell this story, tears ran down my cheeks. I rejoiced and worshipped. What a beautiful picture of Jesus! He said, "I am the DOOR." Then He presented Himself as "the Good Shepherd," and He DID give His life for the sheep. He gave His life that *we* might *have* life. Because HE lives, WE live—and no enemy can steal us from Him because no enemy can pass over or through the Door, the Good Shepherd who protects us! I am so thankful I know Him as my Shepherd. I am not worried about entering heaven, because I have the DOOR to heaven in my heart. If you do not have Christ in your heart, you *have* no hope.

The Jews understood the illustration of the Good Shepherd. They understood that by presenting Himself as the Good Shepherd, He was announcing Himself as their Messiah, Shepherd of their souls. In Genesis 49:24 we read, "But His bow abode in strength, and the arms of His hands were made strong by the hands of the mighty God of Jacob; *(from thence is the SHEPHERD, the Stone of Israel)*." The twenty-third Psalm is one of the strongest presentations of Jesus as the Good Shepherd—and certainly the Jews were familiar with the Psalms. The thirty-fourth chapter of Ezekiel also would have acquainted them with Christ's reference to Himself as the Good Shepherd. (I have already recommended that you study that chapter, but it would be well to go back and read it again.)

"The Good Shepherd giveth His life for the sheep." Here is shown the basic difference between the Good Shepherd and the hireling. The Good Shepherd would risk His life, as David did when he fought a lion and a bear rather than allow even one lamb to be taken from him (I Sam. 17:34—36). The characteristics of a good shepherd the Jews knew, and they understood that Jesus was saying to them, "I have come to do for you what a good shepherd does for his sheep. I have come to die, that the master thief and robber, the devil, might not destroy you. I have come to lay

down my life that you might have life." But they refused
to hear His words; they had no will to see what He was
showing them.

Verse 12: *"But he that is an hireling, and not the shepherd, whose own the sheep are not, seeth the wolf coming,
and leaveth the sheep, and fleeth: and the wolf catcheth
them, and scattereth the sheep."*

Here Jesus clearly pointed out the difference between a
"hireling"—one who is hired and paid wages to care for
the sheep—and the true shepherd to whom the sheep belong, and who would protect them with his life.

*"An hireling . . . seeth the wolf coming, and leaveth
the sheep, and fleeth."* The hireling, tending the flock for
money and not for love, would have only *his own interest*
at heart and would run away and leave the flock at the
mercy of the wolves, whereas the true shepherd, tending
his sheep in love and dedication, would stay and fight,
forfeiting his life in defence of his sheep, if need be.

The Jews to whom Jesus was speaking understood His
meaning, for there were undoubtedly many hirelings among
the shepherds of Jerusalem. The thirty-fourth chapter of
Ezekiel (already referred to) gives a detailed picture of a
faithless shepherd, and therefore the Pharisees, students of
the Old Testament, would have been familiar with our
Lord's meaning here. He was telling them that they were
no better than the hirelings who would leave the sheep and
allow the wolves to devour them; for they, too, sought their
own profit, they were selfish, self-righteous, interested in
what they could get rather than in what they could *give*,
and they had no care for the souls of men.

Matthew 9:36 tells us that when Jesus came on the scene
of His public ministry, "He saw the multitudes, He was
moved with compassion on them, because they fainted, *and
were scattered abroad, as sheep having no shepherd."* The
Pharisees, scribes, and elders—those who made up the rulers
in Israel—had not protected the flock against the assaults

of the devil and his ravening wolves. They had been as "hirelings," not caring for the welfare of the sheep.

This does not mean that *all* ministers who receive salaries are *hirelings*—far from it. There are many of God's men who preach because they love souls, real true ministers who put souls above salary. It has been most refreshing to me in my evangelistic work to meet some of these men, even some who left churches paying high salaries, and took on a great obligation in a smaller, poorer church, in order to carry on the work God had called them to do.

Certainly ministers must receive a livelihood, and we know that when Jesus sent out the seventy He told them, "The labourer is worthy of his hire" (Luke 10:7). In I Corinthians 9:14 Paul said, "The Lord ordained that they which preach the Gospel should live of the Gospel." But there are many "hirelings" in the ministry today.

Our present verse does not mean that in no instance should a true minister of God flee from danger or attempt to protect himself. When Jesus sent out the twelve, even though they were sent to "the lost sheep of the house of Israel," He said to them, "When they persecute you in this city, flee ye into another . . ." (Matt. 10:23).

The Apostle Paul was one of the boldest, most fearless preachers in all of God's Word, yet on different occasions he wisely fled for his life. (Read Acts 9:20–25,29,30; 14:5,6.) There are other instances recorded in the Scriptures where God's men were forced to move on, under divine direction.

On the other hand, there are spirits of saints in Paradise today who gave their lives for the sake of the Gospel. Some were burned at the stake, others were fed to wild beasts in the arenas. Down through the centuries Christians have sometimes been called upon to lay down their lives for the Church and become martyrs for Jesus Christ. Men have suffered severely—and will continue to do so—for the sake of the Gospel; but there can be no ironclad rule as to how long a minister should *endure* such danger. Each individual must settle this in his own heart, under the leading of the

Holy Spirit. In Acts 15:26 Paul and Barnabas were recommended to the church at Antioch as "men that have haz-
arded their lives for the name of our Lord Jesus Christ."
To the Ephesian elders Paul said, "None of these things
move me, neither count I my life dear unto myself, so that
I might finish my course with joy, and the ministry, which
I have received of the Lord Jesus, to testify the Gospel of
the grace of God" (Acts 20:24). Again in Acts 21:13 he said,
"I am ready not to be bound only, but also to die at Jerusalem for the name of the Lord Jesus." If we listen to the
voice of the Holy Spirit, He will direct us as to when we
should flee from danger, and when we should stand—even to
the death, if that is God's will.

Verses 13 and 14: *"The hireling fleeth, because he is an
hireling, and careth not for the sheep. I am the Good
Shepherd, and know my sheep, and am known of mine."*

Verse 13 is self-explanatory and has been discussed in
the preceding remarks. The person who is simply "hired"
to watch over the sheep will desert them when the wolves
come, *"because he IS an hireling"* and does not love the
sheep.

"I am the Good Shepherd." This statement, given for
the second time in four verses, shows the importance of
the office of the Good Shepherd. God does not need to say
anything but once to make it so, and when a statement is
repeated in Scripture, we may know that the repetition is
extremely important. It IS important that we recognize the
divine fact that Jesus is *"THE Good Shepherd"* in the
same way that He is "THE Water . . . THE Bread . . .
THE Light . . . THE Truth . . . THE Author of eternal
life . . . THE Author and finisher of our faith . . . THE
Alpha and Omega." *He is THE great I AM!*

"I . . . know my sheep, and am known of mine." Here
is clearly pointed out the difference between the "hireling"
and the true shepherd, and no doubt this statement cut
deeply into the consciousness of the Jews. They realized

that Jesus was telling them, "You do not *know* me, therefore you are not mine. Moses wrote of me, Abraham saw my day and rejoiced in it; but YOU refuse to accept me as the Good Shepherd, you refuse to hear my voice, and by your actions you testify that you are not of my fold."

Jesus knows (and cares for) every child of His *personally.* He knows each individual—the weaknesses, temptations, trials, and disappointments that beset each of His children. He knows the day-to-day *need* of the sheep of His pasture, and every true believer knows "the Good Shepherd," hears His voice, follows His leading, and therefore recognizes "hirelings" and false teachers. There are multitudes in churches today who know that Jesus *came,* they acknowledge Him as *the Son of God,* and they know that He died on the cross to save sinners—but that does not necessarily mean that they know Him as their personal Saviour. The person who has been truly born again and washed in the blood of Jesus *knows Him personally as THE Saviour.*

Verse 15: *"As the Father knoweth me, even so know I the Father: and I lay down my life for the sheep."*

This verse should be read in conjunction with the preceding verse, with no division between them. The meaning is that the mutual knowledge between Christ the Good Shepherd and born again believers is like the mutual knowledge between God the Father and Christ the Son—a knowledge so intimate, so deep, so incomprehensible, there are no words to describe it. The full nature of the divine and infinite knowledge possessed of each other by God the Father and God the Son is one of those deep mysteries we will never fully understand: *"The secret things belong unto the Lord our God: but those things which are revealed belong unto us and to our children for ever . . ."* (Deut. 29:29). Yet this knowledge and communion that is beyond the finite, known only to the Infinite, exists *between Christ and His children,* and can be compared *only* to the knowledge existing between God the Father and God the Son.

Earth—the finite—has *nothing* by which such comparison can be made!

"I lay down my life for the sheep." Here our Lord speaks of His atoning death on the cross, the propitiation He is soon to make through the shedding of His blood on the cross—the highest proof of His love for the sheep. Jesus on the cross was God's love on display—God's best for man's worst.

In John 15:13 Jesus said, "Greater love hath no man than this, that a man lay down his life for his friends"— but HE did more than that: *He laid down His life for His enemies!* "God commendeth His love toward us, in that, while we were yet sinners, *Christ DIED for us"* (Rom. 5:8).

However, *"sheep"* in this passage does not teach limited atonement—i. e., that Jesus died only for a limited number. If He had not laid His life down, *ALL would have died,* for "the wages of sin is death." If the Good Shepherd had not laid down His life for the sheep, none could ever have entered the fold. John 1:29; 3:16; 6:33; and I John 2:1,2 certainly are more than ample proof that this verse of Scripture does not teach that Jesus died only for believers. *"WHOSOEVER WILL, let him take the water of life freely"* (Rev. 22:17).

Verse 16: *"And other sheep I have, which are not of this fold: them also I must bring, and they shall hear my voice; and there shall be one fold, and one Shepherd."*

"Other sheep I have" applies to the Gentiles. Jesus did not die for the Jews only, although the message was"to the Jew first" (Rom. 1:16); but it was also to the Greek (Gentile).

"This fold" refers to the believing Jews among the nation Israel. In this Dispensation of Grace, the Church is made up of believing Jews and Gentiles. All believers are members of the New Testament Church. Before Jesus came, Gentiles were without hope, aliens from the commonwealth

of Israel, strangers to the covenants of promise, and without God. "But now in Christ Jesus ye who sometimes were far off are made nigh by the blood of Christ. For He is our peace, who hath made both one, and hath broken down the middle wall of partition between us; having abolished in His flesh the enmity, even the law of commandments contained in ordinances; for to make in Himself of twain *ONE NEW MAN*, so making peace; and that He might reconcile both unto God IN ONE BODY BY THE CROSS, having slain the enmity thereby: and came and preached peace to you which were afar off, and to them that were nigh. For through Him we both have access by one Spirit unto the Father" (Eph. 2:11–18 in part).

When Jesus spoke the words, "other sheep I have which are not of this fold," the Gentiles were at that time aliens from the commonwealth of Israel, strangers to the covenants of promise; but Jesus changed all that when He laid His life down that "whosoever" could become a member of the family of God—in this dispensation, a member of the New Testament Church.

The "other sheep" speaks of the Gentiles who would hear the Gospel and would believe on Jesus after His death, burial, and resurrection. These "other sheep" were not saved at that time—but since God is sovereign and knows the end in the beginning, and since the New Testament Church was given to Jesus before the world was, they would be saved when they heard the preaching of the Gospel of the grace of God.

Lest someone misunderstand, let me explain here that the New Testament Church *as a body* was elected and promised before God created the world. (Study I Peter 1:18–23.) The New Testament Church as a body of which Jesus is the head and the foundation (Eph. 5:21–33) was foreordained, elected to be. When Jesus said to Peter, "Upon this rock I will build my Church; and the gates of hell shall not prevail against it" (Matt. 16:13–18) He was speaking of the New Testament Church, the *body*. He did not say that the devil would not attack—and even cause some born again individuals to stumble—but *not fall!* "Let him that thinketh he standeth take heed lest he fall" (I Cor. 10:12).   However, the Church *as a body* is just as sure to be spotless as God Himself is spotless, because it was foreordained of God that the Church as a body be presented to Jesus without spot or wrinkle or any such thing (Eph. 5:27). The New Testament Church is made up of individuals who believe on the Lord Jesus Christ.   The Church *as a body* was elected before the foundation of the world. *Individuals* who make up the body, believe on the Lord Jesus Christ when they hear the Gospel. Not all who hear will be saved, but all who DO *hear and believe* are saved.

Each individual who believes the Gospel and personally receives the Lord Jesus, is predestined to be conformed to the image of God's dear Son.   Paul tells us, "We know that all things work together for good to them that love God, to them who are the called according to His purpose. For whom He did foreknow, He also did predestinate to be conformed to the image of His Son, that He might be the firstborn among many brethren" (Rom. 8:28,29).

When *all* things that happen to a born again believer are added up, they have all happened that the individual believer might be molded and shaped, made like unto the Son of God, the firstborn among many brethren. Whom the Lord loves, He chastens, and scourges every son.   Chastening and scourging are for our good and God's glory. Chastening molds us and makes us fit for the kingdom of heaven.

"Other sheep I have, which are not of this fold" does not mean that some Gentiles were elected to be saved, while others were not elected and therefore could NOT be saved. It means that both Jews and Gentiles who hear the Gospel and receive Jesus in this day of grace, become members of the one true Church.

It is clear that the New Testament Church was given to Jesus in the eternal councils of the Godhead before the foundation of the world, and is being formed now. It began at Pentecost and will continue until the Rapture. Each individual who hears the Gospel and receives the Lord Jesus on the terms of the Gospel will become part of the body of Christ. Believers are united to the body of Christ by the Holy Spirit: "For by one Spirit are we all baptized into one body, whether we be Jews or Gentiles, whether we be bond or free; and have been all made to drink into one Spirit. For the body is not one member, but many" (I Cor. 12:13,14).

Dear friend, if you spend eternity in the lake of fire it will not be because you were not elected (or predestined) to be saved. It will be because you WOULD NOT come to Jesus and allow Him to save you!

"Them also I must bring"—that is, the Gentiles who were at that time heathen *would become* members of the body of Christ, and the Lord Jesus Christ is the One who brings them in.

"They shall hear my voice." Here is both prophecy and promise. I do not doubt that Jesus spoke these words to encourage His disciples in their ministry. What He actually said was, "I have also come to save other than the Jewish fold. I came to 'seek and to save that which was lost' (Luke 19:10). When you preach the Gospel, the *'lost'* among the Gentiles will *hear* the Gospel, and in hearing the *Gospel* they will *hear my voice*, they will recognize the call of the Good Shepherd, they will come to me and I will save them." To the seventy He said, "He that heareth you heareth me; and he that despiseth you despiseth me; and he that despiseth me despiseth Him that sent me" (Luke 10:16).

"There shall be one fold, and one Shepherd"—(the Greek reads "one *flock*"). There is but one Church—the Church of God (Acts 20:28)—and when I say, "the Church of God" I am not referring to a denomination but to THE Church of the living God, the Church of which Jesus is the head and the foundation. All believers are members of His body, bone of His bone and flesh of His flesh, baptized *into* that

body by the Holy Spirit, and made to drink into one Spirit (I Cor. 12:12,13). There is only *one true Church*—one Lord, one faith, one baptism, one flock, one Shepherd.

In speaking of the one true Church (one fold, one flock) we dare not be too narrow or too liberal. If we are too narrow we will be guilty of the sin of the Pharisees, scribes, and elders. If we are too liberal we will classify all local church members as Christians, and this is not true. Not all church members are *Christians,* but some true Christians can be found in almost all churches. Regardless of what denominational church one belongs to, if he is washed in the blood and saved by God's grace, truly born again, he is a member of the one flock, the one true Church; but even though a person holds membership in a very *outstanding* church, if he is not born again he is NOT a member of the one true Church.

Verse 17:   *"Therefore doth my Father love me, because I lay down my life, that I might take it again."*

Here is another divine mystery relating to the unity, fellowship, and love between God the Father and God the Son. It is a statement that must be taken by faith—*believe it because Jesus said it.* He used earth's language pertaining to love.

Before God created the world or anything therein it was predestined that Jesus would leave the Father's bosom, take a body, and shed His blood for the redemption of sinners (I Pet. 1:18—23); but while we thank the Lord Jesus for purchasing salvation, while we praise His name and sing, "Sweetest name on mortal tongue, sweetest carol ever sung," we must not forget that it was GOD who "so loved the world that He gave His only begotten Son." It was GOD who commended His love toward us in that "while we were yet sinners" He allowed Christ to die for us (Rom. 5:8). It was GOD who set forth Jesus to be a propitiation for our sins (Rom. 3:25). Therefore we should also *"JOY IN GOD through our Lord Jesus Christ, by whom we have now re-*

ceived the atonement" (Rom. 5:11).

"Therefore doth my Father love me, because I lay down my life." Because of Jesus' willingness to lay His life down we read, "Wherefore God also hath highly exalted Him, and given Him a name which is above every name: That at the name of Jesus every knee should bow, of things in heaven, and things in earth, and things under the earth; and that every tongue should confess that Jesus Christ is Lord, to the glory of God the Father" (Phil. 2:9—11).

Through the inspired pen of the prophet Isaiah we read, "Therefore will I divide Him a portion with the great, and He shall divide the spoil with the strong; because He hath poured out His soul unto death: and He was numbered with the transgressors; and He bare the sin of many, and made intercession for the transgressors" (Isa. 53:12).

"That I might take (my life) again" points to the resurrection of the Lord Jesus, thereby reminding His hearers that He differed from even the best of *earthly shepherds.* They might lay down their life for the sheep, but they could not take that life again; their death would be the end of their ministry. But not so with Jesus. He laid His life down, *He took it again,* and seated at the right hand of God the Father He ever lives to make intercession for us. He is the one Mediator between God and men (I Tim. 2:5).

The theme of every minister of the Gospel should be the death, burial, and resurrection of the Lord Jesus *"according to the Scriptures."* The devil cares not how fervently we preach if we leave out the main theme of the Gospel message—the blood of Jesus; for without shedding of blood is no remission (Heb. 9:22). The blood of Jesus cleanses from ALL sin, and the blood is the ONLY cleansing power. The blood of Jesus is the center, soul, and heartbeat of the Gospel message, and therefore a sermon without the message of the cross is an empty sermon. A bloodless gospel is the gospel of Satan, not the Gospel of God.

The Jews thought Jesus was nailed to the cross because God was displeased with Him. They thought God had

forsaken Him and given Him over to them to be crucified.
On the contrary, it pleased Jehovah God when Jesus willingly went to the cross to pay the sin-debt. "It pleased
the Lord to bruise Him; He hath put Him to grief." Only
"with His stripes" are we healed, only through *His bruises*
are we made whole. (Read Isaiah 53—the entire chapter.)

Who Killed Jesus?

Verse 18: *"No man taketh it from me, but I lay it down
of myself. I have power to lay it down, and I have power
to take it again. This commandment have I received of
my Father."*

The death of Jesus was voluntary. He willingly gave
His life for sinners, another respect in which He differs
from an earthly shepherd. A good shepherd may give his
life for his sheep—but it will be given *against his will*. No
sane person wants to die. The Christian is not *afraid* of
death, but all of us love life, we want to live in order to
fellowship with our friends and family, and to serve God.
But the Good Shepherd, the Great Shepherd of all believers,
willingly laid His life down, *willingly* made His soul an
offering for sin. He was not compelled to do it, He did it
to please the heavenly Father; and in return God saves
sinners who put their faith in the shed blood of Jesus—He
saves us for Christ's sake (Eph. 4:32).

The *Jews* did not kill Jesus, nor did the *Romans* kill
Him. It is true the Jews demanded His death, and the
Romans nailed Him to a cross; but they did not take His
life. He would still be hanging on the cross had He not
literally given His spirit back to God the Father. *No man*
took the life of Jesus; He laid His life down *that WE might
have life.* No person could have killed Jesus had He not
been willing to die, for Jesus was God in flesh and GOD
CANNOT DIE! It was the love of Jesus for poor, lost,
hell-deserving sinners that held Him to the cross—not the
decree of the Sanhedrin, not the command of Pilate or the

power of the Roman soldiers, not the nails in His hands and feet; *but the power of His love for US.* Jesus died at the very moment He desired to die. No man struck the fatal blow; He *laid His life down* that He might take it again. He was "smitten of God" (Isa. 53:4).

"I have power to lay it down . . . I have power to take it again." Here Jesus declared His divine nature. He had full power to lay His life down when He pleased, at the very moment it was planned; and He had power to *take that life again* when He pleased. He promised to rise the third day—and that is exactly what He *did.* Thus we see that not only were His life and His death in His own hands, but His resurrection as well.

Acts 2:24 and 32 attribute the resurrection to God the Father. In I Peter 3:18 it is attributed to the Holy Spirit. In our present verse we read that Christ raised *Himself* from the dead under His own power; but there is no contradiction here. The Godhead was in perfect unity in every part of Christ's mediatorial work. The three Persons of the Godhead cooperated fully, and each detail of Christ's ministry concerning redemption was the work of the Godhead in complete and perfect unity.

"This commandment have I received of my Father." The fact that Jesus received commandment from the Father does not mean that the Son is *inferior* to the Father. "Commandment" simply means that this was part of the commission Jesus received from the heavenly Father when He came into the world to pay the sin-debt. This is part of the work given Him to do when He came to "work the works of God." He emphasized over and over again that He had not come into the world to do His own will nor work His own works, but to do the will of God the Father— and finish the work the Father gave Him to do.

The statement here also refers to the entire doctrine Jesus had just declared to the Jews in this discourse—the doctrine He had received from His Father and which He preached because His Father commanded Him to preach it:

"Believest thou not that I am in the Father, and the Father in me? The words that I speak unto you I speak not of myself: but the Father that dwelleth in me, He doeth the works. Believe me that I am in the Father, and the Father in me: or else believe me for the very works' sake" (John 14:10,11).

"For I have not spoken of myself; but the Father which sent me, He gave me a commandment, what I should say, and what I should speak" (John 12:49).

Verse 19: *"There was a division therefore again among the Jews for these sayings."*

I stated earlier in these studies that Jesus is the great Divider of men—and this is as it should be, for there is no neutrality where God is concerned. We have already seen (chapter 7, verse 43) that "there was a division among the people because of Him." In chapter 9 verse 16, there was "a division among (the Pharisees)," and in our present verse *"there was a division . . . among the Jews."* That Jesus would be a divider of men was prophesied in Isaiah 8:14 and also in Luke 2:34. If the proud Pharisees, scribes, and elders had known their Old Testament Scriptures as they claimed to know them, they should have realized that the division Jesus caused everywhere He taught was proof positive that He was more than man, that He was their Messiah, the Son of God.

"These sayings" points to the discourse in the foregoing verses, when Jesus had so plainly pointed to God as His Father, had proclaimed Himself the Good Shepherd, and made plain declaration of His deity. We noted previously that some of the people did acknowledge Him as a prophet, others were of undecided mind about Him, but still others— those of the sect of the Pharisees and members of the San-hedrin—rejected Him completely. They simply would not accept this humble, unassuming, supposed "impostor" as Messiah—King of kings and Lord of lords.

Therefore, there was a division among them.

Verse 20: *"And many of them said, He hath a devil, and is mad; why hear ye Him?"*

No person on earth can be as harsh and cruel as a re-ligionist—one who is strictly religious but sadly lost. Sinners are kinder to each other than religionists are to people who live godly in Christ Jesus. What the Jews said amounted to this: "Who are YOU? You are a poor Galilaean, son of an ordinary carpenter, brought up in a carpenter's shop—and you have the audacity to call yourself 'the Good Shepherd'! You talk about laying your life down and taking it again; you say you received such commandment from Almighty God. You have a devil; you are MAD—*insane.*" Then turning to the multitudes who had been listening to Jesus, they demanded, *"Why hear ye Him?"* Why do you listen to such a person?"

The same accusation was brought against Paul when he made his defence before Agrippa. *Festus* said to him, "Paul, thou art beside thyself; much learning doth make thee mad" (Acts 26:24). Paul preached a God-felt, know-so, positive salvation—yet what Festus said to him was, "Paul, you have spent too much time in school. You have too much education, too much learning, and it has driven you *insane!*" (*Today,* when a minister preaches the pure, un-adulterated truth, the liberals and modernists say the op-posite about him—they say, "He did not go to school long enough, he needs more training." Or perhaps they say, "He did not attend the *right* school.") The world loves a smooth, toned-down, easy-going Gospel that would hurt no one's feelings—not even the devil's. Unconverted religion-ists have always hated the pure Gospel, they have always criticized the fundamental minister, and they always will. The only minister who escapes their criticism is the min-ister who preaches a social gospel instead of preaching the pure unadulterated Word of God. Jesus was criticized—*and crucified.* With the exception of John the Beloved, the *apostles* were criticized, imprisoned, martyred for the cause of Christ—and even *John* was exiled to Patmos for his testimony. Yes, the world *still* "exiles" ministers who dare to preach the pure Word of God without fear, favor, or compromise.

Verse 21: *"Others said, These are not the words of him that hath a devil. Can a devil open the eyes of the blind?"*

There are many reasons why I know the Bible is the Word of God, not the work of ordinary men—and our present verse is one of these reasons. It simply says, *"OTHERS said . . . ."* If I had written that verse of Scripture I would have *named* these people because I believe they were worthy of being named; but God's ways are not our ways, and we do not question His wisdom. I suppose if the Bible *had* listed these names, many churches and denominations would be named after these men.

Those who were disposed to believe that Jesus was more than man defended Him on two counts:

His words: "These are not the WORDS of him that hath a devil."

His works: "Can a devil OPEN THE EYES OF THE BLIND?"

The devil and demons do not glorify God in either works or words. They do not strive to do good and to save men's lives. They have but one desire—to damn the souls of men and slander God and His only begotten Son. The works Jesus had wrought among these people and the words He spoke were just the opposite of the works and words of a demented man. Those who befriended Jesus were using good reasoning and good common sense, but the Pharisees refused to be reasonable and they refused to face sensible facts.   They were familiar with Isaiah 35:5 which said, "Then the eyes of the blind shall be opened, and the ears of the deaf shall be unstopped." This clearly pointed to their Messiah, but they refused to admit that the words Jesus spoke and the works He performed were not the words and works of a lunatic, a man possessed of a devil.

In the Greek, the word here translated *"words"* actually

reads *"sayings"*—not only the words Jesus had just spoken, but His sayings—*all* the wonderful words He had said. The sayings of Jesus were like the sayings of no other person who ever lived ("Never man spake like this Man"); but the Jews refused to face this fact.

Jesus Declares His Deity

Verses 22 and 23: *"And it was at Jerusalem the feast of the dedication, and it was winter. And Jesus walked in the temple in Solomon's porch."*

Many Bible scholars believe that the *feast of dedication* was in commemoration of the rebuilding of the temple in Jerusalem in Ezra's time, just after the Babylonian captivity: "And the children of Israel, the priests, and the Levites, and the rest of the children of the captivity, kept the dedication of this house of God with joy" (Ezra 6:16).

It is interesting that only John records the Lord's attendance at four of the great feasts of the Jews: The Passover (ch. 2, v. 13); Pentecost (ch. 5, v. 1); Feast of Tabernacles (ch. 7, v. 2); and in our present verse, the Feast of Dedication.

"It was winter." No doubt the Holy Spirit inserts the time of year to explain why Jesus walked under the cover around the temple, *"in Solomon's porch."* He walked in *the outer court,* not within the temple walls. The area known as "Solomon's porch" was where the Jews gathered for discussions on religious matters, and it was probably here that Jesus sat among the doctors when He was twelve years old: "And it came to pass, that after three days they found Him in the temple, sitting in the midst of the doctors, both hearing them, and asking them questions" (Luke 2:46).

"Solomon's porch" was what we would call a *veranda*— a long, covered walk, under a roof supported by columns on one side. The roof kept out the hot sun in the summertime, and when the cold rains came, people could walk under the roof for protection from the rain. The historian

Josephus tells us that Solomon's porch was the only part of the great temple that was not completely destroyed.

Verse 24: *"Then came the Jews round about Him, and said unto Him, How long dost thou make us to doubt? If thou be the Christ, tell us plainly."*

As Jesus walked in Solomon's porch, the Jews came and surrounded Him until He stood in the midst of them, and then they asked Him, *"How long dost thou make us to doubt?"* (We would ask, "How long will you hold us in suspense?") What more could Jesus do or say that would tell them plainly whether or not He was the Christ of God? They had witnessed the healing of a man born blind—a miracle never before wrought since God created Adam! They had witnessed the miraculous feeding of the five thousand, along with many other wonderful miracles. They had heard His wonderful, life-giving words. Yet they asked, "Why do you keep us in suspense? Why do you not tell us plainly whether or not you are the Christ?"

The Greek word translated *"plainly"* does not necessarily mean "in plain words," but *"boldly, without mystery."* They refused to understand the parables He gave, they refused to see the presentation of Himself as the Good Shepherd, the One who had power to lay His life down and power to take it again. So now they asked, "Why keep us in this state of uncertainty and excitement? Tell us boldly, without any mystery, whether or not you are the Christ."

Verse 25: *"Jesus answered them, I told you, and ye believed not: the works that I do in my Father's name, they bear witness of me."*

"I told you, and ye believed not." Without a doubt, Jesus was referring here to what He had said to the Sanhedrin in chapter 5, after the healing of the man at the pool of Bethesda. In that discussion He had clearly declared that God was His Father, and that the Son did only what He saw the Father do. "For the Father loveth the

Son, and sheweth Him all things that Himself doeth . . .
All men should honour the Son, even as they honour the
Father. He that honoureth not the Son honoureth not the
Father which hath sent Him . . . He that heareth my word,
and believeth on Him that sent me, hath everlasting life,
and shall not come into condemnation; but is passed from
death unto life . . . As the Father hath life in Himself; so
hath He given to the Son to have life in Himself." He
pointed out the fourfold witness of His messiahship: John
the Baptist, the works Jesus did, the witness of the heavenly
Father, and the witness of the Scriptures. *These four testified* that He was truly the Son of God, "that Prophet" who
should come as prophesied by Moses.

You will notice that the Jews had asked Jesus, "How
long wilt thou make us to doubt?" His reply showed them
that they were not doubters—they were *unbelievers*. There
IS a difference between doubting and sheer unbelief. I really think God has more respect for an infidel than He has
for a skeptic or an agnostic.

*"The works that I do in my Father's name, they bear
witness of me."* In other words, Jesus said, "If you cannot
believe what I say, then believe me *for the works I do.*"
In other places the miracles of Jesus are offered as divine
proof positive that He was more than a man, He was THE
Christ, the great I AM. Read again John 3:2; 5:36; 7:31;
9:33. Also read Acts 2:22.

Jesus said to these unbelievers, "If you will not believe
what I have already said and done, if you will not admit
that my miracles prove me to be Messiah, Son of God, then
regardless of what *else* I might do or say you still would
not be convinced."

Notice that He said, *"The works which I do in my
FATHER'S name*—not works of my own choosing, not
things I have chosen to do, but works the Father *appointed*
me to do." Jesus was always careful to remind the Jews
that He was not speaking or working independently of the
Father, but in perfect harmony with Him. The miracles

He performed and the words He spoke were the works the Father gave Him to finish and the words the Father gave Him to speak, words that are spirit and life.

Verse 26: *"But ye believe not, because ye are not of my sheep, as I said unto you."*

(We are told that in the Greek this verse reads, "Ye neither believe my words nor my works, FOR ye are not in the number of my sheep. If you were my sheep you would believe; faith is one of their marks.")

Here is the meaning of the verse: The fact that these persons were not among Christ's sheep was not the *cause* of their unbelief. On the contrary, their unbelief was evidence that they were not of Christ's *sheep.* Jesus said clearly, "Ye WILL NOT come to me, that ye might have life" (John 5:40). They were not of His sheep—not because they were not elected or predestined, but because of their *unbelief.*

The closing words of this verse—*"As I said unto you"*—without a doubt point back to chapter 8, verse 47: "He that is of God heareth God's words: ye therefore hear them not, because ye are not of God." These words also point back to verses 3 and 4 of our present chapter. The people to whom Jesus spoke these words had made up their minds to reject Him. They said, "We will not have Him. We know this Man, we know His brothers and sisters. He is an impostor, an illegitimate, and we refuse to believe on Him."

Verse 27: *"My sheep hear my voice, and I know them, and they follow me."*

Here Jesus describes the character of those who are in the fold—His sheep. Having already stated to the Pharisees that THEY were NOT sheep, He now points out the characteristics of those who ARE sheep. This is one of the richest verses in all of the Gospel of John.

Jesus refers to His children as *"sheep."* All true believers are "the sheep of His pasture, the sheep of His fold"—and this is not by accident. We are helpless and hopeless apart from the Shepherd, we are wholly dependent on Him. Sheep at best are foolish, weak, given to wandering away if the shepherd does not protect them and keep them in the flock.

We see another precious truth here: Jesus calls the sheep *"MY sheep."* Every born again believer is the personal possession of the Good Shepherd. He purchased us at the tremendous price of His own blood and we belong to Him by redemption and purchase. We are His precious, peculiar property, and since that is true, *we are also His responsibility.* I say this in fear and trembling: the Good Shepherd is a million times more interested in our protection, care, and success than we ourselves are interested. He leads us into paths of righteousness "for His name's sake."

"My sheep hear my voice." We are "sheep" because we DID hear His voice (John 5:24). We hear the Word, and that is the beginning of our salvation. We heard His voice when He called us to repentance. When He called us to believe, He called us unto Himself:

"Come unto me, all ye that labour and are heavy laden, and I will give you rest. Take my yoke upon you, and learn of me; for I am meek and lowly in heart: and ye shall find rest unto your souls. For my yoke is easy, and my burden is light" (Matt. 11:28–30). But these people to whom Jesus was speaking would not hear His voice, they refused to come when He called. Therefore they were "not of (His) sheep."

". . . And I know them." Jesus knows each of His children by name. He loves us with a peculiar love and knows us with a special knowledge. He knows everything about us; every hair of our head is numbered—and He knows the number! He knows the secrets of our hearts, the burdens, the longing. Not one tear falls from the eyes of a believer but He knows it.

"And they follow me." Jesus is the Good Shepherd, and true believers—like sheep—follow their Shepherd. As sheep

obey and trust the shepherd, so do believers obey and trust the Lord Jesus Christ.   A true believer can sing from the heart:

> "I'll go where you want me to go, dear Lord,
>   O'er mountain, or plain, or sea;
> I'll say what you want me to say, dear Lord,
>   I'll be what you want me to be!"

It is said that sheep are the most simple of animals — but they are also *superior* to other animals in love and trust.   At the slightest sound of the shepherd's voice the sheep will follow him, but they will not follow strangers. Sheep cannot find pasture and would starve without a shepherd.   Sheep cannot protect themselves and without the shepherd's care the wolves would devour the flock.   There is no other animal so dependent upon another for livelihood and protection.

In the Greek, the meaning of this verse is, "My sheep are one body, which hears my voice — one body (singular) — but the *individual sheep* in the fold follow me."   In verse 16 of this chapter Jesus said, "There shall be one fold and one Shepherd."   There IS one fold and one Shepherd; the sheep *as a body* hear His voice, and *as individual sheep* they follow Him.

Verse 28:   *"And I give unto them eternal life; and they shall never perish, neither shall any man pluck them out of my hand."*

Tremendous truth, clearly stated!   The Good Shepherd gives unto His sheep *"eternal life,"* the precious gift of God, salvation by grace.   Grace brings salvation, pardon, justification — and then, while "goodness and mercy shall follow us all the days of our lives," that is not the end: WE SHALL "DWELL IN THE HOUSE OF THE LORD FOREVER!"

Notice, the Good Shepherd said, *"I GIVE unto them eternal life"* (present tense) — not "I *have* given," not "I *will give* at some future date," but "I GIVE — *right NOW* —

eternal life." Eternal life is the present possession of every born again, blood-washed child of God. We are not *hoping to receive* eternal life at the end of this life's journey, we do not pray, "Lord, *at last* save us in heaven." Born again believers are saved NOW. The split second an individual puts his faith in the shed blood and finished work of the Lord Jesus, that very second he comes into possession of eternal life.

"And they shall NEVER PERISH!" I see no reason for anyone to argue over the meaning of this statement. Jesus simply declares, "My sheep hear my voice . . . I know them . . . They follow me . . . I give them eternal life . . . and they shall NEVER perish."

"NEITHER SHALL ANY MAN PLUCK THEM OUT OF MY HAND." The Greek reads, "any person or any one" — that is, "Neither man, devil, angel, nor any other person or thing shall pluck them out of my hand." Suppose we let the Holy Spirit give further explanation, through the pen of Paul:

"What shall we then say to these things? If God be for us, who can be against us? He that spared not His own Son, but delivered Him up for us all, how shall He not with Him also freely give us all things? Who shall lay anything to the charge of God's elect? It is God that justifieth. Who is he that condemneth? It is Christ that died, yea rather, that is risen again, who is even at the right hand of God, who also maketh intercession for us.

"Who shall separate us from the love of Christ? shall tribulation, or distress, or persecution, or famine, or nakedness, or peril, or sword? As it is written, For thy sake we are killed all the day long; we are accounted as sheep for the slaughter. *Nay, in all these things we are more than conquerors through Him that loved us. FOR I AM PERSUADED, THAT NEITHER DEATH, NOR LIFE, NOR ANGELS, NOR PRINCIPALITIES, NOR POWERS, NOR THINGS PRESENT, NOR THINGS TO COME, NOR HEIGHT, NOR DEPTH, NOR ANY OTHER CREATURE,*

SHALL BE ABLE TO SEPARATE US FROM THE LOVE OF GOD, WHICH IS IN CHRIST JESUS OUR LORD" (Rom. 8:31—39).

Notice the position of the sheep: the sheep do not hold to the Shepherd, the hand of the Shepherd holds the sheep. Instead of the believer trying to "hold on" or "hold out," we need to realize that we are in the Shepherd's hand, and the fact that His mighty hand holds us is the secret of the Christian's victory.   It is the spiritual birthright of every blood-washed, born again believer to enjoy this sweet peace, the gift of God's love and grace.

Verse 29:   *"My Father, which gave them me, is greater than all; and no man is able to pluck them out of my Father's hand."*

The truth declared here adds strength to the truth declared in the preceding verses.   This same truth is also declared in Colossians 3:3—"Your life is hid with Christ in God."   Jehovah, the heavenly Father, gave the sheep to Jesus; therefore they are HIS—but they are the Father's also, and Jesus assures us that the Father *"is greater than all."*   He is not just "mighty," He is ALMIGHTY!   There is none in heaven, in earth, or under the earth as mighty as God the Father.   He is omnipotent, He possesses *all power.*   Therefore nothing—life, death, principalities, powers, or persons—can pluck the sheep out of the Father's hand.

These precious words bring unshakable assurance to the heart of the true believer.   It causes me to rejoice with joy unspeakable to know that God the Father is just as interested in me as Jesus the Son is interested in me.   It was God the Father who loved me and permitted Jesus to die for me (John 3:16), God saved me for Christ's sake (Eph. 4:32), therefore God the Father is interested in my welfare as His child, a member of His Church.

The *"one fold"* (the New Testament Church) was given to Jesus by God the Father before ever the world was. That fold is now being made up of individuals who hear the voice of the Shepherd and come to Him *in faith believing.* The gates of hell shall not prevail against *The Church of the living God.* It will be completed and presented to Jesus "a glorious Church, not having spot, or wrinkle, or any such thing; but that it should be holy and without blemish." (Please study Ephesians 5:22—33.)

Verse 30: *"I and my Father are one."*

This does not destroy the Godhead. There is ONE God, manifested in three Persons: Father, Son, and Holy Ghost. In Matthew 16:16,17, when Peter said to Jesus, "Thou art the Christ, the Son of the living God," Jesus replied, ". . . Flesh and blood hath not revealed it unto thee, but *my Father which is in HEAVEN."* Jesus was on earth, yet He said, "my Father which is *in heaven."* Someone may ask, "Why don't you *explain* the Godhead?" My answer to that question is that if I could explain the Godhead, the Holy Trinity, I would be equal with God. I am thankful that I cannot explain the Trinity. It is one of the deep mysteries which God will explain to us in the great heavenly Bible class. In the meantime, we take it by faith. We believe it because the Bible teaches it.

In our present verse Jesus is saying, *"I* am one, *the Father* is one, yet *the TWO of us are ONE*—one in love, one in power, one in dignity, one in nature, one in essence, one in word." Thus the sheep of the Good Shepherd are doubly secure, doubly protected. Their safety is as certain as the fact that God the Father and God the Son *live.* In his second epistle, verse 8, John the Beloved wrote, "Look to yourselves, *that we lose not those things which we have wrought,* but that we receive a full reward." But this speaks of stewardship, not salvation. We did not "wrought" our salvation; salvation is the gift of God.

The Jews understood clearly what Jesus said when He declared, "I and my Father are one." They understood that He was claiming to be God in flesh.

Verse 31: *"Then the Jews took up stones again to stone Him."*

This is the second time the Jews took up stones to stone Jesus. (See also chapter 8, verse 59.) When He said, "I and my Father are one," they accused Him of blasphemy— and had He not spoken the truth, had He not *been* one with the Father, *God in flesh,* He would have been *guilty* of blasphemy. The Old Testament commanded, "He that blasphemeth the name of the Lord, he shall surely be put to death, and all the congregation shall certainly stone him: as well the stranger, as he that is born in the land, when he blasphemeth the name of the Lord, shall be put to death" (Lev. 24:16). See also Numbers 15:36 and I Kings 21:13. So, claiming that Jesus blasphemed, the Jews took up stones to stone Him, although in the true sense they had no power to put anyone to death. They were under Roman rule, and if they had stoned Jesus they would have been outside the law and their action would have corresponded to our lynch mobs.

In chapter 8, verse 59, the Greek means that the Jews actually *took up* stones, but in our present verse we find a different Greek word which means that they *carried* stones. In other words, they already had the stones in their hands, hoping for an excuse to stone Jesus. Since they were surrounding Him in Solomon's porch, it does not stand to reason that there were stones in that immediate location; therefore they must have brought stones with them, hoping for an opportunity to use them. But they could not cast the stones, because Jesus did not come into the world to die by stoning. He came to die on a cross, and all hell could not stop Him.

Verse 32: *"Jesus answered them, Many good works have I shewed you from my Father; for which of those works do ye stone me?"*

On many occasions the Jews had asked for signs to prove that Jesus was Messiah. He had wrought many miracles (signs) in their presence, and now He asks them which of these good works had so angered them that they were about to stone Him. He had harmed no one, He had fed the hungry, clothed the naked, healed the sick, raised the dead, opened the eyes of the blind, unstopped the ears of the deaf, straightened withered limbs. Did they plan to stone Him for these good deeds? and if so, for *which* of His miracles would they stone Him?

"Many good works have I shewed you from my Father." "I have shewed" means "I have publicly performed these miracles, I have publicly put on exhibition before you these mighty and marvelous works. They were not done in a corner nor in seclusion, but openly—in your streets, in your temple, in your homes."

Here, as in all of His ministry, Jesus reminded the Jews of the solemn and divine fact that it was the *Father's* work that He was doing. Over and over He stressed the truth that what He did and said was in obedience to the will of the heavenly Father. He had come to work the works of the Father, not His own works.

His reference to *"many* good works" suggests that Jesus worked many miracles not recorded in the Gospels (see also John 21:25), and no doubt even in Jerusalem He performed many miracles that are not recorded; but in spite of His mighty works the Jews refused to believe Him or receive Him.

"For which of those works do ye stone me?" The Jews put evil men to death by stoning, but Jesus had done no evil and they knew it. What He asked them was, "Are you really seeking to put me to death for doing good? Which of you convinceth me of *sin?* For which of my good works would you stone me?"

Verse 33: *"The Jews answered Him, saying, For a good work we stone thee not; but for blasphemy; and because that thou, being a man, makest thyself God."*

Here, Jesus challenged His enemies. He had done no

evil, and certainly they could not stone Him for doing good. So they answered that they were not going to stone Him for His *good works*, but because He was a blasphemer— *"because that thou, being a man, makest thyself God."* In chapter 5, verse 18 of this study, we read that the Jews sought to kill Jesus "because He not only had broken the Sabbath, but said also that God was His Father, *making Himself equal with God."*

We must remember that from the standpoint of the flesh, Jesus was a Jew. He grew up in Joseph's carpenter shop at Nazareth, reared in a community with other Jewish children; and though we know almost nothing of His boyhood and youth, the Scripture tells us that He "increased in wisdom and stature, and in favour with God and man" (Luke 2:52). No doubt some of these Jews remembered Him as a boy and they simply could not bring themselves to believe that He was very God in flesh! They refused to acknowledge that He spoke as no man had ever spoken, that His miracles were such as to make them unheard of since man was created. Jesus wanted them to forget everything they knew about Him from the human standpoint and believe Him for the work's sake, for the miracles He was performing. He wanted them to recognize, as Nicodemus did, that no man could do such miracles within his own power.

But the Jews *understood* Him when He spoke of unity of nature with Jehovah God, and they therefore said, "Thou makest thyself GOD!"

Verse 34:   *"Jesus answered them, Is it not written in your law, I said, Ye are gods?"*

The defense Jesus used here against His enemies is remarkable—i. e., if great men (princes, but *men* nevertheless) were called gods, could they accuse *HIM, the SON of God,* of blasphemy because He *called Himself the Son of God?* Jesus took His quotation from the Eighty-Second Psalm, where Asaph, referring to the position and duty of princes and rulers, called them "gods" because their responsibility was so great as compared with the responsibility of other men, and they were so high *above* other men—as in II Samuel 1:14: "David said unto him, How wast thou not afraid to stretch forth thine hand to destroy *the Lord's anointed?*" Also in II Chronicles 19:4—6 we read where Jehoshaphat "set judges in the land . . . and said to the judges, Take heed what ye do: *for ye judge not for man, but for the Lord, who is with you in the judgment.*"

The *"law"* to which Jesus refers in our present verse was the Scriptures. The Jews divided the Old Testament into two parts—The Law, and The Prophets—and The Law included the books of Moses as well as other books, from Genesis through the Song of Solomon. In Matthew 5:17 Jesus said, "Think not that I am come to destroy THE LAW, OR THE PROPHETS: I am not come to destroy, but to fulfil." In Matthew 22:40 He said, "On these two commandments hang all THE LAW and THE PROPHETS." In Luke 24:44 He referred to the Old Testament Scriptures as The Law, Psalms, and The Prophets: "And He said unto them, These are the words which I spake unto you, while I was yet with you, that all things must be fulfilled, which were written in THE LAW of Moses, and in THE PROPHETS, and in THE PSALMS, concerning me."

In His defense against His enemies here, Jesus used their own sacred, honored writings—writings of Moses and David, men whom the Jews honored very highly. In fact, it is most interesting to note that in Christ's public ministry He often used the Scriptures as the sole judge of controversy. When He met Satan on the Mount of Temptation in Matthew 4:1—11 He answered the tempter on each occasion by quoting Old Testament Scriptures. He did not need to quote Scriptures that were already written because anything He said would have been the Word of God. He spoke only as the Father gave Him words, and therefore His words were the words of God. But throughout His ministry He used the Old Testament Scriptures freely.

Jesus asked, *"Is it not written?"* meaning "Do you not

know what your Scriptures say concerning men who are princes and magistrates being called gods?" If the Old Testament, with its profound sense of God's incomparable majesty, did not shrink from calling such men gods, was He blaspheming in calling Himself *Son of God?* Jesus did not argue with His enemies; He simply gave them the Word of God. Hebrew authorities tell us that the word rendered "judges" in Exodus 22:8,9 in the Hebrew is actually "gods." In connection with this, also read Exodus 21:6 and 22:28.

Verses 35 and 36: *"If he called them gods, unto whom the Word of God came, and the Scripture cannot be broken; say ye of Him, whom the Father hath sanctified, and sent into the world, Thou blasphemest; because I said, I am the Son of God?"*

What Jesus is saying here is simply this: If princes and magistrates—appointed, anointed, and receiving this honor by grace—were not in fault when they called themselves gods (or when they were referred to as gods) then how could HE, the only begotten SON of God, deserve to be stoned because He rightfully declared Himself to BE God in a tabernacle of flesh?

They *"unto whom the Word of God came"* refers to those commissioned by God and placed in the position of princes and magistrates. They were persons to whom God had spoken, to whom He had given commandment to rule for Him. Greek authorities tell us that the language used here in the original is almost identical to that in Luke 3:2 where we are told, "the Word of God came unto John...." God gave John a special commission, and the same is true of those referred to as "gods" in Psalm 82.

"The Scriptures cannot be broken." It was an acknowledged principle among the Jews that the Word of God could not be broken, annulled, or destroyed, and Jesus reminded them of this fact. Everything in the Word should receive reverence, not one jot or tittle should be refused or disregarded. The Jews believed this; they believed that every-

thing in their Scriptures was to be given full weight, not one word was insignificant, not one word should be removed, passed over, or evaded because every word was the Word of Jehovah God. Since that were true, and since in Psalm 82 ordinary men such as princes and magistrates were called "gods," then certainly it was not wrong for Jesus to say, "I and my Father are ONE."

In verse 36 Jesus simply repeats the truth He had already declared. *"Say ye of Him . . . ."* The Greek leaves it open and could be read, *"Say ye of ME."* Thus Jesus referred to Himself, leaving no room for doubt of whom He spoke.

"Whom the Father hath sanctified" simply means "whom God has set apart and appointed from all eternity, the One whom God appointed in the covenant of grace, our High Priest, the one Mediator between God and men." Jesus became "Son of man" when He was born of the virgin Mary, but He was *the Son of GOD* from all eternity.

Jesus speaks of Himself as the One *"sent into the world."* He came into the world on a singular mission—to be *Saviour* of the world. "Thou shalt call His name JESUS: for He shall save His people from their sins" (Matt. 1:21). *Jesus* is His earthly name, meaning SAVIOUR. He came into the world to seek and to save that which was lost, to give His life a ransom for many. He came to die that WE might live. He was the Father's "Sent One," the One whom God sent forth to be a propitiation for sins (Rom. 3:25).

All born again believers are sanctified *positionally* the moment they are born again; they are taken out of the kingdom of darkness and placed over into the kingdom of light (Col. 1:13), set apart for God. But the sanctification referred to here is much more excellent than OUR sanctification. Jesus alone was separated from all others. He was *THE ONLY begotten Son of God, THE Lamb of God* which taketh away the sin of the world, and His sanctification was far superior to anything we will ever know in this life.

There is only ONE Jesus, ONE Saviour; He did in a body
what no man had ever done or ever could do. Jesus put
on display the grace of our God, the Spirit and majesty of
God. He was singular in all things—birth, life, ministry,
healing, teaching, power, and words. Indeed, "HIM hath
God the Father sealed" (John 6:27).

"WHEREFORE He is able also to save them to the uttermost that come unto God by Him, seeing He ever liveth
to make intercession for them. For such an High Priest
became us, WHO IS HOLY, HARMLESS, UNDEFILED,
SEPARATE FROM SINNERS, and made higher than the
heavens; who needeth not daily, as those high priests, to
offer up sacrifice, first for His own sins, and then for the
people's: for this He did ONCE, when He offered up Himself. For the law maketh men high priests which have infirmity; but THE WORD OF THE OATH, WHICH WAS
SINCE THE LAW, MAKETH THE SON, WHO IS CON-
SECRATED FOR EVERMORE" (Heb. 7:25—28).

Verse 37: *"If I do not the works of my Father, believe
me not."*

Again Jesus appeals to the evidence of His mighty miracles worked in the presence of His enemies. He said, "If
my works do not prove that I am more than man, then I
do not ask you to believe that I am the Son of God; but
if my works DO prove that I am more than man, more than
an ordinary prophet, you have no right to call me a blasphemer!"

Please notice that Jesus referred to His works as *"the
works of my FATHER."* He refused to compromise His
former statement that He and God the Father were ONE.
From the very outset of His public ministry He made it
clear to His listeners that He was on earth on business for
His Father, and that whatever He said or did, or wherever
He went, He was about the work of God the Father, seeking to do the Father's will. He said, "He that sent me is
with me: the Father hath not left me alone; for I do always

those things that please Him" (John 8:29).

Verse 38: *"But if I do, though ye believe not me, believe the works: that ye may know, and believe, that the Father is in me, and I in Him."*

Here Jesus brings His argument against His enemies to a close, and what He said in the end of His testimony was simply this:

"You confess that no man has ever spoken as I speak. It is true that my words are spirit and life. But if you refuse to *believe* my words or accept my testimony, I appeal to you to observe and accept the evidence of my mighty works, the works the Father gave me to do. My works will prove to you that I am the Son of God, that I and my Father are one, that the Father is in me and I in Him."

What communion! What union and fellowship! Jesus was equal with the Father in every way—in power, holiness, righteousness, in ALL things.

The enemies of Jesus understood perfectly what He said. They understood that He was claiming equality with Jehovah God, the God of their fathers. They understood that He was telling them if they knew God as they *claimed* to know Him, then they would recognize and accept His Son. The very fact of their rejection of Him and their refusal to hear His words or recognize His miracles testified that they did not know God. They understood all of this, as proved by the next verse.

Verse 39: *"Therefore they sought again to take Him: but He escaped out of their hand."*

In Isaiah 1:18 God invited, "Come now, and let us reason together," but the enemies of Jesus refused to reason. Hard-hearted, blinded by the god of this age, willfully ignorant of the signs and prophecies given in the Old Testament concerning their Messiah, they were determined to arrest Jesus and put Him to death, regardless of what He said or did.

"But He escaped out of their hand." The death of Jesus, and the manner in which He would die, was settled before ever God created the earth or anything therein. Therefore, even though His enemies sought to take Him, they could not. I personally believe that He miraculously walked through them unnoticed. The Greek here reads, "He came forth out of their hand"—definitely a miraculous escape. His enemies could not put their hands on Him. Either He was taken out of their company through a miracle, or they were blinded for a moment and could not see Him. He disappeared out of their company.

Jesus Returns to the Site of His Baptism

Verse 40:   *"And went away again beyond Jordan into the place where John at first baptized; and there He abode."*

That Jesus *"went away again beyond Jordan"* refers to the beginning of the public ministry of Jesus when He came to John the Baptist who was then baptizing "in Bethabara beyond Jordan" (ch. 1, v. 28). There is no record that Jesus had visited that place since the day John baptized Him.

Our Lord was divine—yes; but I love the fact that He was also human, and in returning "again beyond Jordan" it would seem that He wanted to bring His ministry to a close in the same place where it began.

Also in returning to the place where He began His ministry, Jesus reminded the Jews that John the Baptist had declared Him as the Lamb of God who would take away the sin of the world. They recognized *John* as a prophet and believed that he came to them by divine appointment on a divine mission.

The return of Jesus to the scene of His baptism would also remind His disciples of the first lesson they learned from Him as He taught them there. How precious and touchingly human, that *Jesus, very God,* wanted to return to the place where He began His earthly ministry!

"And there He abode." Bible scholars believe that He

spent three or four months there—the time between the feast of dedication and the last Passover, which would be from winter to Easter. We do not know where or with whom He lived, but if God had wanted us to know, it would have been recorded in His Word.

Verse 41ᵣ *"And many resorted unto Him, and said, John did no miracle: but all things that John spake of this Man were true."*

From this verse we know that Jesus did not stay in seclusion nor hide Himself from the people. *"Many"* came to hear Him—*how* many we are not told; possibly hundreds, possibly thousands. They came to hear Him on the very spot where John the Baptist had preached and baptized so many. Those who had heard John were reminded of his testimony concerning Jesus, and probably remembered the day He was baptized when the Holy Ghost descended in bodily form like a dove and remained upon Him.

The sermons of Jesus, delivered at the scene of His baptism, evidently brought these things to the memory of the people, and they said, *"John did no miracle: but all things that John spake of this Man were true!"* John's ministry was short, but the Jews did not forget his sermons. Herod had him beheaded at the request of an ungodly woman, thus sealing the lips of John the Baptist; but he could not destroy the sermons John had preached. "The Word of God is not bound" (II Tim. 2:9). A true sermon never dies; it lives on.

It is true that not one word is recorded concerning any miracle ever wrought by John the Baptist. He was a special servant of God, appointed, anointed, and *sent*—a voice to announce the coming Messiah. He did his work and then went to Paradise. He is resting from his labor, but his works follow him. Ministers today still give out the marvelous truths he proclaimed!

If I should go on to be with the Lord today, I wonder if it could be said of me, as it was of John the Baptist,

"All things that he spoke of this Man (Jesus) were true!"

Verse 42: *"And many believed on Him there."*

I do not believe it is possible to say whether these people believed with the heart or with the head. Probably *some* believed with the heart, and others believed only intellectually. The same expression is found in chapter 8, verse 30, and in chapter 11, verse 45.

I personally believe that many of the Jews secretly believed Jesus to be their Messiah, but they feared the Sanhedrin and therefore did not publicly make their belief known. They were afraid to confess Him openly. Certainly after Jesus was raised from the dead, many of the Jews DID publicly confess their faith and were baptized:

"Howbeit many of them which heard the Word believed; and the number of the men was about five thousand. . . And the Word of God increased; and the number of the disciples multiplied in Jerusalem greatly; and a great company of the priests were obedient to the faith. . . And when they heard it, they glorified the Lord, and said unto him, Thou seest, brother, how many thousands of Jews there are which believe; and they are all zealous of the law" (Acts 4:4; 6:7; 21:20).

No doubt many of those who *"believed on Him"* (in our present verse) believed as far as it was possible for them to believe at that point. They became "learners" and seekers, and on the Day of Pentecost, as well as later, many of those who believed intellectually that day became true believers and were born again. There is no doubt that we will meet many of these dear people in that glorious resurrection morning!

CHAPTER XI

1. Now a certain man was sick, named Lazarus, of Bethany, the town of Mary and her sister Martha.

2. (It was that Mary which anointed the Lord with ointment, and wiped his feet with her hair, whose brother Lazarus was sick.)

3. Therefore his sisters sent unto him, saying, Lord, behold, he whom thou lovest is sick.

4. When Jesus heard that, he said, This sickness is not unto death, but for the glory of God, that the Son of God might be glorified thereby.

5. Now Jesus loved Martha, and her sister, and Lazarus.

6. When he had heard therefore that he was sick, he abode two days still in the same place where he was.

7. Then after that saith he to his disciples, Let us go into Judaea again.

8. His disciples say unto him, Master, the Jews of late sought to stone thee; and goest thou thither again?

9. Jesus answered, Are there not twelve hours in the day? If any man walk in the day, he stumbleth not, because he seeth the light of this world.

10. But if a man walk in the night, he stumbleth, because there is no light in him.

11. These things said he: and after that he saith unto them, Our friend Lazarus sleepeth; but I go, that I may awake him out of sleep.

12. Then said his disciples, Lord, if he sleep, he shall do well.

13. Howbeit Jesus spake of his death: but they thought that he had spoken of taking of rest in sleep.

14. Then said Jesus unto them plainly, Lazarus is dead.

15. And I am glad for your sakes that I was not there, to the intent ye may believe; nevertheless let us go unto him.

16. Then said Thomas, which is called Didymus, unto his fellow-disciples, Let us also go, that we may die with him.

17. Then when Jesus came, he found that he had lain in the grave four days already.

18. Now Bethany was nigh unto Jerusalem, about fifteen furlongs off:

19. And many of the Jews came to Martha and Mary, to comfort them concerning their brother.

20. Then Martha, as soon as she heard that Jesus was coming, went and met him: but Mary sat still in the house.

21. Then said Martha unto Jesus, Lord, if thou hadst been here, my brother had not died.

22. But I know, that even now, whatsoever thou wilt ask of God, God will give it thee.

23. Jesus saith unto her, Thy brother shall rise again.

24. Martha saith unto him, I know that he shall rise again in the resurrection at the last day.

25. Jesus said unto her, I am the resurrection, and the life: he that believeth in me, though he were dead, yet shall he live:

26. And whosoever liveth and believeth in me shall never die. Believest thou this?

27. She saith unto him, Yea, Lord: I believe that thou art the Christ, the Son of God, which should come into the world.

28. And when she had so said, she went her way, and called Mary her sister secretly, saying, The Master is come, and calleth for thee.

29. As soon as she heard that, she arose quickly, and came unto him.

30. Now Jesus was not yet come into the town, but was in that place where Martha met him.

31. The Jews then which were with her in the house, and comforted her, when they saw Mary, that she rose up hastily and went out, followed her, saying, She goeth unto the grave to weep there.

32. Then when Mary was come where Jesus was, and saw him, she fell down at his feet, saying unto him, Lord, if thou hadst been here, my brother had not died.

33. When Jesus therefore saw her weeping, and the Jews also weeping which came with her, he groaned in the spirit, and was troubled,

34. And said, Where have ye laid him? They said unto him, Lord, come and see.

35. Jesus wept.

36. Then said the Jews, Behold how he loved him!

37. And some of them said, Could not this man, which opened the eyes of the blind, have caused that even this man should not have died?

38. Jesus therefore again groaning in himself cometh to the grave. It was a cave, and a stone lay upon it.

39. Jesus said, Take ye away the stone. Martha, the sister of him that was dead, saith unto him, Lord, by this time he stinketh: for he hath been dead four days.

40. Jesus saith unto her, Said I not unto thee, that, if thou wouldest believe, thou shouldest see the glory of God?

41. Then they took away the stone from the place where the dead

was laid. And Jesus lifted up his eyes, and said, Father, I thank thee that thou hast heard me.

42. And I knew that thou hearest me always: but because of the people which stand by I said it, that they may believe that thou hast sent me.

43. And when he thus had spoken, he cried with a loud voice, Lazarus, come forth.

44. And he that was dead came forth, bound hand and foot with graveclothes: and his face was bound about with a napkin. Jesus saith unto them, Loose him, and let him go.

45. Then many of the Jews which came to Mary, and had seen the things which Jesus did, believed on him.

46. But some of them went their ways to the Pharisees, and told them what things Jesus had done.

47. Then gathered the chief priests and the Pharisees a council, and said, What do we? for this man doeth many miracles.

48. If we let him thus alone, all men will believe on him: and the Romans shall come and take away both our place and nation.

49. And one of them, named Caiaphas, being the high priest that same year, said unto them, Ye know nothing at all,

50. Nor consider that it is expedient for us, that one man should die for the people, and that the whole nation perish not.

51. And this spake he not of himself: but being high priest that year, he prophesied that Jesus should die for that nation;

52. And not for that nation only, but that also he should gather together in one the children of God that were scattered abroad.

53. Then from that day forth they took counsel together for to put him to death.

54. Jesus therefore walked no more openly among the Jews; but went thence unto a country near to the wilderness, into a city called Ephraim, and there continued with his disciples.

55. And the Jews' passover was nigh at hand: and many went out of the country up to Jerusalem before the passover, to purify themselves.

56. Then sought they for Jesus, and spake among themselves, as they stood in the temple, What think ye, that he will not come to the feast?

57. Now both the chief priests and the Pharisees had given a commandment, that, if any man knew where he were, he should shew it, that they might take him.

Verse 1: *"Now a certain man was sick, named Lazarus, of Bethany, the town of Mary and her sister Martha."*

This verse gives the keynote of the entire chapter. It

introduces *"a certain man"* not mentioned before, a man *"named Lazarus."* He was an *obscure* believer; sacred record bears no history of him, and we know nothing about him except what John records here and in chapter 12.

From what is recorded in our present study we know that Lazarus was a disciple of the Lord Jesus Christ, and that he lived in the little village of Bethany, *"the town of Mary and her sister Martha."* Bethany was situated on the eastern slope of the Mount of Olives, about two miles eastward from Jerusalem toward Jericho. Its former location is well known today, and is accepted without dispute. It was my privilege to visit the area where this small town stood, where our Lord raised Lazarus from the dead. It is not mentioned in the Old Testament, but the events recorded in our present chapter caused it to become well known in the annals of Christian history.

Bethany was also the place where Jesus spent the night just before the Passion, and from whence He began His triumphal entry into the Holy City.

It was also from this little town that Jesus ascended back to the heavenly Father: "And He led them out as far as to *Bethany,* and He lifted up His hands, and blessed them. And it came to pass, while He blessed them, *He was parted from them, and carried up into heaven"* (Luke 24:50,51). It was in this little village that Lazarus lived, with his sisters, Mary and Martha.

Verse 2: *"(It was that Mary which anointed the Lord with ointment, and wiped His feet with her hair, whose brother Lazarus was sick.)*

Four "Marys" are mentioned in connection with our Lord's ministry: the virgin Mary, mother of Jesus; Mary, wife of Cleophas; Mary Magdalene; and Mary the sister of Martha and Lazarus. Therefore, so that we might know *which* of these women was the sister of Martha and Lazarus, John explains that it was the Mary *"which anointed the Lord with ointment, and wiped His feet with her hair."*

Bible scholars do not agree as to the number of times the Lord Jesus was anointed. Some say three times, some say twice. It is clear that He was anointed during the early part of His ministry, and again near its close. He was anointed in the house of Simon the *Pharisee,* and He was anointed in the house of Simon the *leper* in the village of Bethany. He was anointed by a woman who was a great sinner, and He was anointed by the sister of Martha, the "Mary" about whom we are studying at present. It is certain that there were at least two anointings, and it seems probable that there were three. In the Gospel of Mark (chapter 14) we read that a woman anointed Jesus *two* days before the Passover, and on this occasion she poured the ointment on His *head.* John tells us that He was anointed *six* days before the Passover, and that the ointment was poured on His *feet.* If we agree that the Lord was anointed *twice* during His last week on earth before His crucifixion—once *six* days before the Passover, another time *two* days before the Passover—then we have no difficulty to overcome; and the anointing of Luke 7:37,38 by the woman "which was a sinner" makes the third anointing. Some Bible scholars believe that it was Mary of Bethany who anointed Him both times during the last week before the Passover.

Be that as it may, I am thankful that whether He was anointed once, twice, or three times, His anointings have nothing to do with our salvation! The blood of Jesus Christ cleanses us from all sin, and minor difficulties or disagreements will be overcome and made plain in that great heavenly Bible class when we sit at the feet of Jesus. I am not troubled by the things I do not understand, but by what I DO understand; for the things I can grasp and comprehend keep me so busy, and show me that I fall so far short of God's glory, they leave me no time to fret or worry about whether Jesus was anointed twice or three times! (Study Matthew 26:7, Mark 14:3, and John 12:3.)

We will learn in this chapter that born again believers

can be sick to the glory of God. I do believe that in some instances sickness comes upon believers because of sin, for there are some Christians who refuse to look up until God puts them flat on their back in a hospital bed; but some of God's dearest, most consecrated saints sit in wheelchairs or lie in sanatoriums, rest homes, and hospitals. Sickness befalls the best of Christians, and sickness in the life of a believer is not necessarily a sign of unconfessed sin in that life. I repeat—sickness in the life of a believer can bring glory to God.

Verse 3:   *"Therefore his sisters sent unto Him, saying, Lord, behold, he whom thou lovest is sick."*

Mary and Martha knew exactly where Jesus was—indicating a deep love with precious communion and fellowship between this family and the Lord—and they sent word to Him: *"Lord . . . he whom thou lovest is sick!"* Notice the respect these women had for Jesus as shown in their humble message. They did not demand that He heal their brother, they did not frantically insist that He come quickly and "do something." They simply sent Him a message that Lazarus was sick.

Notice another singular thing about this message: The women did not say, *"Lazarus* is sick," they did not call their brother by name. They said, "He *whom thou lovest* is sick." There was such devotion and understanding between Jesus and Lazarus that Martha and Mary knew their message would be understood when they said, "He whom thou lovest is sick."

I am so glad that the love of God and of the Lord Jesus Christ is not of the same manner as man's love. In I John 3:1 we read, "Behold, what manner of love the Father hath bestowed upon us, that we should be called the sons of God . . . ." In Hebrews 13:8 we read, "Jesus Christ the same yesterday, and to day, and for ever." OUR love changes; HIS love will *never* change. "Having loved His own . . . He loved them unto the end" (John 13:1).

The message Mary and Martha sent to Jesus was not made up of flowery words; it was short and simple, but clear and understandable. When we pray, we do not need to dress up our petitions with "frills" and fancy words. We can come to Jesus and talk with Him as we would talk with our nearest and dearest earthly friend. We should never *dictate* to God in prayer; we must pray as Jesus prayed, "Father, not my will, but thine, be done." We need to remember that He knows the end in the beginning. *We* know only this moment, but HE knows all the moments of all the hours of all the days that lie ahead. It is not necessarily the long, flowery prayer that gets an answer, but the *sincere* prayer, the sincere desire of an earnest heart. It may be but a few words, but if it makes the needs of our heart and life known to God, that is all that is necessary. Of course He *knows* our needs even before we ask, but it delights God the Father to have His children come to Him in prayer and communion.

God can heal, He *does* heal—but not in every case. The Apostle Paul was a God-fearing, dedicated, anointed servant of God, yet two of his dearest friends, Epaphroditus and Timothy, were both in poor health. If he could have healed them through prayer, he would have done so. Paul himself prayed thrice that the Lord would remove his "thorn in the flesh." God did not remove the thorn, in spite of Paul's fervent prayers, but said, "My grace is sufficient for thee." To tell a child of God that he cannot be healed because he lacks *faith* is nothing short of cruelty! God can heal, He does heal, but He does all things according to His will and His eternal purpose.

Verse 4: *"When Jesus heard that, He said, This sickness is not unto death, but for the glory of God, that the Son of God might be glorified thereby."*

Mary and Martha probably sent their message to Jesus by word of mouth, a verbal message; and in this verse Jesus gave the messenger an answer to carry back. The message

He sent to Mary and Martha was this: "Lazarus is sick, but his sickness will not bring death in the sense that his body will return to dust. *This* sickness is for the glory of God, and through it *the Son of God* will be glorified."

Jesus could have said to the messenger, "You return to Mary and Martha and tell them that Lazarus will die, but that I will *raise* him from the dead." He did not send such a message, however, because He knew that even if He told the sisters of Lazarus exactly what was going to happen, they would not understand, and their hearts would be crushed by it.

Verse 5: *"Now Jesus loved Martha, and her sister, and Lazarus."*

One thing we learn here is that all born again, blood-washed believers are loved alike by the Lord, regardless of temperament. Jesus showed no partiality in this family; He loved all three the same. Many sermons have been preached about Mary and Martha, and—no doubt because of the incident of Luke 10:38—42—Mary is frequently spoken of more favorably than Martha. In our present chapter, however, it seems that Martha in her behavior far outshone Mary, for while Mary sat in the house and refused to come out to meet Jesus, Martha ran out to meet Him the moment she heard that He was coming.

Not all believers display the same emotions under like circumstances. Some are active-minded while others are quiet. Sometimes, when a loved one departs this life, one member of the family will weep until he can weep no more while another member of that family may not shed a tear. Yet the one who does not weep may feel as much or more sorrow than the one who weeps. We cannot judge people by their emotional demonstrations.

The Greek word translated "loved" in verse 5, describing the love of Jesus for this family, is not the same as the word rendered "lovest" in verse 3. The Greek word used in this verse denotes a deep, noble, excellent love, while the word used for "lovest" in verse 3 indicates love as between a child and its parents, or between husband and wife. (The same Greek word is rendered "kiss" in Matthew 26:48, Mark 14:44, and Luke 22:47.) It is understandable therefore that this same Greek word should not be used in referring to the love of Jesus for Mary, Martha, and Lazarus, for if it had been used there are some who would put a question mark around Jesus' love for these sisters—expecially in light of the fact that He did visit this home often and enjoyed fellowshipping there. The Holy Ghost gave John the word to use here to avoid any appearance of evil. How precious it is to know that the Holy Ghost guarded every word penned down in our Bible—another evidence that the Scripture is verbally inspired, dictated to holy men by the Holy Spirit and penned down by them according to God's instructions.

Verse 6: *"When He had heard therefore that he was sick, He abode two days still in the same place where He was."*

Jesus was omniscient and He knew that Lazarus was sick even before He received the message from Martha and Mary. He also knew *why* he was sick, and He knew what would happen. Therefore He made no haste to reach Bethany. He intentionally *"abode two days still in the same place where He was."* Thus when He finally arrived at Bethany, Lazarus had been dead for four days.

Mary and Martha did not have Romans 8:28 as we do, and they must have wondered why Jesus did not come. Surely they were disappointed that He would tarry so long when they had sent Him the message that Lazarus was sick. Sometimes even the most dedicated of believers asks, "Why?" when God delays the answer to prayer. If we pray in faith believing, He *will* answer—in His own time, according to His own will, and to His glory. But like Mary and Martha, we sometimes wonder and ask, "Why?" One day passed after the message was sent, the second day passed, the third day—and still Jesus had not come. Then the fourth day, He arrived.

Jesus knew the anxiety of these two sisters, He knew their agony of soul and spirit; yet He tarried in Bethabara. Sometimes God allows His saints to suffer in order to bring glory and honor to His name and to bless other believers. Jesus could have prevented the anxiety and suffering on the part of Mary and Martha, but He *allowed* it because He had a purpose in it. He could easily have reached the home of Lazarus before he died, He could have healed him and prevented his death. He could have healed him as He healed the nobleman's son—without even *going* to Bethany. But if He had done so, we would not have this glorious chapter—one of the greatest in all the Word of God.

I repeat—sickness and suffering on the part of a believer does not mean that God does not love us or that Jesus has forsaken us. Lazarus was sick to the glory of God—and God can be glorified through the sickness and suffering of His saints today. Knowing this, knowing that "all things work together for good to them that love God, to them who are the called according to His purpose," we should be able to say with Paul, "Most gladly therefore will I rather glory in my infirmities, that the power of Christ may rest upon me" (II Cor. 12:9).

Verse 7: *"Then after that saith He to His disciples, Let us go into Judaea again."*

The Greek language here is more emphatic than the English, denoting an interval of time; and would read, *"Afterwards, after this,* Jesus said to His disciples, Let us go into Judaea again."

"Let us go" is the language of a kind father speaking to his children, or as the Good Shepherd speaking to His sheep. Jesus did not say, *"I* will go," He did not say, *"You go."* He said, "Let US go. We will go together as one group." This indicates that the disciples were permitted to make a decision or offer an opinion about going to Jerusalem, thus showing how close they were to Jesus and how

intimately they lived in fellowship and communion. They answered Him in words that clearly expressed their feelings and their fears.

Verse 8: *"His disciples say unto Him, Master, the Jews of late sought to stone thee; and goest thou thither again?"*

The Greek word here translated *"Master"* is rendered "Rabbi" in many other places. There is nothing discourteous in the disciples' referring to Jesus as "Master"; that form of address was often used in showing honor and respect for a teacher or leader.

"The Jews of late sought to stone thee." This speaks of the Sanhedrin, the Jewish leaders, not the ordinary run of the Jewish people. The word translated *"of late"* is usually rendered "now, at this time." It had been but a short time since the Jews had tried to stone Jesus, and now He was returning to that very place. The meaning here then would be, "Master, the Jews *even now* seek to stone thee!"

"And goest thou thither again?" The tone of the question here indicates that the disciples were surprised to the point of amazement. "Did we *hear* you correctly? Do you really intend returning to Judaea so soon? The Jews will stone you and take your life!" The disciples loved Jesus, they were concerned about His welfare—and it might be supposed that they were also afraid for their *own* lives since they were openly His followers and close companions. I am not intimating that there was hypocrisy on the part of the disciples. They were genuinely apprehensive on behalf of Jesus, and they did not yet fully understand what lay ahead of Him.

Verse 9: *"Jesus answered, Are there not twelve hours in the day? If any man walk in the day, he stumbleth not, because he seeth the light of this world."*

Jesus did not answer their question directly; He answered in a most remarkable way. He could have said, "Be not afraid, I will take care of you—and you need not

fear for *my* life because I will be divinely protected." But
He did not say that. Instead, He quoted a proverb, and
then drew from that proverb lessons about the person who
is planning a journey, and the time that person will choose
for traveling. He drew no conclusion, but left the application to the disciples. This would seem more strange to us
than it did to the disciples. Even today orientals often
quote proverbs in answer to questions.

"Are there not twelve hours in a day?" A day, generally
speaking, has twelve hours of daylight and twelve hours
of darkness. When one is about to make a journey, if he
travels in the daylight hours he can see where he is going,
he can avoid pitfalls, and he will not fall into the hands
of robbers because the sun is shining and he can see the
path clearly. But if he chooses to walk at midnight he
may stumble, he may fall into the hands of thieves and
robbers. An intelligent man traveling by foot will travel
in the daytime—and this was particularly applicable in the
day when Jesus walked on earth.

Jesus had frequently told His disciples, "Mine hour is
not yet." They had witnessed several occasions when the
Jews had tried to kill Him, and every time He had miraculously escaped out of their hands. They should have known
that had it been possible to destroy Jesus He would already
have been destroyed. What He was saying to them here
was simply, "You need have no fear. There is no need to
be troubled because mine hour has not yet come. My day
of twelve hours is not yet over, and as long as I walk in
that day my enemies cannot harm me. In returning to
Bethany I will be as a man traveling in the bright sunlight. My night will soon appear, my hour will soon come;
but there are twelve hours in my ministry and my twelfth
hour has not yet arrived. Yes, we are going to Bethany
again."

I have always believed and preached that a born again
believer who walks in the light (a Christian completely
yielded to Christ) is indestructible. He cannot be destroyed

until his work is done. It is true that there IS a sin unto death (I John 5:16), and a disobedient believer may be cut off; but an obedient Christian is immortal until his work for Jesus is finished here on earth. The devil and all the demons of hell cannot destroy him until he has completed the ministry God gave him to perform.

Verse 10: *"But if a man walk in the night, he stumbleth, because there is no light in him."*

This verse is self-explanatory. There were no street lights, flashlights, or lanterns such as we have today, and the disciples understood clearly that a person who walked in the night would stumble. That was the practical application of what Jesus said. Actually, He was assuring them that He could not be destroyed until His day of work was over, and as long as they walked with Him *they* could not be hurt or destroyed. Later, in the end of His life and ministry on earth, He said to His enemies, "This is your hour, and the power of darkness" (Luke 22:53). Then they arrested Him and led Him away, and the disciples fled. But that was only after His "twelve hours" were ended.

Verse 11: *"These things said He: and after that He saith unto them, Our friend Lazarus sleepeth; but I go, that I may awake him out of sleep."*

(The Greek reads, "Lazarus, the friend of us, has been laid asleep," and the Greek word rendered "sleepeth" means "is dead.") Jesus used this gentle way of breaking the news to the disciples that Lazarus was dead. Our word "cemetery" comes from the same Greek word the Lord used here, and means literally "a sleeping place."

It is interesting that the word "sleep" is never used in reference to the death of an animal; only to man. *Death* is not annihilation; we are not annihilated when we die— we only lie down to rise again. Study Daniel 12:2; Matthew 27:52; Acts 7:60; 13:36; I Corinthians 11:30; 15:1—18; and I Thessalonians 4:13,14.

I am so glad Jesus referred to Lazarus as "friend"! We are servants of God, bondslaves to Jesus Christ; but we are also "friends." In John 15:15 Jesus said to His disciples, "Henceforth I call you not servants; for the servant knoweth not what his lord doeth: but I have called you *friends; for* all things that I have heard of my Father I have made known unto you."

Notice that Jesus did not say, *"MY friend Lazarus,"* but *"OUR friend Lazarus,"* denoting the unity in the body of Christ. In I Corinthians 12:12,13 we read, "For as the body is one, and hath many members, and all the members of that one body, being many, are one body: so also is Christ. *For by one Spirit are we all baptized into one body,* whether we be Jews or Gentiles, whether we be bond or free; and have been all made to drink into one Spirit." Since we all make up one body, when one member of the body suffers, all members suffer; and when one member rejoices, all members are made to rejoice.

"I go, that I may awake him out of sleep." (The Greek reads "that I may *unsleep* him.") Thank God, one of these days—it may be soon—Jesus is coming back to "unsleep" all who have died in the Lord! In the first resurrection the bodies of all who sleep in Jesus will be raised incorruptible and the living saints will be changed "in a moment, in the twinkling of an eye" (I Cor. 15:51–53; I Thess. 4:13–18).

Jesus never made a bolder, more direct declaration than He made here, for in this statement He announced to His disciples that He was going to Bethany *for the express purpose of raising a dead man to life!* Notice in verse 7 He said, "Let US go into Judaea"; but in this verse He said, *"I go,* that I may awake him out of sleep." No one but Jesus could waken Lazarus from the sleep of death. Had this been an ordinary sleep, an ordinary man could have wakened him; but only Jesus has power *within Himself* to raise the dead.

Verse 12: *"Then said His disciples, Lord, if he sleep, he shall do well."*

I do not see how the disciples could misunderstand this statement concerning the death of Lazarus, but evidently they did. Surely they knew that the common expression "fallen asleep" meant death, and they had often heard the dead referred to as being "asleep"; but they were slow to believe and hard of understanding.

The Greek language here translated *"he shall do well"* is sometimes rendered "shall be made whole" and in other places is translated "healed." If the disciples knew what disease Lazarus had and knew that sleep was profitable for one who had that disease, they would naturally have thought that since Lazarus was sleeping, he was getting better and there was no need of their going to Judaea. They had no idea that Jesus was going to Bethany to raise their friend from the dead.

Verse 13: *"Howbeit Jesus spake of his death: but they thought that He had spoken of taking of rest in sleep."*

Peter, James, and John had heard Jesus refer to the dead daughter of Jairus as "sleeping" (Matt. 9:24), yet when He used the same expression about Lazarus they thought He meant that Lazarus was *"taking of rest in sleep"*—natural sleep, not the sleep of death. They misunderstood Jesus on many occasions. They misunderstood Him when He spoke of leaven (Matt. 16:6—12), and again when He said, "I have *meat* to eat that ye know not of" (John 4:32). We may wonder how these disciples could have been so slow of understanding—but many of US are slow to believe, many of us fail to grasp the deep things of God, and WE have the written Word, the complete and perfect law of liberty! We have opportunity to study and ponder these things from the Word of God, whereas the disciples had only the spoken Word, albeit whatever Jesus said was *the Word of God*. We look *back* to Calvary, we are told what happened there, and WHY. Yet many times we fail to comprehend the truths set forth in the Word, just as the disciples misunderstood the parables and figurative language Jesus used on many occasions.

Verse 14:   *"Then said Jesus unto them plainly, Lazarus is dead."*

He had tried to deal tenderly with them, He had tried to break the news to them gently.   "For we have not an High Priest which cannot be touched with the feeling of our infirmities."   Jesus was made "like unto His brethren" in all things, sin apart, that He might be faithful and compassionate.   He is just as gentle and compassionate today as He was when He attempted to break the news of Lazarus' death gently to His disciples.   But He found it necessary to tell them plainly, "Lazarus is *dead.*"   ("Plainly" means that He had to tell them "openly, unreservedly, and without mystery.")

Verse 15:   *"And I am glad for your sakes that I was not there, to the intent ye may believe; nevertheless let us go unto him."*

If Jesus had been present when Lazarus was taken sick, He would no doubt have healed Him because He was in close fellowship with this family and Lazarus was a beloved friend.

You will notice that Jesus did not say, "I am glad Lazarus is *dead.*"   He said, "I am glad . . . that I was not there."   He knew that the experience the disciples would go through because of the death of Lazarus would increase their faith in a marvelous way.   Their hearts were sad because of the loss of their dear friend, they grieved with Mary and Martha; but out of this sad experience much good would come to them.   Their faith would be strengthened and they would be made better witnesses through the raising of Lazarus.   Jesus has no joy in the suffering of His children, He has no pleasure in loved ones weeping over a casket; but He *allows* sickness, suffering, even death, that believers may be strengthened and drawn closer to God. Therefore He said to the disciples, "I am glad *for YOUR sakes* that I was not there."

"To the intent that ye may believe" does not mean that
the disciples would here exercise faith for the first time.
They did have faith in Him, they did believe on Him; but
through this experience they would believe more heartily
and unhesitatingly, they would fully realize that He was
able to do exceeding and abundantly above anything they
could think or ask.

Faith is the first step on the stairs of salvation, the first
rung on the ladder of redemption. To believe on Christ,
to believe in His death, burial, and resurrection "according
to the Scriptures" is to take the first step toward the Pearly
White City. The secret of Christian power, the secret of
becoming an effective soul winner, is to pray, "Lord, *I believe*. Help thou mine unbelief and increase my faith!"

"Nevertheless let us go unto him." Jesus knew Lazarus
would be in the grave when He reached Bethany, but He
said, "Let us go unto him." He knew exactly why He
was going to Bethany and He knew what He would do
when He arrived there.

(It is refreshing to note that in the Scriptures no person
ever died in the presence of Jesus. It is also refreshing to
note that no person *remained* dead in His presence. He
broke up every funeral He attended!)

Verse 16: *"Then said Thomas, which is called Didymus,
unto his fellowdisciples, Let us also go, that we may die
with Him."*

I am sure there are those who find comfort in studying
the life of Thomas. He is mentioned in chapter 14 verse 5
of our present study, and again in chapter 20, verses 24
through 29—and in both instances he is mentioned as being
in the same state of mind as in our present verse. Evidently Thomas was a person who looked on the dark side of
life, always expecting the worst, always seeming to have
doubts and fears. However, it was in answer to Thomas's
question, "Lord, we know not whither thou goest; and how
can we know the way?" that Jesus gave the wonderful

answer, *"I am the way, the truth, and the life: no man cometh unto the Father, but by me!"*

And now it is Thomas saying, *"Let us also go, that we may die with Him."* Even though he was looking on the gloomy side of things, Thomas is to be commended. He was saying to the other disciples, "Come on, let's go with Him even if we *die!* More than likely He will be killed, and we will be killed also. But if He is going to die, we will die *with* Him."

Dear fellow Christian, if you are weak, take courage. One can be weak and have many infirmities, and still be a disciple of Jesus Christ! There is no more common failure among believers than despondency and discouragement. It is foolish to think that all believers possess the same qualities.   Thomas and Peter belonged to the same little disciple band, yet they were exactly opposite in personality. Peter was overzealous, overconfident, impetuous; Thomas was doubtful, hesitant, cautious. But both were disciples of Jesus, both had grace, both were born again believers.

"Thomas, which is called Didymus . . . ." In the Greek, "Didymus" means *two,* or *double.* Many Bible scholars think this name was given to Thomas because of his double character—i. e., he had *faith,* yet he was weak.

This is the only verse in the entire New Testament where the Greek term *"fellowdisciples"* is used. Thomas said to his fellowdisciples, "Let us also go, that we may die with Him." Jesus is not calling on us to *die* for Him today. He wants us to live for Him; but we must admire Thomas, that he was willing to lay down his life if it should come to that.

Verse 17:   *"Then when Jesus came, He found that he had lain in the grave four days already."*

We do not know how long it took Jesus to travel from Bethabara to Bethany. It was a distance of some twenty or thirty miles, about a day's journey for anyone traveling on foot, which was no doubt the way Jesus traveled from

Bethabara "beyond Jordan" to Bethany. When He arrived at Bethany He found that Lazarus *"had lain in the grave four days already."*

It was not the custom of the Jews in that day to embalm the dead—especially those who were not wealthy or in an outstanding social position. Thus it was impossible for a corpse to "lie in state," and without a doubt Lazarus was buried the same day he died.

In the days of our Lord, the Jews believed that when a person died, the spirit stayed beside the tomb for three days and then departed—either to Paradise, or to hell. If Jesus had come to Bethany two or three days after Lazarus died, His enemies might have claimed that the miracle He wrought was counterfeit, that Lazarus had not actually been dead, that he was only unconscious or in a trance. But Jesus intentionally stayed away until the fourth day, and after four days even the Jews could not deny the miracle. The daughter of Jairus was raised immediately after she died (Mark 5:21—42; Luke 8:41—55), and the son of the widow of Nain had been dead only long enough to be on the way to the grave (Luke 7:11—15); but Lazarus had been in the tomb for four days, and his body had already begun to decay.

We can easily point out those four days: Lazarus probably died the same day the messenger left Bethany to carry the news of his illness to Jesus. It was about a day's journey from Bethany to Bethabara beyond Jordan, Jesus tarried *two* days before starting back to Bethany, and it would have taken Him another day to make the journey. So we can count the day the messenger traveled to reach Jesus, the two days Jesus tarried at Bethabara, and the day He traveled to reach Bethany—making a total of four days.

I have often been asked, "What happened to the *spirit* of Lazarus those four days he was in the grave?" There is only one Bible answer to that question: *"absent from the body . . . present with the Lord"* (II Cor. 5:6—8).

Verse 18: *"Now Bethany was nigh unto Jerusalem, about fifteen furlongs off."*

In this verse the Holy Spirit speaks through John to those of us who might not be familiar with Jerusalem and Bethany—and notice how carefully He speaks in the language of man so that we can understand: Bethany was *"nigh unto Jerusalem, ABOUT fifteen furlongs off."* (Fifteen furlongs is about two miles.) The Holy Spirit uses man's terminology: In John 2:6 we read that the waterpots contained *"two or three* firkins apiece." In John 6:19, the the disciples rowed *"ABOUT five and twenty or thirty furlongs."*

Verse 19: *"And many of the Jews came to Martha and Mary, to comfort them concerning their brother."*

Bethany was very near the city of Jerusalem, which partially accounts for the great number of Jews who came from Jerusalem to Bethany to comfort Mary and Martha. Who these Jews were we are not told, but it stands to reason that they were not members of the Sanhedrin; they were not the chief priests, scribes, or elders.

We are told that mourners at a funeral in that day were primarily women, and no doubt this was true in the mourning for Lazarus. In the days when our Lord tabernacled among men it was common practice among the Jews for neighbors and friends to assemble in and around the home for several days to mourn with the relatives when a member of the family died. This custom still prevails in various parts of the world today.

Since *"many"* came to comfort Mary and Martha, we know that the miracle of raising Lazarus from the dead was witnessed by a great company of people who evidently came out from Jerusalem. No doubt some of them came out of curiosity, others came in deference to custom; but regardless of *why* they came, they witnessed one of the greatest miracles wrought by Jesus during His brief earthly ministry.

Verse 20: *"Then Martha, as soon as she heard that Jesus was coming, went and met Him: but Mary sat still in the house."*

No doubt someone was acting as "lookout" for Mary and Martha, watching in the direction from which Jesus would appear, expecting Him at any moment; and His appearance was immediately reported to the sisters. The moment Martha heard the cry, "Jesus comes!" she hurried out to meet Him outside the village.

"But Mary sat still in the house." There is no doubt in my mind that both sisters received the news at the same time. Martha was grieved and sorrowing just as deeply as Mary; but the moment she heard that Jesus was coming she literally *ran* to meet Him. She forgot the anxious days of waiting, the disappointment that He had not come sooner, she was so happy that He had finally arrived. She did not know, of course, that He would bring Lazarus back from the dead, but she did know that He would better the situation in one way or another. She took comfort in the fact that He had come, and she ran to meet Him before He even came into the village—but Mary waited in the house.

It is much easier for Jesus to raise a dead person than it is for Him to heal a wounded spirit—and Mary was wounded, grieved, hurt. Perhaps she said to herself, "He has waited so long, there is really no need for His coming now. Why should I run out to meet Him? I will wait until He comes to where I am." Yes, Mary loved Jesus, just as Martha did. These sisters were true disciples of the Lord Jesus Christ. Mary had shown more grace on a former occasion when she sat at the feet of Jesus and fed from the living bread while Martha was cumbered and anxious about many things; but in our present passage, Martha seems to have displayed more grace than Mary. We previously mentioned the differences in temperament among believers. We are all *saved* alike—through faith in the finished work of Jesus; but we do not all act alike emotionally. Some be-

lievers are quiet and others are demonstrative. We need
Marthas and we need Marys. We should not condemn the
"Marthas" because they are not like the "Marys"—and
vice versa. But in this particular instance I can see no excuse for Mary's attitude. She appeared to be "pouting"
with Jesus.

Verse 21: *"Then said Martha unto Jesus, Lord, if thou
hadst been here, my brother had not died."*

Here Martha made known the true feelings of her heart—
which is what any Christian should do. Uppermost in her
mind was the thought that if Jesus had come when He first
received her message, Lazarus would not have died. Oh
yes, it is possible for even the best of us to become a little
bit grieved, a little bit discouraged, when our prayers are
not answered as we think they should be, when we pray
for some specific need that we think is tremendously important and should be supplied immediately. But when we
become grieved toward our Lord, we should immediately
confess it and unburden our heart to Him as Martha did.

If Martha had had complete confidence, if her faith had
not been tainted with a touch of unbelief, she would not
have said, *"Lord, IF thou hadst been here* my brother
would not have died." She had undoubtedly heard of the
healing of the nobleman's son, and of the healing of the
centurion's servant. In both instances Jesus had simply
spoken the word and those two people were healed. But
Martha's knowledge of the Saviour was limited; therefore
her faith was limited, and in her grief she did not stop to
think. If she had, she would have known that Jesus knew
Lazarus was sick before she sent word to Him and that
His powers were not limited to His presence.

Many times in our own lives we add to our grief by
suggesting what *might* have been done. We say, "IF we
had gotten our loved one to the hospital in time," or "IF
we had called another doctor." We forget that there are
no accidents with God, and whatever comes in the life of

a believer comes because God wills it or allows it. When His will is uppermost in our hearts and minds, then our business is to submit to whatever happens, knowing that God allowed it for a purpose.

Verse 22: *"But I know, that even now, whatsoever thou wilt ask of God, God will give it thee."*

In these words Martha unmistakably declared her faith in Jesus. She hoped against hope; she assured herself that *somehow* this thing would come out all right. She did not know how, but she believed that somehow Jesus would work it out *"even NOW"*—that is, "In spite of the fact that you let our brother die, in spite of the fact that if you had arrived in time he would *not* have died, since he IS dead I know that somehow, through your power with God, you will do something to help us!"

Martha did not realize that Jesus could do anything GOD could do, that He had the same power GOD had to work miracles. She expected Him to pray to God, and God would do something for them in that sad hour.

I say this with a humble heart, but it needs to be said: There are many who have exercised faith in the saving grace of Jesus, they love God, they are truly born again— but there is much leanness of soul because of *ignorance*. They are ignorant of the Scriptures, ignorant of the power of God, ignorant of His will. In I Thessalonians 4:13 Paul refers to ignorance among believers: he said, "I would not have you to be ignorant, brethren . . . ." Many believers miss their spiritual birthright because of spiritual ignorance— which is inexcusable since we have the Word of God, and born again believers possess the *Teacher* of the Word (the Holy Ghost) who can reveal the deep things of God: "Ye have an unction from the Holy One, and ye know all things. . . . But the anointing which ye have received of Him abid- eth in you, and ye need not that any man teach you: but as the same anointing teacheth you of all things, and is truth, and is no lie, and even as it hath taught you, ye shall abide in Him" (I John 2:20,27).

How *much* faith does it take to bring salvation? Just FAITH—*period.* We simply believe God—and *believing,* we are SAVED; but after we are saved we are only babes in Christ and we are commanded, "As newborn babes, desire the sincere milk of the Word," that we may grow thereby (I Pet. 2:2). Paul instructs, "Study to shew thyself approved unto God, a workman that needeth not to be ashamed, rightly dividing the Word of truth" (II Tim. 2:15). There are *degrees* of faith and degrees of *knowledge.* Proverbs 1:7 says, "The fear of the Lord is the *beginning* of knowledge—but we should not stop there. We should desire to *grow* in faith and *grow* in knowledge. We should pray for God to *give us a desire* to know more about His Word and more about His will for our lives.

Verses 23 and 24: *"Jesus saith unto her, Thy brother shall rise again. Martha saith unto Him, I know that he shall rise again in the resurrection at the last day."*

Martha's faith was weak; therefore Jesus began to lead her, tenderly and gently, into the full truth of Himself—His Person and His office. "Faith cometh by hearing, and hearing by the WORD." Jesus was feeding Martha the bread that would cause her little faith to grow. He said, *"Thy brother shall rise again"*—but He did not say WHEN. He did not say, "Stop worrying. I am going to raise your brother immediately."

Martha replied, *"I know that he shall rise again in the resurrection at the last day."* From the Old Testament Scriptures she knew about the resurrection and was assured that her brother would be raised from the dead at that "last day"; but she did not understand that she was standing in the very presence of "the Resurrection and the Life." Martha did not have the epistles of Paul, she did not have the marvelous account of the Rapture as given in I Corinthians chapter 15 and in I Thessalonians chapter 4. She had only the Old Testament Scriptures—but even so, she still had more knowledge of the works of God than do some of the liberals and modernists today who deny the bodily resurrection! She *believed* in the resurrection—but with a vague understanding. In her deep sorrow, "the last day" seemed far off and of little comfort. We who have the complete, perfect Word of God have a "better hope" and a clearer view of the resurrection. We know that believers will be raised in the Rapture (the first resurrection), and the wicked will not be raised until a thousand years later (the second resurrection). See Revelation 20:4—6.

It seems to me there was a note of disappointment in Martha's reply. She said, "Oh, yes—I *know* he will rise again, but that is a long way off, *in the last day.* We loved him so much, we miss him so much, and we need comfort NOW, not cold comfort for the future."

Verses 25 and 26: *"Jesus said unto her, I am the resurrection, and the life: he that believeth in me, though he were dead, yet shall he live: and whosoever liveth and believeth in me shall never die. Believest thou this?"*

Martha believed that GOD would raise the dead in the great resurrection morning, but Jesus here declared to her, *"I AM the resurrection."* He was showing her that He needed no help to raise the dead. He was not just a *teacher* of the resurrection, He was THE resurrection. He IS the divine Author of the resurrection; He is THE life, whether physical or spiritual. Jesus is the source of life, He is the spring of life; and whatever life one possesses—eternal, spiritual, or physical—is because of Him. It is He who quickens us (Eph. 2:1), it is He who will raise us from the grave. *Without* Him there IS no life. Revelation 1:18 proclaims, "I AM HE THAT LIVETH, AND WAS DEAD; AND, BEHOLD, I AM ALIVE FOR EVERMORE, AMEN; AND HAVE THE KEYS OF HELL AND OF DEATH!"

"He that believeth in me, though he were dead, yet shall he live." In the Greek this statement reads, "Though he has died." Therefore what Jesus said to Martha was

this: *"Believers*—even though they die and are laid in the grave, and even though the body has returned to dust—shall live again. They shall be raised by MY POWER, for I AM the resurrection. All who believe in me cannot be holden of death. Because I live, they shall live also." Just as surely as death could not hold the body of Jesus, just that surely all who believe in Him will be delivered from the grave—bodily. (The spirit never goes to the grave. The split second a *believer* departs this life he is in the presence of God; and when an *unbeliever* dies, he immediately opens his eyes in hell. Read Luke 16:22,23.)

When Jesus returns for His Church in the Rapture, the dead in Christ will be raised first (I Thess. 4:16,17). Their *bodies* will be raised, Jesus will bring their spirits with Him—all the saints who are now resting in Paradise. Living saints will be changed "in the twinkling of an eye" (I Cor. 15:51—53), and together we will be caught up in the clouds to meet the Lord in the air, and we shall live and reign with Him a thousand years. "But the rest of the dead (the wicked dead) lived not again until the thousand years were finished" (Rev. 20:4—6).

In the previous verse, Jesus spoke of those believers who had died, and of a physical resurrection. In our present study, He speaks of living believers and makes the comforting and assuring declaration that *"whosoever believeth in me shall never die"*—that is, he shall not die *eternally.* The moment a person accepts Christ as Saviour, he begins a life that will never end. The second death will have no power over him. His body may be laid in the grave for awhile, but the *sting* of bodily death is removed (I Cor. 15:55).

Jesus asked Martha, *"Believest thou this?"* There are many today—even entire denominations—who claim to be Christian and yet do not believe in the bodily resurrection; but regardless of what various religions teach, *God's Word* teaches bodily resurrection, and God's Word is *forever settled in heaven.*

In other words, Jesus asked Martha, "Do you believe that I can and will raise your brother from the dead? Do you believe that I am the resurrection and the life—very God in flesh?"

It is interesting to note that the words "I AM" occur at least twenty times in the Gospel of John, with reference to Jesus. Sometimes we read, "I AM He" (with "He" in italics, denoting that it is not in the original text). Sometimes we read, "I AM" in connection with other words, such as "I AM the way," but *always* the "I AM" identifies Jesus with Jehovah God, the great "I AM" in Exodus 3:14: "And God said unto Moses, I AM THAT I AM: and He said, Thus shalt thou say unto the children of Israel, I AM hath sent me unto you."

"I AM the bread of life" (ch. 6, v. 35).

"I AM that bread of life" (ch. 6, v. 48).

"I AM the living bread" (ch. 6, v. 51).

"I AM the light of the world" (ch. 8, v. 12).

"I AM from above . . . I AM not of this world" (ch.8, v. 23).

"If ye believe not . . . I AM" (ch. 8, v. 24).

"Ye shall know that I AM . . . and that I do nothing of myself" (ch. 8, v. 28).

"Before Abraham was, I AM" (ch. 8, v. 58).

"As long as I AM in the world, I AM the light of the world" (ch. 9, v. 5).

"I AM the door of the sheep" (ch. 10, v. 7).

"I AM the door: by me if any man enter in, he shall be saved, and shall go in and out, and find pasture" (ch. 10, v. 9).

"I AM the Good Shepherd" (ch. 10, v. 11, v. 14).

"I AM the resurrection, and the life" (ch. 11, v. 25).

"Ye call me Master and Lord: and ye say well; for so I AM" (ch. 13, v. 13).

"Now I tell you before it come, that, when it is come to pass, ye may believe that I AM" (ch. 13, v. 19).

"I AM the way, the truth, and the life: no man cometh

unto the Father, but by me" (ch. 14, v. 6).

"I AM the true vine" (ch. 15, v. 1).

"I AM He!" (ch. 18, vv. 4—8). These were the words that caused the enemies of Jesus to go backward and fall to the ground when they came to arrest Him in the Garden of Gethsemane. Yes, Jesus was the great "I AM," very God in flesh.

Verse 27: *"She saith unto Him, Yea, Lord: I believe that thou art the Christ, the Son of God, which should come into the world."*

The Greek here reads, "I *have* believed and *do* believe." In other words, "I not only believe this moment, I also *have believed* that you are the Christ, the Son of God, the promised Redeemer." Martha's answer seems to be only a general confirmation of her belief that the Lord was the promised Messiah; but even so, she gave a wonderful testimony here, a marvelous confession of faith, considering that she lived before the death, burial, and resurrection of Jesus Christ. How different from the parents of the man born blind (ch. 9), who refused to confess Jesus as the Healer of their son because they feared they would be expelled from the synagogue! Where they were cowardly and seemingly thankless, Martha was extraordinarily bold and courageous in her confession of what faith she had.

Verse 28: *"And when she had so said, she went her way, and called Mary her sister secretly, saying, The Master is come, and calleth for thee."*

I do not know what Jesus said to Martha, nor when and how He gave her a message for Mary. He had not yet gone into the village, but since Martha *"called Mary her sister secretly"* we know that Jesus *did* send a personal message to her, and Martha's manner of delivering that message points again to the close fellowship this family enjoyed with our Lord. Martha did not run into the house and excitedly call out the message Jesus sent to Mary. She told her *"secretly"*—(she whispered). Whatever message Jesus sent to Mary was for the comfort and encouragement of these two sisters, and when Mary left the house to go to the edge of the village where Jesus was, no one but Martha knew where she was going, or why. *"The Master is come, and calleth for thee."*

Verse 29: *"As soon as she heard that, she arose quickly, and came unto Him."*

The Greek here reads, "She, when she heard, arises and quickly comes to Him," both verbs being in the present tense. Mary's sudden action was not because Jesus had arrived at the edge of the village, but because of the personal invitation He had sent her. She was crushed under the grief and sorrow she had borne for the four days since Lazarus died, but the personal message from Jesus caused her to rise up and quickly go out to meet Him.

Verse 30: *"Now Jesus was not yet come into the town, but was in that place where Martha met Him."*

Mary immediately responded to the invitation of Jesus to come to where He was, just outside the village of Bethany. His invitation is still "Come . . . Come unto me, and I will give you rest." God invited Noah, "Come thou, and all thy house, into the ark"—and if Noah had not accepted that invitation he would have perished in the flood. Personally, I believe if Mary had remained in the house, if she had refused to go where Jesus was, her brother would have remained in the grave!

Verse 31: *"The Jews then which were with her in the house, and comforted her, when they saw Mary, that she rose up hastily and went out, followed her, saying, She goeth unto the grave to weep there."*

No doubt the house of Mary and Martha was crowded with those who had come to mourn with them and to offer what comfort they could; but since Martha *"secretly"* de-

livered the Lord's message to Mary, these Jews did not
hear the message and they did not know Jesus was at the
edge of the village. They did not know where Mary was
going when she rose up and left the house so quickly, and
they followed her—thereby witnessing one of the greatest
miracles of Christ's entire ministry.

They said, *"She goeth unto the grave to weep there."*
It was customary in those days for people to go to the grave
and weep over loved ones who had departed this life. They
did not have the light we have today concerning the resurrection; they did not have the marvelous epistles of Paul,
declaring that to be absent from the body is to be present
with the Lord. So they went often to the tomb of a departed loved one, sometimes spending many hours there,
weeping and mourning over their dead.

Verse 32: *"Then when Mary was come where Jesus was,
and saw Him, she fell down at His feet, saying unto Him,
Lord, if thou hadst been here, my brother had not died."*

Mary used the same words Martha had uttered (v. 21).
Both sisters were confident that if Jesus had arrived in time,
Lazarus would not have died, and both were disappointed
that He had tarried so long before coming to them. But
notice the difference in the two sisters when they *met* Jesus:
When Martha met Him she simply said, "If you had been
here, Lazarus would not have died." When Mary saw Jesus, *she fell at His feet.* Does this mean that Mary was
more deeply grieved than Martha? Does it mean that she
was more *humble* than Martha? I think it simply shows
the difference in the emotional makeup of the individual.
Martha was no doubt as deeply grieved as Mary was by
her brother's death; but Mary was easily moved, less ret-
icent about showing her emotions, more prone to give way
to her feelings. Thus, completely overcome with her grief,
she fell down at the feet of Jesus and cried, "Lord, if thou
hadst been here, my brother had not died!" Mary, too,
failed to recognize the divine power of Jesus; she was not

aware that He was the resurrection and the life. No doubt she, like Martha, believed that Lazarus would be raised in the "last day," but she had no assurance that Jesus could raise him at that moment, in His own power.

Verse 33: *"When Jesus therefore saw her weeping, and the Jews also weeping which came with her, He groaned in the spirit, and was troubled."*

Jesus was God in flesh—but He was also *man*; and we see here that He could sympathize with His people. He was, as we are, capable of feeling and weeping. When He saw Mary's grief, and the Jews weeping with her, He was touched and *"He groaned in the spirit."*

I am glad Jesus was God, but I am also glad that He was man. I am glad He was so human, so like us, that He could be stirred by the tears of those He loved; and when He saw Mary and the Jews weeping, He wept in sympathy! *"For verily He took not on Him the nature of angels; but He took on Him the seed of Abraham. Wherefore in all things it behoved Him to be made like unto His brethren, that He might be a merciful and faithful high priest in things pertaining to God, to make reconciliation for the sins of the people"* (Heb. 2:16,17).

When Jesus ascended back to the Father He did not leave behind Him His ability to sympathize with us. He is now in a *glorified body,* but He still feels as human nature feels. Sitting at the right hand of the Majesty on high, He is touched with the feeling of our infirmities. He understands when we weep, when we are filled with sorrow. He understands as perfectly today as when He stood at the tomb of Lazarus. He is able to save and able to keep—yes; but He is also able to feel our sorrows and our heartaches. He walked this path before He called upon believers to walk it, and He knows every grief and pitfall that comes across our pathway.

When Jesus, in sympathy with Mary and her friends, *"groaned in His spirit, and was troubled,"* He was expressing the deepest inward agitation of mind and spirit, agitation in which compassion, grief, and holy hatred of sin's work in the world were mingled together in the groan He gave forth in His spirit. Seeing the tears of Mary and the Jews, He thought of the sorrow sin had brought upon the human race. He was thinking with the brokenhearted sisters as He groaned in His spirit, troubled because He saw sorrow, disappointment, and pain on the faces of those who were weeping because sin had claimed the physical life of a loved one. Physical death is the result of Adam's disobedience. Through the disobedience of Adam, death moved upon all men.

In Mark 14:33,34, in the Garden of Gethsemane, Jesus "taketh with Him Peter and James and John, and began to be sore amazed, and to be very heavy; and saith unto them, *My soul is exceeding sorrowful unto death . . . .*" But there is a difference between the suffering of Jesus at the tomb of Lazarus and His agony in the Garden. At the tomb of Lazarus He groaned in His spirit, thinking with the grieving Mary and Martha. In the garden *He was pouring out His SOUL* to save sinners, loving *a world* of sinners, so burdened that in His prayer His perspiration became as drops of blood. He "groaned in His spirit" when the grief of a family rested heavily upon Him; but His *soul* was sorrowful unto death when the sins of all sinners of all ages pressed down upon Him in the Garden of Gethsemane, pressed so heavily that blood stained His perspiration.

Jesus not only *"groaned in His spirit,"* He was also *"troubled."* *Why* was He troubled? He was God in flesh, He knew what He would do, so why should He be *troubled?* The answer is clear: Jesus was man as well as God, and *as man* He had all the feelings, passions, and affections of man—but He also had perfect control of those feelings, passions, and affections. He did not allow them to overcome Him as Mary did (and as WE often do). He was moved with the sight before Him—He saw the Jews weeping, He saw Mary and Martha weeping; but He was also moved because of the warm place held in His heart by Mary, Martha, and Lazarus.

Certainly this shows us that it is not wrong to weep when we are filled with sorrow. Some people think it is "dignified" to be cold and without feeling, refusing to shed a tear; but I thank God that Christ could weep with those who wept. Sympathy is Christ-like. It is lack of faith to allow sorrow to *overcome* us, for if we are born again Jesus is willing, ready, and anxious to carry our sorrows and griefs; but it is not wrong to be sympathetic and understanding, and may God pity the person who cannot show sympathy or shed a tear.

Verse 34: *"And said, Where have ye laid him? They said unto Him, Lord, come and see."*

Jesus the divine Son of God, knowing all things, did not need to ask where the tomb of Lazarus was; but He was *"very MAN"* and as man He asked where His friend was buried, just as you or I would do. No doubt He asked the question in the presence of the Jews, so that they would know He had had nothing to do with the choice of the tomb and that it was not pre-arranged that Lazarus be brought *out* of the tomb. Had Jesus gone to the grave without asking where it was, some of His enemies would have ridiculed and persecuted Him, saying that it was all planned and pre-arranged, that Lazarus was not really dead and it was only a "publicity stunt."

In the Garden of Eden, the God who *created* Adam certainly knew where Adam was when He walked in the garden in the cool of the day after Adam had sinned and was hiding among the trees; but He called out, "Adam, *where art thou?"* Jesus asked in the same spirit, although He knew where the body of Lazarus had been laid, just as God knew where Adam was. They *asked* because, although God, they were dealing with men.

"They said unto Him, Lord, come and see." Of course these people were unaware that Jesus was about to raise

Lazarus from the dead. No doubt they thought that He was going to the grave with Mary and Martha to weep and mourn there. His question, "Where have ye laid him?" created an interest, and I am sure there was quite a congregation at the tomb to witness the tremendous miracle.

Verse 35: *"Jesus wept."*

This is the shortest verse in the Bible—and to me it is also one of the greatest. Every Bible student appreciates the miracles of Jesus and marvels at His power to perform them; but tears on the cheeks of our Lord are a sight to the human eye that no words can explain! The finite mind of man cannot understand how the King of angels could weep, nor why He *should* weep—the only begotten Son of God, God in flesh, *weeping*—tears streaming down His face. It is almost beyond our comprehension that He who was in the beginning, He who knew eternal splendor, should become acquainted with the sorrows and tears of sinful men. But such is His love! and as He approached the tomb of Lazarus, He wept.

There is no doubt in my mind that Jesus wept in sympathy with His friends whom He loved so dearly; but I am sure He also wept for the suffering sin had brought to the world and upon mankind. There were many graves near the place where Lazarus was buried, and there would be many more in days to come. Each tomb signified that there was a home filled with sorrow and grief-stricken loved ones, all because of man's sin. The scene upon which Jesus looked that day was anything but what God had *intended* this world to be! Sin had hurt the world, sin had brought grief to the friends of Jesus, and sin would nail the Saviour to the cross—not His sins, *but ours!* These things Jesus saw as He stood with the bereaved sisters and wept.

The Word of God gives three accounts of Jesus weeping. In our present passage He wept in sympathy with friends. In Luke 19:41—44 He wept because of what sin was doing to His own people:

"And when He was come near, He beheld the city, *and wept over it,* saying, If thou hadst known, even thou, at least in this thy day, the things which belong unto thy peace! but now they are hid from thine eyes. For the days shall come upon thee, that thine enemies shall cast a trench about thee, and compass thee round, and keep thee in on every side, and shall lay thee even with the ground, and thy children within thee; and they shall not leave in thee one stone upon another; because thou knewest not the time of thy visitation."

Israel had rejected the Messiah, and *because* they had rejected Him God had no alternative but to destroy the city of David. Jesus knew that when Titus the Roman moved in upon Jerusalem, tens of thousands of the Jews would be slaughtered in the streets, and the Holy City would be leveled to the ground. Therefore, looking out over the city, He wept tears of sorrow.

Paul gives us the other account of Jesus weeping. In Hebrews 5:7 we read, "Who in the days of His flesh, when He had offered up *prayers and supplications with strong crying and tears* unto Him that was able to save Him from death, and was heard in that He feared . . . ."

In Luke's account of the agony in the garden, we read, "And being in an agony He prayed more earnestly: and His sweat was as it were great drops of blood falling down to the ground" (Luke 22:44). Paul adds the significant fact that bitter tears were mingled with the blood! As Jesus prayed in the Garden of Gethsemane He faced all the demons of hell, and felt the weight of all the sin of all the world pressing down upon Him. Already He had begun to taste the bitterness of the cup of sorrow He was to drink. In the garden He faced all that hell could throw against Him, and we will never know until we sit in the heavenly Bible class just how much our sins hurt the Saviour as He wept, His perspiration stained with blood.

This little verse, "Jesus wept," the shortest verse in all of the Word of God, assures us that our Lord was just as human as He was divine. Not only did He hunger, thirst, eat, drink, speak, sleep, walk, grow weary, feel indignation, and rejoice like other men; He did all of these things *without sin,* and above all, He wept. We do not read in the Scriptures where angels, cherubim, seraphim, or any heavenly creature ever shed tears. Weeping is peculiar to mankind.

Verse 36:   *"Then said the Jews, Behold how He loved him!"*

Of all graces, love is the most powerful in arresting the attention of men and in influencing the opinion of the world. Love is the most powerful force known to God or man. It was love that brought Jesus from the Father's bosom to a world of sin and sorrow. It was love that held Him to the cross as He paid the sin-debt. The love Jesus revealed here for Mary, Martha, and Lazarus touched the hearts of even His enemies and made them cry out, "Behold, how He loved him!" (*"Behold"* denotes surprise. They were surprised that Jesus loved Lazarus so much that He wept tears of sorrow at the graveside.)

Verse 37:   *"And some of them said, Could not this Man, which opened the eyes of the blind, have caused that even this man should not have died?"*

There seems to be a note of sarcasm here—that is, "Could not this fellow, if He *really* opened the eyes of the blind, have kept Lazarus from dying? If He loved him so much that He weeps over his death, could He not have *prevented* his dying? If He can really perform miracles, and if He loved Lazarus so much, why did He not prove His love by coming and preventing this death?"

Verse 38:   *"Jesus therefore again groaning in Himself cometh to the grave. It was a cave, and a stone lay upon it."*

We find the same Greek word here translated "groaning" as in verse 33 where Jesus "groaned in the spirit." Here,

He groaned *"in Himself"* — He groaned inwardly, spiritually, under the influence of deep, inward emotion as He *"cometh to the grave."*

The Jews did not bury their dead within the boundaries of their cities or villages; they buried them outside the town, on hillsides and in the countryside. We are told here that the grave of Lazarus *"was a cave, and a stone lay upon it."* The Jews seldom buried their dead in graves as we do in this country. Sometimes they dug a grave (Luke 11:44), but usually they buried their dead in tombs hewn from rock in the side of a hill, or in caves. The body of Jesus was laid in a tomb cut from a rock, and a large stone was rolled across the opening to the tomb. The *caves* were sloping, and this appears to have been the kind of grave in which Lazarus was buried, for the Scripture tells us that "a stone lay *UPON it."*

Verse 39: *"Jesus said, Take ye away the stone. Martha, the sister of him that was dead, saith unto Him, Lord, by this time he stinketh: for he hath been dead four days."*

"Take ye away the stone." The same Greek word is used here as is used in verse 41 where Jesus "lifted up His eyes," suggesting that the stone was *lifted* from the grave and placed over beside it. (We note in Matthew 28:2 that the stone was *"rolled back"* from the sepulchre of Jesus.)

Jesus did not need to tell anyone to take away the stone; He could have spoken a word and the stone would have been removed, but He called upon others to take it away in order that they might be more deeply impressed with the miracle. When He performed His first miracle at the marriage in Cana, in changing the water into wine He called upon the servants to fill the pots with water. He did not need anyone to fill the waterpots; He could have spoken the word and the wine would have been there — but He called on the servants to do what they could. They could not change the water into wine, but they *could* fill the waterpots in obedience to His instructions.

No doubt the stone over the tomb of Lazarus was a very large stone and would have required a number of men to move it.   I wonder how many of them later told far and wide of the part they had in assisting the Lord Jesus when He raised Lazarus from the dead?

"Lord, by this time he stinketh."   Martha's statement here proved beyond any doubt that Lazarus was really dead, and those who helped remove the stone had assurance that there was a corpse in the grave—the odor from the decaying body would have convinced them of that.

Although Martha was a devout disciple of Jesus—she loved Him, she believed that He was Messiah—she again revealed her incomplete knowledge of His Person and His power.   When He commanded the stone to be taken away from the tomb, she suggested to Him that He did not realize just how long Lazarus had been dead! ("By this time *he stinketh!"*)   If she had had complete faith in the power of Jesus, God in flesh, she would have known that He could raise Lazarus after he had been dead four days just as easily as He could have raised him after he had been dead four minutes.

The same is true in the spiritual aspect: one who has been a sinner for a long lifetime is no more difficult for Jesus to save than a child who has just reached the age of accountability.   It is more difficult for a hardened sinner to *receive the Gospel* than it is for a child to receive it, but so far as God's part is concerned, He finds no difficulty in saving "whosoever will," regardless of how long that person has been dead in trespasses and sins.

Verse 40:   *"Jesus saith unto her, Said I not unto thee, that, if thou wouldest believe, thou shouldest see the glory of God?"*

Without faith it is impossible to please God (Heb. 11:6). If we would see the miracles of God, we must first believe. The natural man wants to SEE—and then believe; but God's formula for miracles is *"Believe* and you will SEE."

"Said I not unto thee . . . ?" This reminds us how prone we are to forget what Jesus has said to us. We read the Word, we read His wonderful promises, but we forget so easily! Jesus has said many things to us, but how many of them do we keep in our hearts, *constantly believing?*

Bible scholars do not agree as to what Jesus meant here when He referred to a previous message. There are various ideas about *when* He said this, or what else was said in connection with it. We know that He sent word back to the sisters that "this sickness is not unto death, but to the glory of God," and perhaps it was something in that message that He referred to here. We can safely assume that Jesus had taught many times in the home of Mary, Martha, and Lazarus, and no doubt His teaching included the marvelous truth that "all things are possible to him that believeth" (Mark 9:23). Surely these dear friends and the Lord Jesus had often discussed the things of God.

Unbelief limits the power of Omnipotence and ties the hands of God. In Matthew 13:58 we read that Jesus could not do mighty miracles and mighty works in His home town because of the unbelief there. Unbelief is the ugliest sin mortal man can commit against a holy God. It is the sin that has damned every soul that begs for water in hell today: "He that believeth on Him is not condemned: but he that believeth not is condemned already, because he hath not believed in the name of the only begotten Son of God" (John 3:18).

Verse 41: *"Then they took away the stone from the place where the dead was laid. And Jesus lifted up His eyes, and said, Father, I thank thee that thou hast heard me."*

"THEN they took away the stone." It seems that what Martha said in the previous verse caused the men who were about to remove the stone to pause for a moment. When she made the statement that Lazarus had been dead for

four days and had begun to deteriorate, the men who were about to lift the stone must have stopped; but after Jesus assured Martha that if she would only *believe* she would witness a glorious thing, *"then"* they removed the stone.

As soon as the stone was removed, *"Jesus lifted up His eyes, and said, Father I thank thee that thou hast heard me."* Who but the Son of God would pray a prayer like this? Even before He prayed He thanked God that His prayer was already heard—and therefore He did not really need to pray *at all!* He prayed the prayer for the sake of the Jews who were listening, those who thought that He was an enemy to God, an impostor. By His prayer He assured the Jews that He was *not* God's enemy but God's beloved Son, and that God would hear and answer His prayer.

Beloved, this was a breathless moment! Can you picture that company of Jews standing around the mouth of this tomb after the stone was removed? In the prevailing quietness people could hear their own hearts beating. They waited expectantly. Was Jesus really going to bring a dead man back to life, a man who had been dead for four days and had deteriorated to the point where they could smell the stench of his dead body? Then as they stood waiting, *Jesus began to pray.* He lifted His eyes toward heaven, and prayed in an audible voice to the heavenly Father— first giving thanks, assuring the Father that He knew His prayer was answered when He prayed it.

It is most interesting to me to notice that Jesus *"lifted up His eyes."* Also in John 17:1 we read, "These words spake Jesus, *and lifted up His eyes to heaven . . . ."* Almost all of us *bow* our heads when we pray—and rightly so; but Jesus lifted His eyes to heaven. It is not *necessary* that we close our eyes when we pray. I believe that in public prayer, in a group or in a public place, we *should* bow our head and close our eyes to shut out all interference; but if we are praying alone, in private, we can pray with our eyes open. It is wonderful to look toward the

sky and talk to God! He is there—we cannot see Him with
the human eye, but we can look toward the place where
we know He is.

Jesus first *gave thanks* to God. Most of us are too busy
asking to thank God for what He has already done for us.
We should thank God, worship and praise Him for answered prayers. Jesus prayed on many occasions; sometimes He prayed all night—and if HE, the Son of God,
spent so much time in prayer, how much more do WE
need to be in communion with God! We should make
our requests and our needs known to Him, for even though
He knows our needs even before we ask, it pleases Him
for us to call upon Him; but it also pleases Him for us to
praise Him, worship Him, and give thanks to Him. I am
afraid believers are much more ready to *ask* than to give
thanks.

Verse 42: *"And I knew that thou hearest me always:
but because of the people which stand by I said it, that
they may believe that thou hast sent me."*

Tremendous words, deep in meaning! *"Thou hearest
me ALWAYS."* Jesus came into the world on a singular
mission—to do the Father's will, to work the works the
Father gave Him to do. He came because He was the
only one who could take the sinner's place, pay the sin-
debt, and open the door of salvation for all who will believe. Therefore He had the assurance *before the world
was* that God the Father would hear and answer His prayer.

It stands to reason that there was a great company of
people around the tomb of Lazarus—and by His prayer
Jesus announced to them that the great miracle He was
about to perform was a work God the Father had given
Him to do, and that it would prove to them that God had
sent Him, commissioned and empowered Him, and that
He was truly God's Christ, their Messiah, the Sent One.
In the earlier part of the Lord's ministry (Matt. 12:24) His
enemies had accused Him of performing miracles by the

power of Beelzebub, prince of devils. He wanted them to know that this last great miracle was a work that the Father had sent Him to do, and *through* this work they would see divine proof that He was God's Christ, their promised Messiah.

The meaning in the prayer Jesus prayed seems to be this: "Father, I am not giving thanks because I doubted that you would hear me.   I am giving thanks because I know that you ALWAYS hear and answer my prayers.   I am praying publicly for the sake of these poor unbelieving Jews, that they may *see and believe* that I do what I do to bring glory to your name.   I am praying this prayer audibly that these poor, blinded, unbelievers may know that I perform this last great miracle as THE SENT ONE. I do this as the last visible evidence that I am your Son, God in flesh, the Messiah."

Certainly God the Father heard the prayers of Jesus always, because God the Son and God the Father are one— in essence, in nature, in will.   The prayer Jesus prayed here proved to His enemies that what He was about to do would be done with God's approval.

Verse 43:   *"And when He thus had spoken, He cried with a loud voice, Lazarus, come forth."*

I wonder how the expectant crowd felt when Jesus cried out with a loud voice.   Personally, I believe His voice could have been heard by hundreds as He called, "LAZARUS, COME FORTH!"   The Greek word translated "cried" means a very loud and piercing cry.   Every person around the tomb heard Jesus call the name of Lazarus, and you may rest assured that every eye was fixed on the open tomb.   This is the last stage of the last great public miracle recorded by John.

It is interesting that Jesus did not say, "Father, *bring* Lazarus forth," or "Father, raise Lazarus from the dead." Jesus Himself spoke the words that brought Lazarus from the grave—His last effort to convince the Jews that He was their Messiah. Lazarus was addressed *personally*. If Jesus had simply said, *"Come forth,"* all believers in the graves would have been raised from the dead.

Verse 44: *"And he that was dead came forth, bound hand and foot with graveclothes: and his face was bound about with a napkin. Jesus saith unto them, Loose him, and let him go."*

When I read verse 43, and then read, *"He that was dead CAME FORTH,"* I do indeed marvel at the power of the Word of God. We will never know the power of the Word this side of heaven, but we do know that the Word is "the power of God unto salvation," it is "the incorruptible seed" that brings the new birth, and we can understand why the devil has done everything in His diabolical power to *discredit* the Word of God. Those who deny the complete truth of the Word—the miracles of Jesus, His Incarnation and virgin birth—are ministers of Satan. They are called, commissioned, sent, and energized by the devil, and they will surely burn in hell because of their preaching of error:

"For such are false apostles, deceitful workers, transforming themselves into the apostles of Christ. And no marvel; for Satan himself is transformed into an angel of light. Therefore it is no great thing if his ministers also be transformed as the ministers of righteousness; *whose end shall be according to their works"* (II Cor. 11:13—15).

Lazarus had been dead for four days, his body was already in the process of decomposition, and the horrible odor of corruption came from the opened tomb. Yet three words from Jesus—"Lazarus, come forth"—brought this man immediately out of the grave, *alive!* A more distinct, unmistakeable miracle could not have been possible. Anyone who witnessed the raising of Lazarus certainly knew that only Almighty God could perform such a miracle.

Lazarus came forth from the grave *"bound hand and foot with graveclothes: and his face was bound about with a napkin."* This does not necessarily mean that Lazarus was bound so tightly, or that his legs were so tied together, that he could not have *walked* out of the grave. It is not impossible that he came out *without* walking, but personally, I believe his graveclothes did not prevent him from coming out on his own feet. To me it would have been much greater to see him come forth under his own power, walking slowly, than for him to float out like a spirit. Jesus had given life, health, and strength back to Lazarus, and I believe they watched him as he slowly came forth, bound hand and foot, with a napkin around his face—the customary way of preparing people for burial in that day.

In verse 39 Jesus had said, "Take ye away the stone," and now He says, *"Loose him, and let him go!"* Those who took away the stone from the door of the tomb could not deny the fact that a *dead* man lay in the tomb; and those who removed the napkin from the face of Lazarus, those who removed the graveclothes that bound him, knew that they were touching a real, live man—they could feel his flesh, they were convinced that he was not a ghost or a spirit. It is entirely possible that the men who carried the body of Lazarus *to* the grave were among those who helped to remove the graveclothes from him. When Jesus healed the blind man (chapter 9) the Jews questioned the man's parents, doubting that he had really been born blind, thus putting a question mark around the miracle; but certainly no one could question the raising of Lazarus! There could be no doubt that this man from whom they removed the graveclothes was the same man they had prepared for burial four days before. *This* miracle was attested to by the senses—they had *smelled* the odor of the decaying body when the tomb was opened, they had *heard* Jesus call, "Lazarus, come forth," they had *seen* Lazarus as he came from the tomb, and they had *touched* him as they removed the graveclothes. There was no denying that the miracle had taken place, and there was no denying that only GOD could have wrought such a miracle. Thus the enemies of Jesus were silenced for a time.

Some Believe

Verse 45: *"Then many of the Jews which came to Mary, and had seen the things which Jesus did, believed on Him."*

Some of the Jews who had come to comfort Mary and Martha in their sorrow no longer denied that Jesus was truly God's Christ. They believed on Him. I personally believe that this was more than intellectual belief; I think it was "heart belief," and if they were not fully converted at that time they became learners, seekers of truth, and no doubt were among the great number who were saved on the Day of Pentecost. I do not doubt that more rejected Him than believed on Him, but the Scripture says, *"Many* of the Jews . . . believed on Him."

It would be most interesting to know how Mary and Martha reacted when their brother came forth from the grave, but the heavenly Father did not see fit to make this known to us. We cannot doubt that this could be counted as the greatest day of their lives, and certainly their faith was greatly increased through the Lord's raising of Lazarus.

Verse 46: *"But some of them went their ways to the Pharisees, and told them what things Jesus had done."*

The same sun that melts the ice will harden clay into bricks. The Gospel that softens hearts will also *harden* hearts when it is rejected over and over again. Some of the Jews were softened in their hearts by the miracle they had just witnessed, others were hardened. Their minds were already made up, they hated Jesus, and it angered them to see Him perform a miracle they could not explain. Therefore they rushed to the temple to tell the Sanhedrin what had happened at Bethany that day.

Some folk today think that if they could only *see a miracle* they could believe and be saved; but seeing miracles does not necessarily bring men to God. Luke 16:19—31 gives the account of the rich man and the beggar Lazarus.

Lazarus died and was carried by the angels into Abraham's bosom. The rich man also died, and opened his eyes in hell. He begged Abraham to send Lazarus to his father's house to witness to his five brothers and warn them not to come to the place of torment where *he* was; but Abraham replied, "They have Moses and the prophets (the Old Testament Scriptures); let them hear them. . . If they hear not Moses and the prophets, *neither will they be persuaded, though one rose from the dead!"*

We see the same truth illustrated in our present passage. Jesus had just wrought a miracle that only the supernatural power of Almighty God could have wrought—and surely every Jew present that day recognized that fact. But instead of that knowledge *softening* their hearts, they again rejected Jesus and rushed to the authorities to urge them to put an immediate end to the ministry of Jesus.

It is most interesting that there is not one thing mentioned about Lazarus, no record of what happened to him, in the ensuing weeks, months, or years of his life. We do not know how long he lived, we have no record of his life *after his resurrection.* We need not marvel that he did not tell what he saw, heard, and experienced during the period his body was in the grave and his spirit was in Paradise, because Paul tells us in II Corinthians 12:1—4 that he knew a man in Christ who was caught up into Paradise, *"and heard unspeakable words, which it is not lawful for a man to utter."*

It is comforting to know that when Jesus comes in the Rapture the same voice that cried, "Lazarus, come forth!" will call forth the bodies of the saints from graves, wherever they are. *"The dead shall hear the voice of the Son of God: and they that hear shall live"* (John 5:25).

The Enemies of Jesus Plot to Put Him to Death

Verse 47: *"Then gathered the chief priests and the Pharisees a council, and said, What do we? for this Man doeth many miracles."*

This "council" was no doubt the Sanhedrin, governing body of the Jewish religion. It was purely ecclesiastical and had nothing to do with civil rule or politics. Religious dictators have always been the greatest enemies of Christianity. This was true in the days of Jesus, it is true today, and it will be true until the final consummation of all things. The religious leaders (the Pharisees, scribes, and elders), after hearing of the miracle that raised Lazarus from the dead, decided that they must stop Jesus at any cost. So they called a council together, and asked each other, *"What do we?"* In other words, "We must decide what to do, for it is certain that we must do *something!* We cannot sit by and let this Jesus of Nazareth continue His mighty works. His popularity is growing, His followers are fast multiplying, and we must do something immediately. But—*WHAT do we?"*

The Pharisees and religious rulers could not deny the miracles of Jesus—they were too many, they were publicly performed, and they were witnessed by sane, intelligent people. But even though His miracles were not denied, we see that men who stood *in the very presence* of those tremendous miracles were not converted. Miracles do not convert. We are saved by grace through faith—"with the heart man believeth unto righteousness." Seeing with the eye does not convert. The witnessing of a divine miracle such as the raising of Lazarus from the grave did not convert many of the Jews who saw it all. When the council gathered, instead of asking, "What DO we?" they should have said, "In the face of such a miracle, a miracle that only God could bring about, let us all receive this Man as our Messiah!" But these men were blinded by the devil; they had no *will* to believe that Jesus was the Messiah, and they continued their plot to put Him to death.

Verse 48: *"If we let Him thus alone, all men will believe on Him: and the Romans shall come and take away both our place and nation."*

The word *"thus"* means "as at present, and hitherto." That is, the Jews agreed that if they allowed Jesus to continue working miracles, if they simply continued to dispute with Him and took no active measures to stop Him, the mass of the people would believe on Him, His popularity would continue to grow, and He would finally win the majority of the people away from those who ruled in Israel.

"And the Romans shall come and take away both our place and our nation." This was what they feared most! If Jesus should gather enough followers to proclaim Him as King, the leaders in Rome would hear about it and would consider it a rebellion against Roman rule. They would then send an army and destroy Jerusalem with its temple, and destroy the Jews as well—or take them away into captivity as the Babylonians did.

There was no excuse for the members of the council reasoning along such lines. Throughout the ministry of our Lord, in all of His preaching and teaching, He never once mentioned an earthly kingdom, He never suggested a kingdom supported by force. He declared that His kingdom was "not of this world," it was not temporal like the kingdom of Solomon or David. Not once did He intimate that He had come to deliver the Jews from Roman rule. On the contrary, He told the Jews to "render unto Caesar the things that are Caesar's" (Mark 12:17).

If the Pharisees and chief priests had understood their Old Testament Scriptures and the prophecies concerning their Messiah, they would have known that the Romans could never conquer the Lord and His people if Jesus *were* really their Messiah and could work miracles at His will. NO nation had ever been able to conquer the Jews when they served God and walked with Him. The Philistines could not overcome David, and the Romans certainly could not have conquered David's greater Son, the Lord Jesus Christ. If He were truly their King, accepted as their Messiah, He certainly would be victorious over Rome. Their reasoning was the result of their unbelief.

Not only were the Pharisees unbelievers—they were hypocrites as well. They said they were anxious about the temple and the worship of their God; but they were not *really* concerned about the temple and worship; they were afraid their own tyranny would be destroyed! What the chief priests and Pharisees hated most was the doctrine of the Lord Jesus—a doctrine that exposed the evil of their system and weakened their authority in religious matters. Their craft was in serious danger unless they could stop Him from preaching the doctrine He had been preaching. They dared not confess *publicly* what was secretly hidden in their hearts, so they said they were afraid He would excite the Romans to jealousy and cause them to destroy the temple and take the nation into slavery. They said they wanted to stop Him because they feared the Romans, but the truth of the matter was that they found His growing influence with the people disturbing to their peace of mind; they feared He would finally destroy their power over the people and they could no longer dictate their religious doctrine and policy. They used this same scheme when they accused Jesus before Pilate. They said He stirred up sedition, that He made Himself a king.

When the Jews spoke of the Romans coming and taking away their *"place,"* they were speaking of the temple. (Study also Acts 6:13,14 and Micah 1:3.)

Verses 49 and 50: *"And one of them, named Caiaphas, being the high priest that same year, said unto them, Ye know nothing at all, nor consider that it is expedient for us, that one man should die for the people, and that the whole nation perish not."*

"That same year" is extremely important in this verse. That "same year" the high priest's office ended forever. That "same year" the temple veil was rent in twain from top to bottom and the holy of holies laid bare so that *all* could enter. That "same year" the Mosaic economy ended.

When Christ said, "It is finished" He became our High Priest, and now there is one God and one Mediator between God and men, the Man Christ Jesus (I Tim. 2:5). It was "that same year" that Pentecost came, the Holy Ghost was poured out, and He has been in the world ever since to convict, convince, and draw men to God.

From Acts 5:17 we would conclude that Caiaphas was a Sadducee: "Then the high priest rose up, and all they that were with him, (which is the sect of the Sadducees,) and were filled with indignation." If Caiaphas IS the high priest mentioned here—(and most Bible scholars agree that he is)—it accounts for the contemptuous way he answered the argument of the Pharisees: *"Ye know nothing at all . . . ."* But even though Caiaphas came to the defense of Jesus in that respect, it is interesting to notice how they got together and agreed that He should be put to death. The Sadducees and the Pharisees differed on many points of doctrine, but when they set out to destroy Jesus they were in perfect agreement! It is not uncommon for enemies to combine forces when the Gospel and God-fearing men are being attacked.

"Caiaphas being the high priest that same year . . . ." Under the Law of Moses, the office of high priest was held for a lifetime; it changed only when the high priest died. However, it seems that in the days of Jesus, men became high priest by election, but there is no way of knowing whether they served one year, or what their term of office was. It is no wonder then that Paul said on one occasion, *"I wist not brethren that he WAS the high priest"* (Acts 23:2—5). We know Caiaphas was high priest when John the Baptist began to preach in the wilderness: "Annas and Caiaphas being the high priests, the Word of God came unto John the son of Zacharias in the wilderness. And he came into all the country about Jordan, preaching the baptism of repentance for the remission of sins" (Luke 3:2,3). He was also high priest after the Day of Pentecost, and before the persecution and stoning of Stephen (Acts 4:6).

The historian Josephus tells us that the Jews had thirteen high priests from Aaron to King Solomon—a period of 612 years. They had eighteen high priests from Solomon to the Babylonian captivity—460 years. But from the time Herod began to reign until the destruction of Jerusalem (a period of less than 100 years) they had at least twenty-eight high priests. From this, we know that they did not follow the law which they claimed to love and revere so much.

Caiaphas said to the Pharisees, *"Ye know nothing at all."* It seems that Caiaphas emphasized the word "YE," thus expressing contempt for the ignorance and weakness of the Pharisees. "You do not understand the situation. You are wasting time *talking* about stopping this Man from working miracles, and you must take much stronger measures." Then Caiaphas cried out openly and unashamed, *"ONE must die—or THE WHOLE NATION will be destroyed!* This Man with His mighty miracles will cause trouble to come upon our entire nation and we will *all* perish, unless He be put to death. So why discuss the matter further?"

If Caiaphas were living today he would make a marvelous liberal, or an outstanding politician (*politician,* not STATESMAN). His declaration proved that he cared nothing for the law. Notice, he did not say, "It is *lawful* to put this Man to death in order that others might not suffer." He said, "It is *expedient*—(we must do it). This Man must die—it matters not how good He is, how much good He has done or is doing. He may be innocent, He may be just; but He must die, because if we let Him alone He may cause the Romans to destroy our nation." In his statement, Caiaphas violated all the rules of honor, conscience, and truth. Yes, he would certainly have made a marvelous liberal theologian, or a full-fledged politician!

Verse 51: *"And this spake he not of himself: but being high priest that year, he prophesied that Jesus should die for that nation."*

Here and in verse 52 we have John's parenthetical explanation of and amplification upon the saying of the high priest—i. e., although unconscious of what he was doing, Caiaphas had prophesied the truth. In the address he gave the Pharisees there was a very peculiar message of prophecy, given through a man—a Sadducee—who did not believe in the resurrection and who had other misleading ideas concerning spiritual matters; but there is extensive coverage in His prophecy—the fact that Jesus would die for that nation and would gather people from *all* nations.

The office of high priest did not automatically bestow power on men who were high priests, enabling them to prophesy events to come. However, God did bestow such power on certain high priests at certain times, for in the days of David, *Zadok* was certainly referred to as a "seer" (II Sam. 15:27). Also, the *ephod* of the high priest conveyed a certain power to the man who wore it—power to foresee events in the immediate future:

"And David knew that Saul secretly practised mischief against him; and he said to Abiathar the priest, *Bring hither the ephod.* Then said David, O Lord God of Israel, thy servant hath certainly heard that Saul seeketh to come to Keilah, to destroy the city for my sake. Will the men of Keilah deliver me up into his hand? will Saul come down, as thy servant hath heard? O Lord God of Israel, I beseech thee, tell thy servant. And the Lord said, He will come down. Then said David, Will the men of Keilah deliver me and my men into the hand of Saul? And the Lord said, They will deliver thee up" (I Sam. 23:9—12).

The "urim and thummim" in the breastplate of the high priest appeared to have given the wearer peculiar powers of understanding and discernment; but these seemed to be withdrawn and cease, when the first temple was destroyed. After that, we read of no such power pertaining to the high priest. There is not one word in the New Testament suggesting that a Jewish high priest had power such as they had in David's day. We have no reason to believe that Caiaphas was possessed of any special anointing from God. He was a Sadducee, he denied the resurrection—and if we deny the resurrection our faith is vain. (Study I Corinthians chapter 15.) We know God spoke through Balaam's donkey, and to backslidden Peter He spoke through the crowing of a rooster. It is not surprising therefore that He used Caiaphas as an instrument through which to speak, even though Caiaphas did not understand what he said—"this spake he *not of himself.*" The words he spoke were words of prophecy, as proved by events that followed shortly. He prophesied that which was about to come to pass, but he did not realize that Jesus would die on the cross to pay the sin-debt for the whole world. That is not what Caiaphas had in mind when he said, "It is expedient for us, that ONE Man should die for the people, and that the whole nation perish not."

Verse 52: *"And not for that nation only, but that also He should gather together in one the children of God that were scattered abroad."*

Verse 51 was John's *explanation* of the priest's prophecy, and this verse is his *amplification* of it.

The words spoken by Caiaphas were fulfilled in a most extraordinary manner—not in the way that he wished, intended, or expected. We know that his prophecy was given (and fulfilled) by the overruling providence of a sovereign God. Through the power of the Holy Ghost, Caiaphas was compelled to speak words that he himself did not understand, words that prophesied the redemption that would be purchased through the shed blood of Jesus. He *thought* he was demanding only that a man be put to death lest the Jewish nation suffer because of that man; but in reality he was prophesying that Christ would die for Jews and Gentiles and pay the ransom for "whosoever will."

"The children of God that were scattered abroad" refers to the Gentiles who would be born again through hearing the Gospel, from that day until the Rapture of the Church.

These "children of God" are here put in contrast with
"that nation," the nation of Israel, the elect of God at
that time.

The gathering *"together in one"* points to that glorious
day when all the members of the body of Christ will be
gathered together in one at the second coming of Christ—
not the Rapture, but the time mentioned by Paul in Ephesians 1:10:   "That in the dispensation of the fulness of
times He might gather together in one all things in Christ,
both which are in heaven, and which are on earth; even
in Him." (Also study John 12:32 and Genesis 49:10.)

We need not marvel that Caiaphas spoke words of prophecy, not knowing what he spoke. God is sovereign, and His
grace made use of the mouth of this high priest although
his heart remained untouched by the grace of God or by
the Holy Spirit. *Balaam* was an evil man, a lover of gain,
a corrupter of others (read Jude 11 and Revelation 2:14);
yet the Spirit forced him to speak true and wonderful things:
"And Balaam lifted up his eyes, and he saw Israel abiding
in his tents according to their tribes; *and the Spirit of God
came upon him"* (Num. 24:2).

Verse 53:   *"Then from that day forth they took counsel
together for to put Him to death."*

The statement of the high priest settled the matter.   From
that day forward it was determined in the minds of the Jews
that Jesus must die.   The only thing remaining was to find
a time and a way, without creating a tumult and revolt
among the common people.   The fact that Caiaphas held
such high position and the boldness with which he made
his declaration convinced the council.   However, they proceeded cautiously in their plans to destroy Jesus, because
the miracle at Bethany had greatly increased the number
of His disciples; many were following Him now, and they
had to be careful as to when, where, and how they carried
out their murderous plan.

Verse 54:   *"Jesus therefore walked no more openly among*

the Jews; but went thence unto a country near to the wilderness, into a city called Ephraim, and there continued with His disciples."

"Jesus therefore . . . ." How much there is in this word "therefore." It shows us plainly that Jesus knew the hearts and minds of these people; He knew their plans, He knew the council had decided to put Him to death—but He also knew that His hour had not yet fully come, and from that moment on He did not appear openly in Jerusalem until the week He was arrested, tried, convicted, and crucified.

He *"went thence unto a country near to the wilderness, into a city called Ephraim, and there continued with His disciples."* The last days of our Lord's ministry on earth were spent in quiet seclusion, in meditation with the heavenly Father and in fellowship and communion with His disciples. We have no record of any further miracles, nor of any further public works. Since the nation Israel had rejected Him, and the religious leaders had made up their minds to crucify Him, He withdrew and made no further attempt to convince them that He was their Messiah.

Verse 55: *"And the Jews' passover was nigh at hand: and many went out of the country up to Jerusalem before the passover, to purify themselves."*

This explanation shows that John's writings were to the Church in general, and would be read by many who were not familiar with the Jewish feasts and customs; therefore he points out that the Passover was near, and *"many went out of the country up to Jerusalem before the passover"*—which was not unusual; they did it every year. They were devoutly dedicated to their feasts and religious festivals, the keeping of "days." They gathered seven days before the Passover, and thus at that time there were more Jews in Jerusalem than at any other time during the entire year.

Many went up to Jerusalem before the Passover *"to purify themselves."* If you will read and study the book of

Leviticus, you will be amazed to learn the many ways in which an Israelite could become ceremonially unclean, and therefore needed to visit the priest to have an atonement made. In II Chronicles 30:18,19 we read, "For a multitude of the people, even many of Ephraim, and Manasseh, Issachar, and Zebulun, had not cleansed themselves, yet did they eat the passover otherwise than it was written. But Hezekiah prayed for them, saying, The good Lord pardon every one that prepareth his heart to seek God, the Lord God of his fathers, though he be not cleansed according to the purification of the sanctuary."

Numbers 9:6–10 tells us, "And there were certain men, who were defiled by the dead body of a man, that they could not keep the passover on that day: and they came before Moses and before Aaron on that day: and those men said unto him, We are defiled by the dead body of a man: wherefore are we kept back, that we may not offer an offering of the Lord in His appointed season among the children of Israel? And Moses said unto them, Stand still, and I will hear what the Lord will command concerning you. And the Lord spake unto Moses, saying, Speak unto the children of Israel, saying, If any man of you or of your posterity shall be unclean by reason of a dead body, or be in a journey afar off, yet he shall keep the passover unto the Lord."

In the days of Jesus, the religious leaders had bound on the people yokes they could not bear—neither could the chief priests and the scribes bear them themselves. The law as it stood in the first place was a yoke that was difficult to bear, but the Pharisees had added legal restrictions and their own religious traditions to the law—they added to it, and they took from it. Thus we can understand that fear caused tens of thousands of Jews to come into Jerusalem before the Passover to be made ceremonially clean in order to be fit to partake of the feast of the Passover. These Jews were extremely interested in becoming ceremonially clean, but at the same time, in their hearts they were planning to crucify the Lord Jesus Christ.

I might add that the Jews were not the last to be guilty of this sin. There are many church members today who are extremely strict about form and ceremony, baptism and ritual; but they are extremely *reckless* about sin! The devil cares not how religious nor how conscientious a person is, if he stops short of the new birth through the cleansing power of the Lord Jesus Christ.

Verse 56: *"Then sought they for Jesus, and spake among themselves, as they stood in the temple, What think ye, that He will not come to the feast?"*

If some of the Jews who had come to Jerusalem to prepare for the Passover had not *seen* Jesus they had certainly *heard* about Him, for His fame had spread throughout Palestine. Those who had not seen Him were anxious TO see Him, and as they stood in the temple court waiting for the ceremonial purification, they discussed Him among themselves. The paramount question among them seemed to be, "Will He really come to the Passover this year?" (On at least one other occasion He had not, as we learned in chapter 6.) No doubt many of the Jews—especially those who knew the Sanhedrin had decreed His death—felt that He would not come.

"What think ye?" It is interesting to note that the Greek word used here is the same as that used in the question Jesus asked the Pharisees in Matthew 22:42: "What think ye of *Christ?* Whose Son is He?" Here, it no doubt means, "What think ye of His *position,* especially at this time? Do you think He will or will not come to the Passover feast?"

Verse 57: *"Now both the chief priests and the Pharisees had given a commandment, that, if any man knew where He were, he should shew it, that they might take Him."*

Here is recorded the first step taken by the council after the high priest commanded that Jesus be put to death. A general order was issued to the effect that if any person knew where Jesus was, he was to bring that information to them, that Jesus might be arrested and brought in.

Bible scholars believe that this order had to do with Jerusalem only—in other words, if anyone *in Jerusalem* knew where Jesus was, they were to bring that information to the Sanhedrin. It does not seem reasonable to suppose that Jesus left Bethany and traveled to Ephraim without His enemies tracing His journey and knowing where He was; but it is doubtful that they would risk stirring up a tumult among the people by arresting Him outside the walls of Jerusalem.

CHAPTER XII

1. Then Jesus six days before the passover came to Bethany, where Lazarus was which had been dead, whom he raised from the dead.

2. There they made him a supper; and Martha served: but Lazarus was one of them that sat at the table with him.

3. Then took Mary a pound of ointment of spikenard, very costly, and anointed the feet of Jesus, and wiped his feet with her hair: and the house was filled with the odour of the ointment.

4. Then saith one of his disciples, Judas Iscariot, Simon's son, which should betray him,

5. Why was not this ointment sold for three hundred pence, and given to the poor?

6. This he said, not that he cared for the poor; but because he was a thief, and had the bag, and bare what was put therein.

7. Then said Jesus, Let her alone: against the day of my burying hath she kept this.

8. For the poor always ye have with you; but me ye have not always.

9. Much people of the Jews therefore knew that he was there: and they came not for Jesus' sake only, but that they might see Lazarus also, whom he had raised from the dead.

10. But the chief priests consulted that they might put Lazarus also to death;

11. Because that by reason of him many of the Jews went away, and believed on Jesus.

12. On the next day much people that were come to the feast, when they heard that Jesus was coming to Jerusalem,

13. Took branches of palm trees, and went forth to meet him, and cried, Hosanna: Blessed is the King of Israel that cometh in the name of the Lord.

14. And Jesus, when he had found a young ass, sat thereon; as it is written,

15. Fear not, daughter of Sion: behold, thy King cometh, sitting on an ass's colt.

16. These things understood not his disciples at the first: but when Jesus was glorified, then remembered they that these things were written of him, and that they had done these things unto him.

17. The people therefore that was with him when he called Lazarus out of his grave, and raised him from the dead, bare record.

18. For this cause the people also met him, for that they heard that he had done this miracle.

19. The Pharisees therefore said among themselves, Perceive ye how ye prevail nothing? behold, the world is gone after him.

20. And there were certain Greeks among them that came up to worship at the feast:

21. The same came therefore to Philip, which was of Bethsaida of Galilee, and desired him, saying, Sir, we would see Jesus.

22. Philip cometh and telleth Andrew: and again Andrew and Philip tell Jesus.

23. And Jesus answered them, saying, The hour is come, that the Son of man should be glorified.

24. Verily, verily, I say unto you, Except a corn of wheat fall into the ground and die, it abideth alone: but if it die, it bringeth forth much fruit.

25. He that loveth his life shall lose it; and he that hateth his life in this world shall keep it unto life eternal.

26. If any man serve me, let him follow me; and where I am, there shall also my servant be: if any man serve me, him will my Father honour.

27. Now is my soul troubled; and what shall I say? Father, save me from this hour: but for this cause came I unto this hour.

28. Father, glorify thy name. Then came there a voice from heaven, saying, I have both glorified it, and will glorify it again.

29. The people therefore, that stood by, and heard it, said that it thundered: others said, An angel spake to him.

30. Jesus answered and said, This voice came not because of me, but for your sakes.

31. Now is the judgment of this world: now shall the prince of this world be cast out.

32. And I, if I be lifted up from the earth, will draw all men unto me.

33. This he said, signifying what death he should die.

34. The people answered him, We have heard out of the law that Christ abideth for ever: and how sayest thou, The Son of man must be lifted up? who is this Son of man?

35. Then Jesus said unto them, Yet a little while is the light with you. Walk while ye have the light, lest darkness come upon you: for he that walketh in darkness knoweth not whither he goeth.

36. While ye have light, believe in the light, that ye may be the children of light. These things spake Jesus, and departed, and did hide himself from them.

37. But though he had done so many miracles before them, yet they believed not on him:

38. That the saying of Esaias the prophet might be fulfilled, which he spake, Lord, who hath believed our report? and to whom hath the arm of the Lord been revealed?

39. Therefore they could not believe, because that Esaias said again,

40. He hath blinded their eyes, and hardened their heart; that they should not see with their eyes, nor understand with their heart, and be converted, and I should heal them.

41. These things said Esaias, when he saw his glory, and spake of him.

42. Nevertheless among the chief rulers also many believed on him; but because of the Pharisees they did not confess him, lest they should be put out of the synagogue:

43. For they loved the praise of men more than the praise of God.

44. Jesus cried and said, He that believeth on me, believeth not on me, but on him that sent me.

45. And he that seeth me seeth him that sent me.

46. I am come a light into the world, that whosoever believeth on me should not abide in darkness.

47. And if any man hear my words, and believe not, I judge him not: for I came not to judge the world, but to save the world.

48. He that rejecteth me, and receiveth not my words, hath one that judgeth him: the word that I have spoken, the same shall judge him in the last day.

49. For I have not spoken of myself; but the Father which sent me, he gave me a commandment, what I should say, and what I should speak.

50. And I know that his commandment is life everlasting: whatsoever I speak therefore, even as the Father said unto me, so I speak.

The Supper at Bethany

Verse 1: *"Then Jesus six days before the passover came to Bethany, where Lazarus was which had been dead, whom He raised from the dead."*

The public ministry of Jesus to the unbelieving Jews comes to a close with this chapter, and beginning with chapter 13 John records what the Lord said to His disciples in private.

John omits the interval between the time Jesus departed "into a city called Ephraim" and His return to Jerusalem six days before the Passover, but Matthew, Mark, and Luke record the events and the works He performed during the time He was away from Jerusalem. We do not know why the Holy Spirit did not see fit to have John record all of the events and miracles given by the other Gospel writers, but we do know the Holy Spirit inspired the words he penned down in the Gospel that bears his name. (Study Matthew 20:17—34, Mark 10:32—52, and Luke chapter 18 verse 31 through chapter 19 verse 28.) God instructed John as to what he should write, and He also directed him what NOT to write.

The supper at Bethany was *"six days before the Passover."* Although this statement seems to contradict the statement in Mark 14:1, most Bible scholars believe that there was more than one anointing of Jesus before the Passover, which would eliminate any contradiction between John's mention of *six* days before the Passover and Mark's statement which definitely says *two* days before the Passover.

Six days before the Passover Jesus traveled into Bethany, *"where Lazarus was which had been dead, whom He raised from the dead."* These are important words. They tell us that Lazarus *lived* at Bethany, he was not just a visitor there, and therefore he was known by everyone in and around the village. From this statement we also learn the importance of the miracle Jesus wrought on Lazarus. He had mixed and mingled with the people of Bethany during the weeks since his resurrection, they had seen him, talked with him, no doubt had business dealings with him in whatever his business might have been. Therefore the miracle of his resurrection could not possibly be denied.

Verse 2: *"There they made Him a supper; and Martha served: but Lazarus was one of them that sat at the table with Him."*

I believe *"they"* refers to Mary, Martha, and Lazarus, but some believe that it refers to the *entire community.*

Jesus found a warm reception in the home of Mary, Martha, and Lazarus; He loved them, and I personally believe it was those three close friends of the Lord who gave the supper for Him, and I believe it was given in their home.

We notice that even though it was only six days before the Passover and therefore only six days before His crucifixion, He accepted the invitation to this supper and the hospitality of these friends. Certainly it is not wrong for God's children to enjoy such fellowship when things are done "decently and in order." In Luke 7:36 we read of Jesus' sitting at meat in a Pharisee's house, and Matthew 9:10,11 gives an account of His eating with publicans and sinners—for which action the Pharisees severely criticized Him.

"But Lazarus was one of them that sat at the table with Him." This statement is not put here to fill up space; it is here for our instruction and admonition. These words prove the reality of the raising of Lazarus from the dead. This was not a spirit-being, a ghost, who sat at the table with Jesus; it was a real man with the *attributes* of a real man. He had been raised to life in a real body of flesh, blood, and bone—a body like those of the other guests—and he sat at the table and ate with them.

To me, this is (in type) a beautiful picture of the marriage supper of the Lamb, of which John tells us in Revelation 19:9. All the saints will be there—those who have been raised from the grave, and those who have been changed "in a moment, in the twinkling of an eye" in the Rapture. Jesus will be there, at that grand and glorious feast that will be held immediately after the Rapture of the Church. I wonder, dear reader, if *you* are born again? Are *you* saved by grace? If you are, you will attend that great marriage feast in the sky; but if you are NOT born again you will not be present. Think it over, and if you are not saved by faith in the finished work of Jesus, receive Him, believe on Him; He will save you now and will write your name in the Lamb's book of life! All whose names are written in the Lamb's book of life will be present at the marriage supper in the sky.

Verse 3:   *"Then took Mary a pound of ointment of spikenard, very costly, and anointed the feet of Jesus, and wiped His feet with her hair: and the house was filled with the odour of the ointment."*

The action of Mary deserves our careful study and special consideration.   What she did was not uncommon in that country—nor in other eastern countries in that day.   The heat was oppressive, the roads were not paved, and there were no sidewalks such as we have today.   The travelers wore sandals, and thus their feet were exposed to the heat and the dust as they traveled.   It was a custom in that country for the host or someone in his household to bathe the hot, tired, dusty feet of a guest upon arrival at his home.   In I Timothy 5:10 Paul mentions the washing of the saints' feet as a good Christian service on the part of women believers.   Of course, in this day and in our country there is no need for bathing the feet of those who visit the home.

Mary's action proved that she thought there was nothing too good for her Lord.   He had been such a tremendous blessing to her as she sat at His feet and feasted on the bread of life.   Her home had been filled with unspeakable joy and thanksgiving since Lazarus was raised from the dead, and her personal feelings for Jesus compelled her to do any and every thing for Him, no matter how humble the task might be, in order to show her devotion and bring comfort to Him.   Therefore she took *"a pound of ointment of spikenard, very costly,"* and anointed His feet.

Ointment of spikenard, containing the aromatic oil of the spikenard plant, was very expensive—and from the fact that "the house was filled with the odour of the ointment" we know it was also very potent.   Mary did not use just *a few drops* of this precious ointment; she literally *bathed* the feet of Jesus with it!   She used it so liberally that it was necessary to *wipe* His feet after using it. Such use of anything so expensive could well have represented the savings of her lifetime. There is nothing in the record which gives us reason to suppose that this was a wealthy family, although from the type of tomb in which Lazarus was buried and the manner of his burial we might conclude that they were not necessarily poverty-stricken. *Paupers* could not have given the elaborate *feast* mentioned in these verses, but there is nothing to indicate that Mary did not sacrifice greatly in order to provide the ointment of spikenard with which she anointed the feet of her Lord.

This is not the anointing set forth in Luke 7:36—50, nor is it the same anointing described in Mark 14:1—9. In Mark, the anointing was two days before the Passover—and the ointment was poured on the *head* of Jesus. In our present verse, the ointment was poured on His feet, and it was six days before the Passover.

Although Mary's knowledge was limited, it is entirely possible that she had a deeper understanding of Jesus than did those around her. She must have had a clearer perception of Him as pertaining to redemption, and at least by her unselfish deed she testified that she understood the dignity of the Person she anointed—who He was and why He had come into the world.

Verses 4 and 5: *"Then saith one of His disciples, Judas Iscariot, Simon's son, which should betray Him, Why was not this ointment sold for three hundred pence, and given to the poor?"*

It is well to note that in the account of the anointing as given in Matthew 26:8, His *disciples* murmured, and in Mark 14:4 we read that *some* (more than one) were indignant over Mary's use of the expensive ointment. But here in John's account, only *one* disciple is said to have murmured about it, and that one disciple was Judas. This fact also supports the belief that there were two different anointings at Bethany just before the crucifixion.

The name *Simon* is mentioned frequently in the New Testament, but we do not know who *Simon the father of Judas* was, nor why his name is mentioned here in connection with Judas.

We read of one of the disciples called *Simon Peter* (Matt. 4:18; 16:17,18; Mark 1:16; Luke 5:3—10; and John 1:40).

We read of the *apostle* "Simon the Canaanite" who was also called *Zelotes* (Matt. 10:4; Mark 3:18; Luke 6:15).

We read of Simon *the brother of Jesus*, mentioned along with James and Joses (Matt. 13:55).

"Simon *the leper*" is mentioned in Matthew 26:6.

Simon, *"a man of Cyrene"* was compelled to carry the cross of Jesus (Matt. 27:32).

Simon *the Pharisee* is named in Luke 7:40.

Acts 8:9—24 tells of *Simon the sorcerer* in Samaria, and in Acts 9:43 we read of *Simon the tanner.*

However, there is no Scripture which suggests whether or not any of these men might have been the father of Judas. If the Holy Spirit had wanted us to know exactly who *this* Simon was, I am sure that information would have been revealed here.

"Judas Iscariot . . . which should betray Him." This would be more literally read, "the one who was about to betray Him." Jesus knew from the very beginning that Judas was a traitor. In John 6:70 He said to His disciples, "Have not I chosen you twelve, and one of you is a devil?" Judas was a traitor, a thief, a devil. He was never born again, never saved by grace through faith in the Lord Jesus Christ. There is no record in the New Testament where Judas ever called Jesus *"Lord"*—he always referred to Him as "Master." Judas fell—but he did not fall from grace. He fell from the office of apostleship (Acts 1:25). He was false from the very beginning, he was a devil, he was *never* a son of God.

Why was he chosen among the twelve? John 17:12 answers: ". . . *that the Scriptures might be fulfilled."* We should never question the doings of Almighty God.

It is interesting to note that Judas was greatly disturbed and made quite a fuss about Mary's anointing Jesus with ointment worth "three hundred pence," yet he was about to bargain with the chief priests and the Sanhedrin to sell the Son of God for thirty pieces of silver—about one-third the value of the ointment Mary had poured on the Lord Jesus Christ.

The same situation exists today in many instances. Godly men and women who give to the cause of Christ are accused of giving just to get their names in the church bulletin or over the door of a Sunday school room—and I grant that this is sometimes the case; but not always. If we do good in the name of Jesus, if we give of our best and surrender our *all* to Him as Mary did, we can expect our motives to be questioned and our deeds criticized by the hypocrites in church and community.

In the days of the early Church, giving to the poor was understood to be part of the duty of every Christian (Gal. 2:10; I John 3:17); but that was not the real reason Judas criticized Mary for pouring expensive ointment on Jesus.

Verse 6: *"This he said, not that he cared for the poor; but because he was a thief, and had the bag, and bare what was put therein."*

Here the inspired pen of John the Beloved clearly spells out the true character of Judas, and gives the real reason for his asking why the ointment was not sold and the money given to the poor. On the surface the question seemed reasonable and good, but it came from a wicked heart. Judas was not in love with the poor; he did not ask the question because he wanted to put food in the mouths of hungry children or clothe and feed the poor. He simply used the poor and their interests in a subtle way, to bring gain into his own hands.

There are many people today who excuse themselves from giving to foreign missions because they say, "Charity begins at home." Yet these people do not give to home missions nor do they support their local church—many times they allow their pastor and his family to suffer for things they really need.   There are those who excuse themselves from giving to the work of a Bible-preaching church by saying that they give liberally to organizations which feed the poor and clothe the destitute—and although it is honorable to give to charitable organizations, our first duty is to the kingdom of God, for if we seek first His kingdom and His righteousness, all these other things will be added (Matt. 6:33).

People who find excuses for not supporting the Lord's work—at home *or* abroad—are not really interested in keeping the "home fires" burning.   They are interested in their own gain, and they seldom give liberally to anything.   Like Judas, they make speeches and speak great swelling words about what *ought* to be done, and what *could* be done instead of what *is* being done—but they do nothing to bring it about.   These things are written for our instruction and edification; we need to study them carefully and receive whatever benefit God has for us in such statements.

"This he said . . . *because he was a thief.*"   Certainly there are no "frills" on that statement!   I wonder how far some preachers would get today if they preached as clearly and plainly as this?   Jesus had plainly declared that Judas was a devil (John 6:70), and here we are boldly told that he was also a *thief*—language that is understandable by all.

We see here just how much of an outward show a man can make and how far he may go in Christian profession or church work without actually being born again by the grace of God.   Judas, though never saved, was one of the twelve, and he was just as busy as the rest of them were—if not a little *busier.*   He witnessed the mighty miracles of Jesus, he heard His powerful words which were "the power of God unto salvation."   He lived and walked in the very presence of the sinless Son of God—but in spite of his privileges he remained a devil, a thief, wicked from the beginning.

I fear there are many in our churches today—deacons, stewards, elders, even ministers—who are just as lost as Judas Iscariot! No wonder John penned the last two verses in the second chapter of the Gospel that bears his name: "But Jesus did not commit Himself unto them, because He knew all men, and needed not that any should testify of man: for He knew what was in man!"

Christianity is not the office we hold or the profession we make with our lips; it is what we believe and possess in our hearts—"Christ in you, the hope of glory" (Col. 1:27). Judas was not in love with Jesus; he was in love with what was in the bag—he loved *money*. It is not strange therefore that the Holy Spirit clearly warns that "the *love of money* (not money as such, but *the LOVE for it*) is the root of all evil" (I Tim. 6:10).

I believe God *calls* some men to make money and gives them the *ability* to acquire wealth—but those men *share* their money with missions—home and foreign; they give generously of their income to advance the cause of Christ. When any man (or woman) gives unto the Lord that which rightfully belongs to Him, God will honor that man or woman and bless their efforts in the business world. Money is a wonderful thing to have if we use it in the right way and give to the Lord that which is His, thus supporting the cause of Christ as we ought; but it is a dreadful thing to love money for the sake of money alone, or for the material things it will buy. Love of money will deafen the ears, blind the eyes, cripple the soul, and cause a person to live a life of fruitless sorrow.

Riches do not bring peace, and to be rich does not necessarily mean to be *happy*. It is interesting to read in the Scriptures the many places where money is connected with sorrow, heartbreak, and deceit. A person who makes money his god has a conscience seared as with a hot iron, and many times he destroys the friendship and confidence of those near and dear to him. Money does not damn a soul—but remember, the rich young ruler refused to follow Jesus because he would not trust Him with his earthly possessions. We read that when Jesus said, "One thing thou lackest: go thy way, sell whatsoever thou hast, and give to the poor, and thou shalt have treasure in heaven: and come, take up the cross, and follow me," the young man went away grieved, because he had great possessions, he was very rich, and he was not willing to trust Jesus with his wealth! Read Mark 10:17—22 for the full account.

Judas *"had the bag, and bare what was put therein."* I have often wondered how Judas came to be elected or appointed to the position of treasurer for the disciple band. There must have been something very attractive about him— and why not? The *devil* is the "prince of the power of the air . . . the shining one." He was the most cunning of all the beasts when he came to Eve in the form of a serpent. Paul tells us that the *ministers* of Satan can transform themselves as ministers of righteousness, so it is not abusing the Word of God to suggest that Judas Iscariot was very likely an unusual person in many ways.

The Greek word translated *"bag"* is an unusual word and originally referred to a bag in which musicians carried the mouthpiece of an instrument. There can be no doubt that Judas carried a literal bag, in which was money and perhaps other things which had been given to Jesus and His disciples. In Luke 8:1—3 we read, "And it came to pass afterward, that He went throughout every city and village, preaching and shewing the glad tidings of the kingdom of God: and the twelve were with Him, and certain women, which had been healed of evil spirits and infirmities, Mary called Magdalene, out of whom went seven devils, and Joanna the wife of Chuza Herod's steward, and Susanna, *and many others, WHICH MINISTERED UNTO HIM OF THEIR SUBSTANCE."* Jesus had true friends throughout Palestine, and they contributed to His livelihood. Judas was in custody of the money and gifts; he carried the bag, "and bare what was put therein."

Certainly it is necessary for someone to handle money in the church, but the handling of money is a grave responsibility and should not be placed upon any one person. It can lead to dangerous snares and pitfalls. For the protection of the individual, the church should have a *committee* to count the money, keep the records, make the reports, and see to it that no one person is placed in a position where he could be accused of taking the Lord's money. The handling of money is a snare through which many have been tempted, have sinned, and lost their influence in the church and community, as well as losing their eternal reward through unfaithful stewardship—if they ever were saved at all.

Verse 7: *"Then said Jesus, Let her alone: against the day of my burying hath she kept this."*

Jesus sternly rebuked Judas for his criticism of Mary— *"Let her alone!"* The Lord Jesus Christ longs for true worship, and certainly what Mary did was from a true and honest heart; she was no hypocrite. This verse of Scripture shows us that the Lord Jesus is always tenderly looking down upon those who love and serve Him, those who bring honor and glory to His name.

"Against the day of my burying hath she kept this." The Greek word here translated *"against"* actually reads "FOR"—that is, *"FOR the day of my burying she has kept this."* This verse must not be interpreted to mean that Mary *understood* that the Lord's burial was at hand. I think it signifies that it was a *timely* anointing, and although Mary did not fully understand the depths of the anointing, she nevertheless anointed Jesus for His burial. The meaning of what Jesus said would then be paraphrased thus:

"The precious ointment Mary has poured on my feet, though she did it only to honor ME, is significant of far more than earthly honor or a demonstration of earthly love. Mary did one of the most appropriate things she could

have done at this moment. My death is near, I will soon
be placed in the tomb; and although Mary does not fully
understand what the anointing means, what she has done
is a memorial to me because of the nearness of my departure
from this earth. Therefore her action is right and com-
mendable."

It is possible that Judas understood more than Mary
did of the statement Jesus made here, because the Scripture plainly tells us that he was a devil. Most assuredly
the devil knew why Jesus had come into the world, and
on many occasions he did his best to stop Him before His
mission was fulfilled! Jesus had often told His disciples
that He had come into the world to die. In John 10:18
He clearly declared that He would lay His life down; He
is here reminding them that His death was very near and
that Mary had anointed Him for His burying.

We learn from what Mary did here that believers do not
always understand the meaning of what they do. If we
believe God, then we know that all things work together
for good to those who love God and are called according
to His purpose; but many times we do something—in the
Spirit and to the glory of God—without fully understanding
WHY we did it. If we are led by the Spirit, whatever we
do is for our good and God's glory, and we do not *need*
to question why. For instance, in verse 16 of this chapter
we read, "These things understood not His disciples at the
first: but when Jesus was glorified, *then remembered they*
that these things were written of Him, and that they had
done these things unto Him." Believers are instruments
of God. In this day of grace it has pleased Him to use
men and women who are surrendered to Him, who are led
by the Holy Spirit; and He sometimes uses His children
without their knowing fully at the time just what He is
working out in the things He leads them to do.

Verse 8:   *"For the poor always ye have with you; but
me ye have not always."*

Some of our modern political leaders should read this statement! The poor have always had a warm spot in my heart, and I believe every born again person has a desire to help the needy and destitute; but when politicians promise to banish poverty from the earth and at the same time tax the people beyond reason in order to spend millions in an attempt to wipe out poverty, they are acting against the words of Jesus! HE said, *"the poor ALWAYS ye have with you."* The poor always have been with us, and will be with us until Jesus comes again. Only *then,* when the knowledge of the Lord covers the earth as the waters now cover the sea, when the wicked have been put down and Jesus sits on the throne of David, will there be no poverty. As long as there is sin in the world, there will be poverty. By no means do I mean that all *poor people* are sinners— God forbid! There are many Christian people who are poor and deserving of help—but there are tens of thousands who refuse to try to help themselves and who depend on the government and other agencies to feed and provide for them.

Jesus said, "Seek ye first the kingdom of God, and His righteousness; and all these things shall be added unto you" (Matt. 6:33). Therefore I declare on the authority of God's Word that even though the individual who is poor may not be personally responsible for his poverty, SIN is to blame for ALL poverty everywhere. Poverty is a fruit of sin, not a fruit of righteousness. If present-day politicians would study the Word of God they would know that they can never erase poverty from the earth. Only King Jesus will do that when He comes to reign in glory and power. Neither the government nor "religion" will ever abolish poverty.

Our government officials and political leaders should read Paul's admonition to the Thessalonians: "As touching brotherly love ye need not that I write unto you: for ye yourselves are taught of God to love one another. And indeed ye do it toward all the brethren which are in all Macedonia: but we beseech you, brethren, that ye increase more and more; and that ye study to be quiet, and to do your own business, and to work with your own hands, as we commanded you; that ye may walk honestly toward them that are without, and that ye may have lack of nothing" (I Thess. 4:9—12).

Also, in II Thessalonians 3:7—13 Paul said, "For yourselves know how ye ought to follow us: for we behaved not ourselves disorderly among you; *neither did we eat any man's bread for nought; but wrought with labour and travail night and day, that we might not be chargeable to any of you:* Not because we have not power, but to make ourselves an ensample unto you to follow us. For even when we were with you, this we commanded you, that *if any would not work, neither should he eat.* For we hear that there are some which walk among you disorderly, working not at all, but are busybodies. Now them that are such we command and exhort by our Lord Jesus Christ, *that with quietness they work,* and *eat their own bread.* But ye, brethren, be not weary in well doing."

Yes, there are some poor people among us who need help and who deserve to BE helped; but this should be done in the name of *Jesus,* not in the name of the government.

"But me ye have not always." This statement plainly declares that Jesus did not come to this earth to remain here in a body. It was a high and peculiar honor that this earth was blessed—even briefly—with the presence of Jesus Christ, the Son of God, very God in flesh. He came on a mission, and when that mission was accomplished He returned to the glory He had with the Father before the world was.

This statement made by Jesus also destroys the doctrine of *transubstantiation*—a teaching believed by millions of religionists—that the bread and wine actually become the body and blood of Jesus in the taking of the Lord's Supper. Such doctrine is unscriptural. Since Jesus ascended back to heaven and sat down on the right hand of God, *He has not*

been here in a body.   There is a Man in heaven, the Man
Christ Jesus; but He is not on earth, not even in the bread
and wine.   These are but symbols of His broken body and
His shed blood, and when the bread is broken and the
wine is poured, those elements *do NOT* become the body
and blood of Jesus Christ.   *"ME ye have NOT always."*
Jesus has been—and IS—seated at the right hand of God
the Father (Heb. 1:3; I Tim. 2:5).

From the rebuke Jesus gave Judas, we see that even
though it is honorable to feed the poor (and the church
should be concerned about such things), feeding the hungry
and clothing the destitute is not as honorable as glorifying
the Lord Jesus Christ among them.   There are thousands
in churches, in religious groups—even in *secular* organizations—who believe they will enter heaven because they have
done so much good on earth!   But the Bible makes it very
plain that good works will not save.   (Read Isaiah 64:6,
Ephesians 2:9, and Titus 3:5.)   It is much easier to offer
charity toward man than it is to talk to him about his soul.
It is easier to give of our earthly means than it is to surrender soul, spirit, and body to Jesus, be completely controlled by the Holy Spirit, and give God first place in our
lives.

When Jesus said, "Me ye have not always," He was not
referring to the Holy Spirit who abides in the heart of every
believer.   He meant that He would not always be on earth
in the body He was in at that time.   When He completed
the ministry God foreordained for Him before the foundation
of the world, He laid that body down.   He rose from the
grave on the third day and ascended into heaven *in a body,*
but it was a body of flesh and bone, not *blood,* flesh, and
bone.   He gave His blood for the salvation of sinners; it
was through His blood that redemption was purchased.
From the standpoint of His majesty and divine nature Christ
Jesus is with His people every minute of every day; He
will never leave us nor forsake us—but from the standpoint
of His human nature He is now seated at the right hand

236   *The Gospel According to John*

of God.

In Luke 24:39—45 we read, "Behold my hands and my feet, that it is I myself: handle me, and see; for a spirit hath not flesh and bones, as ye see me have. And when He had thus spoken, He shewed them His hands and His feet. And while they yet believed not for joy, and wondered, He said unto them, Have ye here any meat? And they gave Him a piece of a broiled fish, and of an honeycomb. And He took it, and did eat before them. And He said unto them, These are the words which I spake unto you, while I was yet with you, that all things must be fulfilled, which were written in the law of Moses, and in the prophets, and in the psalms, concerning me. Then opened He their understanding, that they might understand the Scriptures."

Verse 9: *"Much people of the Jews therefore knew that He was there: and they came not for Jesus' sake only, but that they might see Lazarus also, whom He had raised from the dead."*

It is understandable that *"much people"* knew Jesus had arrived in Bethany. The news of His arrival there had spread rapidly—first because the village was so near Jerusalem, and also because it was at Bethany that He had raised Lazarus from the dead.

"They came not for Jesus' sake only, but that they might see Lazarus also." Here is revealed a truth concerning human nature. There are folk today who will travel *two thousand miles* to see someone healed, but they would not walk a city block to invite a poor lost sinner to a revival meeting. There are church people who spend money and time, who travel many miles, to attend a meeting where they hope to see something spectacular; but those same people are much less zealous concerning the dead "in trespasses and sin."

Oh, yes—I believe God is able to heal the sick. I believe He is THE Healer, and apart from Him there IS no healing. I shall never cease to thank Him for doctors, nurses, and hospitals; but unless HE touches the body, it will die. All healing is of the Lord; but the most important thing on earth is to get *souls and spirits* healed by the grace of God. Today the masses attend services where they are promised something spectacular, some outward show, and the humble places of worship where the man of God preaches the Word of God, the grace of God, and salvation by grace through faith suffer for attendance. A great multitude of people rushed out to Bethany—not only because Jesus was reported to be there, but because it was at Bethany that He had raised a man from the dead, and they wanted to see that man. Curiosity is a powerful force in the natural man. Men love the sensational. The resurrection of Lazarus was a sensational event, but in just a few days a far *more* sensational thing would occur: the Lord Jesus would come forth from the tomb—in spite of the Roman seal on the door and the Roman guard stationed there, He would rise from the dead just as He had said He would, and He would do it under His own power!

Verse 10: *"But the chief priests consulted that they might put Lazarus also to death."*

Lazarus had harmed no one. He was *a disciple of Jesus,* although there is nothing in the Scripture to suggest that he was an *outstanding* disciple or that he was a fervent preacher of the Gospel. But he *was* a testimony of the power of the Lord Jesus Christ, a testimony that could not be denied. Therefore, since the Sanhedrin could not deny his resurrection or explain away the miracle that brought it about, they were determined to put an end to his testimony by putting an end to his life. So they *"consulted"* as to what means they might use to put him to death.

The word here translated *"consulted"* means to "resolve" or to "determine." The Jews therefore not only *consulted* one with another, they were *determined in their hearts,* and they purposed to put Lazarus to death!

Verse 11: *"Because that by reason of him many of the Jews went away, and believed on Jesus."*

When the Jews stood around the tomb of Lazarus and witnessed his resurrection, some of them were convinced that Jesus was working under the power of Almighty God, and the chief priests and religious leaders knew that unless they did something to stop both Jesus *and* Lazarus, many more would believe on Him and become His disciples. This they intended to prevent at all costs.

I do not doubt that many of the Jews who followed Jesus to the tomb went there as skeptics, but after witnessing the unheard-of miracle that brought Lazarus forth alive from the tomb, they became *believers.* Whether or not these people believed with the heart we cannot say; but if they did not believe from the heart at this time, on the Day of Pentecost they no doubt were in the number who were convinced that Jesus was the Christ, that He had died for the sins of the world, and they would have been in the great number who were baptized at Pentecost.

Surely Lazarus must have given many testimonies not recorded—but even if he had not said a word, the very fact that he was alive was testimony enough to cause the chief priests and members of the Sanhedrin to become angry enough to plot his death!

Jesus Enters Jerusalem As Prophesied by Zechariah

Verses 12 and 13: *"On the next day much people that were come to the feast, when they heard that Jesus was coming to Jerusalem, took branches of palm trees, and went forth to meet Him, and cried, Hosanna: Blessed is the King of Israel that cometh in the name of the Lord."*

Up to this time, Jesus had kept Himself withdrawn from the public eye as much as possible. He retired into the wilderness many times, and on occasions when the people attempted to make Him king by force, He refused. The

rule of His daily ministry was to create as little attention
as possible and not set Himself before the people. It is
true that He had from time to time proclaimed His identity
as the Messiah, the Son of God, but He had sought neither
public acclaim nor popularity with men. NOW, as He makes
His public entry into Jerusalem, great crowds gather around
Him—crowds so great as to cause His enemies to declare,
"Behold, the WORLD is gone after Him!" (v. 19).

The time had now come (His "hour" had come) when
He would pay the sin-debt for the whole world. The true
Passover Lamb would be slain. He was about to make
the true blood atonement, and Messiah would be cut off,
as prophesied in Daniel 9:26: "And after threescore and
two weeks shall Messiah be cut off, but not for Himself...."
The time had come when Jesus would open the way into
the holy of holies and as our true High Priest He would
take His seat at the right hand of the Majesty on high.
That hour had arrived, *and He knew it.* Therefore He
presented Himself publicly, allowing the mass of mankind
to crowd around Him and shout, "Hosanna!" He was
nailed to the cross, giving His life for the sins of the world,
at the time of year when members of all the twelve tribes
were gathered in the Holy City to observe the Passover,
a week when through His unusual and remarkable public
entry into Jerusalem He drew the attention of all Israel to
Himself.

"On the next day" (the day after the supper in Bethany) *"much people"* had come to the feast. This included
the Jews who came up to Jerusalem from Galilee and the
surrounding countryside to observe the Passover. They were
acquainted with the Lord's ministry and miracles in Galilee,
and when they heard that He would be at the feast a great
multitude came to see Him one more time. I do not doubt
that many of the five thousand whom He fed with loaves
and fishes were among the group referred to as "much people." No doubt as Jesus journeyed from Ephraim to Bethany and on into Jerusalem, those who saw Him along the

way sent the news on ahead that He was making His way
up to the Holy City to attend the Passover feast; and the
crowds, thus informed, *"went forth to meet Him,"* and as
they went, they carried branches of palm trees and shouted,
"Hosanna!"

History tells us that palm branches were carried by pro-
cessions when kings marched into a city or when generals
came marching home after winning great success in battles.
In Revelation 7:9, John (in the Spirit) saw the victorious
hosts in heaven, "clothed with white robes, *and palms in
their hands."* Surely, it must have been a sight to behold
as the crowds went forth to meet Jesus, waving palm
branches and casting them in His path as He rode into
the city.

There can be no doubt that some of those who welcomed
Jesus into Jerusalem that day actually believed with all
of their understanding that He was their Messiah. If we
judge by other mass movements, we can be sure that many
carried palm branches because *the crowd* was carrying
them, while still others welcomed Him because they thought
He was about to take over the government and deliver
them from Roman tyranny. Some of the Jews believed
Him to be a prophet raised up by Jehovah God for that
hour, and *as such* they honored Him; but they did not believe that He was the Son of God, their true Messiah.

The people cried, "Hosanna!" as they went out to meet
Jesus. Bible authorities tell us that this is a translation
of a Hebrew word found in Psalm 118:25, and means *"save
now, we beseech thee."* It could be that some of these
people actually believed Jesus to be the One who *would*
save Israel; but it is not for us to say how far the majority
of them entered into the meaning of the words they uttered.

*"Blessed is the King of Israel that cometh in the name
of the Lord."* This sentence would be more literally rendered, "Blessed is He that cometh in the name of the Lord,
King of Israel." These words are taken from Psalm 118:26,
but you will notice that the verse in Psalms says only,

"Blessed be He that cometh in the name of the Lord," and does not mention "King of Israel." The fact that the people added that part of the proclamation leads us to believe that some of them without a doubt believed Him to be their King—but even so, they were expecting a temporal king, one who would deliver them from the Romans. They were not looking for a Saviour to deliver them from the tyranny of Satan and the slavery of sin. However, I think we can safely say that most of those who cried "Hosanna" that day did not know what they were saying, they did not realize the tremendous truth of their words. This is evident in the fact that there were not many days between the cry of "Hosanna!" and their shouts of "Crucify Him! Crucify Him! Let His blood be upon us and upon our children!" The *last* cry testifies that the *first* cry did not come from a heart of faith.

Verse 14: *"And Jesus, when He had found a young ass, sat thereon; as it is written."*

Matthew 21:6,7 gives a more detailed account of this: "And the disciples went, and did as Jesus commanded them, and brought the ass, and the colt, and put on them their clothes, and they set Him thereon."

Even better is the account given in Luke 19:28—36: "And when He had thus spoken, He went before, ascending up to Jerusalem. And it came to pass, when He was come nigh to Bethphage and Bethany, at the mount called the mount of Olives, He sent two of His disciples, saying, Go ye into the village over against you; in the which at your entering ye shall find a colt tied, whereon yet never man sat: loose him, and bring him hither. And if any man ask you, Why do ye loose him? thus shall ye say unto him, Because the Lord hath need of him. And they that were sent went their way, and found even as He had said unto them. And as they were loosing the colt, the owners thereof said unto them, Why loose ye the colt? And they said, The Lord hath need of him. And they brought him to

Jesus: and they cast their garments upon the colt, and they set Jesus thereon.	And as He went, they spread their clothes in the way."

There was nothing unusual about a person riding upon an ass; many men rode little donkeys in that day, and they are mentioned many times in the Word of God. Abraham, Jacob, Job (and others) had many asses. Read Genesis 12:16, 30:43, and Job 42:12. In I Chronicles 27:30 we are told that King David had a special man to care for his asses. Balaam rode upon an ass (Num. 22:21), and so did the Shunammite woman who was very rich (II Kings 4:22—24). It was a mark of *dignity* for one to ride upon a *white* ass (Judges 5:10). So we see that the fact of the Lord's riding into Jerusalem on an ass was not peculiar within itself. What was outstanding about it was that it happened exactly as prophesied by Zechariah hundreds of years before: "Rejoice greatly, O daughter of Zion; shout, O daughter of Jerusalem: behold, thy King cometh unto thee: He is just, and having salvation; lowly, and riding upon an ass, and upon a colt the foal of an ass" (Zech. 9:9).

John tells us that this was "a *young* ass," it was not yet full grown. *Luke* tells us that it was a colt *"whereupon yet never man sat."* Beloved, here is a tremendous miracle! No person had ridden this colt, it was unbroken. The disciples brought the colt to Jesus, and the Scripture tells us that they *"set Jesus thereon."* That means they literally picked the Lord up and set Him on the little donkey. Anyone who knows anything about a young colt that has never been ridden knows how explosive and destructive such an animal can be—yet this young ass was meek and docile as he carried Jesus into the city of Jerusalem. This is even more extraordinary when we consider that in addition to being ridden for the first time, this colt was surrounded by crowds of people shouting, "Hosanna," waving palm branches, and—according to Luke—casting their garments in the way. Certainly things would have been different had Jesus been an ordinary man, very different indeed.

The reason this little donkey did not buck and stampede and literally fling the Rider from his back was because he was being ridden by the One who could calm the most explosive heart, the One whom even the winds and the waves obeyed.

Five hundred years before, Zechariah foretold that the King of Israel would one day ride into the Holy City upon an ass, and at that time there were no kings in Jerusalem. The kingdom had ceased at the captivity, when the Israelites went into bondage. All of the Jews should have recognized the fulfillment of this prophecy, especially should the chief priests, scribes, and elders have recognized it; but if they *did* know it, they ignored it. How *could* they have missed their Messiah? He was born with so many prophetic labels on Him, and everything He said, everything He did, everywhere He went during His life on earth testified that He was "that Prophet" foretold by men of God in the days of their fathers. ALL of the events of the earthly ministry of Jesus were foreknown and foretold by the prophets long before those events took place; and as He rode into the Holy City on a humble little donkey, one of the *greatest* and most outstanding prophecies concerning Messiah, King of the Jews, was literally fulfilled before their eyes!

There are literally *millions* on earth today who are exposed to an open Bible, and events that are transpiring today are just as momentous and outstanding as was our Lord's triumphal entry into Jerusalem more than nineteen hundred years ago. Signs of His second coming are all around us — socially, politically, religiously, and in man's attempts to conquer space. Everything in the Bible that is prophesied to occur before the second coming is either behind us or with us at this very moment: yet millions of people go on as if they would live on this earth forever! They ask, "Where is the promise of His coming? for since the fathers fell asleep, all things continue as they were from the beginning of the creation" (II Pet. 3:4). Peter further declares that such people are "willingly ignorant," as was the case with the Jews when Jesus walked this earth. They had no will to believe on Him.

Verse 15: *"Fear not, daughter of Sion: behold, thy King cometh, sitting on an ass's colt."*

The Holy Spirit did not inspire John to quote Zechariah 9:9 exactly, word by word. The one point He was stressing here is the fact that Jesus was literally doing *at that very moment* what was foretold by one of their honored prophets five hundred years before. God gave this prophecy to Zechariah to comfort the Jews who, broken in spirit, despondent and discouraged, had just returned from the Babylonian captivity. For that reason God gave them this tremendous promise of their Messiah and King, a message designed to take away their fear and depression, and cause them to look forward to the day when they would have a King. However, the prophecy plainly told them that their King would not come as a great warrior and a military leader, but as the Prince of Peace, a holy King, even better than their great king David. He would come—not to deliver them bodily from Babylon, Egypt, or Rome, but to deliver their souls; He would bring salvation. But when their King came, humble, *"sitting on an ass's colt"* instead of coming in the military pomp and splendor they looked for, they refused to receive Him. Instead of crowning Him with a crown of glory, they crowned Him with thorns; and instead of putting Him on a throne, they nailed Him to a cross!

In studying the first and second comings of Christ, it is most interesting that both comings bear a message of comfort. God gave Israel the prophecies in the Old Testament concerning the coming of their Messiah to bring comfort, joy, and hope.   He came the first time *exactly as prophesied.*   Jesus said to His disciples just before the end of His earthly ministry, "Let not your heart be troubled... I go to prepare a place for you. And if I go and prepare a place for you, *I will come again, and receive you unto myself; that where I am, there ye may be also"* (John 14:1—3). And He will do *exactly as He promised!*

In I Thessalonians 4:13—18 Paul tells us not to sorrow "as others which have no hope," for we who believe that Jesus died for our sins according to the Scriptures, and that He rose again according to the Scriptures, also know that our loved ones who have died in the Lord will be with Him when He comes again for His own. One day—it could be today—Jesus will descend from heaven with a shout, with the voice of the archangel and the trumpet of God, and those who have died in the Lord will be raised. Then the saints who are alive will be caught up together with them to meet the Lord in the air—and Paul says, *"Wherefore COMFORT one another with these words!"*

Beloved, if the message of the second coming of Jesus unnerves and frightens you, there is something wrong with your Christian experience. To the born again believer, the message of the second coming does not bring fear and dread —on the contrary, it brings comfort and hope: "For the grace of God that bringeth salvation hath appeared to all men, teaching us that, denying ungodliness and worldly lusts, we should live soberly, righteously, and godly, in this present world; LOOKING FOR THAT BLESSED HOPE, AND THE GLORIOUS APPEARING OF THE GREAT GOD AND OUR SAVIOUR JESUS CHRIST" (Tit. 2:11—13).

Verse 16:   *"These things understood not His disciples at the first: but when Jesus was glorified, then remembered they that these things were written of Him, and that they had done these things unto Him."*

Even those who were *closest* to Jesus did not fully understand who He was and what He was doing. These disciples had lived among Jews who had talked of and looked forward to *a glorious King* who would sit on a throne and deliver them from Roman oppression. This caused them to miss the full meaning of Christ's earthly ministry. *"But when Jesus was glorified"* (after His resurrection and ascension, when the Day of Pentecost came and the mighty miracle of Pentecost was witnessed) *"then remembered they that these things were written of Him."* After Pentecost, they possessed the Holy Spirit, and Jesus had promised that the Holy Spirit would bring these things to mind: "But the Comforter, which is the Holy Ghost, whom the Father will send in my name, He shall teach you all things, *and bring all things to your remembrance, whatsoever I have said unto you"* (John 14:26). After the coming of the Holy Spirit, the little disciple band realized what had taken place during the time they had walked and talked with the Lord Jesus Christ. They realized that everything that happened, from the day He called them to follow Him, until His ascension and glorification, had been foreordained of God; not one thing had transpired "by accident."

Verse 17:   *"The people therefore that was with Him when He called Lazarus out of his grave, and raised him from the dead, bare record."*

Here the people—no doubt a multitude of them—gave testimony that it was *Jesus* who had *"called Lazarus out of his grave,"* and that it was *Jesus* who *"raised him from the dead."* Those who were present to witness that great miracle now *"bare record"* that it was wrought by this same Man who was riding into the Holy City on a young donkey.

Verse 18:   *"For this cause the people also met Him, for that they heard that He had done this miracle."*

A vast multitude of people now surrounded the Lord, many of whom had simply heard the report without actually witnessing the raising of Lazarus. The account naturally created tremendous curiosity, attracting people from far and wide, and it was *"for this cause"* (because of these reports) that the crowds went out to meet Jesus as He rode into Jerusalem.

Verse 19: *"The Pharisees therefore said among themselves, Perceive ye how ye prevail nothing? Behold, the world is gone after Him."*

The enemies of Jesus were baffled; they knew not which way to turn. They had given instructions that anyone who knew of the whereabouts of Jesus should report that knowledge to the council, so that He could be arrested and brought in; but instead of the people reporting where Jesus was, the multitudes were shouting, "Hosanna!" waving palm branches, and calling Him their King. The Pharisees and members of the council dared not attempt to arrest Him at that point, lest they endanger their own lives and be torn to pieces by the crowds. They were forced to stand on the sidelines while the multitudes shouted praises as Jesus entered the Holy City in triumph and victory. I am sure their minds must have gone back to Haman when he was forced to honor Mordecai: "Then took Haman the apparel and the horse, and arrayed Mordecai, and brought him on horseback through the street of the city, and proclaimed before him, Thus shall it be done unto the man whom the king delighteth to honour. And Mordecai came again to the king's gate. But Haman hasted to his house mourning, and having his head covered" (Esth. 6:11,12). For the full account of this incident, read Esther, chapters 5 through 7.

"Perceive ye" is as though we should exclaim, "What a sight!" or "Behold the sight!" And when the Pharisees cried out, "the *world* is gone after Him!" they were not far wrong. According to the historian Josephus, on ordinary occasions as many as three million Jews gathered into Jerusalem, and at this particular time it is believed that at least another million were present! With that many Jews shouting, "Hosanna" and throwing palm branches and garments in the path of Jesus, no doubt it did seem to His enemies that the whole world was there in one body, praising this One whom they so hated and whom they planned to put to death as soon as they could find opportunity.

Great men of God, past and present, believe that the mighty hand of God played an important role in this gala event. The power of God impressed the people to shout out that Jesus was *King,* thus drawing the attention of all men to Him. Their attention would then be focused on Him as He hung on the cross, paying the debt for their sins. All eyes were on Jesus that day, and God wanted all eyes on Calvary when, a few days later, He was crowned with thorns and instead of shouting "Hosanna" these same people were shouting, "Away with Him! Crucify Him!"

Jesus was man, but He was also God, and during His entire earthly ministry He exercised His divine power when He so willed. Habakkuk 3:4 mentions His brightness and His hidden power. In Nazareth His enemies tried to cast Him down over a precipice, but His hour had not yet come; therefore they could not take Him, and "He passing through the midst of them went His way" (Luke 4:30). The angry Jews could not take Him when they would have laid violent hands on Him in the temple in Jerusalem, for His hour had not arrived: "Then took they up stones to cast at Him: but Jesus hid Himself, and went out of the temple, going through the midst of them, and so passed by" (John 8:59). Yes, divine power and divine influence were displayed by Jesus, the power of Almighty God.

Certain Greeks Desire to See Jesus

Verse 20:   *"And there were certain Greeks among them that came up to worship at the feast."*

We do not know who these Greeks were, but we do know they were not heathen, because they had come *"to worship at the feast"*—and certainly a heathen would not have believed in the Passover, nor would one have been admitted to the feast. These men were Gentiles; they were not Jews who had *lived* among the Greeks and then returned to Palestine. They were undoubtedly Greek proselytes; they had turned to the religion of the Jews and were accustomed to attending the religious feasts in Jerusalem. There were many Greek proselytes in that day, according to Acts 17:4: "And some of them believed, and consorted with Paul and Silas; *and of the devout Greeks a great multitude,* and of the chief women not a few."

Men are born with a religious instinct; they want something to worship, they are by nature turned to worship something or someone. The Jewish religion was the strongest religion of that day, and wherever it had been taught and preached there were Greeks—as well as others—who had become proselytes to the Jewish faith.

Jesus "came unto His own, and His own received Him not." This national rejection was about to be publicly evidenced by the Jews' delivering Him up to the Romans to be crucified. As prophesied in Luke 2:25—35, Jesus would visit the Gentiles following His rejection by His own people, "to take out of them a people for His name" (Acts 15:14). It is very striking then that these Greeks came at this time. It was a *"firstfruit,"* so to speak, of a coming harvest, and pointed to those "other sheep" which the Good Shepherd must bring (John 10:16). It is also interesting that Gentiles were among the first to show an interest in Jesus at His birth (the wise men came from the east to worship Him and present gifts); so now these Greeks came to Him shortly before He was crucified.

It would appear that there was a break in events recorded in verses 12 through 19 and events in our present verse. It would be unlikely that the Greeks came seeking Jesus the same day He rode triumphantly into Jerusalem. They would not have said, "We would see Jesus" if they had been looking for Him that same day, for certainly everyone saw Him and knew where He was on that day.

Verse 21: *"The same came therefore to Philip, which was of Bethsaida of Galilee, and desired him, saying, Sir, we would see Jesus."*

The Scripture does not tell us why these Greeks sought

Philip rather than any of the other disciples, nor are we told how they knew Philip *was* a disciple. He lived in a village north of Galilee—and although Peter, Andrew, James, and John were also Galilaeans, Philip's Greek name implied that he had Greek connections, and this could have been the reason the Greeks sought *him* rather than others of the disciples.

The language here implies a true desire in the hearts of these Greeks in seeking to see Jesus. The Greek word translated *"desired"* means "to ask, beseech, or pray." These men were not hypocrites; they were not seeking Jesus for the wrong purpose, as most of the Jews did. They earnestly desired to know the Messiah, the Saviour.

The word here translated "Sir" in most places in the New Testament is rendered "Lord." When it *is* rendered "Sir" it is a form of address used by an inferior when speaking to a superior. In Matthew 13:27 the servants said to the householder, *"Sir,* didst not thou sow good seed in thy field?" Speaking to Pilate, the Jews said, *"Sir,* we remember that that deceiver (Jesus) said, while He was yet alive, After three days I will rise again" (Matt. 27:63). The Samaritan woman, speaking to Jesus, addressed Him as *"Sir"* three times in the course of her conversation with Him (John 4:11,15,19). In our present verse, the Greeks used it as a means of showing their respect for Philip because he was a disciple of the Messiah whom they wanted to see. They had heard enough of the truth from Old Testament Scripture to know that a Redeemer was coming, and I believe they sought Jesus as that One who was to come. It is possible that at the time the Greeks came looking for Jesus, He was in the inner part of the temple, which was not open to Gentiles.

Verse 22: *"Philip cometh and telleth Andrew: and again Andrew and Philip tell Jesus."*

We first met Andrew in chapter 1, verses 35–42, as one of the two disciples of John the Baptist who followed Jesus, went home with Him, and spent the day there. Andrew was never the same again. We touched on his ministry again in the account of the feeding of the five thousand, when he found a lad with a few loaves and fishes which Jesus used to feed the multitudes (ch. 6:1—14). Not much is said about Andrew in the Scriptures, but he brought his brother Simon Peter to Jesus, and Peter became one of the great men of the Bible, a pillar in the early Church. Philip did not know how to handle the situation in which he found himself, but he sought Andrew because he knew that if Andrew did not *know* the answer to his problem, he at least would know where to *find* an answer. So he sought Andrew, and *"Andrew and Philip tell Jesus."*

Verse 23: *"And Jesus answered them, saying, The hour is come, that the Son of man should be glorified."*

Jesus did not receive the Gentiles that day because *in the flesh* He had come into the world as King of the Jews, and it was necessary that He be crucified before Gentiles could be brought into the fold. By not receiving these Greeks into His presence, they would be taught that salvation was not through His wonderful, perfect life, or through His wonderful works, but by faith in the crucified Saviour. They needed to look upon Him as the Lamb of God "slain from the foundation of the world," rather than as the Messiah of Israel.

It was through His death that He broke down the "middle wall of partition," and now both Jews and Gentiles are members of the body of Christ, the New Testament Church:

"Wherefore remember, that ye being in time past Gentiles in the flesh, who are called Uncircumcision by that which is called the Circumcision in the flesh made by hands; that at that time ye were without Christ, being aliens from the commonwealth of Israel, and strangers from the covenants of promise, having no hope, and without God in the world: But now in Christ Jesus ye who sometimes were far off are made nigh by the blood of Christ. For He is our peace, who hath made both one, and hath broken down the middle wall of partition between us; having abolished in His flesh the enmity, even the law of commandments contained in ordinances; for to make in Himself of twain one new man, so making peace; and that He might reconcile both unto God in one body by the cross, having slain the enmity thereby: and came and preached peace to you which were afar off, and to them that were nigh. For through HIM we both have access by one Spirit unto the Father" (Eph. 2:11—18).

"The hour is come." This is the key to our present verse. Jesus had reached that hour when He, as the "corn of wheat," would fall into the ground and die, and *through His death* He would bring forth much fruit, both Jew and Gentile. Because He was very God He knew that many of the Jews expected Him to set up a glorious kingdom. There had been much excitement over His triumphal entry into the Holy City, and the people expected immediate deliverance from the power of Rome. He wanted them to understand that the hour had come—not for Him to sit on a throne, but for Him to die that He might bring forth "much fruit." When He said, *"The hour is come that the Son of man should be glorified,"* He was speaking of His death. He was about to be *glorified,* but He would not sit on a throne of glory in Jerusalem. He would be glorified with the glory He had with the Father in heaven. He had almost completed the work He came into the world to do, and He would soon ascend back to the Father where He was "in the beginning."

The "hour" to which Jesus refers here was appointed and fixed before the world was, and until that appointed hour arrived, all hell could not stop Him from accomplishing His appointed purpose. When that hour *arrived,* He was arrested, tried, condemned, and crucified.

Verse 24: *"Verily, verily, I say unto you, Except a corn*

*of wheat fall into the ground and die, it abideth alone: but
if it die, it bringeth forth much fruit."*

In this verse, another "double verily" stresses the importance of the truth Jesus gives here. It is very likely
that He was speaking to more than Philip and Andrew,
and we must always keep in mind that when Jesus preached
and taught He never preached above the understanding of
those who heard Him. Certainly when He referred to corn—
or a grain of wheat—falling into the ground, He used an
illustration easily understood by the people to whom He
spoke. Every person who heard Him that day knew that
a seed laid on a shelf or kept in a jar would never *produce
fruit!* The seed must be put into the ground, it must die,
and when the heart of that seed springs into life it will
produce a head of wheat with *many* grains. We must be
content to allow the seed to fall into the ground and die
if we expect to produce a harvest of wheat.

This beautiful figure of the seed and the harvest sets
forth a great spiritual truth: *JESUS had to die,* His death
was a divine imperative. The life of the world depended
upon the death of the Saviour. He was that *"corn of
wheat,"* that Seed that must fall into the ground and die.
As long as He tabernacled among men in a body of flesh,
though sinless, perfect, holy, without spot or blemish, He
abode alone. His holiness, His righteousness, His purity
could not save men; those attributes could only show men
how unholy and ungodly they were and how badly they
needed a Saviour. His death on the cross, His shed blood,
was the only way a harvest of souls could be reaped. Unless Jesus, the "corn of wheat," fall into the ground and
die, there would be no harvest; but through His death,
burial, and resurrection "according to the Scriptures" He
would bring forth much fruit. Eternal life for the multitudes of the world depended upon His death.

"Except" is a very strong word as used here. It means
there was no other way, it had to be death—"EXCEPT a
corn of wheat fall into the ground, EXCEPT a corn of

wheat die, there can BE no harvest!'' The sacrificial death
of Jesus was the only way salvation could be purchased for
hell-deserving men and women. Jesus said to Nicodemus,
"As Moses lifted up the serpent in the wilderness, even so
MUST the Son of man be lifted up.'' The "lifting up'' of
Jesus, His dying, was a divine MUST. In verse 32 of this
chapter He said, "And I, if I be lifted up from the earth,
will draw all men unto me.''

Verse 25: *"He that loveth his life shall lose it; and he
that hateth his life in this world shall keep it unto life
eternal."*

Few of the statements made by Jesus are recorded more
frequently than this one. We find it in Matthew 10:39;
16:25; Mark 8:35; Luke 9:24; 17:33; and here in our present
verse—a total of six times these words of our Lord are recorded. The meaning is clear: He who loves his life, he
who thinks more of life in this world than he thinks of the
life to come, shall LOSE that which is the best part of
his life—the inner man, the soul that will never die.

On the other hand, he who puts first things first, he
who cares little for things of this life but puts the kingdom
of God and His righteousness first, will find all things added
unto him. The person who realizes that this life is but a
"dressing room," a place to *get ready* to live, will pre-
serve to eternal glory his spirit and soul which will live
forever. He who lives for self, to get gain and satisfy the
desires of the flesh, will lose his soul—and what shall he
be profited if he shall gain *the whole world* and lose his
own soul? (Matt. 16:26).

By contrast, though a man may never possess the things
of this world, if his soul is saved by his faith in the shed
blood and finished work of the Lord Jesus Christ, he has
gained everything! This life is compared to a vapor that
appears for a little season and then vanishes away. Man's
allotted "threescore years and ten" are but a little span indeed when compared to the unending ages of eternity.

Hear the comforting words of Jesus—spoken first to His disciples, but also given for our instruction and admonition:

"Therefore I say unto you, Take no thought for your life, what ye shall eat, or what ye shall drink; nor yet for your body, what ye shall put on. *Is not the life more than meat, and the body than raiment?* Behold the fowls of the air: for they sow not, neither do they reap, nor gather into barns; yet your heavenly Father feedeth them. Are ye not much better than they?

"Which of you by taking thought can add one cubit unto his stature? And why take ye thought for raiment? Consider the lilies of the field, how they grow; they toil not, neither do they spin: and yet I say unto you, That even Solomon in all his glory was not arrayed like one of these. Wherefore, if God so clothe the grass of the field, which to day is, and to morrow is cast into the oven, shall He not much more clothe you, O ye of little faith?

"Therefore take no thought, saying, What shall we eat? or, What shall we drink? or, Wherewithal shall we be clothed? (For after all these things do the Gentiles seek:) for your heavenly Father knoweth that ye have need of all these things. *But seek ye first the kingdom of God, and His righteousness; and all these things shall be added unto you.*

"Take therefore no thought for the morrow: for the morrow shall take thought for the things of itself. Sufficient unto the day is the evil thereof'' (Matt. 6:25—34).

Dear reader, if you are saving your time, your talents, your love and labors for yourself, you are not saving at all—you are losing *everything!* God grant this be the day you fall in love with Jesus and set your affections on things eternal. This life at best is very brief and eternity is unending. If you receive Jesus and put Him first in your life, you will enjoy the bliss of heaven and the joy of His blessed presence throughout the ceaseless ages of God's eternity!

Verse 26:   *"If any man serve me, let him follow me; and where I am, there shall also my servant be: if any man serve me, him will my Father honour."*

It seems that these words were spoken primarily for the benefit and information of the Greeks who sought to see Jesus, but they were also spoken for all those who desire to become His followers.   Any man who wishes to serve Christ must follow Him, walk in His steps and share His life.   There must be no looking for riches, houses, lands, crowns, honors. To follow Jesus is to deny self, and worldly ambitions. In Matthew 16:24 He said to His disciples, *"If any man will come after me, let him deny himself, and take up his cross, and follow me."*   If we suffer with Him we shall reign with Him. If we deny Him, He will deny US.   If we are faithful stewards we will receive a full reward.   Children of God are *"heirs* of God, and joint-heirs with Christ; if so be that we suffer with Him, that we may be also glorified together"* (Rom. 8:17).

"Where I am, there shall also my servant be."   Blessed promise! All born again believers possess Christ in the Person of the Holy Spirit (Rom. 8:9,16).   All born again believers are citizens of heaven, we sit with Jesus in heavenly places (Eph. 2:6).   All born again believers are hid with Christ in God (Col. 3:3). Thus, *all true believers are NOW where He is in the spirit,* and in the by-and-by, in glorified bodies, we will be in His presence, never to be separated from Him.   The moment one becomes a believer, Jesus takes up His abode in that heart in the Person of the Holy Spirit, and from the moment saving faith is exercised in His shed blood and finished work, He is never separated from His own.

"If any man serve me, him will my Father honour." The Christian is promised divine honor. God the heavenly Father will give to all true believers such honor and glory as this world has never seen, honor and glory this world could not appreciate.   The natural man seeks honor from men, but the born again believer seeks to honor Christ and

will therefore *be honored* in that great rewarding day.

Jesus never bribed any person to follow Him. He never made glowing promises of temporal things to induce men to follow Him. On this particular occasion He knew the disciples were thinking of a glorious political kingdom, more than likely expecting to hold important positions in that kingdom; so He wisely—but kindly—put an end to their unscriptural expectations concerning a powerful earthly kingdom at that time and pointed out to them that if they were to follow Him they must serve Him and walk with Him. It would naturally follow that since the world hated HIM, the world would hate the disciples as well; and since He suffered, they must suffer for His sake. The promise He held out to them was the reward for faithful stewardship—if they followed Him faithfully, there would come a rewarding day when God the Father would glorify them because they had honored His only begotten Son.

However, the honor mentioned here applies to another world, not to this life. God has given us glimpses of that world—the Scriptures emphasize that just being with Jesus will be heaven, and certainly we know there are mansions there (John 14:2). The Word of God tells us enough about heaven for us to know that it is a glorious place—and being with Christ, receiving honor from God, will be the *outstanding* glory of that celestial city!

Listen to these words of inspired revelation:

In John 14:3 Jesus promised, "If I go and prepare a place for you, I will come again, and receive you unto myself; that where I am, there ye may be also."

In John 17:24 He prayed to the heavenly Father, "Father, I will that they also, whom thou hast given me, be with me where I am; that they may behold my glory, which thou hast given me: for thou lovedst me before the foundation of the world."

Let us ask ourselves, "Do I love my life—or have I surrendered it wholly to the One who loved me and gave Himself for me? Am I selfish and self-centered? Am I living for the things of this world? or am I laying up treasures in heaven?" We need to take stock of our lives and determine whether what we do is done to the glory of God, or to the satisfaction of self.

God the Father Audibly Answers the Son

Verse 27: *"Now is my soul troubled; and what shall I say? Father, save me from this hour: but for this cause came I unto this hour."*

There are depths of spiritual truth here and in the following verses that man will never fathom or completely understand. These things, too deep for the mind of man, increase my faith in the Word of God. Peter tells us that the Word of God "came not in old time by the will of man: but *holy men of God spake as they were moved by the Holy Ghost"* (II Pet. 1:21). In II Peter 3:16 we read of "some things *hard to be understood,* which they that are unlearned and unstable wrest, as they do also the other Scriptures, unto their own destruction." If we could understand everything in the Bible, our God would be no greater than *we* are.

Jesus had just said, "If a man love his life, he shall lose it, but if he hates his life in this world he shall keep it unto life eternal." He had said, "If a man would serve me, let him follow me, and where I am there will my servant be." Then suddenly, agony pierced Him and He was troubled. What did He see or feel, what entered His mind and soul, to cause Him to cry out, *"Now is my soul troubled"?* WHY was He troubled? In what form did this trouble grip Him? Was it the sight of the cross He was facing? Was it the *bodily* suffering through which He must pass? I am sure that even though Jesus was God in flesh—sinless and pure, untouched by guile or iniquity—His human body did not look forward to the pain and suffering that lay ahead of Him.

I doubt, however, that it was the physical pain which

He knew would certainly come upon Him that caused His soul to be troubled. I believe it was the imputed sin of the world which was to be laid upon Him that pressed so heavily upon His soul. The sinless Son of God, under the tremendous weight of the sins of the whole world, cried out in agony, "Now is my soul troubled!" This was suffering beyond the description possible in man's language, suffering of the soul of the Saviour of the world.

I do not believe it is possible for mortal man to fully realize what Jesus actually became and what He actually did in order that we might be saved. He did not *become* cursed, He was NOT cursed: He was *"MADE a curse for US"* (Gal. 3:13). I know He did no sin, there was no sin in Him, yet God *"hath made* Him to BE sin for US" (II Cor. 5:21). How is it possible to read those two passages of Scripture and still deny the divine Bible doctrine of substitution, imputation, and atonement? The ONLY way atonement, imputation, substitution, and redemption can be explained is to believe in the Bible doctrine concerning Jesus' being made a curse for us, made to be sin for us. There WAS no sin in Jesus—no, not in thought, word, or deed; but He came to *take away* the sin of the world (John 1:29). He came—not to be ministered unto, but to minister, and to give His life a ransom for many (Matt. 20:28). He came to lay His life down that WE might have life (John 10:18).

Sin is to blame for *all sorrow.* Trouble, sorrow, and heartaches come upon US because of our *own* sins, and we know the wrath of God should fall upon us *because* of our sins; but Jesus was not troubled because of HIS sins—He HAD no sin; He was troubled for the divine wrath of Almighty God due man because of *man's* sins. Many times we are troubled and sorrowful because we know we have grieved God; but *Jesus* did always those things that *pleased God.* HE was troubled because of the things WE have done to offend God. Mortal man fears death. *The wages of sin is death,* and unsaved men fear death because they know eternal damnation awaits them. But Jesus was not *afraid* of death; no condemnation awaited Him because there was *no sin* in Him. Yet He was troubled because He came to bear *our* fears, He came to *take away* fear, and to destroy him who had the power of death, through which power he caused men to fear (Heb. 2:9,14,15). Because of His stripes we are healed; because of His troubled soul and His life laid down, we have peace with God, we have life eternal, and we have "joy unspeakable and full of glory" (I Pet. 1:8).

We accept *by faith* the fact that Jesus was both human and divine. He was God in flesh, He and the heavenly Father were one; but He took a body of flesh, a body as human as yours and mine, sin apart. From the standpoint of *physical* needs—hunger, thirst, weariness, grief—He was made "like unto His brethren" in every detail (Heb. 2:17).

Someone may ask, "How then could Jesus be troubled if He were God in flesh? Since He was divine, all-powerful, why would He say, 'My soul is troubled'? Was His divine nature divided asunder from His human nature?" No, it was not divided asunder, but contained itself, held passive while the *human* nature was suffering. God knew in the beginning what He would do, and He knew the results of His doing. Jesus was to suffer the wrath of a sin-hating God, and was to be "made a curse for us," the prospect of which troubled Him. The *human* nature of Him suffered every pain, heartache, sorrow, and disappointment any man has ever suffered or will ever suffer—either in this world or in hell! In the body God gave Him He took the sinner's place; and in order to do that He suffered all the misery any poor sinner will ever suffer, in this life or in an eternal hell. Yes, He took our place FULLY, not partially. The sins of all the world were laid upon Him by imputation. No wonder He was troubled and amazed! No wonder His prayer in Gethsemane brought forth perspiration stained with blood!

"And they came to a place which was named Gethsemane: and (Jesus) saith to His disciples, Sit ye here, while I shall pray. And He taketh with Him Peter and James and John, and began to be sore amazed, and to be very heavy; and saith unto them, My soul is exceeding sorrowful unto death: tarry ye here, and watch" (Mark 14:32−34).

"And being in an agony He prayed more earnestly: and His sweat was as it were great drops of blood falling down to the ground" (Luke 22:44).

What was it that caused Jesus to be "sore amazed" in the Garden? What caused Him to be "very heavy . . . exceeding sorrowful unto death"? I believe that whatever He saw in Gethsemane, He saw (to some degree) in our present verse. I believe what He experienced to a degree here, He experienced fully in Gethsemane, as described in Psalm 22. Lest you fail to read this passage in your Bible, I quote it here and ask that you study it carefully, prayerfully. You will notice that it is a prophetic Psalm, pointing to Jesus, and it begins with the words He spoke from the cross:

"My God, my God, why hast thou forsaken me? Why art thou so far from helping me, and from the words of my roaring? O my God, I cry in the daytime, but thou hearest not; and in the night season, and am not silent. But thou art holy, O thou that inhabitest the praises of Israel. Our fathers trusted in thee: they trusted, and thou didst deliver them. They cried unto thee, and were delivered: they trusted in thee, and were not confounded.

"But I am a worm, and no man; a reproach of men, and despised of the people. All they that see me laugh me to scorn: they shoot out the lip, they shake the head, saying, He trusted on the Lord that He would deliver Him: let Him deliver Him, seeing He delighted in Him. But thou art He that took me out of the womb: thou didst make me hope when I was upon my mother's breasts. I was cast upon thee from the womb: thou art my God from my mother's belly.

"Be not far from me; for trouble is near; for there is

none to help. Many bulls have compassed me: strong bulls of Bashan have beset me round. They gaped upon me with their mouths, as a ravening and a roaring lion. I am poured out like water, and all my bones are out of joint: my heart is like wax; it is melted in the midst of my bowels. My strength is dried up like a potsherd; and my tongue cleaveth to my jaws; and thou hast brought me into the dust of death. For dogs have compassed me: the assembly of the wicked have inclosed me: they pierced my hands and my feet.

"I may tell all my bones: they look and stare upon me. They part my garments among them, and cast lots upon my vesture. But be not thou far from me, O Lord: O my strength, haste thee to help me. Deliver my soul from the sword; my darling from the power of the dog. Save me from the lion's mouth: for thou hast heard me from the horns of the unicorns.

"I will declare thy name unto my brethren: in the midst of the congregation will I praise thee. Ye that fear the Lord, praise Him; all ye the seed of Jacob, glorify Him; and fear Him, all ye the seed of Israel. For He hath not despised nor abhorred the affliction of the afflicted; neither hath He hid His face from Him; but when He cried unto Him, He heard. My praise shall be of thee in the great congregation: I will pay my vows before them that fear Him. The meek shall eat and be satisfied: they shall praise the Lord that seek Him: your heart shall live for ever. All the ends of the world shall remember and turn unto the Lord: and all the kindreds of the nations shall worship before thee. For the kingdom is the Lord's: and He is the governor among the nations. All they that be fat upon earth shall eat and worship: all they that go down to the dust shall bow before Him: and none can keep alive his own soul. A seed shall serve Him; it shall be accounted to the Lord for a generation. They shall come, and shall declare His righteousness unto a people that shall be born, that He hath done this" (Psalm 22).

In Gethsemane Jesus was compassed by demon monstrosities—"many bulls," *demon* bulls that gaped upon Him with their mouths like ravening lions. I personally believe the devil called together all the demon monstrosities in hell, and they pressed down upon the Saviour in the Garden of Gethsemane until even His soul was "exceeding sorrowful unto death." To some degree, this is what He saw in our present chapter when He cried out, "Now is my soul troubled!" In Gethsemane, hell made its last massive drive to stop the seed of the woman, He who would bruise Satan's head. No wonder He cried, "My soul is troubled!" No wonder He was "sore amazed." No wonder He was in such agony that His perspiration became as drops of blood. He faced such agony for you, for me—and all anyone need do to burn in hell forever is to reject the finished work of the Lord Jesus Christ. To reject Him is enough sin to damn a soul to the lowest hell. If you have not received Him, dear reader, receive Him NOW and let Him save you.

The physical agony Jesus suffered was not His most excruciating pain. Agony of soul and spirit outweighed the physical part of His death. Paul tells us that "in the days of His flesh, when He had offered up prayers and supplications with strong crying and tears unto Him that was able to save Him from death, and was heard in that He feared; though He were a Son, yet learned He obedience by the things which He suffered; and being made perfect, He became the author of eternal salvation unto all them that obey Him; called of God an high priest after the order of Melchisedec" (Heb. 5:7—10).

These finite minds of ours cannot conceive of how much God hates sin and how terrible sin is! Sin made God's only begotten Son to be troubled, exceedingly sorrowful, amazed, sweating drops of blood, and sin caused Him to cry out, "My soul is troubled!" Yes, sin is horrible beyond our understanding.

In Genesis 1:1 we read, "In the beginning God created

the heaven and the earth." In Hebrews 1:2 we read that all things were made by Jesus. God spoke the word and the earth was formed. He said, "Let there be light," and there was light. He said, "Let there be a firmament," and there was a firmament. But when mankind needed a Saviour, even Almighty God in all of His omnipotence, omniscience, and omnipresence, could not say, "Let there be a *Saviour*"—and a Saviour appear! Beloved, God is holy, God is righteous—and because of His holiness and righteousness He could not acquit the wicked (Nah. 1:3); and since God could not *acquit* the wicked, it was a divine imperative that He provide a substitute who could completely satisfy His holiness and righteousness, in order that He might be just and yet justify (save) the ungodly:

"But now the righteousness of God without the law is manifested, being witnessed by the law and the prophets; even the righteousness of God which is by faith of Jesus Christ unto all and upon all them that believe: for there is no difference: For all have sinned, and come short of the glory of God; being justified freely by His grace through the redemption that is in Christ Jesus: Whom God hath set forth to be a propitiation through faith in His blood, to declare His righteousness for the remission of sins that are past, through the forbearance of God; to declare, I say, at this time His righteousness: THAT HE MIGHT BE JUST, AND THE JUSTIFIER OF HIM WHICH BELIEVETH IN JESUS. Where is boasting then? It is excluded. By what law? of works? Nay: but by the law of faith. *Therefore we conclude that a man is justified by faith without the deeds of the law*" (Rom. 3:21–28).

Jesus speaks of *His soul* only three times in the Gospels. In Matthew 26:38 He said to Peter, James, and John, "My soul is exceeding sorrowful, even unto death: tarry ye here, and watch with me." In Mark's account of the same event He said, "My soul is exceeding sorrowful unto death: tarry ye here, and watch." Then in our present verse He said, "Now is my soul troubled."

"And what shall I say?" That Jesus was very God and very man is unmistakably taught in the Scriptures, as can be clearly seen when we compare the language used in chapter 5 and chapter 17 with the language used here in this verse. In chapters 5 and 17 Jesus spoke as God, but here He speaks as *man.* Human nature loves when loved; we befriend those who are friends to *us.* But Jesus was about to die for those who hated Him, and the human part of Him cried out, "What shall I say?" As GOD, He *knew* what He would say, He knew what He would do—He was equal with God in knowledge, and He knew the end in the beginning. But *as man* He had reached a height of anguish and perplexity that caused Him to ask the question. His God-nature answered, and thus Jesus found deliverance in prayer.

"Father, save me from this hour." As man, Jesus shrank from suffering and physical pain. If this had not been true, He would not have been truly MAN. If He had not dreaded pain He would not have been made "like unto His brethren" in all things. His prayer here is almost the same as His prayer in Gethsemane—"Father, if thou be willing, remove this cup from me: nevertheless not my will, but thine, be done" (Luke 22:42). Jesus prayed to be delivered from pain and suffering, which shows us that it is certainly not wrong for *believers* to pray for deliverance from sickness, pain, and sorrow. We need to remember, however, that in everything we must be submissive to the will of God, and in praying to be delivered from the oppression of illness—in ALL of our prayers, for that matter— we must pray as the Saviour prayed: "Not my will, but thine, be done."

You will notice that Jesus did not ask, *"What shall I CHOOSE?"* Even *as man* He knew exactly what He had come into the world to do, and everything He said and did had been foreordained in the eternal councils of the God- head before the world was ever created. Over and over again in His ministry He told the people that He did nothing independently of the Father. He said, "I and my Father are one." (In fact, in the Gospel of John, Jesus speaks of "MY Father" or "THE Father" more than one hundred times.)

In other words, in this portion of the verse Jesus said, "No, I will not pray to the Father to save me from this hour because I took a body and came *into* the world *for* this very hour! I came to lay my life down for the sins of the world. I know that I came to suffer and die, I now face that hour of suffering and my soul is now in agony; but I will drink the bitter cup, I will not pray to my Father to save me from this hour."

Verse 28: *"Father, glorify thy name. Then came there a voice from heaven, saying, I have both glorified it, and will glorify it again."*

As Jesus cried out, "Father, glorify thy name," He forgot the suffering He faced in the flesh. The one desire concerning His mission on earth was, first of all to glorify the Father, and secondly to lay His life down that through His death WE might have life. Believers should follow His example in everything we do, doing all to the glory of God. Our prayer should be, "Father, glorify thy name in me in all that I do and say, and in all that I am." It is God's will that in the end *all things* should glorify Him. To the glory of God all things were created. From a Roman prison Paul wrote to the Philippians, "According to my earnest expectation and my hope, that in nothing I shall be ashamed, but that with all boldness, as always, so now also Christ shall be magnified in my body, *whether it be by life, or by death*" (Phil. 1:20).

"Then came there a voice from heaven, saying, I have both glorified it, and will glorify it again." Three times during the earthly ministry of Jesus, God spoke from heaven in an audible voice. In Matthew 3:17, at the baptism of Jesus, God's voice from heaven said, "This is my beloved Son, in whom I am well pleased." On the Mount of Trans-

figuration, as Moses and Elijah met Jesus and conversed
with Him, a bright cloud overshadowed them and God
spoke from the cloud: "This is my beloved Son, in whom
I am well pleased; hear ye Him" (Matt. 17:5). And in our
present verse He again spoke from heaven, acknowledging
His beloved Son.

"I have both glorified it and will glorify it again" speaks
of the Incarnation, the miracles, the words, and the works
of Jesus. He had already glorified God the Father—but in
the crucifixion, resurrection, and ascension God would be
further glorified; and when Jesus puts Satan into the pit
and seals him there for a thousand years (Rev. 20:1—3), the
Father will be even further glorified. I do not feel that
it is wrongly dividing the Word to say that God not only
spoke here of the Incarnation and the Lord's work on earth,
but also of the entire course of His works, beginning with
creation and extending down to the moment when He spoke
to Jesus as recorded here. All things were created by Jesus
and for Jesus (John 1:3; Heb. 1:2). God glorified His name
in the flood, through the patriarchs, judges, and kings; and
He will once more glorify His name at the end of this dispensation, when Jesus comes to receive His bride.

Verse 29: *"The people therefore, that stood by, and
heard it, said that it thundered: others said, An angel
spake to Him."*

The multitude did not agree on what happened here.
Some of them, probably remembering Sinai, said, *"It thundered!"* Others said, *"An angel spake to Him."* But on
one thing they agreed: *the voice they heard, whether of
thunder or of an angel, belonged to no one in the crowd.*
Something very extraordinary had happened!

Verse 30: *"Jesus answered and said, This voice came
not because of me, but for your sakes."*

Not only had Jesus *taught* the Jews, He also had performed many mighty miracles during His earthly ministry

to convince them that He was their Messiah, the Son of God, "that Prophet that should come"; but in spite of all that He said and did, they rejected Him—and the voice of Almighty God was but one more public announcement that what Jesus had done and was doing was ordered by God the Father. God did not speak in an audible voice to assure Jesus of what He, as God's Son, already knew. He spoke as a witness to the *people,* testifying that He was with Jesus—yea, that Jesus was God in flesh.

Verse 31: *"Now is the judgment of this world: now shall the prince of this world be cast out."*

The hour had arrived when a sentence of condemnation was to be passed upon the whole order of things that had prevailed in the world since creation, a sentence passed by and through the death of Jesus on the cross. What the first Adam lost through disobedience in the Garden of Eden, the last Adam—the Lord Jesus Christ—reclaimed through His blood shed on Calvary. It is true that the whole creation groans and travails in pain even up to this present moment, but through the death of Jesus the whole creation *will be* delivered:

"The creature itself also shall be delivered from the bondage of corruption into the glorious liberty of the children of God. For we know that the whole creation groaneth and travaileth in pain together until now. And not only they, but ourselves also, which have the firstfruits of the Spirit, even we ourselves groan within ourselves, waiting for the adoption, to wit, the redemption of our body" (Rom. 8:21—23). There will be a new earth, and the curse will be lifted.

In the statement Jesus made in this verse, He clearly declared that He was going to spoil "principalities and powers," overcome the rulers of darkness and wickedness and upset the Godless order of things which had prevailed upon the earth since Adam sinned in the Garden of Eden. For many centuries God had winked at these things and tolerated them; but the hour had come when they would be tolerated no longer. Through His death, Jesus would bring the sentence of condemnation upon world systems. Oh, yes, they are still operating, *Satan* is still operating; *but they are defeated.* Satan is a defeated foe, and in the fulness of time Jesus will personally see to it that he is put into the pit and chained there for one thousand years. In the final consummation of all things, Satan will be "cast into the lake of fire and brimstone, where the beast and the false prophet are, and shall be tormented day and night for ever and ever" (Rev. 20:10).

We must take into consideration the terrible condition of the world when Jesus came into it. With the exception of Palestine, the whole world was without God—a world of idolatry, worshipping devils and demons in open rebellion against God. (If you doubt this, read the first chapter of Romans and I Corinthians 10:20.) When Jesus died on the cross His death passed a sentence of condemnation on all these things.

The *"judgment"* here has to do with the sin which overflowed the world at the time Jesus came as a babe in the manger. Sin had reigned, but this continual, *undisturbed* reign of ungodliness and idolatry was to be brought to an end by the death of Jesus. It is not yet completely done away with, but *it will be* when Jesus comes the second time.

The devil controlled the masses of mankind from Eden to Calvary. He held men captive and dominated their hearts and minds, leading them to worship the creature more than the Creator. God had given them up—soul, spirit, and body. But Jesus came, and through His death, burial, and resurrection, tens of thousands were delivered from Satan's bondage: "We see Jesus, who was made a little lower than the angels for the suffering of death, crowned with glory and honour; that He by the grace of God should taste death for every man. . . Forasmuch then as the children are partakers of flesh and blood, He also Himself likewise took part of the same; that through death He might destroy him that had the power of death, that is, the devil; and deliver them who through fear of death were all their lifetime subject to bondage" (Heb. 2:9,14,15).

"Now shall the prince of this world be cast out." The prince of this world could be none other than the devil himself. In Ephesians 2:2 Paul called him "the prince of the power of the air," and in II Corinthians 4:4 he referred to him as "the god of this age." In a sense, the whole world was under the dominion of Satan until Jesus came— and then the devil met his match! He could not lead Jesus into sin, although he tried every avenue of temptation (Matt. 4:1—11). When Jesus died on the cross, Satan's power was broken and heathenism and idolatry no longer control the whole world. On the cross Jesus spoiled Satan's set-up, "and having spoiled principalities and powers, He made a shew of them openly, triumphing over them in it" (Col. 2:15).

Certainly in our present verse Jesus refers to the victory He won on the cross. He did not mean that Satan would be completely shut out of the world at that very hour, but it *was* at that hour that he received his death sentence. He is still in the world, but he has been stripped of much of his power. A careful study of the Old Testament Scriptures will reveal the fact that Satan had tremendous dominion over the souls of men before Jesus came. There were "familiar spirits," wizards, witches. In the Old Testament era the Holy Ghost came upon men and then departed; He did not remain on earth as He does today, abiding in the hearts of believers. The Holy Spirit is in the world now, restraining Satan, and will *remain* in the world until the Rapture. When the saints are taken out of the world, the Holy Spirit will be taken out with them as described in II Thessalonians 2:7: "He who now letteth will let, until He be taken out of the way." After the Holy Spirit is taken out of the world (when the Church is raptured) the Man of Sin will be revealed and the Great

Tribulation will be ushered in.

A personal Jesus met a personal devil on the Mount of Temptation—and I believe with all of my heart that He met a personal devil and all the demons of hell in the Garden of Gethsemane, as well as on Calvary; but praise God, He won the victory! Jesus overcame the world, the flesh, the devil, death, hell, and the grave. He stripped the devil of a great portion of his authority and power and cast him out of a great part of his dominion—and in the by-and-by Satan will be doomed to the lake of fire for all eternity.

Because of the victory Jesus established for us, believers are more than conquerors through HIM: "There hath no temptation taken you but such as is common to man: but God is faithful, who will not suffer you to be tempted above that ye are able; but will with the temptation also make a way to escape, that ye may be able to bear it" (I Cor. 10:13).

In our present verse Jesus foretells what He knew would occur after His death, burial, and resurrection. He knew that thousands would be saved when Peter preached at Pentecost, other thousands would believe and be saved day by day. He knew the Holy Spirit would come into many hearts, and men once controlled by the devil would hear the Gospel, receive its message, and renounce Satan. Thus the devil would be cast out of the individual heart. What had taken place in only a few hearts before the death, burial, and resurrection of Jesus would be repeated by tens of thousands—even *millions* in the years to come, up to this present hour.

Verse 32: *"And I, if I be lifted up from the earth, will draw all men unto me."*

Here, as in chapter 3 verse 14, Jesus plainly speaks of His crucifixion. The statement that He would draw *"all men"* unto Himself does not mean that all men will be *saved.* It simply means that the death, burial, and resur-

rection of Jesus broke down the middle wall of partition
and there is no longer Jew or Gentile. The blood of Jesus
draws men from all races, creeds, and colors, the world
over. His blood is the center of Christianity, the one true
religion. ALL who will come to Him through the drawing
power of the Gospel message will be released from Satan's
power and set free.

The Greek word here translated *"draw"* is the same
word used in John 6:44. Without the drawing power of
the Word of God, as the Holy Spirit *applies* the Word, no
one would ever come to Jesus. It is impossible for any
person to be saved without first hearing the Word (John
5:24; 6:44).

Even while Jesus hung on the cross, His words began
to draw the souls of men. Two thieves were crucified with
Him, one on each side of Him. They both heard His words,
and *one* of them listened attentively. The words of Jesus
brought faith to his heart and he cried out, "Lord, remember me when thou comest into thy kingdom!" Jesus replied, "Verily I say unto thee, To day shalt thou be with
me in Paradise" (Luke 23:42,43).

Another individual heard the words of Jesus and was
saved that day. In Mark 15:37—39 we read, "And Jesus
cried with a loud voice, and gave up the ghost. And the
veil of the temple was rent in twain from the top to the
bottom. *And when the centurion, which stood over against
Him, saw that He so cried out, and gave up the ghost, he
said, Truly this Man was the Son of God!*" I expect to
meet the converted thief and the Roman centurion in that
great day when Jesus comes.

Verse 33:   *"This He said, signifying what death He
should die."*

This explanatory comment leaves no doubt as to what
Jesus meant in the preceding verse when He spoke of being
"lifted up." He was speaking of the cross that would be
raised on Golgotha, the cross on which it was foreordained

that He should die. From the moment He entered His public ministry until He cried out, "It is finished!" His one goal, His one aim and desire, was to finish the work the Father gave Him to do, and bring honor and glory to God. The work the Father sent Him to do was to pay the sin-debt—and there was only one way to pay it: it had to be paid by the death of Jesus on the cross.

Verse 34: *"The people answered Him, We have heard out of the law that Christ abideth for ever: and how sayest thou, The Son of man must be lifted up? Who is this Son of man?"*

This verse shows how hard the Jews were, how willingly ignorant and blind. They knew Jesus was speaking of His death on a cross, for under Roman law criminals paid for their crimes by crucifixion. But they pretended inability to reconcile the prophecies of the Old Testament concerning the Messiah, and what Jesus said concerning His dying on a cross. They believed Messiah would come, but they refused to accept a *suffering* Messiah. They expected Him to be a glorious King, a conqueror of those who oppressed Rome—and this was in spite of their familiarity with Isaiah 53.

"Christ abideth for ever." In this they were correct—and Jesus did not deny it. The Old Testament *prophesied* a Christ who would abide forever. In Isaiah 9:7 we read, "Of the increase of His government and peace *there shall be no end*, upon the throne of David, and upon His kingdom, to order it, and to establish it with judgment and with justice from henceforth even *for ever*. The zeal of the Lord of hosts will perform this."

Psalm 110:4 tells us, "The Lord hath sworn, and will not repent, Thou art a priest *for ever* after the order of Melchizedek."

Daniel prophesied, "There was given Him dominion, and glory, and a kingdom, that all people, nations, and languages, should serve Him: His dominion is an everlasting dominion, which shall not pass away, and His kingdom that which shall not be destroyed" (Dan. 7:14).

In Micah 4:7 God said, "I will make her that halted a remnant, and her that was cast far off a strong nation: and the Lord shall reign over them in Mount Zion *from henceforth, even for ever."*

Gabriel announced to the virgin Mary that she would bring forth a Son who would "reign over the house of Jacob for ever; and of His kingdom there shall be no end" (Luke 1:33). But the Jews refused to see the cross before the crown, they refused to see the sufferings of Christ before His glory and honor. They were blind to Isaiah's prophecy that He would be wounded for our transgressions, bruised for our iniquities. They would not accept Him as the Passover, the substitute sacrifice that would forever satisfy the holiness and the righteousness of God. They were sticklers for the Law of Moses, they claimed to live by the law; and yet the same law that declared the coming of Messiah, eternal King of glory, also declared that He would be "led as a lamb to the slaughter." They closed their eyes to the sufferings of their Messiah and looked only for the glory.

"Who IS this Son of man?" The Jews could not reconcile the statements Jesus had just made. The law said, *"Christ abideth for ever,"* yet Jesus had just said that the Son of man must die on a cross. They were asking Him, therefore, how He expected them to believe such a contradiction. Not once did they entertain the thought that He would be raised in glorious resurrection, victorious over death, hell, and the grave! They were blinded to the fact that these two things could be reconciled, that they could happen to one Person since that Person was the Son of God, very God in flesh.

The title *"Son of man"* is first found in Daniel 7:13: "I saw in the night visions, and, behold, *one like the Son of man* came with the clouds of heaven, and came to the Ancient of days, and they brought Him near before Him." The religious leaders among the Jews had studied the book of Daniel; they were familiar with the title "Son of man," and yet they attempted to use the Scriptures to prove that Jesus was not the Christ. The Old Testament Scriptures prophesied an *eternal* Christ, a glorious King of kings and Lord of lords who would reign forever; but the same verses that prophesied His glory also prophesied His suffering, and the Jews took only the part that proved their point, rejecting other truth set forth in the same passage.

Some people today do the very same thing. For example, in Luke 1:31 we are told, "And, behold, thou shalt conceive in thy womb, and bring forth a Son, and shalt call His name JESUS." (This happened literally, *and millions BELIEVE it.*) Then in verse 32 of the same chapter we read, "He shall be great, and shall be called the Son of the Highest: and the Lord God shall give unto Him the throne of His father David." Tens of thousands believe that Jesus was "great," that He was called "the Son of the Highest"—but they *spiritualize* "the throne of His father David." David was a *literal king,* he sat on a literal *throne;* and the same Scripture that declares "thou . . . shalt call His name Jesus" also declares that He will *sit on the throne of David*—a literal throne as surely as the throne of the Caesars was literal. Many religious leaders today accept *part* of these verses literally, and *spiritualize* the rest. They take the portion that proves what *they* believe, and spiritualize what they *refuse* to believe.

Many ministers today read the clear statement in John 14:1−3 where Jesus comforted His disciples by saying, "I go to prepare a place for you. And if I go and prepare a place for you, I will come again, and receive you unto myself; that where I am, there ye may be also." And then those same ministers proclaim that Jesus is not coming back *literally,* that His second coming is a *spiritual* coming which takes place when people are saved or when a Christian dies. Sometimes they say it occurred at Pentecost. They suggest many things—but Jesus plainly said, "I go away... *I will come again.*" The same Jesus who walked and talked with men on earth for forty days after His resurrection will come again exactly as He went away; He will not break His promise. He will come to receive us unto Himself, that where He is, there we may be with Him throughout eternity.

The Jews said to Him, "We are familiar with our Scriptures. We have read (and we *believe*) that the Son of man will come; *but He will be eternal.* Who is the 'Son of man' of whom YOU speak, the One to be lifted up on the cross? We cannot understand your words."

Verse 35: *"Then Jesus said unto them, Yet a little while is the light with you. Walk while ye have the light, lest darkness come upon you: for he that walketh in darkness knoweth not whither he goeth."*

Notice that Jesus did not say, "I am that Son of man." He had already *said* that—many times, in many ways. Why should He repeat what they had stedfastly refused to believe? Therefore He answered them with a very solemn warning of the danger they were in, danger of allowing their day of salvation to slip away.

"Yet a little while is the Light with you." John the Baptist had announced that *he* was not "that Light," but that he came *to bear witness* of that Light, *"the TRUE Light,* which lighteth every man that cometh into the world" (John 1:6–10). Jesus had declared Himself to be that Light, "the Light of the world," and in this present statement to the Jews He was saying, "I, the Light of the world, will be with you for a little season, but that season cannot last much longer. My day with you will soon come to a close. I am the Light of the world, I am the Sun of Righteousness; but for you, that Sun is about to set."

"Walk while ye have the light." Instead of quibbling and arguing, the Jews should have been walking in the light, walking in the footsteps of Jesus. When He returned to the heavenly Father and took His seat at the Father's right hand, the Jews were left in a state of judicial dark-

ness. As a nation, they were blinded and scattered to the four corners of the earth, and they have lived in hardship and misery ever since. In 70 A. D. — about forty years after the crucifixion — Titus the Roman overran Jerusalem so completely that not one stone was left upon another, and Jews were butchered wholesale in the streets. When Pilate asked them, "Whom shall I release unto you — Jesus or Barabbas?" they cried, "Release Barabbas! Crucify Jesus — let His blood be upon us and upon our children!" They chose the darkness of the damned rather than the Light of the world. Some of the Jews who made that choice were no doubt still living when Titus levelled their Holy City.

"He that walketh in darkness knoweth not whither he goeth." In that day, people did not have the lighting facilities we have today, and a man who tried to make a journey at night certainly had a difficult time of it. He could not see his way, he was likely to fall into the hands of thieves and robbers who prowled the highways and byways at night. He might stumble into a pit or a ditch, he could even fall over a precipice and lose his life! And that is exactly what happened to Israel after Jesus left this world. According to Josephus, in the period between the crucifixion of Jesus and 70 A. D. when Titus conquered the Holy City, Israel was a nation of madmen. They were judicially blinded, seeking for peace that could not be found in their ceremonies; they had no hope, no rest, they lived in misery and heartache.

Verse 36:   *"While ye have light, believe in the light, that ye may be the children of light. These things spake Jesus, and departed, and did hide Himself from them."*

In the previous verse, Jesus had invited the Jews to walk while they had the Light, warning them that darkness would soon overtake them. Here, He is again crying out, beseeching them to *see* the Light, *receive* the Light, and become *children of light*. We must believe right about Jesus before we can become children of God. No person can be

saved unless he accepts the truth about Jesus. It is the
Son who sets us free, and the way to know the Son is to
know the truth. The truth is the Word of God—and "the
Word was with God, and the Word was God." Jesus was
the Word in flesh; He was full of grace and truth. He
was the Light that "shineth in darkness; and the darkness
comprehended it not" (John 1:5). *Believing* is the one needful
step if we would be children of light. "Believe on the
Lord Jesus Christ, and thou shalt be saved" (Acts 16:31).
To believe on the Lord Jesus Christ is to be a child of light
because *HE IS light and life.*

*"These things spake Jesus, and departed, and did hide
Himself from them."* Most Bible scholars believe that Jesus
departed to Bethany at this time. His departure could have
been a miracle, as on other occasions when He withdrew
Himself from their sight.

Verse 37: *"But though He had done so many miracles
before them, yet they believed not on Him."*

The reference to *"so many miracles"* indicates that John
by no means recorded all of the miracles Jesus did in and
near the city of Jerusalem. (I refer you again to John 21:25:
"And there are also many other things which Jesus did,
the which, if they should be written every one, I suppose
that even the world itself could not contain the books that
should be written.") But in spite of these "many miracles,"
miracles that proved His messiahship beyond any possible
doubt, the people remained wilfully ignorant, wilfully blind,
refusing to believe Him, even for the work's sake.

The Greek word here translated *"before"* is translated
"in the *sight* of" in I Thessalonians 1:3, and in I Thessalonians
2:19 it is translated "in the *presence* of." Jesus
performed these miracles "before" the Jews, meaning that
He wrought the miracles in their sight and in their presence.
They *witnessed* the working of the miracles that
clearly proclaimed Jesus as more than man; but because
they hardened their hearts, because their consciences were

seared, they had no will to believe that He was their Messiah. *"They believed not on Him."*

Verse 38: *"That the saying of Esaias the prophet might be fulfilled, which he spake, Lord, who hath believed our report? and to whom hath the arm of the Lord been revealed?"*

This does not mean that the Jews rejected their Messiah in order that Isaiah's prophecy might be fulfilled. This would be fatalism, and the Bible does not teach fatalism. The meaning here is that the Jews' willing and wilful rejection of Him, their deliberate refusal to believe, was the fulfillment of Isaiah's prophecy. Through Isaiah, God prophesied the unbelief of the Jews—but that prophecy was not the CAUSE of their unbelief. Their unbelief was the result of their own willing ignorance and blindness. Even after seeing the mighty works of Jesus, they refused to believe that He was more than man.

The days in which WE live were prophesied by Paul, Peter, and others. We are living in "perilous times," days when men are lovers of their own selves, still willingly ignorant concerning the second coming of Jesus Christ. But the fact that these things are prophesied to come to pass in the last days does not *cause* them to come to pass. The Lord's foreknowledge of man's future sins does not compel men to believe not, nor to sin. The cause of present world conditions is the fact that men *reject the Word of God* today, refusing to believe on the Lord Jesus Christ.

"Lord, who hath believed our report? and to whom hath the arm of the Lord been revealed?" This quotation is from Isaiah 53:1. The Jews had the scroll of Isaiah; Jesus Himself stood in the temple and read from this marvelous fifty-third chapter which describes the sufferings of our Lord and Saviour in perfect accuracy. On the basis of this chapter alone, the Jews should have recognized their Messiah, so clear and understandable is its description of Him.

Our present verse—and those that follow—can be easily

understood when we accept the sovereignty of God. God has known all things from the beginning, and the fact that the Jews *would be* unbelieving is foretold just as clearly as the suffering of Jesus is foretold. The unbelief of the Jews is the fulfillment of Scripture, but let it be clearly understood that the prophecy did not *cause* them to be unbelievers.

"The arm of the Lord" refers to the Lord Jesus Christ. He was the strong arm to save, He was very God in flesh; but the religious leaders in Israel refused to see the light and believe on Him.

Verses 39 and 40: *"Therefore they could not believe, because that Esaias said again, He hath blinded their eyes, and hardened their heart; that they should not see with their eyes, nor understand with their heart, and be converted, and I should heal them."*

Does this statement mean that the Jews *could not* believe, that it was *impossible* for them to believe even if they had wanted to? Did Isaiah's prophecy prevent their believing? Indeed this is NOT what this passage means!

Again I declare that we must accept the sovereignty of God. Before the earth was, God knew every minute detail of all things from the beginning to the end. God spoke to Isaiah, and Isaiah prophesied concerning the fact already known by a sovereign God. Because the Jews rejected Jesus, because they continued in their sins and were wilfully blind, they had no power whatsoever to receive salvation by faith. Rejection of the Gospel hardens hearts, and it is possible for one to go so far in sin and reject the Gospel so long, until God says, *"Ephraim is joined to idols: let him alone!"*

"Therefore" (on account of this) *"they could not believe"* (they were not *able* to believe). Because of their continuous rejection of the mighty words and works of Jesus, they had come to the place where they were not *able* to believe. They had rejected Him so long that God gave them over

to judicial blindness and hardness of heart. For so long, they *would* not believe, and they had now come to the place where they *could* not believe.

This should be a warning to us in this present day. It is dangerous to live in this land of the open Bible where the Word of God is preached daily—and *reject the message* of that Word. As the message of the Gospel is rejected day by day, the *will* becomes less sensitive, hardened and darkened by sin; and when a person *by choice* continues in sin over a long period of time, that person will have no *will* to live a holy life and follow righteousness. The conscience becomes seared, and he is left without feeling as having to do with spiritual things. Such a one is most pitiful because he is hopeless. Apart from God's grace and mercy, man is hopeless, helpless, hell-bound. The very desire to *become* a Christian is planted in the heart through hearing the Word of God. *Apart* from the Word, there can be no *desire* to be saved—no quickening, no drawing to God, no new birth. The Word of God is "the power of God unto salvation to every one that believeth; to the Jew first, and also to the Greek" (Rom. 1:16).

The words in verse 40 are taken from Isaiah 6:9,10: "And He said, Go, and tell this people, Hear ye indeed, but understand not; and see ye indeed, but perceive not. Make the heart of this people fat, and make their ears heavy, and shut their eyes; lest they see with their eyes, and hear with their ears, and understand with their heart, and convert, and be healed." The meaning is simply that God had given the Jews over to judicial blindness, and through this blindness was punishing them for their continued rejection of His Word, His warning, and His only begotten Son, the Lord Jesus Christ.

God hardened *Pharaoh's* heart, but it was not God's *will* to harden Pharaoh's heart any more than it is His will to harden the heart of any other person. Pharaoh was warned, and continually rejected the warning God sent to him. Because of that, his heart became hard.

We find another such instance in Joshua 11:20: "For it was of the Lord to harden their hearts, that they should come against Israel in battle, that He might destroy them utterly, and that they might have no favour, but that He might destroy them, as the Lord commanded Moses."

In Deuteronomy 2:30 we read, "But Sihon king of Heshbon would not let us pass by him: for the Lord thy God hardened his spirit, and made his heart obstinate, that He might deliver him into thy hand, as appeareth this day."

In Romans 9:17,18 Paul said, "For the Scripture saith unto Pharaoh, Even for this same purpose have I raised thee up, that I might shew my power in thee, and that my name might be declared throughout all the earth. Therefore hath He mercy on whom He will have mercy, and whom He will He hardeneth."

God knew what these men would do even before they were born, but this had nothing to do with the will of the individual. Man was created a free moral agent—not a puppet or a machine, but *a living soul!* God cannot do wrong. He will judge in righteousness; the Judge of all the earth will do right toward all men. When we read that a person or a nation is spiritually blinded, we will always discover that the person or nation has been warned again and again, but refused to hear the warning of God and repent. God declares that when He calls and we refuse, when He stretches out His hand and we do not regard it, when we set at nought His counsel and refuse to listen to His reproof, He will laugh at our calamity and mock when our fear cometh. (Study Proverbs 1:22—33.) There is no record in the Bible where God ever hardened the heart of people or nations and gave them over to blindness until He had given them ample warning and time to repent.

In the thirteenth chapter of Matthew we find parables concerning the mysteries of the kingdom of heaven. The disciples asked Jesus *why* He spoke in parables, and He replied that it was given to *them* to know the mysteries of the kingdom of heaven, but to the unbelieving Jews it was *not* given: "For whosoever hath, to him shall be given, and he shall have more abundance: but whosoever hath not, from him shall be taken away even that he hath. Therefore speak I to them in parables: because they seeing see not; and hearing they hear not, neither do they understand. And in them is fulfilled the prophecy of Esaias, which saith, By hearing ye shall hear, and shall not understand; and seeing ye shall see, and shall not perceive: For this people's heart is waxed gross, and their ears are dull of hearing, and their eyes they have closed; lest at any time they should see with their eyes and hear with their ears, and should understand with their heart, and should be converted, and I should heal them. *But blessed are your eyes, for they see: and your ears, for they hear*" (Matt. 13:12—16).

We know that God has no pleasure in the death of the wicked. It is not His will that any perish, but that all come to repentance. God is willing to soften hearts that have been hardened by sin, willing to open the mind that has been blinded by the god of this age; but unless the individual is willing, God's hands are tied. God is LOVE, and love does not drive nor force. Love leads, love invites— and God's invitation is to "whosoever will." The Jews had the message of the Gospel first. They were exposed to the preaching of John the Baptist, and to the teaching of Jesus Himself. They shut their own eyes and hardened their own hearts; and because of this, because they closed their eyes and their hearts against the words and works of Jesus, God gave them over to their own lusts, permitted their hearts to be hardened and allowed their eyes to be blinded. Then they could not repent, they could not believe, they could not return unto God. But it was not God's will that this be so. "He came unto His own, *and His own received Him not.*" Since they refused to receive Him, He withdrew His grace and mercy from them.

Verse 41: *"These things said Esaias, when he saw His glory, and spake of Him."*

To fully appreciate the truth of this verse, we must read the entire sixth chapter of Isaiah. The first five verses of that chapter are given here:

"In the year that king Uzziah died I saw also the Lord sitting upon a throne, high and lifted up, and His train filled the temple. Above it stood the seraphims: each one had six wings; with twain he covered his face, and with twain he covered his feet, and with twain he did fly. And one cried unto another, and said, Holy, holy, holy, is the Lord of hosts: the whole earth is full of His glory. And the posts of the door moved at the voice of him that cried, and the house was filled with smoke. Then said I, Woe is me! for I am undone; because I am a man of unclean lips, and I dwell in the midst of a people of unclean lips: for mine eyes have seen the King, the Lord of hosts" (Isa. 6:1—5). Isaiah saw Christ's glory and spoke of Him. It was such magnificent glory that the seraphim veiled their faces and Isaiah cried out, *"Mine eyes have seen THE KING, the Lord of hosts!"*

Many Bible scholars see in Isaiah's vision here the glory of the Lord Jesus Christ when He comes the second time to punish the Jews in the end of the age. They note that *"the posts of the door" being shaken* seems to indicate terrifying judgment. The temple being *"filled with smoke"* speaks of judgment. The Jews will suffer untold, indescribable misery during "the time of Jacob's trouble"—the last half of Daniel's seventieth week of prophecy. They will finally see Jesus coming in glory and will recognize Him because of the prints of the nails in His hands. Study Zechariah 13:6 through Zechariah chapter 14.

Verse 42:   *"Nevertheless among the chief rulers also many believed on Him; but because of the Pharisees they did not confess Him, lest they should be put out of the synagogue."*

The Holy Spirit, through the inspired pen of John the Beloved, does not overlook a fact that God would have us know concerning the Jews and their unbelief. Some were not utterly blinded or hardened, and these were willing to receive Jesus as sent from God. They did not understand all about Him, but they secretly believed that He was the Christ. Even some of the chief religionists believed, but they were afraid to *confess* that belief. They dared not confess publicly that they believed Jesus to be the Messiah; they were afraid of the Pharisees, and like the parents of the blind man, they feared being put out of the synagogue. They were cowards, overcome by the fear of man: "The fear of man bringeth a snare: but whoso putteth his trust in the Lord shall be safe" (Prov. 29:25).

The New Testament emphasizes open confession: "If thou shalt confess with thy mouth the Lord Jesus, and shalt believe in thine heart that God hath raised Him from the dead, thou shalt be saved. For with the heart man believeth unto righteousness; and with the mouth confession is made unto salvation" (Rom. 10:9,10). These who believed Jesus to be the Christ were afraid to confess openly because, to them, being put out of the synagogue was equal to being shut out of heaven! They feared excommunication as they feared nothing else on earth; but after the Day of Pentecost this fear was taken away, and they testified and preached with holy boldness. Many of them were martyred, many were thrown into prison, they suffered severely; but they continued to witness. They were no longer secret disciples!

Verse 43: *"For they loved the praise of men more than the praise of God."*

Uppermost in the minds of these Jews was the desire to be loved and respected by their fellowmen. They wanted a good report of themselves from men; they could not bear to be ridiculed, persecuted, reviled, and laughed at by other Jews—and most of all they shrank from being put out of the synagogue. They sacrificed their own personal convictions, they paid no attention to the voice of their God-given conscience, they feared man greatly; and therefore they refused to confess openly that Jesus was their Messiah and Saviour, "that Prophet that should come into the world."

These Jews were not the last to seek the praise of men. There are thousands upon thousands today who had much rather receive the praise and plaudits of men than to know God and receive His approval and the everlasting life He gives.

Verse 44: *"Jesus cried and said, He that believeth on me, believeth not on me, but on Him that sent me."*

Here again the Greek denotes a very loud cry, such as one would send out to call people to attention. There is nothing said as to the time and place when the Saviour made this statement, but in the light of verse 36, which says, *"These things spake Jesus, and departed, and did hide Himself,"* I am inclined to believe with most Bible scholars that Jesus began a new address here—probably the day after God spoke from heaven in an audible voice. The message Jesus gave here is probably one of the last public addresses delivered by Him in the city of Jerusalem. It concludes His ministry in that city and brings to a close the public testimony of Jesus to His own people. Here He proclaims His divine office, His divine dignity, and the purpose for which He came into the world. He points out to the Jews the extreme danger of neglecting His words, His testimony to them, and once more assures them that the words He has spoken and the miracles He has wrought were not His own, but were spoken and wrought in perfect cooperation with the power of God the Father. Here again He proclaims to the Jews the perfect unity between Himself and Jehovah God—such unity and oneness that he who believes on Jesus also believes on God who sent Him.

True Bible doctrine concerning the Godhead teaches that there is such perfect unity between Father, Son, and Holy Spirit that when we receive ONE, we receive ALL. When we possess one, *we possess ALL*. Jesus was speaking to a group of Jews who believed that He was more than man, yet were afraid to confess Him as Messiah. He was therefore saying to them, "You need not consider it a small thing to believe on me, because when you believe on me you also believe on God the Father—God of Abraham, Isaac, Jacob, and Moses. To know ME is to know HIM. I am not inferior to the God of your fathers; I am co-equal with Him from the beginning; and when you believe on me, you believe on God."

Verse 45: *"And he that seeth me seeth Him that sent me."*

Jesus repeats here the teaching that it is impossible to separate God the Father and God the Son. He said, "He who sees me does not see me *only,* but through and by me he also sees the Father who sent me. We are ONE." When we believe on Christ we believe on God the Father, and when we see Christ we *see* the Father—not physically, but with the eye of faith, the eye of the inner man. This was possibly the last time He would speak to such a group before He went to the cross, and He wanted all who heard Him to know that when they put their faith and trust in Him, they were resting not only on Him, but on the Father also. Believers rest not only in the hand of Jesus, but in the Father's hand as well. In John 10:28—30 He had told them, "I give unto them eternal life; and they shall never perish, neither shall any man pluck them out of my hand. My Father, which gave them me, is greater than all; and no man is able to pluck them out of my Father's hand. *I and my Father are ONE."*

Verse 46: *"I am come a light into the world, that whosoever believeth on me should not abide in darkness."*

Here Jesus again compares Himself to the sun which illumines the earth physically. As the Light of the world, He is saying here, "I, the Son of God, have come into a world filled with the darkness of sin and ungodliness. I am **THE** Light, the very source of life, and I offer this life to everyone who will receive me, to all who will believe on me. All who believe on me will be delivered from the power of darkness and translated into the kingdom of light."

When Jesus said, *"I am come a light into the world"* He was declaring His pre-existence. He was the light *before* He came into the world. He said to His disciples, *"Ye are the light of the world,"* but they did not *come* "a light into the world"; they *became* light when they received **THE** Light of life, the Lord Jesus Christ.

Just as the sun illumines the whole world and sheds its light upon *all mankind,* Jesus came, *the spiritual light* which "hath appeared to all men" (Tit. 2:11), that "whosoever will" may be saved. He loved the whole world, He is the propitiation for the *sins* of the whole world (John 3:16; I John 2:2). Just as the sun shines for the good of *all,* Jesus came into the world to give His life a *ransom* for all, and whosoever will see the light with the eye of faith and will believe on Jesus will receive life. Salvation is for "whosoever." Romans 10:13 says, "Whosoever shall call upon the name of the Lord shall be saved!"

Christ is *the only light* that can penetrate the darkness of sin that engulfs this world, and the only way to become one with Him is by faith in His shed blood and finished work. All who exercise faith in the Lord Jesus Christ become children of light; they no longer walk in darkness, they walk in the light as **HE** is in the light (I John 1:7). All who reject Jesus abide in darkness, and at the end of their earthly life they will plunge into the blackness of darkness forever.

Verse 47: *"And if any man hear my words, and believe not, I judge him not: for I came not to judge the world, but to save the world."*

Here is pointed out the danger of hearing the words of

Jesus and refusing to believe them. It is a terrible thing to hear the Word of God and reject it. "He that believeth on the Son of God hath the witness in himself: *he that believeth not God HATH MADE HIM A LIAR; because he believeth not the record that God gave of His Son*" (I John 5:10).

When Jesus said, *"I judge him not,"* He meant "I judge him not NOW." He was trying to show the Jews that He came the first time to *save*, not to judge. He did not come to drive the Romans out of Palestine, but to seek and to save that which was lost. He came not as the Great Conqueror, but as the "Great Physician." He came to heal souls, not to destroy men in battle.

He came the first time, a Babe in a manger, a Lamb for the slaughter. He came to lay His life down. When He comes the second time He WILL come in judgment. He will come as the Lion of the Tribe of Judah, King of kings and Lord of lords. He will smite the nations, and His enemies will become His footstool. He will judge in righteousness, He will punish His adversaries, and He will *reign* in righteousness; but that day is yet in the future.

The key to full understanding of this verse is the contrast between the first coming of Jesus and His second coming. He came the first time to set up a throne of grace and mercy, and all who will come to Him in faith believing will become *recipients* of His grace and mercy. When He comes the second time He will set up a throne of *judgment:*

"And I saw a great white throne, and Him that sat on it, from whose face the earth and the heaven fled away; and there was found no place for them. And I saw the dead, small and great, stand before God; and the books were opened: and another book was opened, which is the book of life: and the dead were judged out of those things which were written in the books, according to their works. And the sea gave up the dead which were in it; and death and hell delivered up the dead which were in them: and they were judged every man according to their works. And death and hell were cast into the lake of fire. This is the second death. And whosoever was not found written in the book of life was cast into the lake of fire" (Rev. 20: 11—15). (The "dead" in this passage refers to the wicked dead.)

Jesus provided enough grace to save every sinner who has ever been born or ever will be born. He provided enough blood to cleanse every wicked heart that has ever been or ever will be. He paid the ransom in full, He *finished* redemption; but we must come to Him. The reason men are lost today is that they will not believe on the Lord Jesus Christ: "For God sent not His Son into the world to condemn the world; but that the world through Him might be saved. He that believeth on Him is not condemned: *but he that believeth NOT is condemned already, because he hath not believed in the name of the only begotten Son of God*" (John 3:17,18).

Verse 48: *"He that rejecteth me, and receiveth not my words, hath one that judgeth him: the Word that I have spoken, the same shall judge him in the last day."*

No wonder Satan hates the Word of God! No wonder he has worked so zealously through liberals and modernists to change the Word, take from it, destroy it. Here, Jesus clearly and positively declares that there is a *future judgment*, with condemnation to those who reject Him after they are exposed to His Word.

The Greek word here translated "rejected" has the same meaning as to *despise or set at nought* the Word of God: "He that heareth you heareth me; and he that despiseth you despiseth me; and he that despiseth me despiseth Him that sent me" (Luke 10:16).

He who rejects Jesus and refuses to believe His words will, at the end of life, find that he faces the judgment of Almighty God! He may live to a ripe old age physically; he may be successful in business, politics, or whatever walk of life he has chosen. He may seem to be "getting by" with rejecting Jesus and spurning the Word of God; but such a person is under the wrath of God, and in that great judgment morning he will face God to give an account for that which he has heard of the Word of God, but refused to believe.

John, under inspiration, wrote, "In the beginning was the Word, and the Word was with God, and the Word was God. . . And the Word was made flesh, and dwelt among us . . ." (John 1:1,14). Jesus Himself said, "The words that I speak unto you, they are spirit, and they are life" (John 6:63). And now in our present verse He said, *"The Word that I have spoken, the same shall judge . . . in the last day."* These Jews heard Jesus speak, they listened to His teaching, and when they stand before God at the Great White Throne the words Jesus spoke in their presence will be there to judge and condemn them.

In Romans 3:19 Paul said, "Now we know that what things soever the law saith, it saith to them who are under the law: *that every mouth may be stopped, and all the world may become guilty before God!"* Dear reader, take warning: This verse speaks of the Mosaic system; but if *the Law of Moses* is a mouth-stopper, how much *more* powerful are the words of Jesus, spoken here on earth and penned down by holy men? WE have the New Testament, the perfect law of liberty. We have the Scriptures, God's completed Word; and if we refuse to hear the message of the Scriptures and refuse to *receive the Christ* of the Scriptures, those very Scriptures will stand at the judgment to condemn us and we will hear Jesus say, "Depart! I never knew you!"

Verse 49: *"For I have not spoken of myself; but the Father which sent me, He gave me a commandment, what I should say, and what I should speak."*

"I have not spoken of myself" means that Jesus was not speaking FROM Himself. He once more declared the

truth which He had so often declared before—the intimate relationship and union between God the Father and Jesus Christ the Son.   The words of Jesus were the words the Father gave Him to speak, and to refuse His words was to refuse God because Jesus was God Incarnate.

"The Father which sent me, He gave me a commandment, what I should say, and what I should speak."   The words of Jesus since He entered His public ministry were words agreed upon by the Godhead even before the foundation of the world.   The works He had accomplished were works foreordained by God the Father, to be wrought by Jesus the Son when He should take a body and come into the world to do what the law could *not* do because of the weakness of the flesh.   All that Jesus said and did was pre-arranged by the Godhead, *and therefore was arranged by perfect wisdom.*

When we read in the Word of God that "God sent the Son," and "God set forth the Son," and when Jesus says that His words are the commandment of the Father, we may know that these expressions are used by the Holy Spirit in condescension to our weak, natural minds, our weak faculties of understanding.   Such expressions are used in order that we might understand, as far as it is possible for mankind TO understand, the perfect oneness of the Godhead—Father, Son, and Holy Ghost.   This does not mean that Jesus is inferior (or secondary) to God the Father; but in speaking of Persons in the Divine Trinity it is impossible for the finite mind of man to fully understand and appreciate the Godhead.   We cannot explain one God manifest in three Persons, but we believe it because the Bible declares it, it is Scriptural truth, and we accept it by faith.

When we read that God gave commandment to the Son, this does not mean that the Son had no part in the commandment except to obey.   The commandment God gave to the Son was a commission arranged by the Trinity, arranged in the covenant of redemption, and the Son was as willing to execute the commandment as the Father was to give it.

In Deuteronomy 18:18,19 Moses wrote words given to Him by Almighty God, prophesying, *"I will raise them up a Prophet from among their brethren, like unto thee, and will put my words in His mouth; and He shall speak unto them all that I shall command Him. And it shall come to pass, that whosoever will not hearken unto my words which He shall speak in my name, I will require it of him."* Jesus spoke words the Father had commanded Him to speak, thus fulfilling the prophecy given to Moses and penned down centuries before Jesus came into the world.

Verse 50: *"And I know that His commandment is life everlasting: whatsoever I speak therefore, even as the Father said unto me, so I speak."*

In effect, Jesus said to the Jews here, "Whether or not you believe what I say, whether or not you receive my message, the words I speak were commanded of God the Father. Regardless of what you believe about what I have said, those who *receive* my words have everlasting life and those who reject my words will reap eternal condemnation in the lake of fire." In John 6:68 *Peter* asked, *"Lord, to whom shall we GO? THOU hast the words of eternal life"*—but Peter was one of the few who believed the words of Jesus.

"Whatsoever I speak therefore, even as the Father said unto me, so I speak." With these words, Jesus brings to a close His public messages to the Jews in Jerusalem. From the beginning of His public ministry throughout the three and one-half years He had walked among them, He had given them the message the Father *gave* Him to give to them. Therefore in *rejecting* the message they not only rejected HIM, they also rejected *the God of their fathers.* In rejecting the words of Jesus, they rejected the Word of God—and apart from the Word of God there is no salvation. We are plainly told that "faith cometh by hearing, *and*

hearing by THE WORD OF GOD" (Rom. 10:17).

Jesus said to Nicodemus, "Except a man be born again, he cannot see the kingdom of God. . . Except a man be born *of water* (the Word) *and of the Spirit,* he cannot enter into the kingdom of God" (John 3:3,5).

We are born again "not of corruptible seed, but of *incorruptible, BY THE WORD OF GOD,* which liveth and abideth for ever" (I Pet. 1:23).

Jesus said, *"He that heareth MY WORD,* and believeth on Him that sent me, *hath everlasting life, and shall not come into condemnation;* but is passed from death unto life" (John 5:24).

"Wherefore lay apart all filthiness and superfluity of naughtiness, *and receive with meekness THE ENGRAFTED WORD, which is able to save your souls"* (James 1:21).

Jesus said to His disciples, *"Now ye are clean THROUGH THE WORD WHICH I HAVE SPOKEN UNTO YOU"* (John 15:3).

To the unbeliever, the Word of God is the *power* of God unto salvation (Rom. 1:16).

To the believer, the Word is a lamp unto the feet and a light unto the pathway (Psalm 119:105).

And finally—I thank God that we have the promise that His Word cannot be destroyed, regardless of what the devil and all hell may do against it:

"FOR EVER, O LORD, THY WORD IS SETTLED IN HEAVEN!" (Psalm 119:89).

The Word of God is the sum and substance of all the teachings of Jesus. To reject and despise the Word is to reject and despise all that He taught—yea, all that He *was,* because He was the Word Incarnate. To reject the Word of God brings divine sentence of condemnation. He who rejects the Gospel today rejects everything Jesus preached, taught, and wrought, because the Gospel proclaims the doctrine and teaching of the Lord Jesus Christ, Son of God, Saviour of sinners.

The gravity of rejection of the Word lies in the fact that

every word Jesus spoke was commanded by God the Father. Christ declared clearly and frequently that He was not Himself the source of His teaching, but His teaching was the commandment of God the Father who sent Him into the world to declare the Father and bring light and life to all who would believe in His finished work.

We have now come to the close of the first part of the Gospel of John. Chapter 13 opens with, "Now before the feast of the passover, *when Jesus knew that HIS HOUR WAS COME* that He should depart out of this world unto the Father, having loved His own which were IN the world, *He loved them unto the end."*

Jesus has given His public witness, His public testimony. The works which God the Father sent Him to do, *He has done.* The message God the Father gave Him to give *has been given.* Judgment has been declared, and from here on out His ministry will be concentrated upon that little band of men whom He called to walk with Him while He ministered here on earth.

CHAPTER XIII

1. Now before the feast of the passover, when Jesus knew that his hour was come that he should depart out of this world unto the Father, having loved his own which were in the world, he loved them unto the end.

2. And supper being ended, the devil having now put into the heart of Judas Iscariot, Simon's son, to betray him;

3. Jesus knowing that the Father had given all things into his hands, and that he was come from God, and went to God;

4. He riseth from supper, and laid aside his garments; and took a towel, and girded himself.

5. After that he poureth water into a bason, and began to wash the disciples' feet, and to wipe them with the towel wherewith he was girded.

6. Then cometh he to Simon Peter: and Peter saith unto him, Lord, dost thou wash my feet?

7. Jesus answered and said unto him, What I do thou knowest not now; but thou shalt know hereafter.

8. Peter saith unto him, Thou shalt never wash my feet. Jesus answered him, If I wash thee not, thou hast no part with me.

9. Simon Peter saith unto him, Lord, not my feet only, but also my hands and my head.

10. Jesus saith to him, He that is washed needeth not save to wash his feet, but is clean every whit: and ye are clean, but not all.

11. For he knew who should betray him; therefore said he, Ye are not all clean.

12. So after he had washed their feet, and had taken his garments, and was set down again, he said unto them, Know ye what I have done to you?

13. Ye call me Master and Lord: and ye say well; for so I am.

14. If I then, your Lord and Master, have washed your feet; ye also ought to wash one another's feet.

15. For I have given you an example, that ye should do as I have done to you.

16. Verily, verily, I say unto you, The servant is not greater than his lord; neither he that is sent greater than he that sent him.

17. If ye know these things, happy are ye if ye do them.

18. I speak not of you all: I know whom I have chosen: but that the scripture may be fulfilled, He that eateth bread with me hath lifted up his heel against me.

19. Now I tell you before it come, that, when it is come to pass, ye may believe that I am he.

20. Verily, verily, I say unto you, He that receiveth whomsoever I send receiveth me; and he that receiveth me receiveth him that sent me.

21. When Jesus had thus said, he was troubled in spirit, and testified, and said, Verily, verily, I say unto you, that one of you shall betray me.

22. Then the disciples looked one on another, doubting of whom he spake.

23. Now there was leaning on Jesus' bosom one of his disciples, whom Jesus loved.

24. Simon Peter therefore beckoned to him, that he should ask who it should be of whom he spake.

25. He then lying on Jesus' breast saith unto him, Lord, who is it?

26. Jesus answered, He it is, to whom I shall give a sop, when I have dipped it. And when he had dipped the sop, he gave it to Judas Iscariot, the son of Simon.

27. And after the sop Satan entered into him. Then said Jesus unto him, That thou doest, do quickly.

28. Now no man at the table knew for what intent he spake this unto him.

29. For some of them thought, because Judas had the bag, that Jesus had said unto him, Buy those things that we have need of against the feast; or, that he should give something to the poor.

30. He then having received the sop went immediately out: and it was night.

31. Therefore, when he was gone out, Jesus said, Now is the Son of man glorified, and God is glorified in him.

32. If God be glorified in him, God shall also glorify him in himself, and shall straightway glorify him.

33. Little children, yet a little while I am with you. Ye shall seek me: and as I said unto the Jews, Whither I go, ye cannot come; so now I say to you.

34. A new commandment I give unto you, That ye love one another; as I have loved you, that ye also love one another.

35. By this shall all men know that ye are my disciples, if ye have love one to another.

36. Simon Peter said unto him, Lord, whither goest thou? Jesus answered him, Whither I go, thou canst not follow me now; but thou shalt follow me afterwards.

37. Peter said unto him, Lord, why cannot I follow thee now? I will lay down my life for thy sake.

38. Jesus answered him, Wilt thou lay down thy life for my sake? Verily, verily, I say unto thee, The cock shall not crow, till thou hast denied me thrice.

In chapter 1, verses 1 through 14 of John's Gospel, we studied the Eternal Word Incarnate in Christ Jesus the Lord, our Saviour.

In chapter 1, verses 15 through 34, we studied the testimony of John the Baptist, forerunner of our Lord.

In chapter 1, verse 35, through chapter 12, verse 50, we studied the public ministry of Christ Jesus as He walked the dusty roads of Judaea, Galilee, and the surrounding countryside. We studied His miracles and His wonderful words of life.

We come now to His private ministry to His twelve disciples, *His own.* It is true that all Scripture is given by inspiration and is profitable to us, but these words in chapter 13 were spoken by Jesus directly to the twelve disciples in private.

The Last Passover

Verse 1: *"Now before the feast of the passover, when Jesus knew that His hour was come that He should depart out of this world unto the Father, having loved His own which were in the world, He loved them unto the end."*

As we study the Gospels, we notice that John's account of the Lord's last six days before His crucifixion omits many things mentioned by Matthew, Mark, and Luke. We know the Holy Spirit directed in this, because John was as truly inspired of God as were the other Gospel writers. Therefore we do not ask *why* he omitted certain things; we accept this as God's will and His plan foreordained before the foundation of the world.

We might list here some of the things recorded by Matthew, Mark, and Luke, but not found in John's Gospel:

The parable of the prodigal son (Luke 15:11—32).

The parable of the householder who let his vineyard to husbandmen (Matt. 21:33; Mark 12:1; Luke 20:9).

The parable of the wedding garment (Matt. 22:1; Luke 14:16).

The parable of the ten virgins, five wise and five foolish (Matt. 25:1).

The parable of the talents (Matt. 25:14).

The separation of the nations (sheep and goats) (Matt. 25:31).

The second cleansing of the temple (Matt. 21:12; Mark 11:15; Luke 19:45).

The cursing of the fig tree (Matt. 21:18; Mark 11:12—14).

The public discussion with the chief priests and elders about the baptism of John the Baptist (Matt. 21:25; Mark 11:30; Luke 20:4).

The time when Jesus silenced the Pharisees, Sadducees, and lawyers (Matt. 23:13; Mark 12:38; Luke 20:47).

The institution of the Lord's Supper (Matt. 26:26; Mark 14:22; Luke 22:17).

All of these things are found in either Matthew, Mark, or Luke, *sometimes in all three,* but John records none of them.

One other account omitted by John the Beloved is the prophecy given by Jesus on the Mount of Olives, although Matthew goes into detail concerning this prophecy. Again, we do not ask *why,* because we remember the words of Job 33:13, that God "giveth not account of any of His matters." God is sovereign; His ways are not our ways, His thoughts are not our thoughts. But personally I believe the reason the Holy Spirit did not give John the prophetic

words spoken by Jesus on the Mount of Olives was because
John was to receive and pen down the great book of the
Revelation, the book that tells of "the things that shall be
hereafter." Chapters 2 and 3 of Revelation contain the
prophecy of the Church from beginning to end, and beginning with chapter 4 John wrote "the things that shall
be hereafter," as instructed by the Holy Spirit: "Write
the things which thou hast seen, and the things which are,
and the things which shall be hereafter" (Rev. 1:19). Since
the Holy Spirit knew John would pen down the twenty-two
chapters of Revelation there was no point in giving him
the prophecy Jesus spoke on the Mount of Olives concerning the end time and His second coming.

I also personally believe that the reason the Holy Spirit
did not have John pen down the account of the Lord's
Supper as it is recorded in the other Gospels is that even
in that day there was a growing tendency to idolize the
sacraments — and Jesus never intended that to be. Christianity is *not* ceremonies: it is Christ in the believer, and the
believer in Christ (Col. 1:27; 3:3). True Christianity does
not exalt outward ordinances, holy days, and such. Christianity is not a "form," it is a living Person—CHRIST.
He is the head, the foundation, the heart, the bloodstream,
the life. Christ IS Christianity, and apart from Him there
IS NO Christianity.

Now beloved, we know John's Gospel is "the salvation
book" (John 20:31), and yet the Holy Spirit did not inspire
John to even *name* the Lord's Supper. This is proof positive that this ordinance is not (as many would have us believe) the first, foremost, and most important thing in Christianity. The fruit of the vine does *not* become the literal
blood of Jesus, nor does the unleavened bread become His
flesh! That is not the reason Jesus instituted this ordinance
and instructed believers to observe it until He comes again:
*He did it to show forth His death, burial, and resurrection
until His return.* Paul said to the Corinthian church, "As
often as ye eat this bread, and drink this cup, ye do shew

the Lord's death till He come" (I Cor. 11:26).

John's Gospel plainly instructs us in the way of salvation—we are instructed concerning the *necessity* for the new
birth, the *"how"* of the new birth, and all other things
essential to salvation; so if the Lord's Supper is of primary
importance IN our salvation, then why did the Holy Spirit
allow John to remain completely silent concerning it? There
is an evident and understandable *reason* why John did not
pen down the words concerning this ordinance, words which
were given to Matthew, Mark, and Luke: *The Lord's Supper is NOT essential to salvation, nor is it the primary thing
in Christianity;* it is secondary, just as *water baptism* is
secondary.

Yes, I believe in water baptism for believers, and I also
believe in observing the Lord's Supper; but I do not observe
it in order to be saved, nor to help me be saved—nor to
help me reach heaven. I do it for the express reason that
Jesus *said* do it in remembrance of Him until He comes
the second time.

"Now before the feast of the Passover . . . ." As we
study the four Gospels we notice that the feast of the Passover is always mentioned by each Gospel writer as being
at the exact time of year when Jesus was crucified. This
was foreordained of God, for the Passover lamb was the
most striking, most remarkable *type* of the Lord Jesus Christ
of all the Jewish ceremonials. The Passover lamb was a
type of the Lamb without spot or blemish, the Lamb to
whom John the Baptist pointed when he said, *"Behold the
Lamb of God, which taketh away the sin of the world"*
(John 1:29), and the entire history of the Passover was to
make men understand the redemptive work of the Lord
Jesus Christ.

Then, too, at this particular time of year, the greatest
company of Jews would be gathered in Jerusalem to observe the Passover and thus would be eyewitnesses to the
crucifixion of Jesus. Those who did not come to Jerusalem
at that time would certainly receive *news* of the crucifixion

when their friends and relatives returned home from the Passover, and the news would spread to the ends of the earth in a very short time.

The chief priests and religious leaders said, "Not on the feast day," but the sovereign God in His omnipotence and omniscience foreordained that "the Lamb of God" should be slain at the time of the Passover feast. We do not know the date of the birth of Jesus, we do not know for certain the dates of most of the events of His life, but we do know that He was crucified at Passover time—which according to the Jewish calendar was April (Ex. 12:1—11).

"When Jesus knew that His hour was come that He should depart out of this world unto the Father . . . ." In many ways, *ignorance* is a blessing in disguise. If some of us knew the suffering that lies ahead of us, it would break our hearts and completely destroy our peace of mind; but Jesus knew perfectly well what He faced. He knew every pain, every heartache, every tear. He knew the exact moment *when* He would suffer, *how* He would suffer, and when He would give up the ghost and literally pass His spirit back to the heavenly Father; and I believe this knowledge added to His suffering.

Jesus saw the cross even when, at the age of twelve, He said, "I must be about my Father's business." The cross was before Him every step of His earthly journey— and yet, seeing it and knowing the agony of it, He walked straight to it. His crucifixion was no surprise to *Him.*

Notice that death is here spoken of as a journey, moving from one place to another: Jesus knew that the time had come *"that He should depart out of this world unto the Father."* The same is true in the death of every born again believer. The Christian departs this world to be with Jesus in Paradise. The Apostle Paul said, "To be absent from the body is to be present with the Lord," which is a great and and glorious truth for every born again believer. Regardless of what "religions" teach, regardless of what preachers preach, *I believe the Word of God.* I believe the split second a believer departs this life, he is at home in Paradise and will rest from his labors until that grand and glorious resurrection morning when Jesus comes in the Rapture. True, when a Christian dies the *body* goes back to dust; but the spirit returns to God who gave it, and at the resurrection the mortal body will be raised in immortality, *glorified.*

Beloved, the spirit of a departed believer is not unconscious. Jesus said that "there is joy in the presence of the angels of God over one sinner that repenteth" (Luke 15:10). I ask you, *Who* could be joyful, who *could* rejoice over the repenting of a sinner *except another person who has repented* and known the joy of salvation? *Angels* do not *know* the joy of being born again.

I love the last part of our present verse: *"Having loved His own which were in the world, He loved them unto the end."* I am so glad the love of Jesus is not like man's love. Christians are so often "up and down . . . hot and cold." We do not always love the Lord as faithfully as we should day by day; but Jesus never changes, His love never varies. He loves us with the love of God, and God's Word tells us that with Him "is no variableness, neither shadow of turning" (James 1:17). The knowledge that His disciples would turn cowards and forsake Him did not cause Him to stop loving them. In spite of their weaknesses and failures He loved them to the end. There is no way to describe the love of Jesus for His own; His love "passeth knowledge" (Eph. 3:19).

"His own which were in the world" is an expression of great depth, of precious comfort to God's own. Believers belong to Jesus, we are His property. He bought us and He cares for us. Yes, even while we are *"in the world,"* while we are here on earth, we are His own. "Beloved, NOW are we the sons of God!"

Jesus Washes the Disciples' Feet

Verse 2: *"And supper being ended, the devil having now*

put into the heart of Judas Iscariot, Simon's son, to betray Him."

"*And supper being ended*" would be more literally rendered, "while supper was going on; while supper was in progress." This would seem to be correct, because in verse 26 we read that Jesus gave a sop to Judas, and it stands to reason that if supper had been completely over He would not have done this.

It is most interesting to note that *our Lord's ministry on earth* climaxed with a supper, and a supper was the last ordinance He appointed to the *Church.* In Revelation 3:20, in the message to the Laodiceans (the *lukewarm* church) we read, "Behold, I stand at the door, and knock: if any man hear my voice, and open the door, I WILL COME IN TO HIM, AND WILL SUP WITH HIM, AND HE WITH ME." In this verse, Jesus is standing at the church door, not at the door of a human heart. He is knocking— and if there is just one true, born again, blood-washed believer in that church Jesus will come in and sup with that believer, and the believer can sup with Him. According to prophecy, in the closing days of this dispensation there will be churches where not even *one true believer* can be found.

It is also interesting that the first thing to take place after the Rapture of the Church will be *the marriage supper of the Lamb:* "And He saith unto me, Write, Blessed are they which are called unto the marriage supper of the Lamb. And He saith unto me, These are the true sayings of God" (Rev. 19:9).

John does not name the supper here in the thirteenth chapter of his Gospel, and Bible authorities differ in opinion on the subject. Some believe that this was the same supper that took place at Bethany in the house of Simon the leper two days prior to the Passover feast. Others believe that this was the Passover supper which Jesus ate with His disciples the night before He was crucified. I agree with the latter. Some few Bible scholars believe that it was at

this point when Jesus instituted *the Lord's Supper,* but I
do not believe that this ordinance was instituted until after
verse 30. (Please see Matthew 26:20—30.) It is highly im-
probable that He would have washed the disciples' feet
after the institution of that ordinance.

"The devil having now put into the heart of Judas Is-
cariot, Simon's son, to betray Him" does not mean that
Judas *became* an apostate, for he was a devil to begin with.
In John 6:70 Jesus clearly said to His disciples, "Have not
I chosen you twelve, and one of you is a *devil?"* The personality of the devil himself (and the devil's character as
the father of all wickedness and all ungodliness) are forcibly
brought to light in Judas at this point.

The Greek word translated "put" literally means *"cast,"*
which more accurately describes Satan's way of operating.
Suggestion is one of his chief tools, and the heart of the
unbeliever is the ground where Satan sows (or casts) his
evil seed.

The Holy Spirit plainly points out that Judas Iscariot is
"Simon's son," no doubt to avoid his being mistaken for
Judas, the brother of James, son of Alphaeus. There are
three *other* places in Scripture where Judas is referred to as
Simon's son, but there is not one suggestion as to who this
"Simon" was.

There is an interesting contrast here: JESUS was born
of *woman*: "When the fulness of the time was come, *God*
sent forth His Son, made of a woman . . ." (Gal. 4:4).
Man had nothing to do with the birth of Jesus. It is true
that the virgin Mary was His mother, but God Almighty
was His Father. The Holy Ghost overshadowed Mary and
she brought forth her firstborn Son and called Him Emman-
uel, "which being interpreted is, *God with us."* But JU-
DAS (the devil in flesh, just as Jesus was GOD in flesh)
is referred to as *the son of Simon,* and he was exactly the
opposite of Jesus in every way. Jesus was *truth;* Judas was
a liar and a thief. Jesus came to *give;* Judas was interested
in *taking all that he could*—even to rebuking Mary when

she anointed Jesus with costly ointment.

Verses 3—5: *"Jesus knowing that the Father had given all things into His hands, and that He was come from God, and went to God; He riseth from supper, and laid aside His garments: and took a towel, and girded Himself. After that He poureth water into a bason, and began to wash the disciples' feet, and to wipe them with the towel wherewith He was girded."*

The marvelous words of verse 3 express the depth of our Lord's infinite condescension and unchangeable love for His disciples. He had a full knowledge of who He was and why He had come into the world. He knew the heavenly Father had committed *all power* into His hands. He knew that as God the Father had life in Himself, the Son had life in *Himself,* for He was with the Father in the beginning and would return to the Father, to be seated in the highest seat in heaven at the right hand of the Majesty. Knowing all these things, He yet condescended to render the most humble service of a servant, and washed the feet of His disciples.

We might notice seven things Jesus did here:

1. He rose from supper,

2. He laid aside His garments,

3. He took a towel,

4. He girded Himself,

5. He poured water into a bason,

6. "And began to wash the disciples' feet,

7. and to wipe them with the towel wherewith He was girded."

Laying aside His garments simply means that Jesus laid aside the long, loose, outer garment (or cloak) which people in that country wore in those days.

Girding Himself means that He tied the towel tightly around His waist, as it was customary for a servant to do. A good servant should have his loins girded and his light burning (Luke 12:35), which means that he is ready for anything His master calls on him to do at a moment's notice.   The actions of our Lord here in our present passage are similar to the words of Luke 12:37: "Blessed are those servants, whom the lord when he cometh shall find watching: verily I say unto you, that he shall gird himself, and make them to sit down to meat, and will come forth and serve them."

What Jesus did here, any good host would have done in that day to show hospitality to his guests. Abraham washed the feet of three angelic messengers who came to him as he sat in the door of his tent in the heat of the day: "And when he saw them, he ran to meet them from the tent door, and bowed himself toward the ground, and said, My Lord, if now I have found favour in thy sight, pass not away, I pray thee, from thy servant: Let a little water, I pray you, be fetched, and wash your feet, and rest yourselves under the tree" (Gen. 18:1—4 in part).   In connection with this, also read I Samuel 25:41.

In the land of Palestine in the days of our Lord, people did not wear socks (or stockings) and shoes as we do today; they wore sandals, and thus a traveler's feet became hot and dusty and it was necessary to wash them frequently. Scripture makes it plain that it was a natural and common thing for the servants in a household to wash the feet of those who were guests in that house. Jesus reminded Simon the Pharisee, "Thou gavest me no water for my feet" (Luke 7:44).   According to I Timothy 5:10, it was a mark of an honorable, deserving widow to have "washed the saints' feet."

The remarkable thing about the entire episode in our present passage is not so much the washing of the feet of the disciples, as *the wonder of what Jesus did.* HE, God in flesh, on such solemn occasion condescending to wash the feet of such weak, cowardly mortals! Knowing the end in the beginning, He knew that in a short time He would be leaving these men—poor, feeble travelers in a wicked, ungodly world—and He gently and lovingly rendered this humble service to them to strengthen and refresh them for the days that lay ahead.

Verse 6: *"Then cometh He to Simon Peter: and Peter saith unto Him, Lord, dost thou wash my feet?"*

Since the Greek word here rendered *"then"* is not used in the sense of "in order," we do not know whether Jesus came to Peter first, or whether He washed the feet of other disciples and *then* came to Peter. We cannot determine whose feet Jesus washed first—and anyway, that is beside the point.

When Jesus came to wash *Peter's* feet, Peter said to Him, *"Lord, dost thou wash MY feet?"* (The Greek reads, "Dost thou, of me, wash the feet?") We might ask the same question in this way: "Dost thou, Jesus Son of God, thou who hast the words of eternal life, wash the feet of such an unworthy one as I?" This is the same, in meaning, as the question John the Baptist asked Jesus when the Lord came to him to be baptized: "John forbad Him, saying, *I have need to be baptized of thee, and comest thou to me?"* (Matt. 3:14).

Verse 7: *"Jesus answered and said unto him, What I do thou knowest not now; but thou shalt know hereafter."*

The statement made by Jesus here gives us a key to many other things which we cannot understand: We may not know *now,* but we shall know "hereafter." We must remember that God's ways are not our ways, His thoughts are not our thoughts. He is so much greater and so much higher than we are, we must simply accept by faith what we cannot fully understand. The just shall live by faith—not by sight or understanding; and we know that whatever comes to us, whatever happens to us, "ALL things work together for good to them that love God, to them who are the called according to His purpose" (Rom. 8:28). When things are not going well with us, when the way seems dark and the burdens are discouraging, we can rest in the assurance that God is looking down upon us, Jesus is still the head of the Church, and we are complete in Him—and whatever we must take by faith now, whatever we do not understand, *we shall know "hereafter."*

Verse 8:   *"Peter saith unto Him, Thou shalt never wash my feet.   Jesus answered him, If I wash thee not, thou hast no part with me."*

Greek scholars tell us that the English translation here fails to give the full meaning and strength of the Greek. Literally it reads, "Thou shalt never wash my feet forever"— meaning "You shall never wash MY feet, *now,* or in the *future,* or *ever."*   Peter's language here denotes humility, but sometimes this species of humility is pretense, and goes to extremes.   Peter actually meant that he would wash the feet of Jesus, but Jesus would never wash HIS feet.   This was not humility born of spirituality, and Jesus knew that. He knew Peter's heart, and He knew that presently Peter would curse and declare that he had never *known* his Lord.

"If I wash thee not, thou hast no part with me."   These words were meant to cut deep into Peter's heart.   Jesus did not mean that unless Peter allowed Him to literally wash his feet that night he would cease to be one of the disciples; the words mean much, much more than that. What the Lord meant was that Peter was speaking in the flesh, not in the Spirit; his words were not the words of the spiritually wise.   He objected to the service Jesus was about to perform, an act that was (and is) symbolic in its meaning.   Jesus wanted Peter to understand that He was not washing his feet simply because they were dusty.   No, the washing was a figurative act with a deeper spiritual meaning: *NO ONE can have any part in Jesus or in His stewardship unless that person is WASHED by Jesus.*   HE

is the One who washes away our sins. Peter had been "washed" (vv. 10,11), but *every soul* that is saved must be washed daily, and only Jesus can do the washing. In John 15:3 He said to His disciples, "Now ye are clean through the word which I have spoken unto you."

It is not enough for us to unite with the church, or to be baptized and receive communion, nor even to profess Christianity. We must have a deeper experience: we must be washed, cleansed, made new—and Jesus is the only One who can meet that need. The great question we should ask ourselves is, "Am I washed and justified?" Paul said to the Corinthian Christians, "Ye are washed . . . ye are sanctified . . . ye are justified in the name of the Lord Jesus, and by the Spirit of our God" (I Cor. 6:11).

I would remind you that the "washing" here has nothing to do with baptism, although some ministers and teachers would have you believe so. John 4:2 plainly states that JESUS did not baptize. The *disciples* baptized *in His name,* but Jesus Himself did not baptize. The reference here is to the washing of the inner man, the cleansing of soul and spirit, not to immersion in the water in a baptistry.

Verse 9:   *"Simon Peter saith unto Him, Lord, not my feet only, but also my hands and my head."*

This change of mind was characteristic of Peter. He was excitable, zealous, impulsive, ardent. He was easily stirred and quick to speak, but at this time in his Christian life he had more feeling and emotion than spiritual depth and discernment. He had more zeal than knowledge—and like many today, he went from one extreme to the other. He was horrified at the suggestion that he might have no part with Jesus, and he cried out, *"Lord, not my feet only, BUT ALSO MY HANDS AND MY HEAD!"* Certainly Peter wanted to have a part with Jesus, although he did not fully understand the spiritual meaning of His words— and in his zeal he spoke of literal washing, bathing his body all over.

From the example Peter set here, we can see that great zeal and great love are perfectly consistent with great spiritual ignorance and slowness to comprehend spiritual truth. Even today there are many who, like Peter, have more zeal than knowledge, more love and devotion than spiritual discernment. The words of Peter—"Lord, bathe me from head to foot, my entire body"—are the words of a zealous, warmhearted, impulsive but uncomprehending disciple, and there are many such in the church today.

Verse 10: *"Jesus saith to him, He that is washed needeth not save to wash his feet, but is clean every whit: and ye are clean, but not all."*

Here Jesus tenderly rebuked Peter's spiritual ignorance. He pointed out to Peter that even if He *had* been speaking of a literal washing, a literal bathing of the entire body, a person who is bathed needs only to wash his *feet* after a journey on a dusty road. In other words, the traveler bathed his body before beginning his journey, and after the journey on the dusty road all he needed in order to be clean was simply to wash his *feet*.

If such is true of literal washing, how much more is it true of spiritual washing, the washing of regeneration! "Not by works of righteousness which we have done, but according to His mercy He saved us, by the washing of regeneration, and renewing of the Holy Ghost" (Tit. 3:5). When Jesus forgives our sins, when He redeems us from the curse of sin—everlasting death and damnation; when He justifies us by faith in His finished work, *we are washed entirely*, cleansed from ALL sin, and we need only daily forgiveness and cleansing from defilement as we travel through this sinful world. It is true that we are IN the world but not OF the world, and many times we need cleansing from sins of omission more than sins of commission, and if we say we have no sin we deceive ourselves (I John 1:8). "And if any man sin, we have an Advocate with the Father, Jesus Christ the righteous: and He is the propitiation for our sins: and not for our's only, but also for the sins of the whole world" (I John 2:1,2 in part).

When Jesus died on the cross He settled the sin-debt in full. When we individually put our faith and trust in His shed blood and finished work, He redeems us from the *penalty* of sin which is eternal death. But we need a *Saviour* as well as a Redeemer. We need one to keep us, cleanse us, forgive us when we fail. "For if, when we were *enemies*, we were reconciled to God by the *death* of His Son, much more, *being reconciled*, we shall be *saved by His life*" (Rom. 5:10). Christ is our Redeemer, but He is also our Keeper and our Deliverer. It is He who washes away the contamination we pick up as we travel through this world. We are pilgrims and strangers on earth, our citizenship is in heaven; but as we mix and mingle with men we become defiled and we need our feet washed, spiritually speaking. We do not need to be SAVED (born again) every day, but our feet do become dusty and soiled as we travel this earthly road.

When a person is washed, justified, cleansed by the precious blood of Jesus, that person is completely forgiven, entirely absolved from all spot or guilt, and he stands blameless before God because when God looks at the believer, He sees the blood that covers the sinful heart. But even though we stand before God justified through the blood of Jesus, we still need to confess our faults and failures, our weaknesses and sins daily. We need to pray for daily pardon. In other words, we need a daily washing of the feet, and Jesus is *the only Person* who can do this for us. "For there is one God, and *one Mediator* between God and men, the Man Christ Jesus" (I Tim. 2:5).

Fellow Christian, if you have not confessed your sins lately, you should do it now, this very moment! for even when we do our very best we come far short of the glory of God. But thank God we have an Advocate who sits at the right hand of the Father to make intercession for us, and He listens tenderly to the child of God as that child confesses his weaknesses, faults, and failures. He is ready, He is able, He is faithful and just to forgive our sins and to cleanse us from all unrighteousness (I John 1:9).

"Every whit" means literally *the whole man.* It is indeed interesting, as well as comforting and assuring, that Jesus said, "Ye are clean" to His poor, weak, faltering disciples. I thank God that *we, too,* are cleansed by the blood and sanctified by the Word (I John 1:7; John 17:17).

"But not ALL" definitely points to Judas Iscariot.

Verse 11: *"For He knew who should betray Him; therefore said He, Ye are not all clean."*

Jesus had perfect knowledge of all that would happen to Him from the beginning of His earthly ministry until He said, "It is finished," and therefore He had perfect discernment of the real character of each of His disciples. He did not suffer because He could not *foresee* His sufferings. He was not taken by surprise; He knew exactly what lay ahead. But it was foreordained of God before the foundation of the world that the blood of *the Lamb without spot* should redeem sinners. Jesus was that Lamb, and AS the Lamb of God He singled His eye on Calvary and walked stedfastly toward it, knowing that every step took Him nearer the agony of the cross. With His perfect foreknowledge of all that would happen to Him, He knew that Judas would betray Him, He knew that Judas, though exposed to the same teaching and association as the other disciples, was not saved; He knew the spirit of Satan dwelt in him, and therefore He said, "Ye are not ALL clean."

Verse 12: *"So after He had washed their feet, and had taken His garments, and was set down again, He said unto them, Know ye what I have done to you?"*

After washing the disciples' feet, Jesus put His outer robe on again, took His place at the table, and gave them a discourse which was intended to prepare them for the Lord's Supper. Personally, I believe the washing of the feet of the disciples was done partially to teach them to examine themselves, as we are commanded in Paul's letter to the Church at Corinth to search our hearts and examine ourselves before partaking of the unleavened bread and the fruit of the vine, lest we eat and drink unworthily. Insofar as redemption and justification were concerned, the disciples were *clean* because they were redeemed and justified; but spiritually speaking, they had "dusty feet."

"Know ye what I have done to you?" Jesus asked this question to stir the disciples, to cause them to ask questions and inquire as to *the meaning* of what He had just done. He wanted them to understand the significance of His actions from a spiritual standpoint.

Verse 13: *"Ye call me Master and Lord: and ye say well: for so I am."*

The Greek here reads, "Ye call me, or speak of me, as the Master and the Lord." This was an expression used by the disciples while Jesus was here on earth, as when Martha said to Mary, "The Master is come" (John 11:28).

"Ye say well, for so I am." The little word *"so"* is not in the Greek. What Jesus said was, "Ye say well, for *I AM.*" And *He was* the great I AM of the Old Testament, the I AM of all eternity. He was "Master AND Lord," and He endorsed the expression by His words "Ye say well." No one but very God in flesh could make such an assertion. He was Master—and He *wants* to be *Lord* of all who will put their trust in His finished work and His shed blood.

Verses 14 and 15: *"If I then, your Lord and Master, have washed your feet; ye also ought to wash one another's feet. For I have given you an example, that ye should do as I have done to you."*

In other words, "If I, whom you call the Lord and the Master, have taken the place of a servant and performed the most condescending, humble act of service to you, you should feel obligated to do the same kind of service for one another." The Greek language here is very emphatic, meaning "It is your duty and debt, you are under *obligation* to do it, one to another." Jesus here teaches a lesson in humility, and certainly if we follow in His steps we will live a life of humility—for even though He was God in flesh, He was the most humble Person who ever lived. There is no place in the heart of a believer for worldly pride, and the more spiritual a person is, the more dedicated and humble he will be.

"I have given you an example, that ye should do as I have done to you." What did Jesus mean here? Did He mean that we should *literally* wash each other's feet? or did He mean that we should *imitate His spirit* in what He had done for the disciples? I realize that several denominations practice literal foot-washing, and I would not wound any sincere soul; but to me it is inconsistent with the teaching of the Lord Jesus to suppose that He would attach that much importance to a mere bodily action of physical service. The Word of God tells us that "bodily exercise profiteth little" (I Tim. 4:8), and Jesus Himself said, "It is the spirit that quickeneth; *the flesh profiteth nothing*" (John 6:63).

Heaven bears me record, I would be willing to bathe the feet of any person who is unable to bathe his own feet. I would be happy to render such service to any fellow Christian if he were for any reason bodily incapable of performing that service himself. But beloved, there are many humble tasks that believers can do which will render real service to the cause of Christ, and which would put time to better use than bathing feet that have already *been* bathed and do not need the dust washed from them.

Believers are pilgrims traveling toward the heavenly home, this world is enemy territory, and our feet (*spiritually* speaking) do become contaminated and dusty. We need to be washed, but *only JESUS* can wash away that contamination. The literal washing of feet among the saints will not cleanse us from sins and shortcomings. I have no quarrel with those who *desire* to bathe feet in the church, but I do not feel that the Lord Jesus *intended* that we should literally bathe each other's feet. He was teaching the spirit of humility and service, and as His followers we should walk in His steps. If we do that, we will be willing and happy to do any task, no matter how humble, if it will help a fellow pilgrim as we travel through this world.

The true interpretation of our Lord's words here may be found in Matthew 20:25–28: "Jesus called them unto Him, and said, Ye know that the princes of the Gentiles exercise dominion over them, and they that are great exercise authority upon them. But it shall not be so among you: but whosoever will be great among you, let him be your minister; and whosoever will be chief among you, let him be your servant: Even as the Son of man came not to be ministered unto, but to minister, and to give His life a ransom for many."

If the Lord Jesus Christ, King of kings, condescended to leave heaven and take upon Himself the body of a man, made like unto sinful flesh, and died on a cross that we might be saved, there is *nothing* too humble for believers to do for each other.

I would point out here that doing humble tasks for the poor and needy will not *save* us, nor will it *help* to save us. There is nothing about *poverty* in the passage we are studying. The disciples were being taught to be humble in their service to each other. It is certainly easier—and perhaps more self-satisfying—to visit the sick, give money to the poor, and render help to those less fortunate than ourselves, than it is to live a dedicated Christian life, sacrificial and humble in all that we do to and for fellow believers. We have much doctrinal orthodoxy today without true Christian love and humility, and such is worthless before God.

The three outstanding truths set forth in the verses we have just studied are:

We are washed clean from all sins in the blood of Jesus.

We need to wash our feet daily, in a spiritual sense, to be cleansed from the contamination of our walk in the world.

Our duty is to make the Lord Jesus Christ our example in all things, and thus *whatever* we do will be done to the glory of God.

Verse 16: *"Verily, verily, I say unto you, The servant is not greater than his lord; neither he that is sent greater than he that sent him."*

Here the "double verily" emphasizes the great importance of the lesson the Lord had just taught His disciples. Love and humility are tremendous, weighty things in the service of God, and Jesus here charged us to remember that the servant, instead of being *greater* than his master, must strictly follow the *example* set by his master. The person who carries a message is not greater than the one who sends him to carry it, therefore the messenger must follow the instruction of the one who sends the message.

If we are to be true and faithful servants of the Lord Jesus Christ we must follow the example He set before us and deliver the message He gave, without adding to or taking from it. He gave us the example of love and humility, and we who are His servants should never be ashamed or too proud to *follow* that example.

Verse 17: *"If ye know these things, happy are ye if ye do them."*

Here is confirmation of what was said in the previous verse. In other words, "Do not be content simply to *know* these things, but practice them as well. If you know and understand the meaning of what I have just done, you will find joy unspeakable and full of glory if you put these things into practice in your daily living." James tells us that *"as the body without the spirit is dead, so faith without works is dead also"* (James 2:26). To know the things

Jesus taught, to be exposed to the examples He set forth, and yet do nothing about it will do us no good, furnish no joy, and bring no reward at the end of life's journey. Certainly there are many believers who know more than they practice, they have been given much more light than they follow, and for that reason they are wretched and miserable, missing the joy of their Christian heritage. According to James 4:17, to know the will of God, to know what He would have us do and then refuse to do it, is certainly sin: "To him that knoweth to do good, and doeth it not, to him it is sin."

Verse 18: *"I speak not of you all: I know whom I have chosen: but that the Scripture may be fulfilled, He that eateth bread with me hath lifted up his heel against me."*

"I speak not of you all" refers to Judas Iscariot. Remember that in verse 10 of this same chapter Jesus said to Peter, "Ye are clean, but not *all.*" Judas Iscariot was never clean, and according to the words of Jesus he was a devil from the beginning. We will study this more fully in chapter 17.

"I know whom I have chosen." Only in that heavenly Bible class will we know fully why Jesus chose Judas as one of the twelve. He knew before God made Adam that Judas would betray Him, but the fact that He knew did not *cause* the betrayal. The fact that God knows the hearts of all men does not change "whosoever shall call upon the name of the Lord shall be saved," nor does it change John 3:16. The sovereignty of God and His omniscience do not change the free will of man, nor do they change our responsibility as free moral agents created in the image of Almighty God.

"That the Scripture may be fulfilled, He that eateth bread with me hath lifted up his heel against me." Here, as in many other places in God's Word, we read that this was done that the *Scripture* might be fulfilled; but we must not suppose that these things happened *in order* that Scrip-

ture be fulfilled. The meaning is that when things were done, Scripture WAS fulfilled—that is, persons who did certain things fulfilled Scriptures (or prophecies) that had been made perhaps centuries before. The sovereignty of God and the free will of man do not clash, they are in perfect harmony. The fact that God is sovereign and knows the end in the beginning does not change the fact that man is made in God's image and is a free moral agent with a will to choose Jesus or reject Him.

The statement of Jesus in this verse is a fulfillment of the prophecy in Psalm 41:9: "Yea, mine own familiar friend, in whom I trusted, which did eat of my bread, hath lifted up his heel against me." But even though Jesus knew in the beginning that Judas would betray Him, that did not change His feelings for His betrayer. He did not disown him, and in the garden when Judas betrayed Him with a kiss, Jesus called him "friend" (Matt. 26:50).

Verse 19: *"Now I tell you before it come, that, when it is come to pass, ye may believe that I am He."*

The purpose of the Lord's words in this verse was to encourage and cheer the eleven *faithful* disciples. Even though Judas would betray Him, He said to the others, "Do not be discouraged, do not be dismayed or sad at heart." He was preparing them beforehand, so that when His betrayal came to pass and one of their number proved unfaithful, they would not be confounded and confused. Instead, they would recognize Jesus as Messiah, very God in flesh, omniscient and revealing things before they happened. Again, in the Greek, the personal pronoun "He" is not there, and Jesus therefore said, "ye may believe that I AM."

Verse 20: *"Verily, verily, I say unto you, He that receiveth whomsoever I send receiveth me; and he that receiveth me receiveth Him that sent me."*

With this statement (preceded by another "double verily")

the Lord Jesus gave dignity to the faithful disciples. What Judas did could have demoralized the other eleven and caused them to become discouraged if they had not been prepared in advance. They could have said, "If Judas, who seemed so faithful and sincere, could do such a thing, *we* may come to the same fate later." But Jesus reassured them by the declaration He made here.

"He that receiveth whomsoever I send receiveth me." These disciples would be sent to carry the Gospel message to all of the known world. After the Lord's resurrection and after Pentecost, they would receive power and they would be His witnesses in Judaea, in Jerusalem, and unto the uttermost parts of the earth. Jesus knew that He would give these men His great commission and send them out, and those who received these faithful disciples would be receiving *Jesus.*

"And he that receiveth me receiveth Him that sent me." God the Father sent Jesus, Jesus would send the disciples, and therefore whosoever received the disciples would receive Jesus, and would receive God the Father as well.

Beloved, we should be very careful how we treat God's faithful ministers. God commands, "Touch not mine anointed," and it is a dangerous thing for the wicked to despise and mistreat a man of God. A minister may be weak, he may be devoid of education, academically speaking; but if that man is called and commissioned of God to preach the Gospel, he carries a message that is royal and divine. He carries that message for Jesus' sake, and such a minister is not to be despised, misused, or abused. He is to be esteemed for the Gospel's sake.

The Apostle Paul said to the Thessalonian Christians, "We beseech you, brethren, to know them which labour among you, and are over you in the Lord, and admonish you; and to esteem them very highly in love for their work's sake. And be at peace among yourselves" (I Thess. 5:12,13). The true minister of God is to be esteemed in love for his work's sake—not because of the man himself but because of the Gospel he carries and because of the Lord God Almighty whom he represents.

Jesus Foretells His Betrayal

Verse 21: *"When Jesus had thus said, He was troubled in spirit, and testified, and said, Verily, verily, I say unto you, that one of you shall betray me."*

"When Jesus had thus said . . . ." The Greek reads, "When Jesus had said these things," referring to all that He had just said to His disciples.

"He was troubled in spirit." This expression, referring to Jesus, is peculiar to John's Gospel. We find it here, and also in chapter 11, verse 33, and in chapter 12, verse 27. It has already been pointed out that though Jesus was God, He was also man; and that He was "troubled in spirit" means that He was sorrowful because Judas, who had been walking with Him for more than three years, was about to betray Him to His enemies. He knew even at that moment that Judas would betray Him with a kiss and sell Him for the price of a slave.

Also, the agony and distress of soul under the pressure of the sin of the world was bearing down upon Him; very soon He would come face to face with the devil and all the forces of hell in the Garden of Gethsemane, and the knowledge of all this caused Him to be troubled in spirit. The Gospel of John is marvelous in many ways. Of all the Gospel writers, John the Beloved is the one who dwells most on the divine nature of the Lord Jesus, and who most fully understood and minutely described for us the reality of the human affections of the Son of God.

Jesus *"testified, and said . . . ."* John uses the word "testified" more than any other of the Gospel writers. It occurs thirty-three times in the Gospel of John, and in all of the other Gospels it appears only three times. That Jesus "testified" here means that He spoke audibly, making an open declaration in a very solemn manner, in the way that a person on the witness stand would give testimony to some fact or occurrence.

"Verily, verily, I say unto you, that one of you shall betray me." The "double verily" used here would serve to arrest the attention of the disciples and cause them to give earnest heed to what the Lord was saying. His announcement was extremely important: *"One of you shall betray me into the hands of my enemies,* I will be arrested, tried, and condemned. This betrayal is the first step in my final march to Golgotha."

Verse 22: *"Then the disciples looked one on another, doubting of whom He spake."*

Our English word "doubting" hardly conveys the full force of the disciples' reaction here. They were "perplexed," or puzzled. The Lord's announcement so amazed them as to render them speechless. They looked at each other in astonishment and wondered who it could be that would betray their Master. Evidently they had no suspicion of Judas, who probably had an excellent record with the other disciples. From outward appearance (and probably from the service he rendered) he had just as good a record as Peter, James, John, Matthew, or any of the other eleven. So far as the other disciples knew, Judas was just as unlikely to betray the Lord Jesus as were any of the others. Man looks on the outward appearance, but God looks on the heart (I Sam. 16:7)—and we cannot tell what men are by looking at them, nor even by listening to their words of testimony. "The heart is deceitful above all things, and desperately wicked: who can know it?" (Jer. 17:9).

Verse 23: *"Now there was leaning on Jesus' bosom one of His disciples, whom Jesus loved."*

"One of His disciples, whom Jesus loved" undoubtedly refers to John the Beloved, but John was a man of an humble heart and he was so devoted to Jesus that he left his own name out of his writings as much as possible. He

refers to himself here as the disciple whom Jesus loved, and this expression is found four other times in John's Gospel—chapter 19 verse 26, chapter 20 verse 2, chapter 21 verses 7 and 20.

There are two words in the Greek language which are translated "love," and Greek scholars tell us that the word used here denotes the highest, most noble love. We note here that even though Jesus loved *all* of His disciples, He had a particular love for John, and there is a reason for this—which we will see as we continue through the remaining chapters of John's Gospel. I believe Jesus loved Mary, Martha, and Lazarus with that same love, but this does not mean that our Lord had respect of persons; we know that He did not (Rom. 2:11). What He does for one of His children He will do for all if they will fully surrender and follow Him. John the beloved disciple did that.

"Leaning on Jesus' bosom" is explained by the fact that in the east in the days of our Lord, people did not *sit* at the table as we do today. Instead of *sitting around* the table, they reclined at the table. Most pictures of the Last Supper are very misleading because of this. Such pictures portray Jesus and His disciples sitting around the table as is our custom today.

Verse 24: *"Simon Peter therefore beckoned to him, that he should ask who it should be of whom He spake."*

The characteristic forwardness and unusual zeal of Peter are seen again here. The Lord's statement concerning His betrayal seemed to excite Peter more than any of the others, and he was very anxious to know the name of the person who would betray Him. Could it be that he wondered if it could be himself? He gave John a sign that he should ask Jesus which of the twelve would be His betrayer.

It might be well to call attention to the fact that some of the religions in the world today claim Peter as their head and leader, and still others teach that Peter was THE Rock upon which Jesus built the New Testament Church.

If these doctrines were true, it would seem strange that Peter should have had to use John as an intercessor between himself and Jesus. If Peter had been as important in establishing the Church as some religionists teach that he was, it would seem that *he*, not John, would have been next to the Lord at the supper table. These are things worth thinking about in this day of apostasy, liberalism, and modernism, this time of the beginning of the forming of the church of Antichrist.

Verse 25: *"He then lying on Jesus' breast saith unto Him, Lord, who is it?"*

The Greek here reads "he having *fallen* upon Jesus' breast . . . ." What John did was move closer to the Lord, leaning toward Him in order to ask the question without being heard by the other disciples. It is evident from verses 28 and 29 that he did not exclaim aloud, "Lord, who IS it?"

Verse 26: *"Jesus answered, He it is, to whom I shall give a sop, when I have dipped it. And when He had dipped the sop, He gave it to Judas Iscariot, the son of Simon."*

Since the question had been asked quietly, Jesus evidently answered in the same manner, for no one save John seemed to notice His reply: *"He it is, to whom I shall give a sop, when I have dipped it."* What Jesus did to show John who the traitor was, was very common in that day at eastern banquets; it was a common way of eating in the days of our Lord, and no one at the table would have noticed it or said anything about it.

Greek scholars tell us that *"sop"* could be translated "morsel" without doing any damage to the Scripture—as in Ruth 2:14: "Boaz said unto her, At mealtime come thou hither, and eat of the bread, *and dip thy morsel in the vinegar.* And she sat beside the reapers: and he reached her parched corn, and she did eat, and was sufficed, and left." Therefore when Jesus gave a morsel (or sop) to Judas,

in the true sense it would denote a favor or compliment
and would attract no undue attention.

*"And when He had dipped the sop, He gave it to Judas
Iscariot, the son of Simon."* The word here translated
"gave" is *"gives"* (present tense), denoting the immediate
action of Jesus following John's question. And again the
Holy Spirit makes it clear that it was Judas, *"the son of
Simon,"* who betrayed the Lord.

Verse 27:   *"And after the sop Satan entered into him.
Then said Jesus unto him, That thou doest, do quickly."*

This does not mean that Satan entered into Judas for
the first time here. It means that at that moment he took
complete control of the heart of Judas.

Someone may ask, "If Judas was a devil, as has been
declared, why does the Scripture say that Satan *entered
into* him?"   I answer in the words of the Lord Jesus concerning God the Father. Jesus said, "I am in the Father,
and the Father in me . . . I and my Father are ONE."
If we believe the Word of God—excluding tradition, "religion," and denominational ideas—then we have no difficulty in believing that Judas Iscariot was the son of the
devil, just like Jesus was the Son of God. Therefore, just
as Jesus was God in flesh (II Cor. 5:19), Judas was the
devil in flesh. Jesus was God, yet man; Judas was devil,
yet man.   It is not strange that Satan abode in the flesh
of Judas Iscariot, in the same way that God abode in the
flesh of Jesus; and on this occasion he took complete control of Judas, causing him to obey his evil wishes to the
fullest extent.

Few of us fully realize the power of the devil. He is a
personality—not just an "influence," and he is unbelievably
powerful. He is our great spiritual foe. He was present
in the person of Judas in the Passover chamber, and we
need not be surprised that he attends the services in our
churches today. He is there every time the doors open!

"Then said Jesus unto him, That thou doest, do quickly."

John wrote under inspiration of the Holy Spirit, but he did not explain the meaning of the words here, as he does in other places; but I personally believe Jesus wanted Judas to understand that He knew exactly what he was about to do. He was not trying to *hasten* the act of wickedness Judas was about to perform, but He wanted Judas to understand that He was ready, He was not afraid, He had come into the world as the Lamb without spot, to be slain for the sins of the world. His hour had now come; therefore He said to Judas, "What thou doest, do quickly"—and notice that He used present tense. He did not say, "What you WILL do," but "what you *are doing* right now." He knew the plans Judas had made, He knew those plans were complete, and just as God said to Balaam in Numbers 22:20, "Rise up, and go," and to Israel in Ezekiel 20:39, "Go ye, serve ye every one his idols," so Jesus said to Judas, "That thou doest, do quickly."

Verse 28: *"Now no man at the table knew for what intent He spake this unto him."*

This verse confirms what was said about John's question in verse 25, and the Lord's reply in verse 26. Whereas no one seemed to hear either John's question or the reply Jesus gave him, *everyone at the table* heard what was said to Judas here. It took them completely by surprise, and evidently they had no idea what Jesus meant.

Verse 29: *"For some of them thought, because Judas had the bag, that Jesus had said unto him, Buy those things that we have need of against the feast; or, that he should give something to the poor."*

This verse is most interesting and enlightening. It shows that the disciples had no suspicions of Judas; he gave no outward indication of being an inferior person—in fact, from the position of trust he held it would seem that he was *superior* insofar as wisdom, prudence, and faithfulness were concerned. We know from the Scriptures that Satan in his original form was "the anointed cherub that covereth," he was Lucifer the shining one; and since Judas was Satan in flesh (John 6:70), it is not unreasonable to assume that he was a very attractive, outstanding person, and he was trusted by the other disciples to carry their money.

We also see in this verse that Jesus did not work miracles to supply the physical needs of Himself and His disciples.   They thought that since Judas had the money, Jesus had instructed him to go and buy supplies for them, or else that He was sending Judas to buy food and other commodities to give to the poor.   Jesus could have spoken a word and there would have been food, clothing, and all other needs supplied.   This teaches us that even though we are sons of God and our Father owns the cattle on a thousand hills, the silver, gold, and wealth of the world, we still must *work* for our livelihood.   We must buy and sell as other people do, take care of our money, and practice prudence and economy in our business activities.

Also very noticeable here is the fact that the disciples had no idea Jesus was so near the end of His earthly ministry.   Had they realized that He was to be crucified within the next twenty-four hours they would not have supposed He was sending Judas to buy supplies.

We also learn from this verse that the Lord Jesus believed in and practiced helping the poor; otherwise the disciples would not have thought He was sending Judas out to "give something to the poor."   We know that the early church practiced helping the poor, for in Galatians 2:9,10 Paul said, "When James, Cephas, and John, who seemed to be pillars, perceived the grace that was given unto me, they gave to me and Barnabas the right hands of fellowship; that we should go unto the heathen, and they unto the circumcision.   *Only they would that we should remember the poor; the same which I also was forward to do.*"

The handling of money—especially the Lord's money—carries a great responsibility and a snare.   Paul warned

Timothy that the *love* of money is the root of all evil (I Tim. 6:10), and therein lies the snare. If we can have money *and not LOVE it,* if what we have is used to the glory of God, then money is a blessing; but if we allow money to become our god, it is a deadly and destructive thing. In Proverbs 30:8,9 we read, "Remove far from me vanity and lies: *give me neither poverty nor riches;* feed me with food convenient for me: lest I be full, and deny thee, and say, Who is the Lord? or lest I be poor, and steal, and take the name of my God in vain." It is not sinful to have money; I believe God calls some men to *make* money—and if they give to Him that which is rightfully His, He blesses them abundantly. It is not *money* that is evil, but the LOVE of money. Some love it and do not have it, others have money and do not love it. We know from the Scriptures—as well as from history past and present—that riches do not bring peace and happiness, nor does money guarantee security.

Verse 30: *"He then having received the sop went immediately out: and it was night."*

Undoubtedly Judas now realized that the Lord knew all about him, knew his devilish plot and what he was about to do; and as soon as Jesus gave him the sop and spoke those remarkable words, Judas immediately left the company of the Lord and the disciple band. He understood what Jesus meant, even though the other disciples did not. Some doubt that Judas Iscariot actually was a communicant at the Passover Supper, but Luke tells us, "Behold, the hand of him that betrayeth me is with me on the table" (Luke 22:21). To me, this proves beyond any shadow of doubt that Judas Iscariot was at the table and did partake of the last supper, along with the other disciples.

"And it was night." Yes, it was night in more ways than one in the life of Judas Iscariot. John the Beloved does not explain these words for us, however. It could be that Judas waited until darkness had engulfed the land

before he set about fulfilling his plans. In Luke 22:53 Jesus said to Judas and those who came to arrest Him in the garden, "This is your hour, *and the power of darkness.*" Just as Jesus is light, Satan is the author of all spiritual darkness. Since Judas was the devil in flesh, he was *darkness,* spiritually speaking.

Verse 31:   *"Therefore, when he was gone out, Jesus said, Now is the Son of man glorified, and God is glorified in Him."*

Here we come to a distinct break in the narrative. Judas withdrew himself from the company of the other disciples and went out into the night. Immediately the Lord Jesus speaks as one relieved from a great burden. There is a distinct difference in the tone of all that He says from this point on.

"Now is the Son of man glorified, and God is glorified in Him."   Greek scholars tell us that both verbs here are in the past tense, and should read *"has been* glorified." His glorification was so near, so sure and certain, that Jesus spoke of it as a thing already accomplished. Knowing in the beginning that He would be glorified and that the Father would be glorified IN Him, it was accomplished *in purpose,* and in a matter of hours it would be accomplished in *reality:*   "I have glorified thee on the earth: I have finished the work which thou gavest me to do" (John 17:4). The time had arrived for God the Father to receive the highest glory He could possibly receive by and through the sacrifice of His Son on Calvary.

It is noteworthy that the Lord Jesus Christ never referred to His death as punishment, disgrace, or humiliation, but speaks of it as the one event that would most glorify both Himself and God the Father. When we look at Calvary through human eyes it is extremely ugly, *but as believers, we can know its glory:*   "God forbid that I should glory, save in the cross of our Lord Jesus Christ, by whom the world is crucified unto me, and I unto the world"

(Gal. 6:14).

Jesus came into the world to do the will of God, to satisfy the holiness and righteousness of God, to satisfy the *law* of God—and therefore He regarded His death on the cross as the most glorious part of His ministry and mission here on earth. He knew that nothing could glorify the Father's attributes of holiness, mercy, faithfulness, and justice as the death of His only begotten Son on the cross would do.

Verse 32: *"If God be glorified in Him, God shall also glorify Him in Himself, and shall straightway glorify Him."*

"If" does not suggest doubt here, and should have been rendered "since." The same is true in Colossians 3:1, where the verse should read *"SINCE ye then be risen with Christ . . . ."* Thus the meaning in our present verse is that SINCE God the heavenly Father is especially glorified in all His attributes by and through the death of Jesus, then He will at once bestow special glory on Jesus the Son because of the Son's work:

"God, who at sundry times and in divers manners spake in time past unto the fathers by the prophets, hath in these last days spoken unto us by His Son, whom He hath appointed heir of all things, by whom also He made the worlds; who being the brightness of His glory, and the express image of His Person, and upholding all things by the word of His power, *when He had by Himself purged our sins, SAT DOWN ON THE RIGHT HAND OF THE MAJESTY ON HIGH"* (Heb. 1:1—3).

In John 10:17 Jesus said, "Therefore doth my Father love me, because I lay down my life, that I might take it again." During His earthly ministry every word He spoke, every step He took, every miracle He performed was for the glory of God the Father. He *finished* the work the Father gave Him to do, He completely satisfied God the Father in every minute detail: "Wherefore God also hath highly exalted Him, and given Him a name which is above every name: that at the name of Jesus every knee should bow, of things in heaven, and things in earth, and things under the earth; and that every tongue should confess that Jesus Christ is Lord, to the glory of God the Father" (Phil. 2:9—11).

"In Himself" points to the special and peculiar glory which in the eternal councils of the Trinity is conferred on Jesus, the second Person of the Trinity—conferred on Him because of His incarnation, His cross, His passion. Here again is seen the perfect unity, harmony, and cooperation of God the Father and Jesus the Son. By His death on the cross, Jesus demonstrated to the world how much God hates sin, and how *ugly* sin is in the sight of God. Then *God* shows the world, through the resurrection of the Lord Jesus and His exaltation to the seat of glory at the Father's right hand, how He delights in the finished work of the Son. God delights in the redemption of poor, lost sinners, which redemption Jesus accomplished through His death on the cross—and you may rest assured that all who glorify God the Father will be glorified *by* God the Father.

Verse 33: *"Little children, yet a little while I am with you. Ye shall seek me: and as I said unto the Jews, Whither I go, ye cannot come; so now I say to you."*

It is interesting that Jesus did not refer to the disciples as *"little children"* until after the departure of Judas Iscariot—and this is the *only* time He called them "little children" in the Gospel of John. These words are like the words of a father speaking to his earthly children whom he is about to leave as orphans in the world. Jesus loved His faithful followers and looked upon them as His little children.

"Yet a little while I am with you." They were nearing the moment when they must separate—Jesus to go to Calvary and return to the heavenly Father, the disciples to remain, pilgrims and strangers, in the world. He was doing all He possibly could to prepare them for His death

because He knew that when He was arrested, tried, and nailed to the cross, the disciples would be amazed, perplexed, confounded. If they were troubled at the announcement of His arrest and death, how much *more* perplexed they would be *after* He was crucified, taken from the cross and placed in the tomb!

"Ye shall seek me . . . whither I go, ye cannot come." Jesus had made the same statement to the Jews earlier, but it had a different meaning then than when it was spoken to the disciples. The Jews were unbelievers and therefore were not *fit* to go where Jesus was going. But to the disciples, He simply meant that where He was going they could not come at that time, immediately, though they would come to Him later. He knew, however, that there would be many anxious hours between the time He was crucified and the time when He should reappear to them as their risen Lord. He had *told* them on numerous occasions that He would rise again, but they were slow to believe—and Jesus knew they would be troubled, perplexed, and disheartened during the hours He lay in the tomb.

This is the only place where Jesus ever used the expression *"the Jews"* when speaking to His disciples. He used it in talking with the Samaritan woman in John 4:22, and in speaking with Caiaphas and Pilate; but this is the only place in which He refers to "the Jews" when speaking to His faithful disciples.

Verse 34: *"A new commandment I give unto you, That ye love one another; as I have loved you, that ye also love one another."*

Here the Lord was speaking to His disciples for the last time before He walked the last step to Calvary. He was giving them His last message, and that message was *"Love one another"*—and notice that they were to love one another *as HE loved THEM*. In John 15:13 Jesus said, "Greater love hath no man than this, that a man lay down his life for his friends"—but Jesus laid down His life for

His *enemies.*   Certainly believers should love one another
with a sacrificial love.   In I John 3:16 we read, "Hereby
perceive we the love of God, because He laid down His
life for us: and we ought to lay down our lives for the
brethren."

Again, in I John 4:7—12, we are told, "Beloved, let us
love one another: for love is of God; and every one that
loveth is born of God, and knoweth God.   He that loveth
not knoweth not God; for God is love.   In this was manifested the love of God toward us, because that God sent
His only begotten Son into the world, that we might live
through Him.   Herein is love, not that we loved God, but
that He loved us, and sent His Son to be the propitiation
for our sins.   Beloved, if God so loved us, we ought also
to love one another.   No man hath seen God at any time.
If we love one another, God dwelleth in us, and His love
is perfected in us."

It is the will of God and the desire of the Lord Jesus
Christ that believers dwell together in love and Christian
unity.   The desire of Jesus to promote such love and Chris-
tian fellowship among His children is plainly declared by
His speaking so much on the subject of love just before
He went to Calvary.

"A new commandment I give unto you."   What did Jesus mean by *"new"?*   He meant the *degree* with which
believers should love each other.   The *law* commanded,
"Thou shalt love thy neighbour as thyself" (Lev. 19:18);
but Jesus commanded His disciples to love one another
"even as I have loved you," thus setting a new and higher
standard of love than had been known on earth under the
law.   Since by taking a body like unto our bodies (sin
apart), Jesus brought God's love down to man, love one
for another is now to be explained and experienced with
new clearness.   The love believers have one for another is
to be enforced by new motives and obligations, illustrated
by a new example, and obeyed in a new manner. We
are now commanded to love each other as Christ loved

US—and that is the highest standard of love ever set forth in this world.

Verse 35: *"By this shall all men know that ye are my disciples, if ye have love one to another."*

No one could misunderstand the truth declared here. Love for each other among believers was to be the glorious characteristic, the divine, distinguishing label, of Christ's disciples; and if they did not love each other, then one and all might know that they were not true disciples.

In this day ministers, evangelists, and missionaries are measured to a large extent by the outstanding works they do, the so-called "miracles" they perform. Oh, yes—I *believe* in miracles. The greatest miracle since the virgin birth of Jesus is the new birth for poor, miserable sinners. When an alcoholic, a doper, a gambler, some poor derelict of humanity receives Jesus and is instantly transformed into a sober Christian gentleman, that transformation is indeed a miracle; but Jesus did not say, "Men will know you are my disciples *by your gifts and your miracles."* He did not say, "Men will know you are my disciples *because of your intellectual attainment and theological training."* He said, "Men will know you are my disciples *because you LOVE ONE ANOTHER."*

The simple (but powerful) grace of love distinguishes between the true and the false in discipleship, and this grace is within the reach of all—the highest, the lowliest, the most learned, the most ignorant—ALL. "If a man say, I love God, and hateth his brother, he is a liar: *for he that loveth not his brother whom he hath seen, how can he love God whom he hath not seen?"* (I John 4:20). The person who is filled with bickering, quarreling, envy, malice, and like characteristics is not a true believer. It is foolishness for one to talk of regeneration, justification, election, sanctification, and then not demonstrate practical Christian love. Paul said, "Though I speak with the tongues of men and of angels, and have not charity (love), I am become as

sounding brass, or a tinkling cymbal. And though I have
the gift of prophecy, and understand all mysteries, and all
knowledge; and though I have all faith, so that I could
remove mountains, and have not charity (love), I am nothing. And though I bestow all my goods to feed the poor,
and though I give my body to be burned, and have not
charity (love), it profiteth me nothing" (I Cor. 13:1—3).
Regardless of how orthodox we may be, regardless of what
outward show we may make, if we do not possess and
exercise love one toward another we do not know Jesus as
our personal Saviour. Let us ask ourselves, "Do those
with whom we come in contact know that we are true believers because of our love for our fellowmen—especially
those who are of the household of faith?"

Jesus Foretells Peter's Denial

Verse 36: *"Simon Peter said unto Him, Lord, whither
goest thou? Jesus answered him, Whither I go, thou canst
not follow me now; but thou shalt follow me afterwards."*

Here, as in many other instances, the impulsive spirit
of Simon Peter prompted him to ask Jesus what He meant
when He said, "Whither I go, ye cannot come." It was
Peter who spoke up, but the same question must have been
in the minds of all of the disciples. They had very little
understanding of the Lord's words here. Even though He
had told them again and again that He must be arrested,
condemned, and crucified, they did not understand what
He meant.

You will notice Jesus did not tell Peter where He was
going. He graciously explained, *"Whither I go, thou canst
not follow me NOW; but thou shalt follow me afterwards."*
He was going where Peter could not follow Him at that
time, but would follow Him after His death. It is possible
that these words are much deeper than we first notice, because in the *last chapter* of John's Gospel Jesus said to
Peter, "When thou wast young, thou girdedst thyself, and

walkedst whither thou wouldest: *but when thou shalt be old, thou shalt stretch forth thy hands, and another shall gird thee, and carry thee whither thou wouldest not. This spake He, signifying by what death he should glorify God"* (John 21:18,19). Bible history tells us that Peter was crucified head downward—and in this statement "thou shalt follow me," *Jesus* also pointed to the manner of Peter's death, the time when he should depart this life for the place where Jesus was going. Jesus said to Peter, "Follow me," and the steps in which he followed were to lead to a cross and to the Father's house.

I believe Peter understood much more about what Jesus said than is recorded here, because in II Peter 1:14 he said, "Knowing that shortly I must put off this my tabernacle, *even as our Lord Jesus Christ hath shewed me.*"

Verse 37: *"Peter said unto Him, Lord, why cannot I follow thee now? I will lay down my life for thy sake."*

Peter's question here shows that he did not fully realize how near was the death of Jesus. But impulsive person that he was, at that moment he *did* love Jesus so much that he was willing to go with Him, walk in His steps, and if necessary *die* with Him. Peter was sincere, his words were well meant. He did not doubt that something dark lay ahead for his Lord, and he was truthful when he said, "I will go with you—even unto death." But Peter was easily stirred, and at that moment there was more emotion than Christian principle in his declaration.

Verse 38: *"Jesus answered him, Wilt thou lay down thy life for my sake? Verily, verily, I say unto thee, The cock shall not crow, till thou hast denied me thrice."*

"Peter, you do not realize what you are saying, you do not know how weak and feeble you are. Will you really and truly lay your life down for me? The cock shall not crow this very night until you have denied me three times!"

Only God in flesh could have answered Peter as Jesus

answered him here, telling him exactly what he would do
and when he would do it.   Yet, here we see the beauty
of the kindness, sympathy, compassion, and condescension
of Jesus. He knew Peter would deny Him, He knew Peter
would play the coward and forsake Him. But in spite of
His foreknowledge, Jesus did not reject Peter, He did not
denounce him and cast him out; and *after* Peter's fall, after
he had cursed and sworn that he had not even *known* the
Lord, Jesus turned and looked at him with such tenderness
and compassion as to melt Peter's heart and cause him to
weep tears of bitter repentance—and then the sinless Son
of God forgave him!

Those of us who profess to be spiritually minded and
strong in the faith should be extremely careful how we
condemn weaker brethren. We should be tender and compassionate toward those who are weak in the faith. There
are some believers who are inconsistent and live very care-
less lives.   They do things that are provoking—but as we
observe their weaknesses and shortcomings, we should not
forget the Lord's feelings toward and His dealings with
Simon Peter after the denial. Even after Peter cursed and
swore and denied Him three times, declaring that he did
not even know Jesus, the Lord loved him; and when Peter
wept tears of repentance Jesus forgave him and restored
him.   How I thank God that He is married to the backslider! (See Jeremiah 3:14.)

CHAPTER XIV

1. Let not your heart be troubled: ye believe in God, believe also in me.

2. In my Father's house are many mansions: if it were not so, I would have told you. I go to prepare a place for you.

3. And if I go and prepare a place for you, I will come again, and receive you unto myself; that where I am, there ye may be also.

4. And whither I go ye know, and the way ye know.

5. Thomas saith unto him, Lord, we know not whither thou goest; and how can we know the way?

6. Jesus saith unto him, I am the way, the truth, and the life: no man cometh unto the Father, but by me.

7. If ye had known me, ye should have known my Father also: and from henceforth ye know him, and have seen him.

8. Philip saith unto him, Lord, shew us the Father, and it sufficeth us.

9. Jesus saith unto him, Have I been so long time with you, and yet hast thou not known me, Philip? he that hath seen me hath seen the Father; and how sayest thou then, Shew us the Father?

10. Believest thou not that I am in the Father, and the Father in me? the words that I speak unto you I speak not of myself: but the Father that dwelleth in me, he doeth the works.

11. Believe me that I am in the Father, and the Father in me: or else believe me for the very works' sake.

12. Verily, verily, I say unto you, He that believeth on me, the works that I do shall he do also; and greater works than these shall he do; because I go unto my Father.

13. And whatsoever ye shall ask in my name, that will I do, that the Father may be glorified in the Son.

14. If ye shall ask any thing in my name, I will do it.

15. If ye love me, keep my commandments.

16. And I will pray the Father, and he shall give you another Comforter, that he may abide with you for ever;

17. Even the Spirit of truth; whom the world cannot receive, because it seeth him not, neither knoweth him: but ye know him; for he dwelleth with you, and shall be in you.

18. I will not leave you comfortless: I will come to you.

19. Yet a little while, and the world seeth me no more; but ye see me: because I live, ye shall live also.

20. At that day ye shall know that I am in my Father, and ye in me, and I in you.

21. He that hath my commandments, and keepeth them, he it is that loveth me: and he that loveth me shall be loved of my Father, and I will love him, and will manifest myself to him.

22. Judas saith unto him, not Iscariot, Lord, how is it that thou wilt manifest thyself unto us, and not unto the world?

23. Jesus answered and said unto him, If a man love me, he will keep my words: and my Father will love him, and we will come unto him, and make our abode with him.

24. He that loveth me not keepeth not my sayings: and the word which ye hear is not mine, but the Father's which sent me.

25. These things have I spoken unto you, being yet present with you.

26. But the Comforter, which is the Holy Ghost, whom the Father will send in my name, he shall teach you all things, and bring all things to your remembrance, whatsoever I have said unto you.

27. Peace I leave with you, my peace I give unto you: not as the world giveth, give I unto you. Let not your heart be troubled, neither let it be afraid.

28. Ye have heard how I said unto you, I go away, and come again unto you. If ye loved me, ye would rejoice, because I said, I go unto the Father: for my Father is greater than I.

29. And now I have told you before it come to pass, that, when it is come to pass, ye might believe.

30. Hereafter I will not talk much with you: for the prince of this world cometh, and hath nothing in me.

31. But that the world may know that I love the Father; and as the Father gave me commandment, even so I do. Arise, let us go hence.

In every part of the world where the Gospel has been preached, the first six verses of this chapter are perhaps loved by more people than any other passage in the Bible, with the exception of the Twenty-Third Psalm. This passage is extremely rich in precious truth, and ever since the day Jesus spoke the words they have been dear to the hearts of believers. These verses have been read in hospital rooms, at gravesides, in times of distress and tribulation. They have enlightened, comforted, and encouraged ministers and laymen alike.

We live in a troublesome world, and even the most spiritual Christian has trouble, heartache, and disappointment. Job 14:1 tells us, *"Man that is born of a woman is of few days, and full of trouble."* But Jesus opened His discourse to His disciples in this chapter with the comforting words, "Let not your heart be troubled!"

In these opening verses of chapter 14 we find the divine remedy for the age-old disease of heart trouble—not the kind of heart trouble that kills physically, but that which disturbs the Christian and takes away the joy to which every believer is rightfully entitled. The remedy for this kind of heart trouble is *FAITH.* Jesus said to His disciples, *"Ye believe in God, believe also in ME."*

The pastoral discourse given by the Saviour in this chapter surpasses all others for depth, tenderness, and comprehensiveness; but we should keep in mind the circumstances under which He delivered the first part of His discourse. There is no break between the last verse of chapter 13 and the first verse of chapter 14. Jesus gave this tender, heart-searching address to His eleven faithful disciples on the last night He spent with them before His death, and it was given to strengthen them for the anxious hours of darkness and despair that lay ahead.

The words of Jesus recorded in the first six verses of this chapter bring out the perfections of the God-man in a most blessed way. His words are like a glorious, golden sunset surrounded by storm clouds, dark and threatening, with streaks of lightning playing through them and claps of thunder causing the earth to tremble and shake. Then in the midst of the tempest, the glowing radiance of the setting sun can be seen.

No mortal could have spoken as Jesus spoke that night. Man would have been thinking of his own sufferings, and he would not have said to his followers, "Let not YOUR heart be troubled." Jesus knew the sufferings He faced, He knew exactly what lay ahead for Him, He knew the torturous death He would die; but in spite of His fore-

knowledge of these things, He was thinking of His followers—yes, even of you and me; and "having loved His own,
He loved them unto the end."

We marvel at the slowness of the disciples to understand
the meaning of some of the teachings of Jesus concerning
His death on the cross. He had told them plainly over
and over again that He had come into the world to lay
His life down, but they could not fully grasp the significance of His teaching. It might be well to take time and
space here to look at some of the Scriptures which so clearly
show His attempts to enlighten His followers in the last
months and weeks of His life here on earth:

In Luke 12:50 He spoke of a baptism He must experience:
"I have a baptism to be baptized with; and how am I
straitened till it be accomplished!"

In John 3:14 He referred to a "lifting up" which He
must endure: "As Moses lifted up the serpent in the wilderness, even so must the Son of man be lifted up."

In Luke 13:32 He spoke of a goal He must reach: "Behold, I cast out devils, and I do cures to day and to morrow, and the third day I shall be perfected."

In Luke 24:7 He spoke of a suffering through which He
must pass: "The Son of man must be delivered into the
hands of sinful men, and be crucified, and the third day
rise again."

In John 12:27 and 13:1 He spoke of an "hour" which
must strike: ". . . For this cause came I unto this hour.
. . . When Jesus knew that His hour was come that He
should depart out of this world unto the Father . . . ."

In John 10:11 and 18 He spoke of laying His life down:
"I am the Good Shepherd: the Good Shepherd giveth His
life for the sheep. . . No man taketh it from me, but I lay
it down of myself . . . ."

In Luke 24:44 He spoke of a fulfillment of Scripture which
He would make: "These are the words which I spake unto
you . . . that all things must be fulfilled, which were written in the law of Moses, and in the prophets, and in the

Psalms, concerning me."

In John 18:11 He spoke of that dark, bitter cup that He must drink: "The cup which my Father hath given me, shall I not drink it?"

In Luke 22:20 He spoke of the shedding of His blood: "Likewise also the cup after supper, saying, This cup is the new testament in my blood, which is shed for you."

In John 3:16 He spoke of a love He would manifest: "For God so loved the world, that He gave His only begotten Son, that whosoever believeth in Him should not perish, but have everlasting life."

In John 12:24 He spoke of the death He must die: "Except a corn of wheat fall into the ground and die, it abideth alone: but if it die, it bringeth forth much fruit."

In Matthew 20:28 He spoke of a vicarious act He would perform: "The Son of man came not to be ministered unto, but to minister, and to give His life a ransom for many."

In John 6:51 He spoke of a gift He would bestow: "The bread that I will give is my flesh, which I will give for the life of the world."

In John 19:30 He told His disciples of a work He would accomplish: "When Jesus therefore had received the vinegar, He said, *It is finished*: and He bowed His head, and gave up the ghost."

In Matthew 26:28 He told of a remission He would secure: "This is my blood of the new testament, which is shed for many for the remission of sins."

In John 7:39 He told them of a power He would communicate to them: "This spake He of the Spirit, which they that believe on Him should receive: for the Holy Ghost was not yet given; because that Jesus was not yet glorified."

In John 16:7 He spoke of a profit He would insure. It would be to the profit of the disciples that He return to the Father: "For if I go not away, the Comforter will not come unto you; but if I depart, I will send Him unto you."

In John 3:14 and 15 He spoke of a life which He would obtain through His death: "As Moses lifted up the serpent in the wilderness, even so must the Son of man be lifted up: that whosoever believeth in Him should not perish, but have eternal life."

In John 17:19 He taught them of a consecration He would assume: "For their sakes I sanctify myself, that they also might be sanctified through the truth."

In John 12:31,32 He made known to them a victory He would win: "Now is the judgment of this world: now shall the prince of this world be cast out. And I, if I be lifted up from the earth, will draw all men unto me."

In Luke 24:46,47 He told them of a forgiveness He would give: "Thus it is written, and thus it behoved Christ to suffer, and to rise from the dead the third day: and that repentance and remission of sins should be preached in His name among all nations, beginning at Jerusalem."

These teachings of Jesus should have opened the spiritual eyes of His disciples; but they were slow to believe, and even in the last hours before His crucifixion they were still perplexed and amazed when He told them that He must go into Jerusalem where He would be arrested, tried, condemned, and put to death. In that dark hour, Jesus bore a burden of anguish that no mortal could help Him bear. He must tread the winepress alone, for He alone could pay the sin-debt. The disciples could not enter into His feelings, they could not know the sorrow of His heart—but HE knew the sorrow and anxiety *they* were feeling, He knew how perplexed and troubled they were; and in spite of His own sorrow, He was thinking of *them*.

The Second Coming Foretold

Verse 1: *"Let not your heart be troubled: ye believe in God, believe also in me."*

As Jews, these men believed in God the Father, but they needed to have more faith in God the Son (the *cru-*

cified Son).

"*Ye believe in God; believe also in ME.*" **Faith** is the answer for perplexity, anxiety, and distress of soul and spirit. The despondency and discouragement of the disciples was evidence that though they believed in God they did not believe what God had told them in the Old Testament through the prophets concerning the coming Messiah. They could not believe the humble Jesus who came as a Lamb was the glorious Messiah and King; but in the fifty-third chapter of Isaiah God clearly spelled out the fact that the Lord Jesus *would* come as a Lamb, to be rejected, despised, wounded, "smitten of God and afflicted." Many other passages in the Old Testament told of the sufferings of the Lamb of God, but they did not believe or accept what the prophets had said about the cross before the crown, the sufferings before the glory.

Not only did God (through the writers of the Old Testament) give warning as to what would occur, but Jesus Himself had warned them and told them what to expect. He plainly told them that He must suffer at the hands of the chief priests and scribes, that He would be "lifted up" (crucified), and He exhorted them to hold fast the faith, confidence, and stedfastness they had shown in the beginning of their discipleship. He said, "These things have I spoken unto you, that ye should not be offended (in me)."

"*Let not your heart be troubled.*" Jesus was not only speaking to the eleven disciples that night; He was speaking to you and me as well. Therefore I say to the discouraged soul who may read these lines, "Let not YOUR heart be troubled. God the Father knows your anxiety, your sorrow, and He possesses the power, wisdom, grace, and goodness to supply your every need and satisfy your every earnest desire. He is the eternal God, He is still on the throne to rule in the affairs of men, and He will see to it that all things work together for good to His own. He is able to give you joy, peace, victory over the world, the flesh, and the devil.

Are *you* discouraged and cast down, dear believer? Hear these words from the pen of the psalmist: "God is our refuge and strength, a very present help in trouble. Therefore will not we fear, though the earth be removed, and though the mountains be carried into the midst of the sea" (Psalm 46:1,2). There is no cause for fear, for when trials and troubles come, we need only remember that God is looking down upon us—and "if God be for us, who can be against us?" (Rom. 8:31).

FAITH is the answer to every problem of the believer. Faith is the *victory* that overcomes the world (I John 5:4). We are *saved* by God's grace through faith (Eph. 2:8). The just shall *live* by faith (Rom. 1:17)—*and whatsoever is NOT of faith is sin* (Rom. 14:23); so "have faith in God" (Mark 11:22). Believe in His absolute sovereignty, believe in His perfect, infinite wisdom, believe in His unchanging faithfulness, believe in His love that cannot be measured.

"Believe also in me." What did Jesus mean when He spoke these words to His disciples? They had walked and talked with Him during the years of His public ministry, they believed Him to be their promised Messiah, God's Christ. But remember, they were believing on One who was *in their midst,* One who had been their daily companion and with whom they had fellowshipped intimately throughout their discipleship. Now this One was soon to be removed from the earth, He would soon return to the Father, He would soon be invisible insofar as the natural eyesight is concerned. So He was saying to them here, "You believe in GOD, and HE is invisible. You have never seen His form, yet you are conscious of His love, mercy, and care. Even though you have never physically *seen* God, you have never touched Him, you *believe* in Him. In that same manner you must have confidence and faith in ME—confidence in my love, my care, even after I am crucified; for death cannot hold me, I will rise again and will ascend unto my Father from whence I came. God is invisible,

but you *believe* in Him. Now in the same way, *believe in ME* when these things shall come to pass as I have told you."

When Jesus said to His disciples, "Believe also in me," He declared His deity in a most unmistakable manner, testifying that He was equal with God and that we should believe in Him exactly as we believe in God. Later, Peter in his first epistle gave words of comfort for believers:

"Blessed be the God and Father of our Lord Jesus Christ, which according to His abundant mercy hath begotten us again unto a lively hope by the resurrection of Jesus Christ from the dead, to an inheritance *incorruptible, and undefiled, and that fadeth not away, reserved in heaven for you,* who are kept by the power of God through faith unto salvation ready to be revealed in the last time. Wherein ye greatly rejoice, though now for a season, if need be, ye are in heaviness through manifold temptations: that the trial of your faith, being much more precious than of gold that perisheth, though it be tried with fire, might be found unto praise and honour and glory *at the appearing of Jesus Christ*: WHOM HAVING NOT SEEN, YE LOVE; IN WHOM, THOUGH NOW YE SEE HIM NOT, YET BELIEVING, YE REJOICE WITH JOY UNSPEAKABLE AND FULL OF GLORY" (I Pet. 1:3−8).

In this chapter Jesus gave His disciples seven distinct promises, thus giving them sevenfold encouragement:

1. He assured them that for the disciples of Christ, *heaven is sure* (vv. 1−3).
2. He told them plainly that in Him they had a sure *way* to heaven (v. 6).
3. He assured them that they need not fear that His works would cease after He left them, because they would do greater works than HE had done (vv. 10−12).
4. In His absence, they would possess the Holy Spirit to help them (vv. 16,17).
5. He would not leave His people forever, but would return to receive them again (vv. 18−23).

6. The Holy Spirit (who would come after Christ's departure) would teach the disciples and bring to their memory all things which Jesus had said (v. 26).

7. He would give them peace that the world could not give—nor take away (v. 27).

These seven promises should encourage Christians today, because we are *recipients* of the same promises, and we should have the same assurance that was guaranteed to these faithful men.

The cure for anxiety and a troubled heart is "Believe in God, believe also in Jesus." You will notice He did not say, "Believe my *deity*." He simply said, *"Believe ME personally."* These men were Jews, and the Jews did not understand about the Trinity. They believed in one God, they believed in the *unity* of God, but they did not understand about the three Persons of the Godhead. Therefore Jesus wanted them to believe in HIM exactly as they believed in GOD. He knew that such faith would put an end to their anxiety, and they would experience the peace of God.

Verse 2: *"In my Father's house are many mansions: if it were not so, I would have told you. I go to prepare a place for you."*

The *"Father's house"* is the third heaven, the place of which Paul speaks in II Corinthians 12:2—4. Paul said, "I knew a man in Christ above fourteen years ago, (whether in the body, I cannot tell; or whether out of the body, I cannot tell: God knoweth;) such an one caught up to the third heaven. . . How that he was caught up into paradise, and heard unspeakable words, which it is not lawful for a man to utter."

The *first* heaven is the atmosphere just above us, the *second* heaven holds the planets and constellations, and the *third* heaven is far above ALL heavens. When Jesus rose from the dead and "led captivity captive," He ascended far up above all heavens, into the Father's house where

He is now seated at the right hand of the Majesty. (Please read Ephesians 4:8–10 and Hebrews 1:3).

"The Father's house" is an expression accommodated to human weakness. God needs no literal house with a roof and floor such as the houses in which *we* live, but His dwelling place is referred to as "God's house" because this is the only language we can understand. God is a Person—the Bible speaks of His eyes, His voice, His arms, His feet; but He is an eternal Spirit and He is everywhere. Therefore He needs no house. (In connection with this please study Deuteronomy 12:5, Psalm 33:14, I Kings 8:13, and II Corinthians 5:1.)

Jesus referred to "the Father's house" three times in the Gospels. In chapter 2 verse 16 of our present study, when He drove the moneychangers from the temple, He said, "Make not my Father's house an house of merchandise." In Luke 15:11–34 the Father's house is represented as a place of joy and happiness, a place of gladness and rejoicing. The third time Jesus mentioned the Father's house is here in verse 2 of chapter 14 of John's Gospel, when He refers to the final abode of the children of God.

In Luke 19:12 and Hebrews 11:16, heaven is called a *"country"*—a word that speaks of its vastness—(and who could describe that vastness in man's language)?

In Hebrews 11:10 and the entire twenty-first chapter of Revelation, heaven is spoken of as a "city"—and when we think of a city we think of many houses, many inhabitants, and much activity.

II Peter 1:11 speaks of heaven as a "kingdom," which points out that God's house is a place of order; for when we think of a kingdom we think of a *king*, with men under the king—a very orderly arrangement.

In Luke 23:43 and Revelation 2:7 we read of "Paradise," and immediately we think of a place that brings joy and happiness, a place that delights the heart.

Then in our present verse, heaven is called "the Father's house"—*home;* and when we think of home, we think of security, warmth, joy, and peace. Heaven is all of those things—*and much, much more!*

"*In my Father's house are many mansions.*" The Greek word for "mansions" literally means *abiding places.* One of the modern Bible translations reads, "In my Father's house are many *rooms.*" I do not believe a God who speaks a world like ours into being would build "rooms" for His children to dwell in forever! That does not sound like the God whom I love and serve. "Abiding places" can be mansions, and Jesus said, "In my Father's house are *many mansions.*"

But notice: The mansions were already there when Jesus spoke these words, and He promised, "*I go to prepare a place for YOU.*" From this, I am led to believe that the place where we, the New Testament Church, will live was not IN the Father's house when Jesus made this declaration to His disciples. He was assuring them that in the Father's house were many mansions, many glorious abiding places, but He was returning to the Father's house, there to prepare a special place for His bride, the born again children of God. Personally I believe the place Jesus spoke of here is the Pearly White City as described in Revelation 21. This will be the home of the Church and we will abide there forever, although we will have access to the Father's house—as well as having access to the new earth and all of God's new creation, the new heaven, the new earth, and the Pearly White City.

When the Bible speaks of a "new heaven" it is not referring to the Father's house, but to the *atmospheric* heaven which will be renovated, burned, and a new heaven created. *The devil* is the "prince of the power of the air," and the air is literally filled with demons. They will all be burned out when Jesus comes in flaming fire, taking vengeance on them that know not God. Satan will be put into the lake of fire and the demons will be destroyed forever. Then there will be a *new* atmospheric heaven, a new earth, and the Pearly White City, which will be the abiding place of the

New Testament Church.

Jesus knew that troublesome times lay ahead for His disciples. He knew they would be severely persecuted, and certainly the world that hated HIM would also hate His followers (Luke 6:22; John 15:18,19). Therefore He assured them that even though they might be outcasts on earth, they might encounter disappointments and suffer persecution, He would personally prepare a place for them, a heavenly home, that where He is, His children may be also. Fellow believer, we may be rejected of men, but in the Father's house (Psalm 115:16; Rev. 21:2,10) there is a place being prepared for those who are prepared by grace through faith in the finished work of Jesus, where we will spend eternity in the eternal abode of the righteous.

"If it were not so, I would have told you." In chapter 13 verse 33 Jesus referred to His disciples as "little children," and here He speaks to them on that basis—as a father might assure his children that he would keep his word. He did this to comfort them, and to reassure them that even though they could not go with Him at that time, they would come to Him later and would be with Him forevermore.

"I go to prepare a place for you." Heaven is a prepared place for a prepared people, and I can guarantee you on the authority of God's Word that no person will accidentally stumble into it. Those who go to heaven will do so because they have prepared for it in this life—and the only way to prepare for heaven is to believe on the Lord Jesus Christ. *HE is the Door,* and there is no other entrance to that eternal home. We enter by and through Him, or we do not enter at all.

Jesus at the right hand of God is our divine guarantee that all born again people will enter the place which is now being prepared for us. Even though we do not fully understand the "preparing" of that place, it is a comforting and assuring thought to know that when we arrive in heaven we will not be strangers there. We will enter a place specially prepared for us, and for which we are specially prepared. We will be very much at home and eternally happy when we enter that celestial city.

God always prepares for His own. He has never allowed His people to enter a place that was not prepared for them — and He never will. It was thus with Adam. "The Lord God planted a garden eastward in Eden" (a prepared place for His created man), and He placed Adam in the garden.

The same was true of Israel when they entered the land of Canaan: "And it shall be, when the Lord 'thy God shall have brought thee into the land which He sware unto thy fathers, to Abraham, to Isaac, and to Jacob, to give thee great and goodly cities, which thou buildedst not, and houses full of all good things, which thou filledst not, and wells digged, which thou diggedst not, vineyards and olive trees, which thou plantedst not; when thou shalt have eaten and be full" (Deut. 6:10,11). God always prepared the way for Israel when they served Him, looked to Him and kept His Word.

"*I go* . . . ." What a comforting thought to know that Jesus Himself is preparing our heavenly home. Dear believer, you may have little of this world's goods, you may live in a rented house or even in a shack; but be of good cheer. If you are born again, saved by the grace of God and covered by the blood of Jesus, you have a home "over there" where Jesus has gone to prepare a place for you, and you may rest assured that it will be there when you arrive. No one can take it from you. Your eternal inheritance is "incorruptible, and undefiled," it will not fade away, it is *"reserved in heaven for you"* (I Pet. 1:4).

Verse 3: *"And if I go and prepare a place for you, I will come again, and receive you unto myself; that where I am, there ye may be also."*

Believers are a *special* people. In the words of Peter, the saints of God are "a chosen generation, a royal priesthood, an holy nation, *a peculiar people"* (I Pet. 2:9 in part). Believers are God's special miracle, and we must have a special place to dwell. Jesus is now preparing that place, and when the Church enters heaven a new thing will have taken place: *men will be brought into the heavenly home.* There is *one* Man there now—the Man Christ Jesus, the "firstfruits":

"For there is one God, and one Mediator between God and men, THE MAN CHRIST JESUS" (I Tim. 2:5).

"But now is Christ risen from the dead, and become the FIRSTFRUITS of them that slept. For since by man came death, by man came also the resurrection of the dead. For as in Adam all die, even so in Christ shall all be made alive. But every man in His own order: *CHRIST THE FIRSTFRUITS;* afterward they that are Christ's at His coming" (I Cor. 15:20—23).

Man is an earthly creature. He was created from the dust of the earth, and God created him to *live* on the earth. But Adam sinned, and through his sin man *lost* the earth. The earth shared the ruin of man, because God not only cursed man, He cursed the earth as well, and everything in it. However, "God so *loved* the world, that He gave His only begotten Son, that whosoever believeth in Him should not perish, but have everlasting life" (John 3:16). Yes, the Son of God left the bosom of the Father and willingly came to earth to pay the sin-debt, that man who had sinned might enter heaven through His shed blood. Therefore, the individual who has trusted in the shed blood and finished work of Jesus is prepared for the prepared place promised in our present verse.

"I will come again." Jesus is not trusting anyone else to prepare the place for His bride, nor will He trust anyone else to come for His bride. He will not *send* for us; He will come in person to direct us to the place He has prepared for us. The Church is the pearl of great price, the most precious possession Jesus has, and He will Himself come for the Church and call His people to meet Him in

the air:

"For the Lord HIMSELF shall descend from heaven with a shout, with the voice of the archangel, and with the trump of God: and the dead in Christ shall rise first: Then we which are alive and remain shall be caught up together with them in the clouds, to meet the Lord in the air: and so shall we ever be with the Lord. Wherefore comfort one another with these words" (I Thess. 4:16—18).

"Behold, I shew you a mystery; We shall not all sleep, but we shall all be changed, in a moment, in the twinkling of an eye, at the last trump: for the trumpet shall sound, and the dead shall be raised incorruptible, and we shall be changed. For this corruptible must put on incorruption, and this mortal must put on immortality. So when this corruptible shall have put on incorruption, and this mortal shall have put on immortality, then shall be brought to pass the saying that is written, Death is swallowed up in victory. O death, where is thy sting? O grave, where is thy victory?" (I Cor. 15:51—55).

The promise here in our present verse is to be distinguished from the return of Jesus in glory to judge the earth and set up His kingdom. We must differentiate between His coming *FOR His saints* and His coming *WITH His saints.* He will come FOR believers (as recorded in I Thessalonians 4:13—18), and then He will come later *to judge the nations* (Matt. 24:29—31). When He comes *for* the saints He will come as "a thief in the night" (I Thess. 5:2). When He comes *with* the saints in the Revelation, every eye shall see Him and "all kindreds of the earth shall wail because of Him" (Rev. 1:7).

Jesus promised His disciples, *"I will come again AND RECEIVE YOU unto myself."* In this dispensation, the Holy Spirit is in charge of believers. He "borns" us, baptizes us, indwells us, anoints us, leads us, seals us, and fills us. But when the Church is completed and caught out of this earth, the Holy Spirit's work will be finished, insofar as the Church is concerned; and He will yield us to the One who died for us and redeemed us—the Lord Jesus Christ. This will be the crowning day for Jesus, the day when He will RECEIVE the Church unto Himself.

"That where I am, there ye may be also." Man has long tried to figure out what heaven will be like, just how grand and glorious heaven will be. Songs have been written about it, books have been penned in an effort to describe it; but the Apostle Paul tells us, *"Eye hath not seen, nor ear heard, neither have entered into the heart of man, the things which God hath prepared for them that love Him"* (I Cor. 2:9).

John the Beloved tells us that the Pearly White City will shine like diamonds and precious gems, the twelve gates will be twelve pearls, and the street will be transparent gold. Heaven will indeed be a glorious place, more glorious than man can describe or understand—but beloved, the most glorious thing of all will be that when Jesus receives His saints unto Himself, *where HE is, WE will be also!* What an assuring, comforting fact are the words of Jesus, His promise that we will be with Him forever. He will come again, and when He comes the second time there will be no more parting. No wonder Paul exclaimed, *"I am in a strait betwixt two, having a desire to depart, and to be with Christ; WHICH IS FAR BETTER"* (Phil. 1:23).

All who have exercised faith in the finished work of the Lord Jesus Christ have the assurance that one day they will enter the place Jesus is preparing for us, and will abide with Him in that eternal home in unbroken fellowship—the most perfect place that Jesus in His perfect power can prepare. The Word of God is solid ground, an unshakable foundation for consolation and assurance in this wilderness of sin as we travel to that land that is fairer than day. Jesus our Mediator is now seated at the right hand of God the Father interceding for us, promoting our interests; and in the fulness of time He will come again and receive us unto Himself, to be with Him forever.

Verse 4: *"And whither I go ye know, and the way ye*

know.''

In other words, Jesus said to them, "You are troubled
and downhearted because you do not know where I am
going, and because I have said that you cannot at this
time come where I am going. I am going to my Father's
house, a place of many mansions, and *I am going to prepare a place for YOU.* Therefore you need not be troubled,
anxious, or fearful, for you will follow me in due time. You
cannot follow me at this moment because the time has not
yet arrived for you to enter that place, the arrangements
are not complete. But when I return to my Father's house
and complete the arrangements for you, I will personally
return for you and receive you, that where I am, there you
may be also.''

In this verse, *"whither"* points to the Father's house
where Jesus was going, and *"the way"* points to the process
by which we will arrive where He has gone. Thus Jesus
pointed out to the disciples the *goal* of their pilgrimage,
and also the way by which they should *reach* that goal.

Verse 5: *"Thomas saith unto Him, Lord, we know not
whither thou goest; and how can we know the way?"*

In spite of the fact that Jesus had been speaking to His
disciples as one would talk to a little child—simply, plainly,
in understandable words—they still did not understand.
He spoke of the heavenly Father, and of the Father's house,
a place of many mansions. He told them He was going
there to prepare a place for His people, and when that
preparation was completed He would come again and receive them unto Himself, that they might be with Him
forever, that they might share with Him the place He would
prepare for them. But Thomas was thinking in the natural,
thinking of earthly things. Perhaps he thought when Jesus
mentioned the Father's house that He was speaking of a
home outside the city of Jerusalem, but evidently he did
not realize that the reference was to an eternal home with
the risen Lord. The Holy Spirit had not yet been given,

nor did Thomas have the "perfect law of liberty" as we do today. Spiritual ignorance is inexcusable on our part, for we have the completed, perfect Word of God, and we have the Holy Spirit to enlighten, guide, and reveal the deep things of God.

I thank God for the question Thomas asked the Lord here, for without it we would not have the answer Jesus gave. I am glad Thomas asked Him, "Lord, since we do not know where you are going, *how CAN we know the WAY?*"

Verse 6: *"Jesus saith unto him, I am the way, the truth, and the life: no man cometh unto the Father, but by me."*

Before Adam sinned, he enjoyed a threefold privilege in his relationship with God: He *knew* God, he had *communion* with God, and he possessed *spiritual life.* He was innocent, clothed with Shekinah glory; but after the fall, after Eve yielded to the temptation of the devil and ate the forbidden fruit, and then gave to Adam and *he* ate, the threefold relationship with God was broken. They were alienated from God, and when Adam heard the voice of God walking in the garden in the cool of the day as was His custom, instead of running *to* the Lord for fellowship and communion, Adam ran *from* God and hid among the trees of the garden. He no longer desired fellowship with his Creator. He had broken God's command and thereby had broken the sweet communion he had enjoyed with God.

When Adam sinned, he sold the entire human family into sin. "Wherefore, as by one man sin entered into the world, and death by sin; and so death passed upon all men, for that all have sinned" (Rom. 5:12). Since Adam is the father of the human race, all descendants of Adam are born sinners. Thus every son of Adam needs illumination, regeneration, and reconciliation.

Illumination comes through the Word: "Thy Word is a lamp unto my feet, and a light unto my path" (Psa. 119:105).

Regeneration comes through the blood of Jesus Christ: "If we walk in the light, as He is in the light, we have fellowship one with another, *and the blood of Jesus Christ His Son cleanseth us from all sin*" (I John 1:7).

We are *reconciled to God* in the Lord Jesus Christ: "And all things are of God, who hath reconciled us to Himself by Jesus Christ, and hath given to us the ministry of reconciliation" (II Cor. 5:18).

Therefore we see that our illumination, regeneration, and reconciliation are in the Lord Jesus Christ. He is our sufficiency; we are complete in Him. He is the Way to the Father, He is the Truth, He is the Life. No man can come to the Father but by Jesus.

"I am the WAY." Proverbs 16:25 tells us, "There is a way that *seemeth* right unto a man, *but the end thereof are the WAYS of death."* The way to heaven is singular: *Jesus is THE Way.* There are many attractive religions, but there is only ONE Way to God. All other "ways" are the product of man's thinking; they are therefore counterfeit, sidetracks of the devil, and they all lead to hell. The way of "religion," the way of church membership, the way of baptism, the way of keeping the Law, the way of resolutions, the way of reformation—none of these "ways" will lead to heaven. Satan cares not how religious a person may be, nor how sincere he is, nor how clean and upright his life may be. These things will never take away sin, and the devil does not oppose them. As long as one does not exercise faith in the Lord Jesus Christ, Satan does not care how many other "good" things he may follow after.

After God had clothed Adam and Eve with the skins of animals (at the price of the life blood of those animals) He promised the Deliverer. To the serpent He said, "I will put enmity between thee and the woman, and between thy seed and her Seed; It shall bruise thy head, and thou shalt bruise His heel" (Gen. 3:15). You see, the sinner could not come to God, but God, in the person of the Lord Jesus Christ, came to sinners. Jesus came to seek and to save the lost. He is the Way, the ONLY Way, to the Father's house, to heaven and eternal life.

"I am the TRUTH." Christ is the full, complete, and final revelation of God. In the Garden of Eden God told Adam exactly what to do and what *not* to do; but instead of believing God, Adam and Eve believed the devil, and ever since Adam sinned, man has been a *victim* of the devil, groping in darkness, ignorance, and error. All men are born in sin and shapen in iniquity. "The way of the wicked is as darkness: they know not at what they stumble" (Prov. 4:19). Writing to the believers at Ephesus Paul spoke of unbelievers as "having the understanding darkened, being alienated from the life of God through the ignorance that is in them, because of the blindness of their heart" (Eph. 4:18).

But to the Ephesian Christians he wrote, *"And YOU hath He quickened,* who were dead in trespasses and sins: wherein in time past ye walked according to the course of this world, according to the prince of the power of the air, the spirit that now worketh in the children of disobedience: among whom also we all had our conversation in times past in the lusts of our flesh, fulfilling the desires of the flesh and of the mind; *and were by nature the children of wrath, even as others"* (Eph. 2:1—3).

Ecclesiastes 7:29 tells us *"that God hath MADE man upright;* but they have sought out many inventions."

The final verdict for unregenerate man is spelled out in Paul's letter to the Romans—and what a sad, sordid picture we find there! In Romans 3:10—18 we read:

"As it is written, There is none righteous, no, not one: There is none that understandeth, there is none that seeketh after God. They are all gone out of the way, they are together become unprofitable; there is none that doeth good, no, not one. Their throat is an open sepulchre; with their tongues they have used deceit; the poison of asps is under their lips: Whose mouth is full of cursing and bitterness: Their feet are swift to shed blood: Destruction and misery

are in their ways: And the way of peace have they not
known: There is no fear of God before their eyes!''

Just before the crucifixion, Pilate asked Jesus, "What IS
truth?" (John 18:38).   You may rest assured that truth is
not to be found in man's systems—philosophy and other
things.   Truth is found in a Person, the Lord Jesus Christ.
HE IS the truth, "in whom are hid all the treasures of
wisdom and knowledge" (Col. 2:3).

The Word of God is the place to find the truth concerning God the Father, Christ the Son, the Holy Spirit, how
to be saved, how to live a victorious life—for the Word is
TRUTH (John 17:17).   Jesus was the Word Incarnate, and
He said, "Ye shall know the Truth, and the Truth shall
make you free. . . If the Son therefore shall make you free,
ye shall be free indeed" (John 8:32,36).   The only way to
be free from fear, free from the dread of eternity when we
shall stand before God, is to hear the truth, believe the
truth, live by the truth, and die by the truth—and the only
place to *find* the truth concerning spiritual things is in the
infallible, unalterable, forever-settled Word of God.   That
is why the devil is trying today to discredit the Word of
God with so many new translations—adding a little, taking
away a little, rearranging words and phrases, until soon
unbelievers will *lose faith* in the Word of God.   We must
not be ignorant concerning the schemes of Satan to destroy
and discredit the truth.   We must remember that *absolute*
Truth is found in the Person of the Lord Jesus Christ.   In
the words of the Apostle Paul, "Let God be true, but every
man a liar" (Rom. 3:4).

"I am the LIFE."   As we studied earlier in this series,
Jesus did not *begin* to live at His birth.   As the Father had
life in Himself, so the Son also had life in Himself.   *God's
Christ* was in the beginning with God; *man's Jesus* was
born of the virgin Mary about twenty centuries ago.   JESUS
is His earthly name, meaning "Saviour."   Joseph was instructed to call the baby "JESUS: for He shall save His
people from their sins" (Matt. 1:21).   CHRIST is His *divine*

name, denoting His deity; and Christ *had* no beginning.
He was IN the beginning with God.

Not only is Jesus "the Life," but He *destroyed* him
who had the power of *death*: "We see Jesus, who was
made a little lower than the angels for the suffering of
death, crowned with glory and honour; that He by the
grace of God should taste death for every man. . . Forasmuch then as the children are partakers of flesh and blood,
*He also Himself likewise took part of the same; that through
death He might destroy him that had the power of death,
that is, the devil; and deliver them who through fear of
death were all their lifetime subject to bondage*" (Heb.
2:9,14,15).

Christ Jesus is therefore the Emancipator from death.
All who have received Him by faith have life eternal; all
who reject Him are dead in trespasses and sins.

The natural man does not fear God, he has no concern
for his soul's salvation, and no man can come to God except the Holy Spirit draw him: "The natural man receiveth
not the things of the Spirit of God: for they are foolishness unto him: neither can he know them, because they
are spiritually discerned" (I Cor. 2:14). Therefore it is natural for the natural man to love the things of the world.
His whole life and desire is self, pleasure, and worldly at-
tractions.

But it is *unnatural* for a *believer* to love the things of
the world, because the believer possesses divine nature,
his citizenship is in heaven, he is a pilgrim and stranger
on earth, and he looks for the Saviour from heaven in that
glorious morning when He shall descend with a shout, with
the voice of the archangel and the trump of God, when the
dead in Christ shall rise and we shall be caught up together with them to meet the Lord in the air.

The prodigal son in Luke 15 presents a clear picture of
the sinner. He was a son from the natural standpoint,
and as such he took his share of the inheritance, took his
journey "into the far country" and spent his substance in

riotous living.   Then as he sat in the swine pen, hungry,
destitute, friendless, he realized what a fool he had been.
He remembered his father's house, he remembered that his
father had *servants* who fared better than he; and in humble
penitence he arose and began his journey back to his father's house.   "But when he was yet a great way off, his
father saw him, and had compassion, and ran, and fell on
his neck, and kissed him."   The son then made his confession: "Father, I have sinned against heaven, and in
thy sight, and am no more worthy to be called thy son."
The father then clothed the boy in the best robe, put a
ring on his hand, put shoes on his feet, and ordered a feast
to be made in honor of his son's return.   He said, "This
my son was DEAD, and is ALIVE again: he was LOST,
and is FOUND."

With such clear Scripture, how can it be said that this
young man was a backslider?   Yet some preachers and
teachers give the parable this interpretation.   Actually, the
prodigal son presents a perfect picture of a young man coming to the age of accountability, and instead of yielding to
the heavenly Father he goes the way of the world, follows
his own will instead of following God's will.   If he *had*
followed the will of God he would not have ended up in
the hog pen.   The father said, "my son"—and from the
standpoint of family relations he *was* the son of the father,
just as we are all *sons of God* from the standpoint of *creation.*   But we are not all sons of God by redemption.
The prodigal was the son of the father from the standpoint
of the human family, but spiritually he was lost and dead.

All who have believed on the Lord Jesus Christ and received His finished work are alive unto God.   They have
passed from death unto life.   Jesus said, "He that heareth
my word, and believeth on Him that sent me, hath everlasting life, and shall not come into condemnation: but
is passed from death unto life" (John 5:24).   Believers have
been translated out of darkness into light, out of the kingdom of Satan into the kingdom of God's dear Son (Col.

1:13). ALL who believe on Jesus have everlasting life, "and he that believeth NOT the Son shall not see life; but the wrath of God abideth on him" (John 3:36).

Have YOU received the Lord Jesus as YOUR personal Saviour? Have you received life from Him? If not, God grant you do it right now. "Believe on the Lord Jesus Christ, and thou shalt be saved" (Acts 16:31). Hear and obey His Word, and He will give you everlasting life!

"No man cometh unto the Father but by me." When God said *"no* man" He meant exactly that. Regardless of how sincere one may be, regardless of how dedicated and consecrated he may be, he cannot see God the Father except through Jesus the Son. Christ is the ONLY way to the Father; there IS no other way, no other truth, no other life: "For other foundation can no man lay than that is laid, which is Jesus Christ" (I Cor. 3:11).

"Neither is there salvation in any other: for there is none other name under heaven given among men, whereby we MUST be saved" (Acts 4:12).

Verse 7: *"If ye had known me, ye should have known my Father also: and from henceforth ye know Him, and have seen Him."*

Jesus was more than a *manifestation* of God the Father: He was *God IN FLESH.* The statement in this verse is connected with the whole of the immediate context. The apostles found it difficult to understand the words of Jesus concerning the Father, Himself, the Father's house, and Jesus' being the only way TO the Father's house. They could not understand these truths because they did not *fully* understand who Jesus was. They believed Him to be the Son of God, their Messiah, but they had never fully grasped the truth that He was *GOD in flesh.*

Knowledge of God the Father is obtained only through Jesus the Son. If we know the Father, we know the Son— and it is equally true that we know the Father *no better than we know the Son.* The more fully we know and understand the Son, the more fully we know and understand the Father.

"From henceforth ye know Him and have seen Him."
In other words He said, "Knowing *me,* ye also know the
Father.   *Seeing* me, ye also see the Father insofar as the
Father can be known and seen by mortal man." The union
between Father and Son is so close, so perfect, that they
who see and know the Son also see and know the Father.
"He that abideth in the doctrine of Christ, he hath both
the Father and the Son" (II John 9b).

This is one of those things which we cannot comprehend
completely.   There is no language to adequately express
it, therefore we accept it by faith.   We believe and reverence the truth, and in our weak way we attempt to explain it, but we will never fully comprehend the Godhead.
However, the more we read the Word and feed upon it,
the more we are enlightened *through* the Word and the
more we know of Christ. It follows that the more we know
of Christ the more we will know of the heavenly Father.

Verse 8:   *"Philip saith unto Him, Lord, shew us the
Father, and it sufficeth us."*

The human mind is unable to grasp the deep things
of God quickly, and Philip did not understand what Jesus
had just said to Thomas.   Undoubtedly he, too, was thinking in terms of the natural and his mind was set on actually *seeing* the Father.   There could be several reasons
for this.   Perhaps Philip was thinking of the experience
of Moses when, in answer to his earnest prayer, he was
allowed to hide in the cleft of the rock and God permitted
him to see His retiring glory as He passed by. Moses
prayed, "I beseech thee, shew me thy glory." And God
said, "Thou canst not see my face: for there shall no man
see me, and live. . . Behold, there is a place by me, and
thou shalt stand upon a rock: and it shall come to pass,
while my glory passeth by, that I will put thee in a clift
of the rock, and will cover thee with my hand while I pass

by: and I will take away mine hand, and thou shalt see my back parts: but my face shall not be seen" (Ex. 33: 18—23 in part).

It could be that Philip was thinking of the time when Moses, Aaron, and others were permitted to witness the tremendous revelation recorded in Exodus 34:5—8:

"And the Lord descended in the cloud, and stood with him there, and proclaimed the name of the Lord. And the Lord passed by before him, and proclaimed, The Lord, The Lord God, merciful and gracious, longsuffering, and abundant in goodness and truth, keeping mercy for thousands, forgiving iniquity and transgression and sin, and that will by no means clear the guilty; visiting the iniquity of the fathers upon the children, and upon the children's children, unto the third and to the fourth generation. And Moses made haste, and bowed his head toward the earth, and worshipped."

Or perhaps Philip was thinking of Isaiah 40:5: "And the glory of the Lord shall be revealed, and all flesh shall see it together: for the mouth of the Lord hath spoken it." This statement from Isaiah was prophetic, but Philip did not have the New Testament as we have it, Pentecost had not come, and therefore the Spirit had not enlightened the disciples. Philip was thinking as the mind of man thinks, and he wanted to *see* the Father.

Verse 9: *"Jesus saith unto him, Have I been so long time with you, and yet hast thou not known me, Philip? He that hath seen me hath seen the Father; and how sayest thou then, Shew us the Father?"*

Here Jesus administered a gentle rebuke. We know from John 1:43 that Philip was one of the first disciples whom the Lord called, and therefore He asked him, "Have I been so long time with you, Philip, and yet you do not know me? Have you walked with me throughout my earthly ministry, and yet you do not understand who I am?" Philip wanted to see God, and he did not realize that he was

standing *in the very presence of God* in flesh. Through
the words He spoke and the miracles He performed, Jesus
had shown forth the glory of God and had manifested Himself as the only begotten of the Father. He was the visible
image of the invisible God (II Cor. 5:19). He was the
brightness of the Father's glory, the express image of His
Person (Heb. 1:3). In Him all the fulness of the Godhead
dwelt (Col. 2:9).

The natural man sees with the natural eye, but the
spiritual man sees with the eye of faith. The deep truth
pointed out here is that we who see Jesus with the eye
of faith, having sincerely believed that He is the only begotten, eternal Son of God, have seen as much of God the
Father as mortal man can understand. The union between
Father and Son is so complete that to see the Son is to
see the Father, and yet we must be very careful to know
and believe that the Father and the Son are two distinct
persons.

Verse 10: *"Believest thou not that I am in the Father,
and the Father in me? The words that I speak unto you
I speak not of myself: but the Father that dwelleth in
me, He doeth the works."*

The words and the works of Jesus were a perfect and
undeniable revelation of Almighty God. His words were
works, because His word was so powerful that when He
spoke, it was done. When He commanded, it stood fast.
At the tomb of Lazarus He simply called, "Lazarus, come
forth!" and the man who had been dead for four days came
forth from the grave.

*"The words that I speak unto you I speak not of my-
self."* Jesus always made it very clear that He did nothing
independently of God the Father. Not only did He live
and act under the Father's will, but the very words He
spoke were given to Him by the Father. The words and
works of Jesus were all settled in the eternal council of
the Godhead before the world was created.

"The Father that dwelleth in me, He doeth the works."
Again we face the infinite truth of the mysterious and insoluble unity of God the Father and God the Son. Although Jesus was very man, He never *ceased* to be God,
and therefore He could say, "The Father doeth the works."

Verse 11: *"Believe me that I am in the Father, and the
Father in me: or else believe me for the very works' sake."*

Here Jesus used almost the same words He had used in
speaking to His enemies in chapter 10, verse 38. To them
He said, "If I do (the works), though ye believe not me,
believe the works: that ye may know, and believe, that
the Father is in me, and I in Him." If Philip did not understand and could not believe that Jesus and God were
one, then he must acknowledge the proof of that union
in the miracles the Lord performed and in the work that
He had done. Surely no one but God could work the works
Jesus had performed in the presence of His disciples.

The disciples did not fully understand the deity of Jesus
until after His resurrection and ascension. The darkness
of their minds is difficult for us to understand, but we
today have the completed, perfect Word of God, and in
I John 5:20 we read, "We KNOW that the Son of God is
come, and hath given us an understanding, that we may
know Him that is true, and we are in Him that is true,
even in His Son Jesus Christ. This is the true God, and
eternal life."

In our present verse, as in many other places, the Lord
Jesus names His words and His works as divine testimony
to His identity, proof of His divine nature and His divine
mission. It is a grave mistake to omit miracles as one
evidence that Christianity is the only religion that will
save us and make us fit for the kingdom of God. Liberals
and modernists *deny* the miracles, but we who believe the
Bible believe the *miracles* of the Bible—in the Old Testament as well as in the New—and we believe that the miracles and works of Jesus prove that He was no less than

God in flesh.

Verse 12:   *"Verily, verily, I say unto you, He that believeth on me, the works that I do shall he do also; and
greater works than these shall he do; because I go unto
my Father."*

The "double verily" in this verse precedes the Lord's
encouraging statement to His disciples that they would
not become weak, helpless ministers after His departure.
On the contrary they would continue to perform miracles,
they would do works which would confirm the fact of their
discipleship.   The miracles recorded in Acts certainly fulfilled the words of Jesus spoken here, for according to the
record the apostles healed the sick, raised the dead, cast
out demons, and did many other mighty miracles.

*"He that believeth on me, the works that I do shall
he do also."*   Certainly this statement was fulfilled, according to Hebrews 2:1—4:

"Therefore we ought to give the more earnest heed to
the things which we have heard, lest at any time we should
let them slip.   For if the word spoken by angels was sted-
fast, and every transgression and disobedience received a
just recompence of reward; how shall we escape, if we
neglect so great salvation; *which at the first began to be
spoken by the Lord, and was confirmed unto us by them
that heard Him; GOD ALSO BEARING THEM WITNESS,
BOTH WITH SIGNS AND WONDERS, AND WITH DI-
VERS MIRACLES, AND GIFTS OF THE HOLY GHOST,
according to His own will?"*   ("Them that heard Him"
refers, of course, to the disciples.)

Paul said to the Corinthian believers, "When that which
is perfect is come, then that which is in part shall be done
away" (I Cor. 13:10).   We who have the perfect Word of
God do not need miracles such as raising the dead and
miraculous healing of the sick.   Yes, I believe in divine
healing.   I know God does heal the sick, and I have personally been delivered from the very jaws of death by the

prayers of God's dear people; but there is no reason to suppose that Jesus meant these mighty miracles to be performed by ministers today.

In the Bible we find the great miracles always at some outstanding crisis, such as God's deliverance of Israel from Egypt, or on the Day of Pentecost when the Church was born, and during the transition period from law to grace as recorded in the Acts of the Apostles. *Paul* healed the sick and raised the dead, and in Acts 5:15 we read that the sick were brought into the streets on beds and couches and they were healed when Peter's *shadow* passed over them. But we do not read in the Scriptures that ministers in this day and hour will continue to raise the dead and heal the sick as those men did. We have the completed Word of God, and "we ought to give the more earnest heed to the things which we have heard."

"And greater works than these shall (ye) do." It could not be truly said that the apostles performed greater physical miracles than our Lord, but after Pentecost by the power of God they did more wonderful works, for the miracle of miracles is the salvation of a sinner! These words of Jesus were fulfilled when Peter and others of the apostles preached. In Acts 2:41 we read that three thousand souls were saved, and in Acts 6:7 we read, "And the Word of God increased; and the number of the disciples multiplied in Jerusalem greatly; *and a great company of the priests were obedient to the faith."*

Greek scholars tell us that this phrase in the Greek reads, "And greater than these shall he do." Notice the word "works" is not there; therefore it stands to reason that Jesus was not referring to physical miracles, but rather to something else that would be of greater magnitude than raising a dead person or healing a sick body. The apostles would do something *greater* than the miracles He had performed, and I do not doubt that He was speaking of the preaching of the Gospel. Preaching the Gospel of a risen and exalted Christ, proclaiming the grace of God to every creature, pointing souls from darkness to light and causing unbelievers to be born of the Spirit is a far greater miracle than healing a leper or causing a withered arm to be made whole. God gave these apostles unusual power and they possessed unusual gifts—but that was during the transition period in the first century of Christianity. God was highly pleased and honored by the work of Jesus the Son, and He honored the Son by giving these men power to do mighty miracles.

I might add that in Acts 3:11−16 we find Peter and the other disciples giving God the glory for the miracles they were enabled to perform. Peter and John had just healed a lame man who sat, begging, at the temple gate. "And as the lame man which was healed held Peter and John, *all the people ran together unto them in the porch that is called Solomon's, greatly wondering.* And when Peter saw it, he answered unto the people, Ye men of Israel, why marvel ye at this? or why look ye so earnestly on us, as though by our own power or holiness we had made this man to walk? The God of Abraham, and of Isaac, and of Jacob, the God of our fathers, hath glorified His Son Jesus; whom ye delivered up, and denied Him in the presence of Pilate, when he was determined to let Him go. But ye denied the Holy One and the Just, and desired a murderer to be granted unto you; and killed the Prince of life, whom God hath raised from the dead; whereof we are witnesses. AND HIS NAME THROUGH FAITH IN HIS NAME HATH MADE THIS MAN STRONG, whom ye see and know: yea, THE FAITH WHICH IS BY HIM HATH GIVEN HIM THIS PERFECT SOUNDNESS IN THE PRESENCE OF YOU ALL."

"Because I go to my Father" points to the outpouring of the Holy Ghost on the Day of Pentecost, after Jesus had ascended back to heaven and taken His seat at the right hand of God. If He had not departed from this earth and returned to the Father, the Holy Spirit would not have come. In chapter 16, verse 7 of this study He said, "I tell

you the truth: It is expedient for you that I go away: for if I go not away, the Comforter will not come unto you; but if I depart, I will sent Him unto you."

The word *"because"* is important in the last phrase of our present verse. I appreciate the fact that our Bible is divided into chapters and verses—but men, not the Holy Spirit, did the dividing, and some verses end at the wrong place. The last phrase of verse 12 should connect with verse 13, thus: "Because I go unto my Father, whatsoever ye shall ask in my name, that will I do . . . ." He was here assuring them that when He ascended back to the Father He would hear and answer their prayers and they would be able to do great and mighty things. He would not leave them alone; He would do mighty miracles through them, in the Person of the Holy Spirit who would come on the Day of Pentecost to indwell, empower, and lead them. Thus was Isaiah 53:10 fulfilled: "Yet it pleased the Lord to bruise Him; He hath put Him to grief: when thou shalt make His soul an offering for sin, He shall see His seed, He shall prolong His days, and the pleasure of the Lord shall prosper in His hand."

Yes, the disciples would do greater things than Jesus did; but these things would be done by Jesus in the Person of the Holy Spirit, working through them. *"AND THEY WENT FORTH, AND PREACHED EVERYWHERE, THE LORD WORKING WITH THEM, AND CONFIRMING THE WORD WITH SIGNS FOLLOWING"* (Mark 16:20).

Verse 13: *"And whatsoever ye shall ask in my name, that will I do, that the Father may be glorified in the Son."*

In this verse we learn an important thing about prayer. We learn that prayer should be made in the name of the Lord Jesus Christ and through His mediation—not through a minister, priest, or pope. There is but one Mediator between God and men, the Man Christ Jesus (I Tim. 2:5).

"Whatsoever" does not mean that believers can pray for vain, selfish things and expect God to answer. A Chris-

tian *praying in the Spirit* will ask for whatsoever things the soul needs, whatsoever can be used to bring glory and honor to God the Father and to the Lord Jesus Christ.

"That the Father may be glorified in the Son" means that Jesus will do whatsoever the believer asks, that God may be glorified through His mediation. Since Jesus fulfilled every desire of God and satisfied God's holiness, righteousness, and law, then the fact that Christ has the power to do anything His disciples ask brings glory and honor to God.

God has never answered a selfish prayer, and He never will. If we pray to bring honor, glory, or gain to ourselves, we need not expect God to hear our prayers; but if we pray in the name of Jesus and if what we ask is for the purpose of bringing glory to God, then He will hear and answer our prayers.

In studying this verse we need to keep the previous verses in mind. We need to remember here that Jesus was comforting His disciples who were troubled and discouraged because of His announced departure. In the preceding verse He had assured them that His cause on earth would not suffer because of His going to the Father, and that greater things would be done by them than they had seen Him do; and now He tells them that the fact of His departure would unite them to Him more intimately and effectually in a spiritual way because through prayer they could reach Him and He would be in their presence at any time. He had shown them by example that there was an intimate connection between His prayers and the miracles He had done, and they were to understand that prayer was essential if they were to do the works He had left them to do. They had heard Him pray on many occasions, as in chapter 6, verse 11, chapter 11 verse 41, chapter 12 verse 28, and many other Scriptures in this Gospel as well as in Matthew, Mark, and Luke. He was here instructing them to follow His example in calling on the heavenly Father.

Verse 14:   *"If ye shall ask any thing in my name, I*

will do it."

Blessed indeed is this promise! If believers ask *anything* in His name, they can count on Him to answer—but again, a born again Christian will not ask for foolish things.

Jesus wanted His disciples to realize that He was not bound to earth; He could be with the Father and be with them at the same time. Even though He would be absent from them in body, He would manifest His deity on earth by answering, if they would pray in His name. He had all power in heaven and on earth, the Father had committed all judgment unto Him, and He had already told His disciples this, as recorded in chapter 5, verse 22 of this study.

What did Jesus mean by telling His disciples to pray in His name? Did He mean that we are simply to close our prayers *"in Jesus' name. Amen"*? No indeed! To pray in Jesus' name means that the believer is praying in His Person, standing in His place, identified with Him. We make our petitions in prayer *by virtue of our very union with Jesus.* We are bone of His bone, flesh of His flesh, hid with Him in God, seated with Him in the heavenlies. Thus when the believer prays in the Spirit and in the name of the Lord Jesus Christ, it is actually Christ who is making the petition.

The only possible way for the believer to reach God the Father is in the Son. He is our High Priest, our Mediator, and when we pray sincerely in the name of Jesus, praying in His will, God looks beyond us and sees His beloved Son and hears the Son making intercession for us.

To pray in the name of Jesus means to pray for the things that will bring glory and honor to Jesus Christ and to God the Father. When we pray in His will, we pray for the things *He* would pray for, we seek the things *He* would seek, and in our prayer life we honor and glorify the things *He* would honor and glorify.

It is interesting, too, that Jesus did not say, "If you ask in my name, my FATHER will do it." He said, "If you ask in my name, *I will do it.*"

Verse 15: *"If ye love me, keep my commandments."*

Jesus is saying simply this: "If you really do love me, then *prove* your love—not by grieving and being despondent because of my going, but by striving to do my will in the things I have taught you."

The same is true of His followers today. We prove our love by what we do. If we love Jesus as we should, we will do our best to keep His commandments—and bear in mind that Jesus was not speaking here of the Law of Moses, but of His own commandments, which include all of His moral teaching during His earthly ministry, especially the truth set forth in the Sermon on the Mount.

The language of Jesus in this verse could be used only by one who was equal with God. *Moses* never said, "my commandments," *Elijah* never said, "my commandments"—but Jesus plainly said, "Keep MY commandments." There is much singing (and talking) in churches today about how we love Jesus, but such sentiment is empty and worthless unless we *show* our love in obedience to His will and His command, as He instructed the disciples to do.

What ARE the commandments of Jesus? His commandments are the entire revelation of His divine will. He came into the world to do the *Father's* will; *we* are sons of God, and therefore the uppermost desire of *our* hearts should be to keep the words of Jesus and do HIS will.

There are scores of commandments in the New Testament. For instance, in Mark 11:22 Jesus said, *"Have faith in God."* In the first verse of our present chapter He said, *"Believe God, believe ME."* When a lawyer asked Jesus, "Master, which is the great commandment in the law?" He replied, *"Thou shalt love the Lord thy God with all thy heart, and with all thy soul, and with all thy mind. This is the first and great commandment. And the second is like unto it, Thou shalt love thy neighbour as thyself"* (Matt. 22:35—39).

The law of God, the will of God, yea, the *commandment* of God is that we love *Him* first and supremely, and that we love our neighbor as we love ourselves. When we love with a love such as this, there is no need for worry concerning the other commandments in either the Old or the New Testament. The true Christian will keep the Lord's commandments impartially; he will not choose some and reject others. If we love Christ as we should, we will keep His commandments *cheerfully,* not of necessity, but simply because He *bids* us do it. And when we keep His commandments because we love Him, we will love His law and His Word the more.

The Promise of the Holy Spirit

Verse 16: *"And I will pray the Father, and He shall give you another Comforter, that He may abide with you for ever."*

Up to this time, *the Lord Jesus Christ* had been their Comforter; but now that He was leaving them He assured them of "another Comforter"—and notice that it is Jesus who will pray the Father to *send* the Comforter. In verses 13 and 14 He had instructed *the disciples* to pray in *HIS* name, and in Luke 11:13 He told them that *the Father* would give them the Holy Spirit if they asked. But in this verse He assured them that He *Himself* would ask God the Father to send the Comforter.

There has been a great deal of controversy over the Greek word here rendered "Comforter"—but if we keep in mind the original meaning of our English word, we see that there could be no better one used. The English word "Comforter" comes from two Latin words which mean "alongside of, strong." Therefore the Comforter (the Holy Spirit) is One who stands alongside of, or who walks alongside, to strengthen, direct, protect, and keep us.

The fact that Jesus spoke of the Holy Spirit as *"another* Comforter" tells us that He was to fill the place Jesus had occupied up to the time of His return to the Father, and that He would *do* for the disciples all that Jesus had done while He was with them here. The only difference would be that the Holy Spirit would abide within them and would *minister* from within, whereas Christ had ministered to them from without. But the Holy Spirit would comfort, strengthen, assure, and guide them, helping them in any and every way they needed help.

The Lord's reference to *"another Comforter"* also gives proof that the Holy Spirit is a *person,* not an "influence." Jesus was the Comforter while He was on earth, and at His departure He promised to send *another* Comforter. The Holy Spirit is a person just as surely as God the Father and God the Son are persons. He is a *divine* person, the third Person of the Trinity.

We see the Holy Trinity very plainly in this verse. Jesus said, "I (the Son) will pray the Father (Jehovah God), and He shall give you another Comforter (the Holy Spirit)."

The same Greek word translated "Comforter" here is rendered "advocate" in I John 2:1—"We have an *Advocate* with the Father, Jesus Christ the righteous." An advocate is one who gives aid, one who *pleads the cause* of his client. Hebrews 7:25 tells us that Jesus ever lives to make intercession for us. Therefore, since the Holy Spirit is within us (Rom. 8:9,14,16,26) and Christ is our Advocate on high, we have *TWO Comforters,* two divine Helpers to strengthen, guide, advise and protect us as we travel through earth to heaven.

What assuring words Jesus gave the disciples in this verse! He would pray the Father, and the Father would send another Comforter *"that HE may abide with you FOREVER."* They had been saddened and discouraged by His announcement that He must needs return to the Father, but He assured them that the Comforter who would come in His place would abide forever—and He will! He came on the Day of Pentecost, and He will remain until the Church, every born again believer, is caught out of the world to meet Jesus in the air, "and so shall we ever be with the Lord" (I Thess. 4:17; II Thess. 2:7).

Verse 17: *"Even the Spirit of truth; whom the world cannot receive, because it seeth Him not, neither knoweth Him: but ye know Him; for He dwelleth with you, and shall be in you."*

In the preceding verse, Jesus promised the disciples another Comforter—but in this verse He accommodates the human mind by patiently and gently explaining that they are not to expect a *visible* person like unto Himself.

There are two things here that we need to see:

First, *"the Spirit of truth"* is used in speaking of both the *written* Word and the *Incarnate* Word. Christ had just told Thomas, "I am the way, the TRUTH, and the life." Then in chapter 17 verse 17 He prayed to the Father (in the presence of the disciples), "Sanctify them through thy truth: thy WORD is truth."

Second, the Holy Spirit is here to glorify the Lord Jesus Christ. Jesus said, "He shall glorify me: for He shall receive of mine, and shall shew it unto you" (ch. 16, v. 14).

The Holy Spirit is the Spirit of Christ because He was sent BY Christ. Jesus told His disciples, "It is expedient for you that I go away: for if I go not away, the Comforter will not come unto you; but if I depart, I WILL SEND HIM UNTO YOU" (ch. 16, v. 7).

The Holy Spirit is also the Spirit of the *written* Word, because we *have* the written Word as the result of the Spirit's moving holy men to pen down the Scriptures as they were inspired of God: "For the prophecy came not in old time by the will of man: *but holy men of God spake AS THEY WERE MOVED BY THE HOLY GHOST"* (II Pet. 1:21).

In this day and hour, the Holy Spirit is the One who interprets the Word: "Howbeit when He, the Spirit of truth, is come, He will guide you into all truth: for He shall not speak of Himself; but whatsoever He shall hear, that shall He speak: and He will shew you things to come" (John 16:13).

When Jesus walked with His disciples in person He was

their teacher; but after His ascension the Holy Spirit became their teacher—*and ours*:   "The Comforter, which is
the Holy Ghost, whom the Father will send in my name,
He shall teach you all things, and bring all things to your
remembrance, whatsoever I have said unto you" (John
14:26).

The Holy Spirit today works through the written Word:
"This is He that came by water and blood, even Jesus
Christ; not by water only, but by water and blood. And
it is the Spirit that beareth witness, because the Spirit is
truth" (I John 5:6).

Jesus speaks of "the Spirit of truth *whom the world cannot receive."*   The world is sold out to the devil. I John
5:19 tells us that *"the whole world* lieth in wickedness"
(or *"in the lap of the wicked one"*). The world demon-
strates its real character in its opposition to everything
God stands for: *"For all that is in the world,* the lust of
the flesh, and the lust of the eyes, and the pride of life,
IS NOT OF THE FATHER, BUT IS OF THE WORLD.
And the world passeth away and the lust thereof: *but he
that doeth the will of God abideth for ever"* (I John 2:16,17).

Now we know that the Holy Spirit is invisible, so why
did Jesus say, "the world *seeth* Him not"?   We find the
answer in I Corinthians 2:14:   "The *natural* man receiveth
not the things of the Spirit of God: for they are foolishness unto him: *neither CAN he know them, BECAUSE
THEY ARE SPIRITUALLY DISCERNED."*

From this we know that Jesus spoke of seeing with the
spiritual eye, not with the physical eye. The unbeliever
cannot see the Spirit because "except a man be BORN
AGAIN, he cannot SEE the kingdom of God" (John 3:3)
and *the unbeliever has not been born again.* Before one
can see with the spiritual eye, he must receive Jesus into
the heart by faith; and when a person trusts in *Jesus,* HE
opens the blinded mind and gives light to the spiritual
eye. For the disciples, the eyes of their understanding had
already *been* opened and Jesus knew they would receive

the Comforter who was to come into the world after the
Saviour's ascension.   This is borne out in the next phrase
of our verse:

*"But YE know Him; for He dwelleth with you, and shall
be in you."*   Here is pointed out the contrast between the
people of God and the people of the world.   Believers are
possessors of the Holy Spirit: *"He dwelleth with you."*   Of
course at that time the disciples did not possess the Spirit
as they did after Pentecost; He was *with* them, but Jesus
said, "He *shall be* IN you"—that is, after Pentecost.   He
would come and take up His abode in the inner man,
making their bodies His temple.

On what grounds does the Holy Spirit come into our
hearts to dwell?   Certainly we are not *fit* for such an abode,
for we are born in sin and shapen in iniquity.   Even after
we are *born again,* the flesh is still with us.   That does not
mean that the believer practices sin, nor that he *wants* to
sin; but we live in a tabernacle of flesh which, if Jesus
tarries, will return to dust.   No, we do not become the
temple of the Holy Spirit because we are FIT for Him to
indwell.   He comes into the heart the very moment we are
saved, and He abides within us *BECAUSE we have trusted
in the shed blood and finished work of the Lord Jesus
Christ!*

In the *Old* Testament, God dwelt in the midst of Israel
even when His chosen people were backslidden, stiffnecked,
and uncircumcised in heart—but He dwelt there on the
grounds of the atoning blood: "And he shall make an atonement for the holy place, because of the uncleanness of the
children of Israel, and because of their transgressions in
all their sins: and so shall he do for the tabernacle of
the congregation, that remaineth among them in the midst
of their uncleanness" (Lev. 16:16).

In the same manner, the Holy Spirit abides within the
believer NOW.   He is there because of the sufficiency and
excellency of the one offering Christ made when He gave
His precious blood, and *through* His blood "perfected for

ever them that are sanctified" (Heb. 10:14).

Believers who are praying for the coming of the Holy Spirit are praying in ignorance. Every born again, blood-washed believer is *already* a possessor of the Holy Spirit (John 3:5; Rom. 8:9,14,16; Eph. 4:30). In the Old Testament era the Holy Spirit came upon men for a purpose and then departed, but since Pentecost He has dwelt in the heart of every believer, and will remain there as long as that believer remains upon this earth. He is here to bring glory and honor to God, and He will guide us in the paths of right living for the name's sake of Jesus.

Verse 18: *"I will not leave you comfortless; I will come to you."*

(The Greek language here bears the message, "I will not leave you orphans.") In chapter 13 verse 33 Jesus spoke to His disciples as "little children," and now He is assuring those little children that they would not be orphaned, because He would send another Comforter that they might not be left as sheep without a shepherd, helpless, wandering among the wolves of an unfriendly world without a leader or defender.

"I will come to you." I believe there is a primary and a secondary meaning here. I believe Jesus is speaking of the time when He came to His disciples after His resurrection, and of the time when He came (invisibly) after His ascension—at Pentecost. But He was also pointing to the time when He would come in glory to receive the Church, as He taught them in verses 2 and 3 of this chapter. However, the New Testament makes it clear that the coming of the Holy Spirit was NOT the coming of Jesus for His Church. Some teach that *Pentecost* was the fulfillment of the second coming, but they teach *error*.

Verse 19: *"Yet a little while, and the world seeth me no more; but ye see me: because I live, ye shall live also."*

The last time this wicked world saw the sinless Son of

God was on Calvary as He died for the sins of mankind!
After His resurrection, He appeared only unto chosen ones—
His own disciples and true children of God.   In Acts 10:
40,41 we read, "Him God raised up the third day, and
shewed Him openly; not to *ALL the people, but unto witnesses chosen before of God,* even to us, who did eat and
drink with Him after He rose from the dead."

The *world* will see Jesus again when He comes in glory:
"Behold, He cometh with clouds; and every eye shall see
Him, and they also which pierced Him: and all kindreds
of the earth shall wail because of Him.   Even so, Amen"
(Rev. 1:7).   The world will not see Him when He comes
for the Church, for He will come "as a thief in the night,"
and "in the twinkling of an eye" it will all be over (I Cor.
15:51—55; I Thess. 4:13—18; 5:1—6).   The Rapture will be
secret, the Church will be taken up into the clouds to meet
Jesus in the air; but when He comes at the close of the
Great Tribulation period, every eye on earth will see Him.

"But ye see me."   The disciples saw Jesus as He spoke
to them, they saw Him again and again after the resurrection, they saw Him as He was caught up into heaven, and
after His ascension *they saw Him by faith* as we see Him
today.   When He comes in the Rapture we shall see Him
as He is and we shall be like Him (I John 3:2).   Believers
will see Him throughout all eternity, never to be separated
from Him.   "They shall see His face; and His name shall
be in their foreheads" (Rev. 22:4).

"Because I live, ye shall live also."   The only reason
Christians have eternal life is because we believe on Jesus.
He abides in our hearts, we are "hid with Christ in God,"
and since *God* can never die, *Jesus* can never die.   Therefore since we are in Him and He is in us, we have eternal
life.   Because HE lives, WE live.   We have life that can
never be destroyed: "Whereby are given unto us exceeding
great and precious promises: that by these ye might be
partakers of the divine nature, having escaped the corruption that is in the world through lust" (II Pet. 1:4).

"What shall we then say to these things? If God be for us, who can be against us? He that spared not His own Son, but delivered Him up for us all, how shall He not with Him also freely give us all things? Who shall lay anything to the charge of God's elect? It is God that justifieth. Who is He that condemneth? It is Christ that died, yea rather, that is risen again, who is even at the right hand of God, who also maketh intercession for us.

"Who shall separate us from the love of Christ? Shall tribulation, or distress, or persecution, or famine, or nakedness, or peril, or sword? As it is written, For thy sake we are killed all the day long; we are accounted as sheep for the slaughter.

"Nay, in all these things we are more than conquerors through Him that loved us. *For I am persuaded, that neither death, nor life, nor angels, nor principalities, nor powers, nor things present, nor things to come, nor height, nor depth, NOR ANY OTHER CREATURE, shall be able to separate us from the love of God WHICH IS IN CHRIST JESUS OUR LORD"* (Rom. 8:31—39).

At the time Jesus was talking with His disciples, He knew that shortly this wicked, Christ-rejecting world would no longer be able to accuse Him nor gaze upon Him. They could no longer follow after Him, seeking something through which they could condemn Him and demand His death. He would soon leave this world to return to the heavenly Father—but even though the world would see Him no more until He should return with tens of thousands of His saints, He wanted the disciples to have the assurance that *they* would see Him—and they *did* see Him—*in person* after the resurrection, and *by faith* after His ascension.

In the Greek, *"I live"* means "the Living One." This means much more than the Lord's resurrection from the dead. It means that as "the Living One" He is the *source* of life, the fountain of life. "In Him was life; and the life was the light of men. . . For as the Father hath life in Himself; so hath He given to the Son to have life in

Himself" (John 1:4; 5:26). Jesus IS the life, and apart from Him *there is no life.*

Verse 20: *"At that day ye shall know that I am in my Father, and ye in Him, and I in you."*

This statement points to His glorious second coming, for only then will we have perfect knowledge concerning the Father, Son, and Holy Ghost—one God manifested in three Persons. *"At that day"* we will know and be able to understand that Jesus and the Father and the Holy Spirit are ONE, though they are THREE.

Verse 21: *"He that hath my commandments, and keepeth them, he it is that loveth me: and he that loveth me shall be loved of my Father, and I will love him, and will manifest myself to him."*

The heart of the message Jesus gave His disciples in this chapter is one of comfort, and that theme runs *throughout* the chapter. His expressions of comfort and assurance are many and varied. He assured them that even though He would be leaving them soon, He would make provision for them and would return for them later. He pointed out *the Way* to where He was going, telling them that He Himself was the Way. He further assured them that He would not withdraw the miraculous power through which He had worked His mighty miracles, but would enable them also to have power to do even greater works than HE had done.

Then He told them that after He departed, whatever they asked in His name He would do, and thus in a spiritual sense would be even more closely and intimately associated with them than before. He promised that He would not leave them "orphans," but would send a divine Person, the third Person of the Godhead, to take His place—a Person who would instruct and guide them, protect and console them, remind them of all that He Himself had said to them, and give them peace that the world could not take away.

He also assured them that the time would come when they *would* fully understand the unity between Himself and God the Father, and also the unity of those who were *sons of God by faith* and the *only begotten* Son of God.

Now in our present verse He returns to the lesson given in verse 15—and when Jesus *repeats* what He says, you can rest assured that the words are of the utmost importance. Here He stresses the fact that the person who knows the commandments of Jesus and puts those commandments into practice is the person who *really LOVES the Lord.* We prove our love by what we do. Oh, yes—*we are SAVED by grace,* works have no part in our salvation; but works are the evidence of saving faith and they prove our love for Jesus. When we serve Him according to His will, when we keep His word and obey His commandments, our obedience is proof of our love for Him. Profession must be backed up with action, for *many profess with their lips* but their hearts are far from God.

"He that loveth me shall be loved of my Father." God loves those who love His only begotten Son. The only possible way we can please and honor God is in the Lord Jesus Christ; therefore the person who truly loves Jesus and proves that love by His life, will be loved by God the Father in a *very special way.* It is Bible truth that "God *so loved the world* that He gave His only begotten Son," but let it be noticed that God loves the believer with a peculiar, very special love, a love over and beyond the general love of God as shown by His compassion toward all mankind. In the spiritual sense, God is the Father of born again, blood-washed believers *only.* Jesus said to the unbelieving Pharisees, *"YE are of your father the devil"* (John 8:44). The Bible teaches no such doctrine as "the Fatherhood of God and the brotherhood of man."

"And I will love him, and will manifest myself to him." The believer who keeps the commandments of Jesus will be loved by Him in a very special way, and He will *mani-*

fest Himself to that believer in a very special way. The obedient Christian will know comfort, joy, and assurance that the nominal Christian does not know or dream of. He will enjoy a special portion of God's grace and favor.

The reason most believers receive so little out of their Christian experience is that they put so little *into* it. They are saved by God's grace—and they let it end there. They are saved, babes in Christ, but they do not love the Lord completely, they do not study to show themselves approved unto Him, they do not feed on the Word, and therefore they do not grow. And the majority of such Christians wonder why *they* cannot have the same experience as the believer who is happy, rejoicing in all things, continually praising God for His goodness. ALL born again people could have such an experience if they would only surrender their all to Jesus, love Him supremely, and let Him be the motivating force in their lives. God loves *all* of His children, and the reason He gives some believers more comfort, peace, and joy than others have, is that those believers love HIM more deeply and follow His steps more closely, study His Word and keep His commandments more faithfully than others do. They walk the walk of obedience, and Jesus rewards them according to their faithfulness.

It is a wonderful experience to know Christ, but it is a much *more* wonderful, richer experience to KNOW that we know Him: "And hereby we do KNOW that we know Him, if we keep His commandments. He that saith, I know Him, and keepeth not His commandments, is a liar, and the truth is not in him. But whoso keepeth His Word, in him verily is the love of God perfected: hereby know we that we are in Him" (I John 2:3—5).

What is meant by Jesus' promise to *"manifest"* Himself to the believer who is obedient to His commandments? Did He mean that He would show Himself *physically* to that believer? that He would appear to him *bodily*? No, that is not what He meant. God is no longer tabernacling in flesh among men. Jesus does not say to us as He said to Thomas, "Reach hither thy finger, and behold my hands; and reach hither thy hand, and thrust it into my side" (John 20:27). In I John 1:1,2 John the Beloved wrote, "That which was from the beginning, which we have heard, which we have SEEN WITH OUR EYES, WHICH WE HAVE LOOKED UPON, AND OUR HANDS HAVE HANDLED, of the Word of life: (For the life was manifested, and we have seen it, and bear witness, and shew unto you that eternal life, which was with the Father, and was manifested unto us.)" We cannot say this today; we do not see Jesus with the physical eye, nor can we *touch* Him in the physical sense.

Nor is the promise Jesus made here to be fulfilled through "visions" or dreams. Jacob had a vision at Bethel; he saw a ladder, set on the earth and reaching into heaven, with the angels of God ascending and descending upon it—(read the account in Genesis 28); but God promises no such visions today. We walk by *faith*, not by sight.

Isaiah had a *glorious* vision: He saw the Lord, *"sitting upon a throne, high and lifted up,* and His train filled the temple. Above it stood the seraphims: each one had six wings; with twain he covered his face, and with twain he covered his feet, and with twain he did fly. And one cried unto another, and said, *Holy, holy, holy, is the Lord of hosts: the whole earth is full of His glory"* (Isa. 6:1—3).

But God does not manifest Himself today through such visions as Isaiah had. We see God today—not with the physical eye, and not through visions and dreams, but in the spiritual revelation of Himself to the eye of the inner man, *by faith.* We see Him with the eyes of the soul, and we have a vivid realization of His being with us, abiding in us, and directing us by the power of the Holy Spirit.

Then how *does* God manifest Himself to us today? *It is through THE WRITTEN WORD OF GOD that the INCARNATE WORD manifests Himself to the believing heart.* We will not know this side of heaven just how important is the Word of God, nor how much it has to do with all that we are spiritually. Fellow believer, this is of the *utmost* importance: The more we read and study the Word, the more we search the Scriptures, *the more fully Jesus manifests Himself to us and the more fully He becomes a glorious reality!* Job said, "I have heard of thee by the hearing of the ear: *but NOW mine EYE* (the eye of the inner man) seeth thee" (Job 42:5).

The TERMS of this glorious manifestation are clearly set forth by the Lord Jesus in the first part of our present verse: *"He that hath my commandments, and KEEPETH them."* When we love Jesus so fervently that we keep His holy Word simply because it IS His Word; when our love for Him leads us to immediate and unreserved obedience to Him; when we reach the place where no sacrifice is too great if it will bring glory to His name; when nothing—houses or lands, family or friends—can come between us and unbroken devotion to Him, THEN and only then will we be able to walk *"as seeing Him who is invisible"* (Heb. 11:27). Such a Christian will be victorious over every doubt, fear, and foe, because *"we are MORE than conquerors through Him that loved us."*

Verse 22:   *"Judas saith unto Him, not Iscariot, Lord, how is it that thou wilt manifest thyself unto us, and not unto the world?"*

It is clearly pointed out here that *this* "Judas" was *not* Judas Iscariot, betrayer of our Lord. This Judas was the brother of James, son of Alphaeus, and was also called *Jude.* He was the writer of the epistle that bears his name. *James* is sometimes referred to in the Scriptures as the brother of our Lord (see Matthew 13:55, Mark 6:3, and Galatians 1:19). Some believe that Mary had no other children after Jesus was born, but I cannot agree with such teaching. Although Jesus was the *firstborn,* and Joseph "knew her not" until she had *brought forth* her firstborn Son and called Him JESUS (Matt. 1:25), I believe other children were born after the Lord's birth, children who were fathered by Joseph.

Be that as it may, the "Judas" spoken of here was the brother of James who is referred to as the Lord's brother, and in other places Jude is spoken of as "Lebbaeus, whose surname was Thaddaeus" (Matt. 10:3).

"How is it that thou wilt manifest thyself unto US, and not unto the world?" How slow this man was to believe— as were the other disciples! Yet in their slowness and ignorance they caused the Lord Jesus to speak words rich in precious truth that blesses our hearts today. Thank God for the questions asked by these unlearned men. Jude was seeking after truth, and his question points back to verse 19 where Jesus said, "The world seeth me no more." He wanted to know the difference between the disciples and the world, and what distinct privilege is given to believers that the world does not and cannot have.

"How is it?" in the Greek reads, "What has happened?" and *"thou wilt"* reads "thou art about." In other words, Jude asked Jesus, "What has happened that thou art about to manifest thyself unto *us*, and not unto the world?" There is indication here that he, like most of the Jews in the days of our Lord's earthly ministry, expected the setting up of a glorious kingdom and deliverance from Roman bondage. If, like Nicodemus, the Samaritan woman, and others, he was thinking in terms of the natural, he would not have understood what Jesus meant by manifesting Himself to the disciples and not to the world.

Verse 23: *"Jesus answered and said unto him, If a man love me, he will keep my words: and my Father will love him, and we will come unto him, and make our abode with him."*

Here is repetition of the truths given in verses 15 and 21. Jesus again emphasizes the fact that the believer who truly *loves* Him will keep His words and obey His commandments. Such a believer will in turn be loved by the Father with a peculiar, very special love, and both Father and Son will make their abode with him.

"WE will come unto him, and make OUR abode with him." Here again is seen the unity between Father, Son, and Holy Spirit, a unity that cannot be broken. So perfect is the union of the three Persons of the Trinity as having to do with our salvation, that if any one of the three were removed, there would BE no salvation.

In Proverbs 8:17 God said, "I love them that love me; and those that seek me early shall find me." God fellowships only with believers who love Him, welcome Him, keep His Word and obey His commandments. True love to God is *manifested* through obedience; true love never puts a question mark around anything the Word of God has to say. If God says it, we believe it and obey it—IF we love Him as we should and as He deserves to be loved.

Paul expressed the attitude of the true believer when he said, "Not as though I had already attained, either were already perfect: but I follow after, if that I may apprehend that for which also I am apprehended of Christ Jesus. Brethren, I count not myself to have apprehended: but this one thing I do, forgetting those things which are behind, and reaching forth unto those things which are before, I press toward the mark for the prize of the high calling of God in Christ Jesus" (Phil. 3:12—14).

Jesus was speaking of heart-obedience, the longing of the inner man to be fully submitted and conformed to God's will. The truly born again believer has a *desire* to keep the Word of God. Paul said in II Corinthians 8:11, "Now therefore perform the doing of it; *that as there was a readiness to will, so there may be a performance also* out of that which ye have."

The believer who loves Jesus with his whole heart will find the expression of His will in His Word and will readily accept it; but for the believer who is prone to love Jesus with reservations, there must be commandments. The same is true in earthly families. For some children when they do wrong, a *look* from a mother or father is sufficient reproof to command obedience. The desire of the parent is recognized by the child, and out of love and respect for that parent's authority the child obeys. For others, there must be *rules*—and chastisement for *breaking* those rules.

The same is true in the spiritual realm. Some believers are moved simply by the thought of God's love, as Peter was on the night he denied his Lord. Jesus turned and looked at him, and that look was sufficient to call Peter to repentance with bitter tears. Some Christians are moved to obedience when they read the Word, while others must face a definite and positive *command* from the Lord before they will acknowledge His authority and respect Him as Lord of their life as well as Saviour of their soul.

Notice that our Lord does not say, "Keep my commandments," but "my *words*," generally including all of His teachings. He promises to *manifest* Himself unto those who keep His commandments (v. 21), but He promises that both He and the Father will come and *make their abode* with those who keep His WORD—and "abiding" means *fellowship*.

We know that John the Beloved knew the joy of fellowship with God, because he wrote, "That which we have seen and heard declare we unto you, *that ye also may have fellowship with us: and truly OUR fellowship is with the Father, and with His Son Jesus Christ. And these things write we unto you, THAT YOUR JOY MAY BE FULL*" (I John 1:3,4).

Abiding fellowship is God's reward to the Christian who practices loving obedience at all times, accepting and keeping God's Word; but he who refuses to accept the reproof and correction of the Scripture need not expect to enjoy life abundantly.

Verse 24: *"He that loveth me not keepeth not my sayings: and the Word which ye hear is not mine, but the Father's which sent me."*

Once more our Lord declares the same great principle

He has already set forth, this time from the *negative* side. If there is no obedience to Christ, then there is no *love* for Christ, *for love begets obedience.* Practical obedience is the evidence of true love—but profession, church membership, baptism, good works, weeping or rejoicing are worthless *without* obedience. There is no middle ground with Jesus; we are either for Him or against Him, we love Him or we hate Him. *We cannot be neutral.* In the Old Testament God told His people that the iniquities of the fathers would be visited upon the children even unto the third and fourth generations of them that hated Him; but He promised to show mercy unto thousands who *loved* Him and kept His commandments (Ex. 20:5,6). In Luke 11:23 Jesus told His disciples, "He that is not with me is against me: and he that gathereth not with me scattereth."

"And the Word which ye hear is not mine, but the Father's which sent me." This statement was to remind the disciples again of the perfect unity of Father and Son. Because the words Jesus spoke were the Father's words, He spoke with authority and divine dignity. His words and His commandments were the words and commandments of Almighty God, and those who *despised* the commandments of Jesus despised the commandments of the Father as well. By like token, those who honored and obeyed the words of Jesus also honored and obeyed the Father.

With this verse Jesus disposes of three questions asked Him by His disciples in previous verses:

Thomas asked, "Lord, *how can we know the way* to where you are going?" Jesus replied, "I AM the way" (vv. 5,6).

Philip was eager for visible manifestations of God, and he said, "Lord, shew us the Father, and it sufficeth us." Jesus said to him, "He that hath seen ME hath seen the *Father*" (vv. 8,9).

Then in verse 22 Jude asked, "Lord, how is it that thou wilt manifest thyself unto us, and not unto the world?" Jesus answered that question with the explanation that the world does not believe Him, the world does not love Him, the world does not keep His words—so how *can* He manifest Himself to the world?

Evidently these three questions were stumblingblocks to the disciples, and Jesus patiently but firmly disposed of them in the foregoing verses.

Verse 25: *"These things have I spoken unto you, being yet present with you."*

"These things" may refer to the things Jesus had taught His disciples in our present chapter, or the reference *could* be to all the things He had taught them up to this point in His public ministry.   Even if it includes only the things recorded in this chapter, there is enough truth to bring assurance to the faintest heart; and if it refers to *all* of His teachings, then the disciples were certainly made aware from the very outset that Jesus had come to declare the Father, to do the will of the Father, and to finish the work the Father had sent Him to do.

He said to them, as WE would talk to our discouraged children, "These—and many other things I have told you since I have been with you—were said to comfort you, and in just a little while after I leave you the Holy Spirit will come, and He will cause you to remember all that I have said to you since I have been with you.

Verse 26: *"But the Comforter, which is the Holy Ghost, whom the Father will send in my name, He shall teach you all things, and bring all things to your remembrance, whatsoever I have said unto you."*

Here is divine proof that the third Person of the Trinity is not an abstract "influence."   He is a *Person*, capable of teaching, leading, counseling.   Jesus said, "HE shall teach you," using the masculine pronoun, and certainly this would not refer to an abstract influence.

"The Comforter . . . whom the FATHER will send in my name . . . ." Notice that the Father sent the Comforter,

but He was sent in the name of Christ. Jesus the Saviour came in the *Father's* name (John 5:43), the Holy Spirit would come in the *Son's* name. He would come in Christ's stead, to take over the interest of Jesus on earth. He would direct, indwell, comfort, lead, assure, and seal believers. Jesus had glorified the heavenly Father in all that He did and said, and in like manner the Holy Spirit came to glorify Jesus the Son. Up to the time of His crucifixion Jesus had supplied the spiritual needs of His disciples; but now that He was leaving them, *"another* Comforter" would provide for their spiritual needs—and for the needs of all believers on down to the end of this Dispensation of Grace.

"He shall teach you all things." The Holy Spirit would make clear to the disciples that which at that point was still a mystery to them. Many of the Lord's sayings were words of mystery to His followers at the time He said them, but after Pentecost the Holy Spirit would remind them of these things and would reveal the mysteries to them.

The Gospel of John contains two examples of the fulfillment of this promise. In chapter 2 verse 22 we read, "When therefore He was risen from the dead, His disciples remembered that He had said this unto them; and they believed the Scripture, and the word which Jesus had said." In chapter 12 verse 16 we read, "These things understood not His disciples at the first: but when Jesus was glorified, then remembered they that these things were written of Him, and that they had done these things unto Him."

In a sense, this promise applies to *all* believers, for the Holy Spirit is our teacher:

"Ye have an unction from the Holy One, and ye know all things. . . But the anointing which ye have received of Him abideth in you, and ye need not that any man teach you: but as the same anointing teacheth you of all things, and is truth, and is no lie, and even as it hath taught you, ye shall abide in Him" (I John 2:20,27).

I have been preaching the Gospel for more than thirty years, and during those years, before going into the pulpit to preach or into the studio for a radio broadcast I have prayed for God to fill me with the Spirit and bring to my memory the things I should declare in my sermon. I can testify that God has heard and answered my prayer, and on many occasions the Holy Spirit has enabled me when without Him I could not have delivered a message. Many times God has worked a miracle in my body, in my mind, and in my heart. I never attempt to preach the Word of God without first praying, "Lord, empty me, fill me with thy Spirit, enlighten my mind, and help me to speak the words I ought to speak and leave unspoken the words I should not speak." The only way any minister can preach or teach in the will of God is to pray for the filling, guidance, and inspiration of the Holy Spirit, because it is He who reveals to us the deep things of God. After all, the Bible came to us through holy men as they were moved of the Holy Ghost to pen down the words of God:

"We have also a more sure word of prophecy; whereunto ye do well that ye take heed, as unto a light that shineth in a dark place, until the day dawn, and the day star arise in your hearts: knowing this first, that no prophecy of the Scripture is of any private interpretation. *For the prophecy came not in old time by the will of man: but HOLY MEN OF GOD SPAKE AS THEY WERE MOVED BY THE HOLY GHOST"* (II Pet. 1:19—21).

The promise to reveal *"all* things" applies of course to all things *needful* to believers, things beneficial to the soul. It does not include such secular knowledge as science, astrology, etc. *"All things"* here must be limited to things needful to be known by the Christian for the welfare of soul and spirit.

The Guarantee of Perfect Peace

Verse 27: *"Peace I leave with you, my peace I give unto you: not as the world giveth, give I unto you. Let not your heart be troubled, neither let it be afraid."*

In the New Testament, *"peace"* is spoken of in a two-fold sense: First, it signifies *reconciliation* as contrasted with *alienation.* Second, it signifies *tranquility* as contrasted with a state of *tumult.* The one is objective, the other is subjective.

In Romans 5:1 we find *peace WITH God:* "Therefore being justified by faith, *we have peace with God through our Lord Jesus Christ."* The wrath of God against us is ended forever. We have *peace* with God, having been justified by faith in the shed blood and finished work of the Lord Jesus Christ. God's wrath is taken away and "there is therefore now no condemnation to them which are in Christ Jesus, who walk not after the flesh, but after the Spirit" (Rom. 8:1). This is the peace we enjoy through reconciliation.

The other sense in which the Christian has peace is found in Philippians 4:7: "The peace of God, which passeth all understanding, shall keep your hearts and minds through Christ Jesus." God has promised to keep us in *perfect* peace if our minds are stayed on Him (Isa. 26:3). When we trust Jesus for salvation, God saves us and forgives us for Christ's sake (Eph. 4:32); and when the wrath of God is taken away, we enjoy tranquility of soul, God puts His peace within us, and thus we are not only *at peace WITH God,* we also possess *the peace OF God.*

Jesus said, *"Peace I leave with you."* This peace is ours as the result of the atonement.

Jesus also said, *"My peace I give unto you."* We enjoy this peace through the indwelling Spirit.

Jesus promised the disciples *personal* peace, *His OWN peace.* If we follow our Lord from the first day of His public ministry until He cried out from the cross, "It is finished!" we will find that He was never disturbed by circumstances. He was *moved with compassion,* yes—but He was never *disturbed,* and He never resisted the will of the heavenly Father. The peace Jesus promised the disciples was the peace that filled His *own* heart here on earth,

peace that was His because of His unbroken communion
and fellowship with God the Father.

Notice Jesus said, *"My peace I GIVE unto you."* We
cannot *merit* this peace of God, we cannot earn it, we cannot buy it; but Jesus GIVES His peace to each and every
believer. The world HAS no peace to give. Pleasure? Yes,
the world gives pleasure—*for a season;* but peace? No.
Only God can give peace to the human heart. He reserves
the sole right to give peace, and He gives it to all who
will put their faith in the finished work and shed blood of
the Lord Jesus Christ.

The world *talks* much about peace—in fact, we hear
more about peace today than any people who ever lived;
but there IS no peace except the peace that exists in the
hearts of believers—*God's peace.* We have peace programs,
peace societies, there is much talk of "world peace," much
talk of *"keeping* the peace"; but in I Thessalonians 5:3 we
read, "When they shall say, Peace and safety; then sudden
destruction cometh upon them, as travail upon a woman
with child; and they shall not escape."

We are living in the age of tranquilizers. Millions of
people live on pills day by day, our institutions for the
feebleminded are filled to overflowing, and tens of thousands
who *should* be in mental hospitals are NOT there simply
because there is no room for them! Tons of tranquilizers
are sold today; people literally live on them to keep from
committing suicide. We live in a troubled world, these
are perilous times; but thank God, *as individuals* we can
have peace—peace *with* God and *the peace OF God*—if we
will only believe on Jesus and trust in His shed blood.

In verse 1 of this chapter Jesus said to His disciples,
"Let not your heart be *troubled."* But here He adds,
"Neither let it be AFRAID." Surely the disciples should
have been comforted, assured, strengthened, and encouraged
to great degree; but not long after this, Peter profanely
denied his Lord and the other disciples forsook Him and
fled. Such is human frailty!

The peace of God removes fear, doubt, worry, and does away with fretting. It is a sin for the Christian to fret and worry and live in fear; there is no reason for it. I John 4:13—18 says, "Hereby know we that we dwell in Him, and He in us, because He hath given us of His Spirit. And we have seen and do testify that the Father sent the Son to be the Saviour of the world. Whosoever shall confess that Jesus is the Son of God, God dwelleth in him, and he in God. And we have known and believed the love that God hath to us. God is love; and he that dwelleth in love dwelleth in God, and God in him. Herein is our love made perfect, that we may have boldness in the day of judgment: because as He is, so are we in this world. *There is no fear in love; but perfect love casteth out fear: because fear hath torment. HE THAT FEARETH IS NOT MADE PER-FECT IN LOVE."*

Then in Hebrews 13:5,6 we read, ". . . He hath said, *I will never leave thee, nor forsake thee. So that we may boldly say, THE LORD IS MY HELPER, AND I WILL NOT FEAR WHAT MAN SHALL DO UNTO ME!"*

Yes, verse 27 of our present chapter is definitely the property of all born again believers.

Verse 28: *"Ye have heard how I said unto you, I go away, and come again unto you. If ye loved me, ye would rejoice, because I said, I go unto the Father: for my Father is greater than I."*

This statement refers to what the Lord had said in chapter 13, verses 33 and 36, and chapter 14, verses 2, 3, and 12. The disciples understood enough of what He said to know that He was about to leave them, and that was the reason they were troubled and perplexed, in spite of His reassurance and words of comfort.

"I go away, and come again unto you." This definitely points to the Lord's second coming. In verses 2 and 3 of this chapter Jesus said, "I go to prepare a place for you. . . . I will come again, and receive you unto myself." If

the disciples had really believed that, they would have been rejoicing instead of being filled with misgivings. Had they loved Him with an intelligent love instead of with a doubting love, if they had fully understood His mission, His nature, and His work, they would have been rejoicing to hear Him say, "I go away, and come again unto you." In that announcement He declared that He had finished the work the Father sent Him to do, therefore salvation was provided for all who would believe and receive His words and His finished work.

"If ye loved me" does not mean that the disciples did not love Jesus at all. They DID love Him, and He *knew* they loved Him. In verses 15, 21, and 23 of this chapter it is certainly assumed that they loved Him.

"My Father is greater than I." These words have to do with our Lord's Incarnation and humiliation. Jesus was one with the Father in the beginning, *co-equal* with God; but when He spoke these words He was dwelling in a body of flesh made like unto man while God the Father is an eternal Spirit. Jesus was—and IS—equal to the Father as touching the Trinity, the Godhead; but He was inferior to God as touching His manhood. Trinitarians believe in the humanity of Christ as strongly as they believe in His divinity. Jesus was very God, but He was also very man. As God, He is equal *with* God from eternity throughout eternity, but as *Man* He was inferior to the Father.

Jesus took upon Himself the form of a servant, but His being in that form was both voluntary and temporary:

"Let this mind be in you, which was also in Christ Jesus: Who, being in the form of God, thought it not robbery to be equal with God: but made Himself of no reputation, and took upon Him the form of a servant, and was made in the likeness of men: and being found in fashion as a man, He humbled Himself, and became obedient unto death, even the death of the cross. *Wherefore God also hath highly exalted Him,* and given Him a name which is above every name: that at the name of Jesus every knee should bow, of things in heaven, and things in earth, and things under the earth; and that every tongue should confess that Jesus Christ is Lord, to the glory of God the Father" (Phil. 2:5—11).

Hebrews 12:2 tells us that "for the joy that was set before Him" Jesus "endured the cross, despising the shame, and is set down at the right hand of the throne of God." If the disciples had fully understood who Jesus was, if they had fully understood His mission on earth, they would have rejoiced that He had finished the work He came into the world to do, and was returning to the Father to reassume the glory He had with the Father before the world was, the glory He had laid aside to become Incarnate, the Saviour of sinners. He was approaching the time when He would lay aside the position of inferiority which He had maintained since He was born of the Virgin Mary and came to tabernacle among men.

He who thought it not robbery to be equal with God had, of His own free will, taken the form of a servant and been made in the likeness of sinful man. As God the Father's servant, it was to God the Father that He would render an account. Yes, He who was rich with all of heaven's splendor at His feet, *for our sakes* became abjectly poor, without place to lay His head or home to call His own. He was a man of sorrows and acquainted with grief, and *as such* He was definitely inferior to God the Father, sitting on the throne in glory. As Jesus walked this earth, the brightness of His glory was eclipsed by human flesh. Thus God the Father was surrounded by the multitudes of worshipping heavenly hosts who praised His holy name, while Jesus the Son was despised, spat upon, insulted, beaten, rejected, and crucified. Jesus knew all of this as He spoke to His disciples, He knew the agony and suffering that lay only a few hours ahead of Him; but looking beyond that, He announced to His disciples that He was about to return to the Father, and in returning would receive again the glory He had had *with* the Father in the beginning.

Verse 29: *"And now I have told you before it come to pass, that, when it is come to pass, ye might believe."*

"I have told you before IT come to pass." To what does Jesus refer here? The disciples *believed*, but their faith was weak—and our Lord made this statement so that when He should finally be nailed to the cross, die, and be buried, they might continue to believe that He was their Messiah, the divinely appointed One, and their faith would not be shaken. They must continue to believe that His words were true and trustworthy, and that every promise He made to them was as certain as the fact that God is God.

Verse 30: *"Hereafter I will not talk much with you: for the prince of this world cometh, and hath nothing in me."*

Jesus knew it was only a short time until His crucifixion. His betrayal was at hand, He would soon be arrested, tried, condemned, and put to death. He was therefore preparing His disciples for that hour. *"Hereafter I will not talk much with you"* refers to the short time before His crucifixion; it has nothing to do with the forty days He remained here on earth after His resurrection, before His ascension.

"The prince of this world cometh . . . ." Satan was about to bruise the heel of the Deliverer (Gen. 3:15). The awful archenemy of God—and of all mankind—was about to begin His final assault on the Saviour, an assault that began in the Garden of Gethsemane when all the forces of hell were marshalled against the Son of God, as we will see when we reach that section of our study.

"And hath nothing in me" speaks of the inherent holiness of the Lord Jesus Christ. The devil could not attack Jesus *from within* because He was very God, even though He was man. There was no guile in Him, He had no evil nature, and therefore Satan was forced to attack Him from without.

To illustrate this, we might use a crude illustration: Suppose we threw a lighted match into a barrel of explosives.

There would be a terrible explosion, a great upheaval. But if we tossed a lighted match into a barrel of *water,* the water would quench the fire. Jesus quenched every fiery dart of the devil, because Jesus was God in flesh, and God cannot be tempted with evil:

"Let no man say when he is tempted, I am tempted of God: *for God cannot be tempted with evil, neither tempteth He any man:* But every man is tempted, when he is drawn away of his own lust, and enticed" (James 1:13,14).

Jesus also made His statement for the consolation and assurance of the discouraged disciples. He told them ahead of time that there was no doubt as to the outcome of the approaching conflict, for He would win the victory. There was no possible chance for Satan to win this battle. The victory was as sure for Jesus as the existence of God was sure. There was no weak point in the Saviour for Satan to attack, therefore our Lord would come forth the conqueror. He had already conquered the world and the flesh, and now He would conquer the devil, death, hell, and the grave. Satan found a weakness in Cain, in Noah, in Abraham, even in the disciple Peter who walked and talked with the Lord in person; but in the spotless Lamb of God he found no weak point through which he could launch an attack, nothing on which to lay hold.

Jesus did not say, *"Judas is coming . . . the Romans are coming . . . the Pharisees and chief priests and rulers are coming."* No, He said, "The *prince of this world* cometh." It is important to remember that *men* are only the *tools* of Satan.

Satan, *"the prince of this world,"* rules and reigns in the hearts of unregenerate men—and that takes in the vast majority of all mankind (I John 5:19). Few of us realize, even in small measure, the extent (or the intensity) of the devil's power and influence on the peoples of this earth.

When Jesus said, "the prince of this world *cometh,"* He did not mean that Satan was coming for the first time, putting in his first appearance. All through the ministry of Jesus here on earth the devil tempted Him, assailed Him, and opposed Him bitterly and consistently through his various tools. Jesus and Satan met face to face after the baptism of Jesus, when our Lord was led of the Spirit "into the wilderness to be tempted of the devil" (Matt. 4:1—11). But now he is coming in a specially vicious attack, making his last all-out drive to frustrate the purpose of God and wreck the plan of salvation. He was the most cunning searcher ever to walk the face of this earth. He searched every nook and corner of the life of Jesus in his attempt to find something through which he could accuse Him, and you may rest assured that had there been anything amiss in the Saviour's life, Satan would have found it—and most assuredly *he would have announced it!*

Verse 31: *"But that the world may know that I love the Father; and as the Father gave me commandment, even so I do. Arise, let us go hence."*

Blessed statement! Even though Jesus knew that "the prince of this world cometh," He did not run from him, but rather advanced to meet him. He had come into the world to pay the sin-debt, and in order to do that He must meet the devil face to face in this last great onslaught, this all-out battle.

In chapter 10, verses 17 and 18, He said, "Therefore doth my Father love me, because I lay down my life, that I might take it again. No man taketh it from me, but I lay it down of myself. I have power to lay it down, and I have power to take it again. *This commandment have I received of my Father."* Therefore, having received commandment from the heavenly Father, the Son went forth to meet the devil.

"That the world may know that I love the Father . . . ." It is most remarkable that this is the only place where it is recorded that Christ spoke of *His* love for His *Father* in heaven. He had willingly left the Father's bosom and taken a body of humiliation, and now IN that body He

was about to give *supreme proof* of His love for the Father.

"As the Father gave me commandment, even so I do."
In His last message to His disciples before He went to
Calvary, Jesus said, "What I am about to do, I do willingly. I set my face toward Calvary and I will *voluntarily*
go to the cross. I do this to prove to you and to the world,
to heaven, earth, and hell, that I love the Father who sent
me into the world to make an atonement for the souls of
sinful men. He gave me commandment—but my love for
Him is so pure, so fully complete, that even though He
has commanded me, I go forward *willingly*, and in my death
on the cross I show my love for the Father, my obedience
to His will and His command. I am determined to finish
the work the Father sent me to do, and in finishing that
work I must die that sinners may be saved."

In Hebrews 12:1–4 we read, "Wherefore seeing we also
are compassed about with so great a cloud of witnesses,
let us lay aside every weight, and the sin which doth so
easily beset us, and let us run with patience the race that
is set before us, looking unto Jesus the author and finisher
of our faith; who for the joy that was set before Him endured the cross, despising the shame, and is set down at the
right hand of the throne of God. *For consider Him that
endured such contradiction of sinners against Himself, lest
ye be wearied and faint in your minds. YE HAVE NOT
YET RESISTED UNTO BLOOD, STRIVING AGAINST
SIN."*

"Arise, let us go hence." It would seem that with this,
Jesus rose from the supper table and started on His way
to the Garden of Gethsemane. No one can know for sure,
but it seems that the rest of His instructions were given
as He walked toward the garden—until the end of chapter
16, when He no doubt paused and offered up the prayer
of chapter 17. (Compare chapter 18, verse 1.)

As we bring this chapter to a close, I am humbled by
the realization of how little I really know and understand
of the full meaning of much of it. Some of the statements

in this chapter are difficult to understand because of our inability as finite creatures to grasp the full meaning of the great mystery of the Godhead—the complete and unbroken unity between Father, Son, and Holy Ghost. We believe in the Trinity but we cannot comprehend the mystery of it. Man's words cannot fully express the meaning of such unity; but even though we cannot explain it, we believe it simply because God said it. It is on His Word that our faith must be based, for His Word is infallible, forever settled in heaven (Psalm 119:89).

As we complete our study of chapter 14, we might note one other outstanding thing about it:

From the outset of His public ministry, Jesus continually called attention to Himself, but in such manner as never to thrust Himself forward. He always pointed to the Father who had sent Him, and over and over again He told His disciples that He came to do the Father's will, to do the work the Father gave Him to do, and that the words He spoke were the words the Father gave Him. But in the chapter we have just studied, we find Him using the personal pronouns "I . . . me . . . my . . . mine . . . myself" almost eighty times. I will list them for you here. It is a very interesting study:

In *verse 1* He used the personal pronoun "me" as the object of faith: "Believe God—believe ME."

In *verse 2* He used "my" and "I": "MY Father's house . . . I would have told you . . . I go to prepare a place for you." Thus He gave the disciples assurance.

In *verse 3* He used "I" three times and "myself" once: "I go . . . I will come again, and receive you unto MYSELF; that where I am, there ye may be also."

In *verse 4* He used "I": "Whither I go, ye know."

In *verse 6* He used "I" and "me": "I am the way, the truth, and the life: no man cometh unto the Father, but by ME."

In *verse 7* He used "me" and "my": "If ye had known ME, ye should have known MY Father also."

In *verse 9* He used "I" once, and "me" twice: "Have I been so long time with you . . . Hast thou not known ME . . . He that hath seen ME hath seen the Father."

In *verse 10* He used "I" three times, He used "me" twice, and "myself" once: "I am in the Father, and the Father in ME . . . I speak unto you . . . I speak not of MYSELF . . . the Father that dwelleth in ME, He doeth the works."

In *verse 11* He used "me" three times and "I" one time: "Believe ME that I am in the Father, and the Father in ME . . . believe ME for the very works' sake."

In *verse 12* He used "I" three times, and used "me" and "my" once: "I say . . . He that believeth on ME . . . the works that I do . . . I go unto MY Father."

In *verse 13* He used "my" and "I": "Whatsoever ye shall ask in MY name, that will I do."

In *verse 14* He used "my" and "I": "If ye shall ask any thing in MY name, I will do it."

In *verse 15* He used "me" and "my": "If ye love ME, keep MY commandments."

In *verse 16* He used "I": "I will pray the Father . . . ."

In *verse 18* He used "I" two times: "I will not leave you comfortless: I will come to you."

In *verse 19* He used "me" twice and "I" once: "Yet a little while, and the world seeth ME no more; but ye see ME: because I live, ye shall live also."

In *verse 20* He used "I" twice, "my" and "me" once: "I am in MY Father, and ye in ME, and I in you."

In *verse 21* He used "my" two times, He used "me" two times, He used "I" and "myself" once: "MY commandments . . . loveth ME . . . he that loveth ME shall be loved of MY Father, and I will love him, and will manifest MYSELF to him."

In *verse 23* He used "me" one time, He used "my" twice: "If a man love ME, he will keep MY words: and MY Father will love him . . . ."

In *verse 24* He used "me" twice, He used "my" and

"mine" once: "He that loveth ME . . . MY sayings . . . is not MINE, but the Father's which sent ME."

In *verse 25* He used "I": "These things have I spoken . . . ."

In *verse 26* He used "my" and "I": "MY name . . . I have said."

In *verse 27* He used "I" three times, and "my" once: "Peace I leave with you, MY peace I give unto you: not as the world giveth, give I unto you."

In *verse 28* He used "I" five times, He used "me" and "my" once: "I said . . . I go . . . If ye loved ME . . . I said, I go unto the Father . . . MY Father is greater than I."

In *verse 29* He used "I": "I have told you . . . ."

In *verse 30* He used "I" and "me": "Hereafter I will not talk much with you: for the prince of this world cometh, and hath nothing in ME."

In *verse 31* He used "I" two times and "me" one time: "I love the Father . . . as the Father gave ME commandment, even so I do."

Only God in flesh could use so many personal pronouns in such a short passage and not display pride and haughtiness; but since Jesus was the fulness of the Godhead bodily, He could say, "I will" — and fulfill what He said.

The Revelation of the Father

The Gospel of John is especially the Gospel which reveals God the Father. By comparison, *Matthew* mentions "the Father" forty-four times, *Mark* mentions "the Father" five times, *Luke* uses the same expression seventeen times; but in *John's* Gospel "the Father" is mentioned one hundred and twenty-two times in one way or another.

As we study the Gospel of John, we find that from the first chapter through the last a *definite thought* may be emphasized in each chapter where the heavenly Father is mentioned; and since chapter 14 closes with emphasis on the thought "that the world may know that I love the

Father . . . ," and chapter 15 opens with the definite statement, "I am the true vine, and my Father is the husbandman," I thought it might be well to point out some of the references and trace a definite line of thought as the Father is mentioned in various ways throughout the "salvation Gospel."

John opens his Gospel with the Son of God in the Father's bosom (ch. 1 v. 18), and in chapter 13 verse 25 we find *the saved sinner* in the bosom of the *Son.* And now let us look at some of the ways in which John's Gospel reveals the Father as the other Gospel writers do not:

1. The Father's Unfolding:

"In the beginning was the Word, and the Word was with God, and the Word was God. . . And the Word was made flesh, and dwelt among us, (and we beheld His glory, the glory as of the only begotten of the Father,) full of grace and truth." Thus in the first fourteen verses of John's Gospel we find the Father's unfolding.

2. The Father's House:

Just after the miracle at the marriage feast in Cana, when Jesus turned the water into wine, He went up to Jerusalem, to the temple; and when He entered there he found the temple polluted, in the hands of moneychangers and sellers of merchandise. "And when He had made a scourge of small cords, He drove them all out of the temple, and the sheep, and the oxen; and poured out the changers' money, and overthrew the tables; and said unto them that sold doves, *Take these things hence; make not MY FATHER'S HOUSE an house of merchandise*" (ch. 2, vv. 15,16).

3. The Father's Trust:

"The Father loveth the Son, and hath given all things into His hand" (ch. 3, v. 35). God the Father had perfect confidence and trust in Jesus the Son. God trusted *Adam*— and Adam failed that trust. But "the last Adam," the

Lord Jesus Christ, was faithful, and God gave Him the wealth of heaven. As our Saviour, Jesus has much to give because He has received all the treasures of the Father. God has "given ALL things into His hand." Our Saviour is abundantly rich, He is able and willing to give us every good gift. "No good thing will He withhold from them that walk uprightly" (Psalm 84:11b).

4. The Father's Worship:

"God is a Spirit: and they that worship Him must worship Him in spirit and in truth" (ch. 4, v. 24). The Spirit-nature of God seeks spiritual worship from His children. He is not concerned about the type of building *in* which we worship, He is not concerned about the *form* of our worship, for God *looks on the HEART,* and He seeks worshippers who love Him supremely and who worship from a dedicated heart, in spirit and in truth.

5. The Father's Will:

Jesus said, "I can of mine own self do nothing: as I hear, I judge: and my judgment is just; *because I SEEK NOT MINE OWN WILL, BUT THE WILL OF THE FATHER WHICH HATH SENT ME"* (ch. 5, v. 30).

Jesus walked in the will of God. Every step He took, every word He spoke, every action He made, were according to the Father's will, and the Father walked with Him in all of His ways. It is still God's will that His children walk according to His direction and subject to His will in every phase of life. *Jesus* is now seated at the right hand of the Majesty on high, an exaltation accorded Him by God the Father because of His obedience to the Father's will; and it is the obedient Christian who will be supremely blessed during his earthly walk.

6. The Father's Provision:

"Jesus said unto them, I am the bread of life: he that cometh to me shall never hunger; and he that believeth on me shall never thirst" (ch. 6, v. 35). In Christ, God provided the bread of life. Jesus was God-given, God-sealed, and God-satisfied; therefore the individual who has Christ will want for nothing; He is our sufficiency and we are complete in Him. When we possess Christ we possess the fulness of the Godhead, we possess divine nature, and we possess the Living Bread. In Philippians 4:19 Paul declared, "My God shall supply all your need according to His riches in glory by Christ Jesus."

7. The Father's Commission:

Jesus said, "If I judge, my judgment is true: for I am not alone, but *I and the Father that sent me. . .* He that sent me is true; *and I speak to the world those things which I have heard of Him"* (ch. 8, vv. 16,26).

The Lord Jesus Christ was set forth by God the Father, His vocation was to *please* God the Father. Even in His earthly ministry He never denied His unity with the Father. He declared that He was in the beginning with the Father, that He proceeded *from* the Father, yea, He was God in flesh (II Cor. 5:19).

8. The Father's Fellowship:

As we study the tenth chapter of John's Gospel, especially verses 15 through 38, with the eye of faith we see the mutual love, mutual knowledge, mutual action, mutual possession, and mutual preservation which mark the fellowship between God the Father and Jesus the Son. Jesus said, "As the Father knoweth me, even so know I the Father . . . Though ye believe not me, believe the works: that ye may know, and believe, that the Father is in me, and I in Him (ch. 10, vv. 15 and 38 in part). Yes, there was *perfect* fellowship between God the Father and Jesus the Son.

9. The Father's Power:

When the stone was taken away from the tomb of Lazarus, "Jesus lifted up His eyes, and said, *Father, I thank thee that thou hast heard me. And I knew that thou hearest me always:* but because of the people which stand by I said it, that they may believe that thou hast sent me" (ch. 11, vv. 41 and 42). No power, not even death, can withstand the prayer of the Son of God, or the Father's power in response to that prayer. When Jesus said, "Lazarus, come forth," Lazarus came forth. God unloosed the power of death, and Lazarus stepped from the grip of death into the open vitality of life.

10. The Father's Glory:

In chapter 12, verse 28, Jesus prayed, "Father, *glorify thy name.* Then came there a voice from heaven, saying, I have both glorified it, and will glorify it again." Jesus on the cross was God's love on display, heaven's best dying for earth's worst. In verse 23 of chapter 12 Jesus said, "The hour is come, that the Son of man should be glorified," and the "hour" to which He referred was *Calvary,* the darkest hour of human history; yet the death of Jesus on the cross brought glory to the heavenly Father. Christ met sin face to face; He met God's claim on mankind, glorified His name and fulfilled every iota of the Father's will concerning the sin-debt. When Jesus cried out, "It is finished," He brought the greatest glory to the heavenly Father that could possibly be brought to God's holy name.

11. The Father's Confidence:

Chapter 13, verse 3 tells us that Jesus *knew* of the Father's perfect confidence in Him, He knew that *"the Father had given ALL THINGS into His hands,"* He knew that He came *from* God and that He would return TO God. The world despised Him, spat upon Him, attempted to stone Him, called Him an illegitimate and an impostor. He was deserted by friends and betrayed by one of His own disciple band. The shadow of the cross was always over Him, and the judgment of God that must be meted out against sin was ever before Him, present with Him. But Jesus had a single eye, fixed on Calvary—and all that the devil, earth, and hell could hurl against Him could not deter His purpose, nor hide the smile of the Father's face, a smile that assured the Son of the Father's perfect faith and confidence in Him, confidence that He would finish the work the Father had given Him to do, and He fulfilled that confidence.

12. The Father's Image:

Jesus said to His disciples, "If ye had known me, ye should have known my Father also: and from hence forth ye know Him, and have seen Him. Philip saith unto Him, Lord, shew us the Father, and it sufficeth us. Jesus saith unto him, Have I been so long time with you, and yet hast thou not known me, Philip? HE THAT HATH SEEN ME HATH SEEN THE FATHER; and how sayest thou then, Shew us the Father?" (ch. 14, vv. 7—9).

Jesus was the brightness of God's glory, "the express image of His Person" (Heb. 1:3). All we need to know about God was in the Lord Jesus Christ. He was God manifest in flesh; therefore any question we ask about God the eternal Father or God the eternal Spirit, we will find the answer in Jesus the eternal Son. He came to declare God, and He did exactly that.

13. The Father's Ministry:

"I am the true vine, and my Father is the Husbandman. Every branch in me that beareth not fruit He taketh away: and every branch that beareth fruit, He purgeth it, that it may bring forth more fruit" (ch. 15, vv. 1,2).

Although Jesus is the true vine, the Father is the Husbandman, and it is the pruning and care of the Husbandman that causes the fruitfulness of the branches. The vine must be cared for, and it must be pruned or there would be no fruit. The Husbandman is the One who does the pruning, and in verse 8 of chapter 15 Jesus said, "Herein is my

Father glorified, *that ye bear MUCH fruit.*"

14. The Father's Love:

"For the Father Himself loveth you, because ye have loved me, and have believed that I came out from God" (ch. 16, v. 27). Because God so loved the world that He gave Jesus to die for us, all that we are as sons of God through His grace is the outcome of the work, ministry, and death of Jesus Christ the Son. All that we possess through salvation is the outcome of Christ's work for us. Christ worked for us, died for us, and perfected the plan of salvation for us because of the Father's love. We are sons of God, we are more than conquerors, and we are victorious over all spiritual enemies *because we overcome IN HIS POWER.* We receive Jesus by faith, and the Father lives IN us in the Person of the Holy Spirit. Thus when we possess Jesus we possess the fulness of the Godhead, "for in (Jesus) dwelleth all the fulness of the Godhead bodily. And ye are complete in Him, which is the head of all principality and power" (Col. 2:9,10).

15. The Father's Keeping:

Jesus prayed, "Holy Father, keep through thine own name those whom thou hast given me, that they may be one, as we are" (ch. 17, v. 11). Throughout the seventeenth chapter of John's Gospel we find assurance of the Father's keeping. Jesus prayed—not only for those who followed and walked with Him during His earthly ministry, but for all believers throughout the Church Age, until the body of Christ is complete and we are caught up to meet Him in the clouds in the air.

The finished work and shed blood of Jesus on the cross is the basis for His prayer as recorded in chapter 17; and because of His finished work and the Father's confidence and faith in the Son, that prayer is our guarantee that we will enter that celestial city and occupy the Holy City, the place Jesus has gone to prepare for us.

16. The Father's Cup:

"Then said Jesus unto Peter, Put up thy sword into the sheath: the cup which my Father hath given me, shall I not drink it?" (ch. 18, v. 11).

In Gethsemane Jesus prayed, "O my Father, if it be possible, let this cup pass from me: *nevertheless not as I will, BUT AS THOU WILT*" (Matt. 26:39). The Saviour saw the cup of our sins, the cup of our woe and misery, and when this bitter, black cup was pressed by God's hand of love to the lips of Jesus, He drank it to the last bitter dregs, that WE might have the cup of blessing and eternal salvation. If He had said, "I will *not* drink it," God the Father would not have *forced* Him to drink it, and we would never have known the cup of salvation. But Jesus took the cup of our woe and sin, in order that WE might have eternal salvation.

17. The Father's Presence:

After His resurrection, Jesus said to Mary, "Touch me not; for I am not yet ascended to my Father: but go to my brethren, and say unto them, I ascend unto my Father, and your Father; and to my God, and your God" (ch. 20, v. 17).

Having paid the sin-debt and made salvation possible for us, Jesus ascended into the Father's presence. "Now that He ascended, what is it but that He also descended first into the lower parts of the earth? He that descended is the same also that ascended up far above all heavens, that He might fill all things" (Eph. 4:9,10). He who ascended into the Father's presence first descended into the depths of darkness, despair, suffering, anguish, and death—but death could not hold Him because He is LIFE. Because HE lives, WE live also. Because *HE died*, we have eternal life by faith in His finished work. He is seated now in the Father's presence, making intercession for you and me, for all believers. But before He went back to the Father and took His seat at the right hand of the Majesty, He left a command for believers: "Go ye therefore, and teach all nations . . . and, lo, I am with you alway, even unto the end of the world" (Matt. 28:19,20 in part). He sends US forth today to make known the good news, the glad tidings, the *riches* of His saving grace and keeping power.

The Father's Specific Acts Recorded in John

The Father's definite seeking (ch. 4, v. 23).

The Father's earnest working (ch. 5, v. 17).

The Father's deep loving (ch. 5, v. 20; ch. 10, v. 17; ch. 16, v. 27).

The Father's powerful raising (ch. 5, v. 21).

The Father's definite and specific sending (ch. 5, v. 23; ch. 8, vv. 16,18).

The Father's divine sealing (ch. 6, v. 27).

The Father's holy giving (ch. 6, vv. 32–37; ch. 10, v. 29; ch. 13, v. 3).

The Father's drawing of the sinner (ch. 6, v. 44).

The Father's recognized honoring (ch. 8, v. 54; ch. 12, v. 26).

The Father's appreciative knowledge (ch. 10, v. 15).

The Father's distinct and definite command (ch. 10, v. 18; ch. 14, v. 31).

The Father's unmistakeable message (ch. 12, v. 50).

The Father's manifested indwelling (ch. 14, v. 10).

The Father's sufficient bestowment (ch. 14, v. 26; ch. 15, v. 26).

The Father's faithful tending (ch. 15, v. 1).

The Father's safekeeping (ch. 17, v. 11).